STATISTICAL HANDBOOK ON ADOLESCENTS IN AMERICA

Edited by Bruce A. Chadwick and Tim B. Heaton

Oryx Press
1996

The rare Arabian Oryx is believed to have inspired the myth of the unicorn. This desert antelope became virtually extinct in the early 1960s. At that time several groups of international conservationists arranged to have 9 animals sent to the Phoenix Zoo to be the nucleus of a captive breeding herd. Today the Oryx population is over 1000, and over 500 have been returned to the Middle East.

© 1996 by The Oryx Press
4041 North Central at Indian School Road
Phoenix, Arizona 85012-3397

Published simultaneously in Canada
Printed and Bound in the United States of America

∞ The paper used in this publication meets the minimum requirements of
American National Standard for Information Science—Permanence of Paper
for Printed Library Materials, ANSI Z39.48, 1984.

Library of Congress Cataloging-in-Publication Data
Statistical handbook on adolescents in America / edited by Bruce A.
Chadwick, Tim B. Heaton.
    p. cm.
    Includes bibliographical references and index.
    ISBN 0-89774-922-7 (cloth)
    1. Teenagers—United States—Statistics. I. Chadwick, Bruce A.
II. Heaton, Tim B.
    HQ796.S8237 1996   96-10514
    305.23'5—dc20   CIP

Contents

List of Tables and Charts

Preface

Casual observation reveals that American adolescents face both a bright and challenging future as well as a dangerous and foreboding one. On the one hand, medical and nutritional advances have greatly improved the health of American teenagers and educational opportunities abound (youth in junior high school now learn to navigate the information highway, which exposes them to vast amounts of information). On the other hand, out-of-wedlock births and divorce have produced a large number of single-parent families. Poverty among children, including adolescents, has greatly increased as a consequence. Physical, emotional, and sexual abuse also are problems threatening the very life of a substantial number of adolescents. Children begetting children and children killing children, by both murder and suicide, are becoming all too frequent occurrences.

Youth in the U.S., at times, shows promise of being able to deal with serious social problems that have, to date, remained intractable. The level of educational attainment, employment preparation, and individual accomplishment of American youth signal a generation ready to make its mark on history. On the other hand, American youth's interest in drinking, drugs, sex, and violence also suggests a generation out of control.

The information contained in this book will be valuable to educators, political and civic leaders, parents, and others either concerned about or interested in America's youth. For our purposes, adolescence is defined by the range of ages 12 to 21. Therefore, our analysis focuses on the experiences of young people from age 12 to the late teens and early twenties, depending on available information. We also include some information on younger children, both as a basis for comparison to adolescents and because experience in early childhood can have profound consequences later in adolescence. For example, poor health care or extended poverty at early ages can have long-term effects. Occasionally, a source will also include data on younger children that we could not separate out, so we had to report on all children.

Major topics covered in this book include family context, sexual behavior, economics, health, education, quality of life, recreation, deviance, and parent-child relationships. The many charts and tables provide in-formation about the opportunities available to older children and their accomplishments, as well as the problems they face and those they create. The reader can form his or her own conclusions about what society is doing right or wrong concerning the training of its youth and whether American youth poses a threat to or is the hope for our future.

When data were available, we included information about the characteristics of adolescents with single, divorced, or married mothers; of teens with white, black, and Hispanic mothers; and of teens whose mothers have different levels of education. Also, when possible, we presented the children's characteristics according to the age and social class of their mothers and the sex of the adolescents. Finally, we included data over time, when available, so that trends can be observed.

Sources Used

The 1990 U.S. Census, especially the public use sample, was used to provide detailed statistics about marriage, childbirth, and family living arrangements. Several public domain national databases were utilized extensively to create detailed tables and charts. We obtained codebooks and data tapes from five national studies of families and children and used them to create many of the tables in this volume.

In 1976, the Foundation for Child Development initiated a national longitudinal survey of children and their parents (referred to as the National Survey of Children). The purpose was to assess the physical, social, and psychological well-being of different groups of American children; to develop a profile of the way children live and the care they receive; and to document the relationships between the conditions of children's lives and measures of their development and well-being. The initial survey interviewed 2,301 children and the parent most knowledgeable about the child. A second wave of interviews was collected in 1981. Ninety percent of the children in Wave I were located and interviewed by telephone along with their parents for Wave II. The third Wave interviewed 80 percent of the children and parents from Wave II.

The 1985 National Family Violence Survey was funded by the National Institute of Mental Health and the National Science Foundation. It provided data comparable to a similar study conducted in 1975. Interviews were obtained from over 6,000 parents. The main objective was to document the level of violence and level of spousal, child, and elderly abuse in American society.

The National Survey of Families and Households' sample of 13,000 households was conducted in 1987–1988. This massive survey was funded by the Center for Population Research of the National Institute of Child Health and Human Development. Black, Hispanic, and single-parent families, families with stepchildren, and cohabiting couples were over-sampled to provide sufficient numbers of these groups to make insightful comparisons. The survey provides a wealth of information about a wide variety of topics including family processes, effects of divorce, child-rearing practices, parent-child interactions, and the behavior of adolescents.

The 1988 National Health Interview Survey on Child Health was conducted by the National Center for Health Statistics and cosponsored by the National Institute for Child Health and Human Development and the Health Resources and Services Administration. Interviews were obtained from 17,110 individuals about child care, geographic mobility, impairments, acute conditions, chronic conditions, sleep habits, school problems, and developmental problems.

The 1990 Survey of Parents and Children was conducted by the national Commission of Children whose members are appointed by the President, the President *Pro Temp* of the U.S. Senate, and the Speaker of the U.S. House of Representatives. It was a national telephone interview survey conducted among 1,738 parents in the continental United States who were living with their children. Data were collected about the current state of family life, the quality of the relationships between parents and their children, and adolescents' interactions with major institutions affecting the family such as schools, the workplace, neighborhoods, and religious organizations.

In addition to these and other government publications, we relied on many other published sources prepared by organizations such as Gallup, The Search Institute, The Alan Guttmacher Institute, The Urban Institute, and the Russell Sage Foundation, as well as reports by other interest groups focusing on children.

The material in this handbook provides the most comprehensive source of information regarding the status of American adolescents available to date.

STATISTICAL
HANDBOOK
ON ADOLESCENTS
IN AMERICA

A. Demographics of Adolescents and Children

Changing patterns of marriage, childbearing, and living arrangements have dramatically altered the demographic circumstances of adolescents. In this chapter, we examine the demographic context of these circumstances. First, we describe the number, age, sex structure, and ethnic composition of young people. Second, we focus on fertility patterns that have given rise to the present number of children and family contexts within which they reside. The next four sections examine various aspects of the family context, including the following: (1) the size of families in which children live, (2) the type of families created by the marital status of parents, (3) the living arrangements of children, and (4) the presence of grandparents.

AI. DEMOGRAPHIC STRUCTURE

The post-war baby boom created a growing number of children in the 1950s and 60s. The number actually declined somewhat between 1970 and 1980. After the year 2000, the number of children is expected to continue to decline slightly, and the decline will be somewhat larger for adolescents than for younger children. Therefore, stability in the number of children combined with an increasingly aging population will lead to a declining proportion of people under age 18 in the decades to come.

In general, more male babies are born than female babies, but the percentage of males usually declines with age because of higher male mortality. Curiously, the current population of children continues to have a disproportionate percentage of males at adolescent ages.

A large majority of children are white and non-Hispanic. Because of higher minority fertility, however, whites are a shrinking percentage of the total number of children and, according to projections, will continue to be so in the future.

A2. FERTILITY PATTERNS

Birth rates and the characteristics of parents are the major factors contributing to the number and social characteristics of children. The actual number of children women have declines at younger ages, partly because younger women have not finished childbearing and partly because birth rates, in general, are declining. A more accurate portrayal of fertility trends is provided by the total fertility rate. This rate calculates the completed family size implied by age-specific birth rates in a given year. The total fertility rate declined throughout the nineteenth and first half of the twentieth century. After the baby boom in the 1950s and early 60s, the fertility rate has now dropped to an all time low. Most women, however, still intend to have at least one child.

Because of an aging population and declining fertility rate, slightly over half of adult women currently have no children under the age of 18, and few women now have more than four children. Also, black and Hispanic women are more likely to have children under 18 than non-Hispanic, white women are.

Only about half of the women who had a baby in 1992 were married at the time. The number of children born out-of-wedlock has increased dramatically since 1970, especially among blacks. Unwed parenthood is now as common or more common in the U.S. than in most other countries of the world.

A3. SIBSHIP SIZE

Family size can be viewed in different ways. Fertility rates are used to gauge population growth, and the total fertility rate measures family size for mothers. From the child's perspective, the number of siblings or sibship size is a more appropriate indicator of family size. Because younger couples have smaller families, older children tend to live in larger families than do younger children. About a fourth of children under age six have no siblings in the home and another 40 percent have only one sibling. Less than half have more than one sibling. In comparison, only about 10 percent of children aged 12 to 17 are the only child, and more than half have at least two siblings. The number of adolescents who are only children, however, has increased as fertility has declined.

The average sibship size of children tends to mirror the long term decline in fertility, the upsurge of the baby boom, and then the continued fertility decline since

1970. Correspondingly, the percentage of only children has increased since 1960. Minority children, however, grow up with more siblings than do white, non-Hispanic children.

A4. FAMILY TYPES

In addition to lower fertility, changing marriage patterns, including rising rates of divorce and unwed parenthood, have altered the family circumstances of children. As declining fertility has reduced the number of families that have children at home, marital disruption and unwed parenthood has increased the number of families with children that are headed by a single parent. Although there is some increase in families headed by a single male (up to four percent in 1990), most of the rise in single-parent families involves mothers.

Remarriage has also created more families with stepchildren. Most of these "blended" families constitute either a biological mother and stepfather or biological and stepchildren of each parent. Black families are more likely to include a biological mother and stepfather than either Hispanic or white, non-Hispanic families. As a result of the above noted changes, only about one-fourth of all households include a married couple with children at home.

A5. LIVING ARRANGEMENTS OF CHILDREN AND ADOLESCENTS

Changing structure and size within each family type has lead to changes in the living arrangements of children. The percentage of children living with two parents who have each married only once dropped from about 70 percent in 1940 to only about 50 percent in 1988. In contrast, the percentage of children living with a single mother because of divorce, separation, or unwed parenthood has increased. Blacks have experienced a greater decline in children living with a biological mother and father, but the decline is also evident among whites and Hispanics. By 1992, over half of black children, about a third of Hispanic children, and about one-fifth of white children lived with only one parent.

The "traditional family" is often discussed, but no single definition of such a family exists. The "Ozzie and Harriet" family, defined as a two-parent family with all the children born after the parents' only marriage where the father works full time and year round and the mother is not in the labor force, has not been a majority since at least 1920. Because of changes in family structure noted above and in female employment (described in the chapter on economics), the percentage of children living with a father who works full time and a mother who is not in the labor force dropped to under 18 percent by 1990.

By 1980, nearly half of all children lived in a single-parent family at some point by age 17. The percentage of children who live in single-parent families is higher in the U.S. than in many other countries. Children who grow up in single-parent families run a higher risk of having less educated parents, living in poverty, having accidents, repeating a grade, being expelled or suspended from school, being treated for emotional problems, and having behavioral problems.

A5. GRANDPARENTS

Various demographic trends have altered the likelihood of children living with grandparents. More adults are now surviving long enough to be grandparents. In addition, growing numbers of single parents are returning to live with their own parents. On the other hand, there is a growing propensity for older people to live either with their spouse and no one else when married or alone when single. The net result of these changes is a modest increase in the percentage of children who live in their grandparents' home, from 3.2 percent in 1970 to 4.9 percent in 1990. A significantly higher percentage of children have a grandparent in their home—7.5 percent in 1990.

Black and Hispanic children are much more likely to live in the grandparents' home or to have grandparents in the home than are white children. Children with single parents are also much more likely to live with grandparents than are other children.

A1. DEMOGRAPHIC STRUCTURE

A1-1. Number of U.S. Children under 18, by Age, 1940–2010

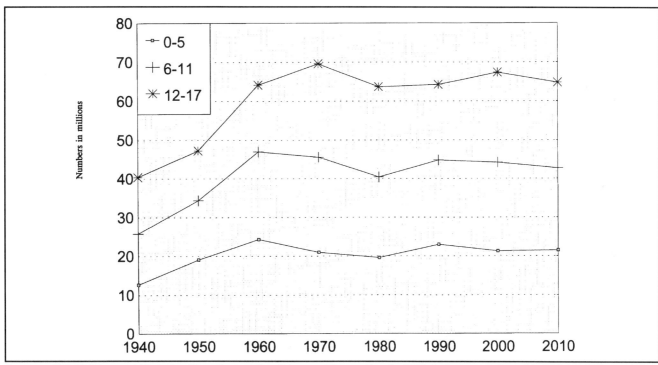

Source: U.S. Children and Their Families: Current Conditions and Recent Trends, 1989. A Report together with Additional Views of the Select Committee on Children, Youth, and Families. U.S. House of Representatives, One Hundred First Congress, First Session (September 1989) page 3.

A1-2. Percent of the Population under Age 25, 1970–2050 (Projected after 1992)

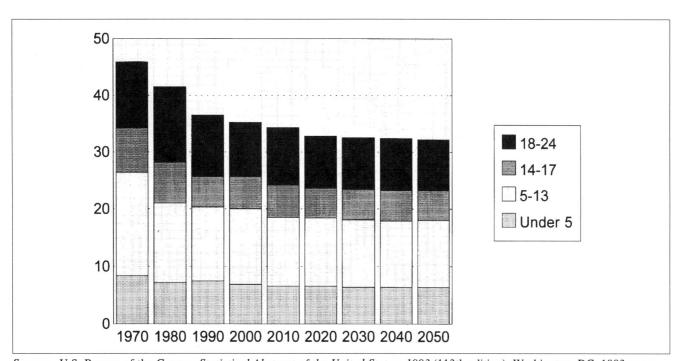

Source: U.S. Bureau of the Census, *Statistical Abstract of the United States: 1993* (113th edition). Washington, DC, 1993 pages 15 and 17.

A1-3. Ratio of Children (0–17) to Elderly (65+), 1970–2050, Projected after 1992

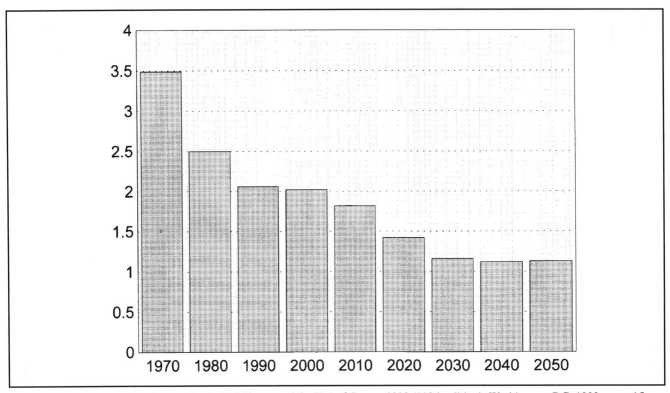

Source: U.S. Bureau of the Census, *Statistical Abstract of the United States: 1993* (113th edition). Washington, DC, 1993 pages 15 and 16.

A1-4. Ratio of Males to Females, by Age, 1991

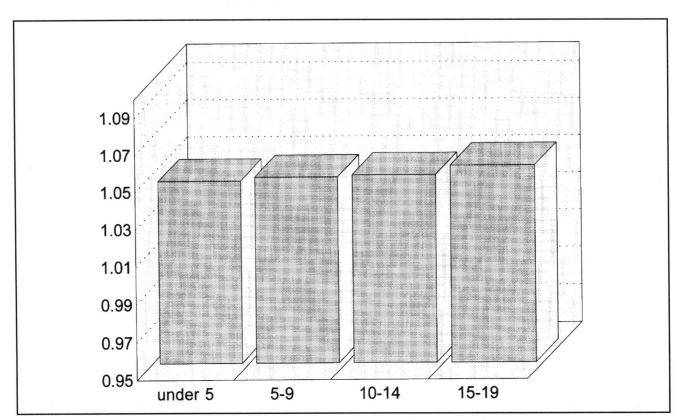

Source: U.S. Bureau of the Census, *Statistical Abstract of the United States: 1993* (113 edition). Washington, DC, 1993, page 16.

A1-5. Number of Children under 18, by Ethnicity, 1940–2010

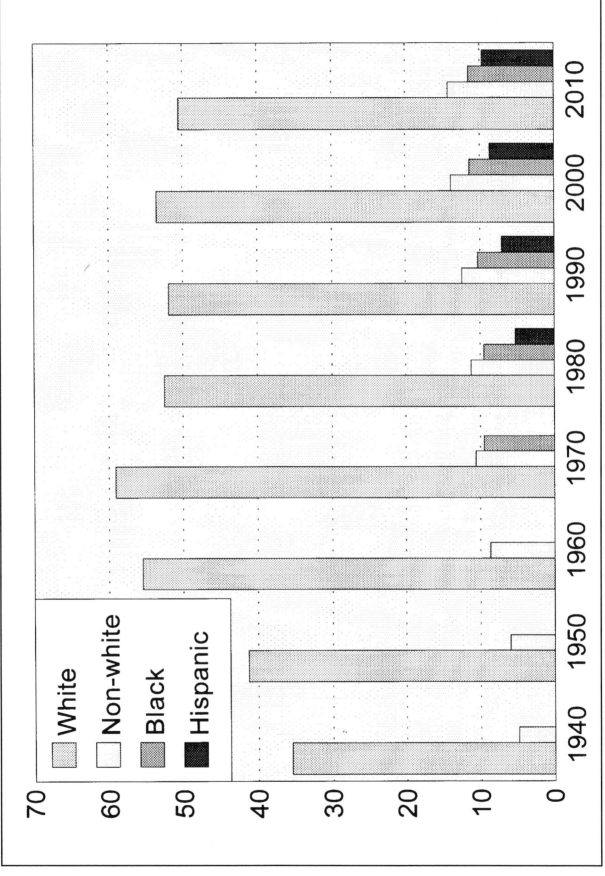

Source: U.S. Bureau of the Census, Statistical Abstract of the United States, 1993 (113 edition), Washington, DC, 1993, page 14.

A1-6. Race and Hispanic Origin of Children, 1990

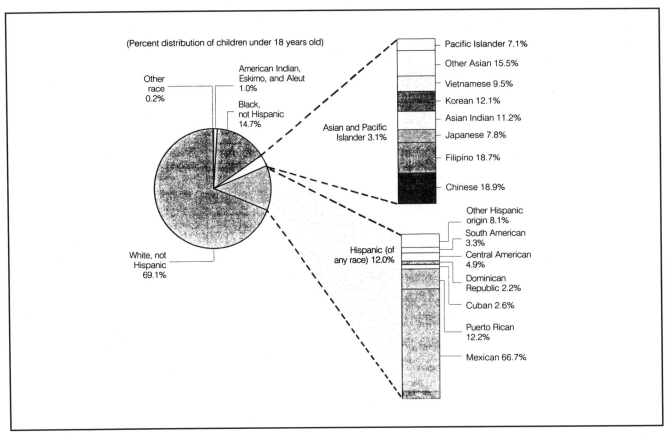

Source: U.S. Bureau of the Census, *We the American Children.* U.S. Department of Commerce, Economics and Statistics Administration. Washington, DC, 1993, page 3.

A1-7. Ethnic/Race Composition of Children, 1991

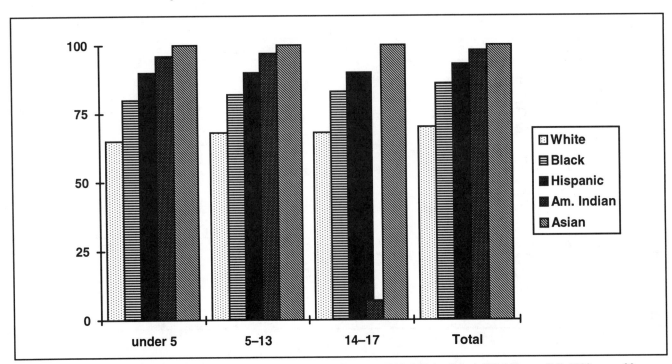

Source: U.S. Bureau of the Census, *Statistical Abstract of the United States: 1993* (113th edition). Washington, DC, 1993, page 22.

A1-8. Ethnic/Race Composition of Children, by Age, 1991 and 2025

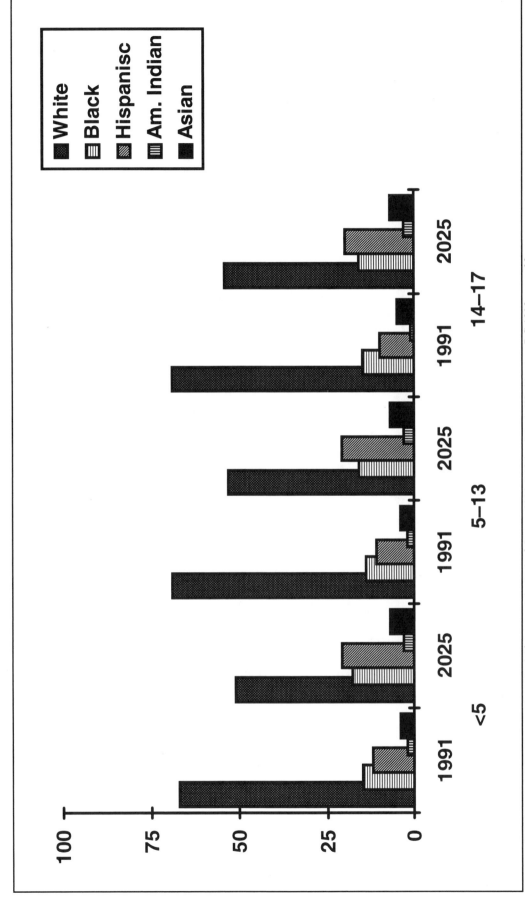

Source: U.S. Bureau of the Census, *Statistical Abstract of the United States: 1993* (113th edition). Washington, DC 1993, page 22.

A2. FERTILITY PATTERNS

A2-1. Live Births—Number and Rate, by State, 1990 and 1991

DIVISION AND STATE	NUMBER (1,000)						RATE PER 1,000 POPULATION[4]					
	1990					1991 prel.[3]	1990					1991 prel.[3]
	All races[1]	White	Black	Hispanic[2]			All races[1]	White	Black	Hispanic[2]		
				Total	Mexican					Total	Mexican	
U.S.	4,158.2	3,225.3	724.6	595.1	385.6	4,111.0	16.7	15.5	22.4	26.7	28.7	16.2
New England	201.2	175.3	19.0	15.5	0.6	189.5	15.2	14.6	30.3	27.2	20.1	14.3
Maine	17.4	16.9	0.2	0.1	(Z)	16.6	14.1	14.0	31.7	18.6	13.0	13.2
New Hampshire	17.6	17.1	0.2	(NA)	(NA)	16.1	15.8	15.7	25.6	(NA)	(NA)	13.9
Vermont	8.3	8.2	(Z)	(Z)	(Z)	7.7	14.7	14.7	19.5	8.2	9.7	13.2
Massachusetts	92.7	78.3	10.2	8.4	0.3	86.3	15.4	14.5	34.1	29.3	22.5	14.5
Rhode Island	15.2	13.1	1.3	1.6	0.1	14.6	15.1	14.3	34.5	34.1	35.7	14.5
Connecticut	50.1	41.8	7.0	5.3	0.2	48.3	15.2	14.6	25.6	25.0	20.1	14.8
Middle Atlantic	591.8	450.1	118.7	75.7	5.1	578.8	15.7	15.0	23.8	23.8	34.9	15.2
New York	297.6	216.8	66.3	53.1	3.8	292.4	16.5	16.2	23.2	24.0	41.0	16.2
New Jersey	122.3	92.6	24.5	17.0	0.9	117.8	15.8	15.1	23.6	22.9	30.4	15.1
Pennsylvania	172.0	140.7	27.9	5.6	0.4	168.6	14.5	13.4	25.6	24.3	16.5	13.9
East North Central	675.5	536.7	123.5	34.7	23.8	662.4	16.1	15.0	25.6	24.1	25.2	15.5
Ohio	166.9	137.1	27.7	2.4	1.0	158.6	15.4	14.4	24.0	17.4	17.5	14.4
Indiana	86.2	74.6	10.3	1.9	1.4	84.7	15.6	14.9	23.8	18.8	20.3	14.9
Illinois	195.8	144.8	45.2	24.2	17.7	194.0	17.1	16.2	26.7	26.8	28.3	16.5
Michigan	153.7	117.5	32.9	4.3	2.6	153.4	16.5	15.2	25.5	21.5	18.5	16.4
Wisconsin	72.9	62.7	7.5	1.9	1.2	71.7	14.9	13.9	30.7	20.0	21.3	14.5
West North Central	270.3	235.4	24.1	5.6	4.1	262.4	15.3	14.5	26.9	19.5	19.8	14.5
Minnesota	68.0	61.0	3.1	1.1	0.8	67.0	15.5	14.8	32.7	19.5	22.5	15.1
Iowa	39.4	37.4	1.3	0.6	0.4	36.0	14.2	13.9	26.6	19.1	15.5	12.6
Missouri	79.3	63.8	14.1	1.0	0.7	78.0	15.5	14.2	25.7	15.7	19.0	15.0
North Dakota	9.3	8.2	0.1	0.1	0.1	9.1	14.5	13.6	33.8	26.4	26.1	14.0
South Dakota	11.0	9.0	0.1	0.1	0.1	11.0	15.8	14.1	41.4	21.5	20.9	15.4
Nebraska	24.4	22.1	1.6	0.8	0.5	23.9	15.4	14.9	27.0	21.7	17.4	14.7
Kansas	39.0	34.0	3.8	2.0	1.6	37.3	15.7	15.3	26.8	20.9	21.0	14.6
South Atlantic	700.3	476.1	207.2	39.4	8.9	689.1	16.1	14.3	23.2	18.5	28.3	15.5
Delaware	11.1	8.2	2.7	0.3	0.1	11.2	16.7	15.4	23.8	20.4	27.2	16.0
Maryland	80.2	51.0	26.0	2.5	0.5	84.5	16.8	15.0	21.9	20.2	29.7	17.5
Dist. of Columbia	11.9	1.7	9.2	0.9	(Z)	10.0	19.5	9.7	22.9	27.2	14.8	17.0
Virginia	99.4	71.1	24.7	3.5	0.6	96.6	16.1	14.8	21.3	21.6	19.1	15.4
West Virginia	22.6	21.5	1.0	0.1	(Z)	22.2	12.6	12.4	17.1	8.6	8.5	12.2
North Carolina	104.5	69.8	31.7	1.8	1.0	102.4	15.8	13.9	21.7	22.9	30.2	15.2
South Carolina	58.6	35.2	22.7	0.6	0.3	57.7	16.8	14.6	21.8	18.7	24.1	16.0
Georgia	112.7	69.7	41.3	2.3	1.3	110.0	17.4	15.1	23.6	20.8	26.7	16.6
Florida	199.3	147.9	48.1	27.6	5.0	194.5	15.4	13.8	27.3	17.5	31.0	14.6
East South Central	236.4	167.5	66.3	1.2	0.6	232.1	15.6	13.9	22.3	12.4	15.9	14.9
Kentucky	54.4	48.5	5.4	0.3	0.2	54.9	14.8	14.3	20.4	12.5	20.5	14.7
Tennessee	75.0	56.0	18.0	0.4	0.2	73.1	15.4	13.8	23.2	13.6	16.6	14.5
Alabama	63.5	40.8	22.0	0.3	0.2	60.5	15.7	13.7	21.6	14.0	16.8	14.6
Mississippi	43.6	22.2	20.9	0.1	(Z)	43.5	16.9	13.6	22.8	7.3	7.0	16.6
West South Central	472.7	366.1	90.2	117.2	103.5	482.0	17.7	18.2	22.9	25.8	25.9	17.7
Arkansas	36.5	27.2	8.7	0.4	0.2	34.6	15.5	14.0	23.2	20.8	19.7	14.2
Louisiana	72.2	40.7	30.0	0.9	0.2	74.6	17.1	14.3	23.1	10.1	8.6	17.2
Oklahoma	47.8	35.6	5.5	(NA)	(NA)	47.3	15.1	13.8	23.7	(NA)	(NA)	14.7
Texas	316.4	262.6	45.9	115.8	103.0	325.6	18.6	20.6	22.7	26.7	26.5	18.8
Mountain	242.8	212.4	10.2	48.7	31.8	243.4	17.8	18.1	27.2	24.4	22.1	17.5
Montana	11.6	9.7	0.1	0.3	0.1	11.5	14.5	13.1	31.5	24.0	17.3	14.3
Idaho	16.4	15.8	0.1	1.4	1.2	17.2	16.3	16.6	27.3	27.1	27.7	16.6
Wyoming	7.0	6.5	0.1	0.5	0.3	6.8	15.4	15.2	29.7	19.8	17.2	14.6
Colorado	53.5	48.1	3.4	9.3	4.7	54.0	16.2	16.6	25.5	21.9	16.5	16.1
New Mexico	27.4	22.2	0.8	12.2	2.8	28.2	18.1	19.3	25.8	21.1	8.6	18.0
Arizona	69.0	58.1	3.2	19.7	18.9	67.7	18.8	19.6	28.7	28.6	30.7	18.3
Utah	36.3	33.9	0.4	2.0	1.2	35.1	21.1	21.0	33.3	24.1	21.8	20.1
Nevada	21.6	18.1	2.2	3.3	2.5	23.0	18.0	17.9	27.4	26.2	29.1	18.8
Pacific	767.2	605.7	65.3	257.0	207.2	755.5	19.6	21.4	26.6	31.7	32.5	18.8
Washington	79.3	68.2	4.1	5.7	3.9	75.7	16.3	15.8	27.7	26.6	24.8	15.2
Oregon	42.9	38.9	1.3	3.0	2.6	42.8	15.1	14.7	27.3	26.4	30.9	14.6
California	612.6	486.3	58.2	245.6	200.1	605.7	20.6	23.7	26.4	31.9	32.7	19.8
Alaska	11.9	7.6	0.7	0.3	0.2	11.2	21.6	18.3	31.9	18.4	21.5	21.1
Hawaii	20.5	4.7	1.0	2.4	0.3	20.0	18.5	12.7	35.3	29.9	24.2	17.5

NA Not available. Z Less than 50. [1]Includes other races not shown separately. [2]Persons of Hispanic origin may be of any race. Births by Hispanic origin of mother. [3]Includes births to nonresidents. Provisional. [4]Based on resident population enumerated as of April 1 for 1990 and estimated as of July 1 for 1991.

Source: U.S. Bureau of the Census, *Statistical Abstract of the United States: 1993* (113th edition). Washington, DC, 1993, page 75.

A2-2. Mean Number of Children Ever Born to Ever-Married Black, White, and American Indian and Alaska Native Women, by Age of Women in 1990

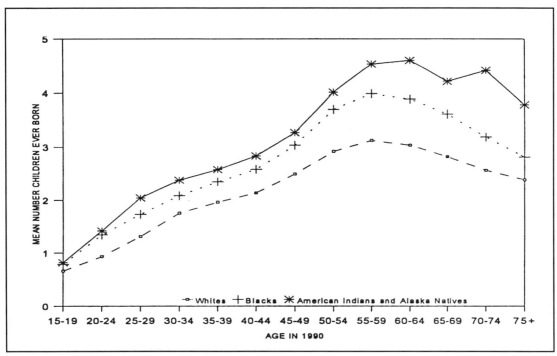

Source: Census of Population and Housing, 1990: Public Use Microdata Samples U.S. Technical Documentation, prepared by the Bureau of the Census. Washington, DC: The Bureau, 1992.

A2-3. Trends in the Total Fertility Rate, 1800–1990

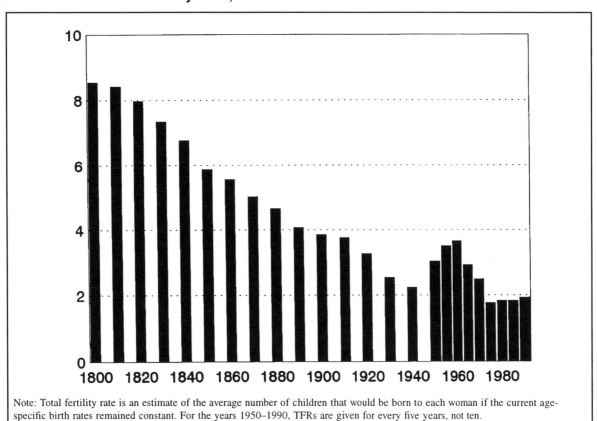

Note: Total fertility rate is an estimate of the average number of children that would be born to each woman if the current age-specific birth rates remained constant. For the years 1950–1990, TFRs are given for every five years, not ten.

Source: Hernandez, Donald J. *America's Children: Resources from Family, Government, and the Economy.* New York: Russell Sage Foundation, 1993, page 22. Used with permission of Russell Sage Foundation.

A2-4. Percent Distribution of Number of Own Children under 18 Years Old, 1970–1992

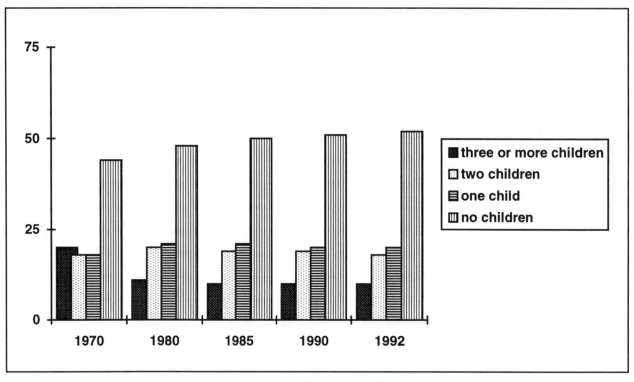

Source: U.S. Bureau of the Census, *Statistical Abstract of the United States: 1993* (113 edition). Washington, DC, 1993, page 61.

A2-5. Percent Distribution of Number of Own Children under 18 Years, by Ethnicity, 1992

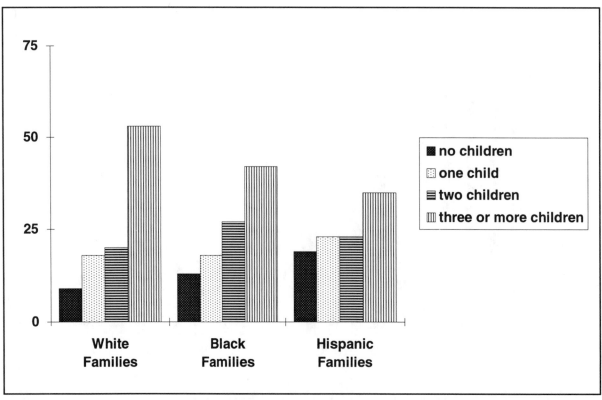

Source: U.S. Bureau of the Census, *Statistical Abstract of the United States: 1993* (113th edition). Washington, DC, 1993, page 61.

A2-6. Distribution of Women and Average Number of Children Ever Born, by Race, Age, and Marital Status, 1992

(Percent distribution. Numbers in thousands).

Characteristic	Total women	Women by number of children ever born								Children ever born	
		Total	None	One	Two	Three	Four	Five and six	Seven or more	Total number	Per 1,000 women
BLACK											
All Marital Classes											
15 to 44 years	8,017	100.0	34.4	21.5	21.4	12.8	5.6	3.5	.7	11,900	1,484
15 to 19 years	1,313	100.0	86.9	8.8	3.4	.8	-	.1	-	242	186
20 to 24 years	1,336	100.0	42.8	29.2	16.5	8.0	2.7	.8	-	1,350	1,011
25 to 29 years	1,422	100.0	31.1	24.6	23.7	10.9	6.1	3.5	.1	2,100	1,477
30 to 34 years	1,493	100.0	19.8	21.7	30.2	17.5	6.2	4.1	.5	2,746	1,840
35 to 39 years	1,345	100.0	13.8	22.3	25.9	20.8	9.9	5.8	1.5	2,932	2,180
40 to 44 years	1,109	100.0	11.1	22.4	28.7	19.3	9.1	7.3	2.2	2,530	2,282
Women Ever Married											
15 to 44 years	3,585	100.0	11.1	23.3	30.2	20.3	8.8	5.2	1.0	7,686	2,144
15 to 19 years	16	(B)	(B)	(B)	(B)	(B)	(B)	(B)	(B)	16	(8)
20 to 24 years	238	100.0	22.1	28.1	26.8	15.0	5.6	2.4	-	384	1,808
25 to 29 years	608	100.0	18.5	27.2	28.6	14.3	8.4	2.8	.2	1,072	1,783
30 to 34 years	858	100.0	11.9	22.4	35.5	19.8	6.7	3.4	.2	1,707	1,888
35 to 39 years	934	100.0	6.8	21.7	27.3	25.5	10.6	6.3	1.7	2,255	2,416
40 to 44 years	930	100.0	6.7	21.8	30.3	21.1	10.3	8.1	1.8	2,251	2,421
Women Never Married											
15 to 44 years	4,432	100.0	53.3	20.1	14.3	6.7	3.0	2.2	.4	4,215	961
15 to 19 years	1,297	100.0	87.5	8.5	3.1	.7	-	.1	-	226	174
20 to 24 years	1,097	100.0	47.3	29.4	14.3	6.5	2.1	.4	-	966	841
25 to 29 years	813	100.0	40.5	22.6	20.1	8.4	4.4	4.1	-	1,028	1,264
30 to 34 years	634	100.0	30.6	20.7	23.0	14.4	5.5	5.0	.9	1,039	1,638
35 to 39 years	412	100.0	29.8	23.7	22.6	10.1	8.2	4.7	1.0	677	1,646
40 to 44 years	179	100.0	33.9	25.6	20.5	9.6	3.0	3.1	4.3	278	1,666
HISPANIC[1]											
All Marital Classes											
15 to 44 years	5,555	100.0	34.0	19.0	22.8	13.9	6.5	3.0	.8	8,570	1,543
15 to 19 years	922	100.0	85.5	12.4	2.1	-	-	-	-	153	186
20 to 24 years	942	100.0	48.6	25.7	19.6	4.3	1.6	.2	-	802	861
25 to 29 years	1,050	100.0	26.9	26.8	27.0	12.5	4.2	2.4	.2	1,568	1,484
30 to 34 years	1,001	100.0	16.4	19.7	31.6	20.0	7.7	3.8	.8	2,001	1,988
35 to 39 years	956	100.0	11.5	14.6	29.7	24.4	14.0	4.6	1.1	2,254	2,367
40 to 44 years	683	100.0	12.7	11.7	26.2	24.5	13.1	8.5	3.4	1,793	2,624
Women Ever Married											
15 to 44 years	3,549	100.0	11.5	22.8	31.5	19.7	9.3	4.1	1.1	7,541	2,125
15 to 19 years	79	100.0	26.2	63.4	10.4	-	-	-	-	66	842
20 to 24 years	436	100.0	22.9	37.3	29.0	7.2	3.1	.4	-	574	1,317
25 to 29 years	768	100.0	15.9	29.4	32.0	15.1	5.1	2.3	.3	1,333	1,736
30 to 34 years	813	100.0	9.3	20.4	35.9	21.6	8.5	3.5	.7	1,749	2,162
35 to 39 years	830	100.0	5.6	15.8	32.1	25.9	14.6	5.0	1.0	2,070	2,486
40 to 44 years	624	100.0	6.9	11.9	28.7	26.0	14.0	8.7	3.7	1,748	2,803
Women Never Married											
15 to 44 years	2,005	100.0	73.9	12.2	7.5	3.6	1.4	1.2	.2	1,029	513
15 to 19 years	844	100.0	91.1	7.7	1.3	-	-	-	-	86	102
20 to 24 years	506	100.0	70.8	15.6	11.5	1.8	.2	-	-	228	460
25 to 29 years	281	100.0	56.8	19.9	13.5	5.3	1.8	2.7	-	235	834
30 to 34 years	188	100.0	47.4	16.5	13.0	12.7	4.0	5.2	1.1	252	1,340
35 to 39 years	126	100.0	49.7	7.1	14.3	14.8	10.3	2.1	1.7	184	1,453
40 to 44 years	60	(B)	(B)	(B)	(B)	(B)	(B)	(B)	(B)	45	(8)

[1] Persons of Hispanic origin may be of any race.

B = base too small to show derived measure

Source: Bachu, Amara. *Fertility of American Women: June 1992, U.S. Bureau of the Census, Current Population Reports, P20-470.* U.S. Government Printing Office, Washington, DC, 1993, page 1.

A2-7. Percent of Children Born out of Wedlock, by Race, 1940–1990

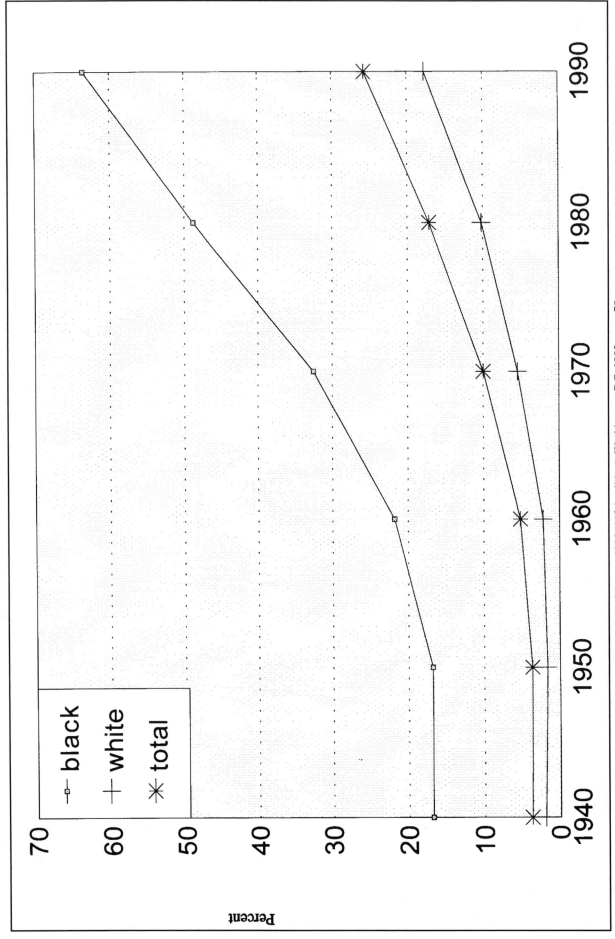

Source: U.S. Bureau of the Census, Statistical Abstract of the United States: 1993 (113th edition). Washington, DC, 1993, page 78.

A2-8. Percentage of Total Births to Unmarried Women, Selected Countries, 1960–1986

Country	1960	1965	1970	1975	1980	1986
France	6.1	5.9	6.8	8.5	11.4	21.9
Germany, Federal Rep. of	6.3	4.7	5.5	6.1	7.6	9.6
Italy	2.4	2.0	2.2	2.6	4.3	5.6
Sweden	11.3	13.8	18.4	32.4	39.7	48.4
United Kingdom	5.2	7.3	8.0	9.0	11.5	21.0
United States	5.3	7.7	10.7	14.2	18.4	23.4

Source: Hobbs, Frank, and Laura Lippman. *Children's Well-Being: An International Comparison.* International Population Reports Series P-95, No. 80. U.S. Department of Commerce, Bureau of the Census. Washington, DC: U.S. Government Printing Office, 1990, page 49.

A3. SIBSHIP SIZE

A3-1. Number of Siblings in the Homes of Children 0–5 Years Old and 12–17 Years Old, by Race and Hispanic Origin, 1990

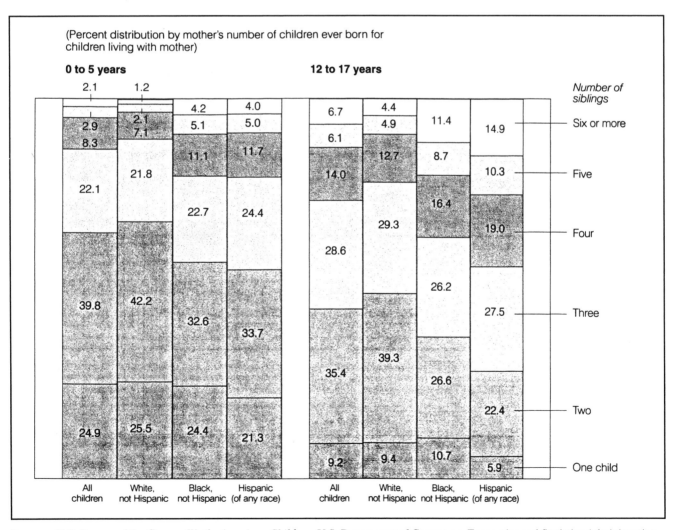

Source: U.S. Bureau of the Census, *We the American Children.* U.S. Department of Commerce, Economics and Statistics Administration. Washington, DC, 1993, page 6.

A3-2. Median Number of Siblings, Children Aged 12-17, 1865–1994

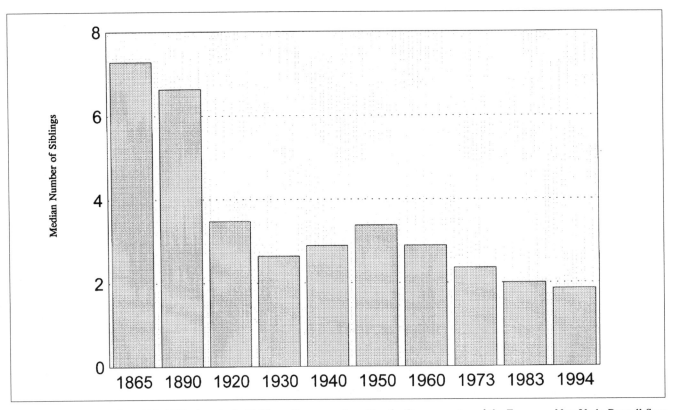

Source: Hernandez, Donald J. 1993. *America's Children: Resources from Family, Government, and the Economy.* New York: Russell Sage Foundation, page 28. Used with permission of Russell Sage Foundation.

A3-3. Median Number of Siblings, by Race, Children Aged 0–17, 1940–1980

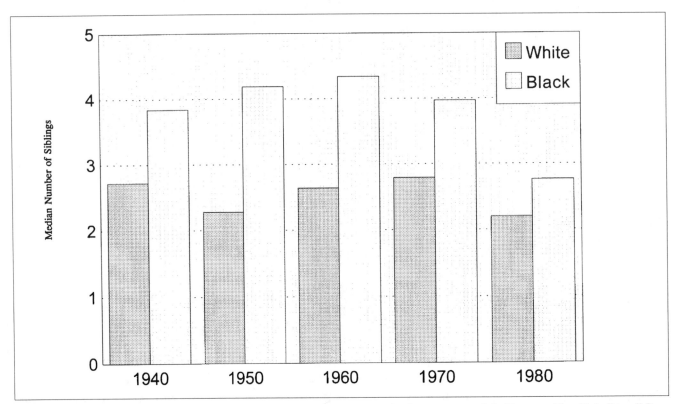

Source: Hernandez, Donald J. 1993. *America's Children: Resources from Family, Government, and the Economy.* New York: Russell Sage Foundation, page 41. Used with permission of Russell Sage Foundation.

A3-4. Percent of Adolescents Aged 12–17 Who Were an Only Child, 1865–1994

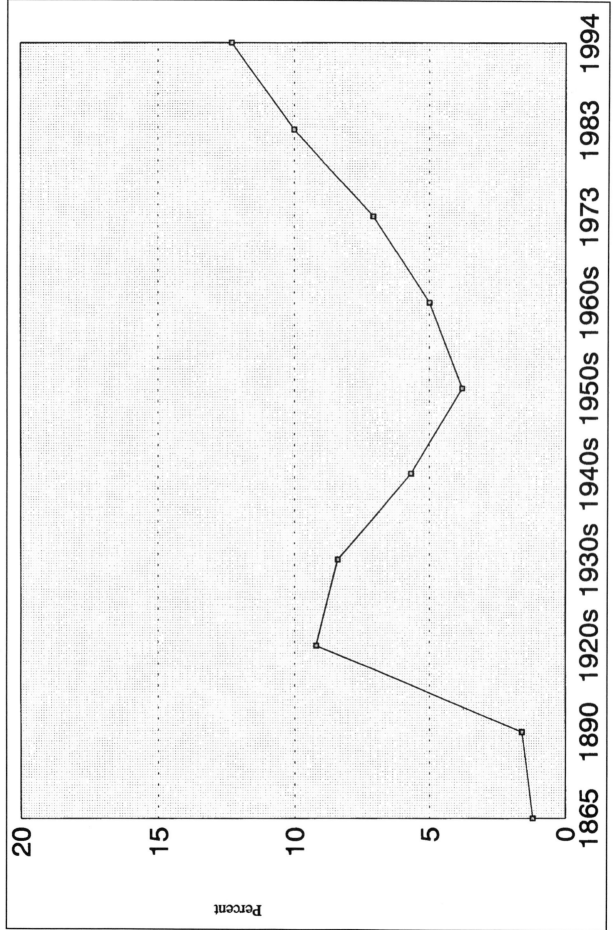

Source: Hernandez, Donald J. 1993. *America's Children: Resources from Family, Government, and the Economy.* New York: Russell Sage Foundation, page 53. Used with permission of Russell Sage Foundation.

A4. FAMILY TYPES

A4-1. Familes, by Number of Own Children under 18 Years Old, 1970–1992

Race, Hispanic Origin, and Year	NUMBER OF FAMILIES (1,000)					PERCENT DISTRIBUTION					Average size of family
	Total	No children	One child	Two children	Three or more children	Total	No children	One child	Two children	Three or more children	
All Families[1]											
1970	51,586	22,774	9,398	8,969	10,445	100	44	18	17	20	3.58
1980	59,550	28,528	12,443	11,470	7,109	100	48	21	19	12	3.29
1985	62,706	31,594	13,108	11,645	6,359	100	50	21	19	10	3.23
1990	66,090	33,801	13,530	12,263	6,496	100	51	20	18	10	3.17
1992	67,173	34,427	13,615	12,364	6,768	100	51	20	19	10	3.17
Married couple	52,457	28,037	9,520	9,728	5,173	100	53	18	19	10	3.23
Male householder[2]	3,025	1,742	768	391	123	100	58	25	13	4	2.77
Female householder[2]	11,692	4,648	3,327	2,244	1,472	100	40	28	19	13	2.98
White Families											
1970	46,261	20,719	8,437	8,174	8,931	100	45	18	18	19	3.52
1980	52,243	25,769	10,727	9,977	5,769	100	49	21	19	11	3.23
1985	54,400	28,169	11,174	9,937	5,120	100	52	21	18	9	3.16
1990	56,590	29,872	11,186	10,342	5,191	100	53	20	18	9	3.11
1992	57,224	30,178	11,204	10,477	5,365	100	53	20	18	9	3.11
Black Families											
1970	4,887	1,903	858	726	1,401	100	39	18	15	29	4.13
1980	6,184	2,364	1,449	1,235	1,136	100	38	23	20	18	3.67
1985	6,778	2,887	1,579	1,330	982	100	43	23	20	15	3.60
1990	7,470	3,093	1,894	1,433	1,049	100	41	25	19	14	3.46
1992	7,716	3,271	1,870	1,429	1,146	100	42	24	19	15	3.43
Hispanic Families[3]											
1970	2,004	597	390	388	629	100	30	20	19	31	4.28
1980	3,029	946	680	698	706	100	31	22	23	23	3.90
1985	3,939	1,337	904	865	833	100	34	23	22	21	3.88
1990	4,840	1,790	1,095	1,036	919	100	37	23	21	19	3.83
1992	5,177	1,843	1,160	1,139	1,035	100	36	22	22	20	3.81

[1]Includes other races, not shown separately. [2]No spouse present. [3]Hispanic persons may be of any race. 1970 Hispanic data as of April and based on Census of Population

Source: U.S. Bureau of the Census, *Statistical Abstract of the United States: 1993* (113th edition). Washington, DC, 1993, page 61.

A4-2. Family Households with Own Children under Age 18, by Type of Family, 1970–1992, and by Age of Householder, 1992

Family Type	1970	1980	1990	Total	1992					
					15 to 24 years old	25 to 34 years old	35 to 44 years old	45 to 54 years old	55 to 64 years old	65 years old and over
NUMBER (1,000)										
Family households with children	28,731	31,022	32,289	32,746	1,707	11,061	13,999	4,994	850	136
Married couple	25,532	24,961	24,537	24,420	822	7,866	10,859	4,064	714	95
Male householder[1]	341	616	1,153	1,283	87	413	506	197	59	21
Female householder[1]	2,858	5,445	6,599	7,043	798	2,781	2,633	732	78	20
PERCENT DISTRIBUTION										
Family households with children	100	100	100	100	100	100	100	100	100	100
Married couple	89	81	76	75	48	71	78	81	84	70
Male householder[1]	1	2	4	4	5	4	4	4	7	15
Female householder[1]	10	18	20	22	47	25	19	15	9	15
HOUSEHOLDS WITH CHILDREN[2]										
Family households with children, total	56	52	49	49	65	77	80	41	9	1
Married couple	57	51	47	47	56	74	80	41	9	1
Male householder[1]	28	36	40	42	33	57	65	38	18	6
Female householder[1]	52	63	61	60	88	94	82	40	7	1

[1]No spouse present. [2]As a percent of all family households, by marital status of householder.

Source: U.S. Bureau of the Census, *Statistical Abstract of the United States: 1993* (113th edition). Washington, DC, 1993, page 61.

A4-3. Married-Couple Family Households with Children, 1980–1990

Type of Family	Number (1,000)			Percent Distribution		
	1980	1985	1990	1980	1985	1990
Total	24,091	23,868	25,314	100.0	100.0	100.0
Biological[1]	19,037	18,470	19,253	79.0	77.4	76.1
Adoptive[2]	429	303	345	1.8	1.3	1.4
Biological mother-stepfather[3]	1,818	2,207	2,619	7.5	9.2	10.3
Biological father-stepmother[4]	171	180	152	0.7	0.8	0.6
Joint biological-step[5]	1,862	2,039	2,475	7.7	8.5	9.8
Joint biological-adoptive[6]	429	223	324	1.8	0.9	1.3
Joint step-adoptive[7]	12	15	8	*	0.1	*
Joint bio-step-adoptive[8]	25	29	*	0.1	0.1	*
Unknown[9]	309	403	137	1.3	1.7	0.5

*Represents or rounds to zero. [1]All the own children were biological children of both parents. [2]All the own children were adoptive children of both parents. [3]All the own children were biological children of the mother and stepchildren of the father. [4]All the own children were biological children of the father and stepchildren of the mother. [5]At least one child was a biological child of both parents, at least one was a biological child of one parent and a stepchild of the other parent, and no other type of child was present; or a stepchild of each parent and no other type of child was present. [6]At least one child was a biological child of both parents, at least one was an adopted child of both parents, and no other type of child was present. [7]At least one child was a biological child of one parent and a stepchild of the other parent, at least one was an adopted child of both parents, and no other type of child was present. [8]At least one child was a biological child of both parents, at least one was the biological child of one parent and the stepchild of the other, and at least one was an adopted child of both parents. [9]At least one child had at least one parent for whom the nature of the relationship could not be designated.

Source: U.S. Bureau of the Census, *Statistical Abstract of the United States: 1993* (113th edition). Washington, DC, 1993, page 62.

A4-4. Family Type of Married-Couple Households, 1980–1990

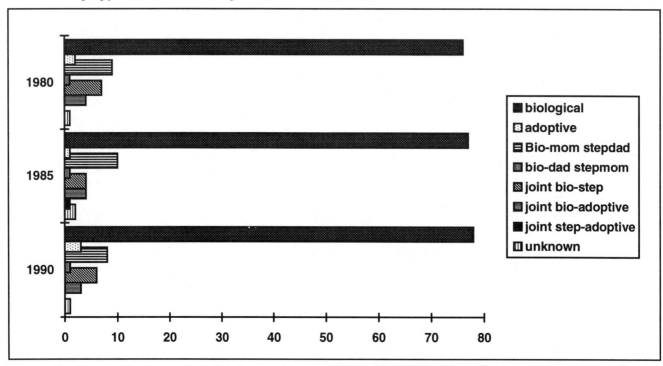

Source: U.S. Bureau of the Census, *Statistical Abstract of the United States: 1993* (113th edition). Washington, DC, 1993, page 62.

A4-5. Family Type of Married-Couple Households, by Race, 1990

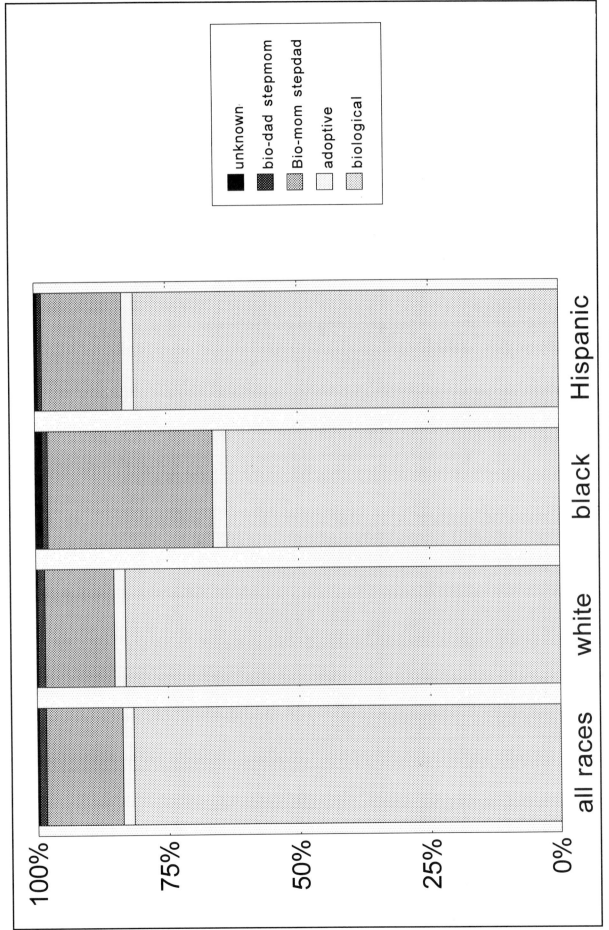

Source: U.S. Bureau of the Census, *Statistical Abstract of the United States: 1993* (113th edition). Washington, DC, 1993, page 62.

A4-6. Family Groups with Children under 18, by Type, Race, and Hispanic Origin of Householder or Reference Person, 1992

(Numbers in thousands)

Subject	All family groups		Family households		All subfamilies		Related subfamilies		Unrelated subfamilies	
	Number	Percent	Number	Percent	Number	Percent	Number	Percent	Number	Percent
ALL RACES										
Family groups with children	35,378	100.0	32,746	100.0	2,633	100.0	2,011	100.0	622	100.0
Two-parent groups	24,879	70.3	24,420	74.6	459	17.4	415	20.6	44	7.1
One-parent groups	10,499	29.7	8,326	25.4	2,173	82.5	1,596	79.4	577	92.8
Maintained by mother	9,028	25.5	7,043	21.5	1,985	75.4	1,462	72.7	523	84.1
Maintained by father	1,472	4.2	1,283	3.9	189	7.2	134	6.7	55	8.8
WHITE										
Family groups with children	28,847	100.0	27,045	100.0	1,803	100.0	1,296	100.0	507	100.0
Two-parent groups	21,909	75.9	21,517	79.6	392	21.7	351	27.1	41	8.1
One-parent groups	6,938	24.1	5,528	20.4	1,410	78.2	944	72.8	466	91.9
Maintained by mother	5,753	19.9	4,488	16.6	1,264	70.1	851	65.7	413	81.5
Maintained by father	1,186	4.1	1,040	3.8	145	8.0	93	7.2	52	10.3
BLACK										
Family groups with children	5,164	100.0	4,445	100.0	719	100.0	621	100.0	98	100.0
Two-parent groups	1,948	37.7	1,926	43.3	22	3.1	21	3.4	1	1.0
One-parent groups	3,216	62.3	2,519	56.7	697	96.9	600	96.6	97	99.0
Maintained by mother	2,994	58.0	2,335	52.5	660	91.8	564	90.8	96	98.0
Maintained by father	221	4.3	184	4.1	37	5.1	36	5.8	1	1.0
HISPANIC*										
Family groups with children	3,771	100.0	3,333	100.0	439	100.0	354	100.0	85	100.0
Two-parent groups	2,473	65.6	2,321	69.6	152	34.6	128	36.2	24	28.2
One-parent groups	1,298	34.4	1,012	30.4	286	65.1	226	63.8	60	70.6
Maintained by mother	1,112	29.5	853	25.6	259	59.0	206	58.2	53	62.4
Maintained by father	186	4.9	159	4.8	27	6.2	20	5.6	7	8.2

*May be of any race.

Note: Family groups comprise family households, related subfamilies, and unrelated subfamilies. A subfamily is a married couple (husband and wife enumerated as members of the same household) with or without never-married children under 17 years old, or one parent with one or more never-married children under 18 years old, living in a household and related to but not including either the householder or the householder's spouse.

Source: Rawlings, Steve W. *Household and Family Characteristics: March 1992.* U.S. Bureau of the Census. Current Population Reports, P20-467. U.S. Government Printing Office, Washington, DC, 1993, page xv.

A4-7. Composition of Family Groups with Children, by Race and Hispanic Origin, 1970–1992

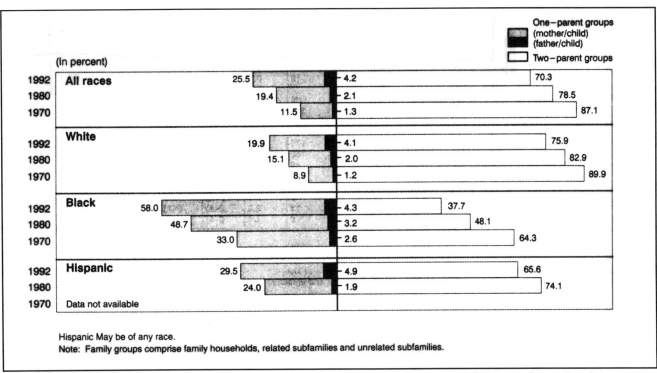

Source: Rawlings, Steve W. *Household and Family Characteristics: March 1992*. U.S. Bureau of the Census. Current Population Reports, P20-467. U.S. Government Printing Office, Washington, DC, 1993, page xv.

A4-8. Living Arrangements of Adolescents, by Age, 1992

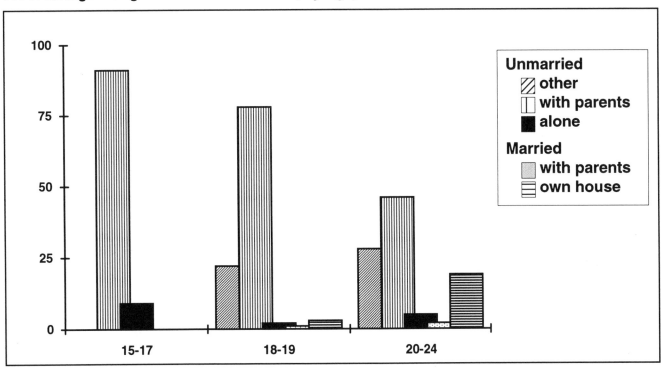

Source: Rawlings, Steve W. *Household and Family Characteristics: March 1992*. U.S. Bureau of the Census. Current Population Reports, P20-467. U.S. Government Printing Office, Washington, DC, 1993, page vii.

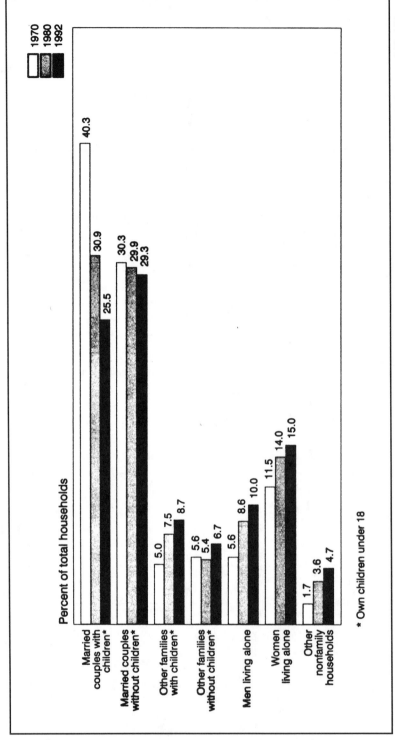

A4-9. Household Composition, 1970–1992

Source: Rawlings, Steve W. *Household and Family Characteristics: March 1992.* U.S. Bureau of the Census. *Current Population Reports*, P20-467. U.S. Government Printing Office, Washington, DC, 1993, page vii.

A5. LIVING ARRANGEMENTS OF CHILDREN AND ADOLESCENTS

A5-1. Children Living with Biological, Step, and Adoptive Married-Couple Parents, by Race and Hispanic Origin of Mother, 1980–1990

Type of Parent	All Races[1]			White			Black			Hispanic[2]
	1980	1985	1990	1980	1985	1990	1980	1985	1990	1990
Number (1,000)										
Own children under 18 years,										
Total	47,248	45,347	45,448	42,329	39,942	39,732	3,775	3,816	3,671	4,568
Biological mother and father	39,523	37,213	37,026	35,852	33,202	32,975	2,698	2,661	2,336	3,703
Biological mother-stepfather	5,355	6,049	6,643	4,362	4,918	5,258	877	952	1,149	699
Stepmother-biological father	727	740	608	664	676	549	46	50	38	38
Adoptive mother and father	1,350	866	974	1,209	754	815	119	76	97	101
Unknown mother or father	293	479	197	242	391	135	35	77	51	27
Percent Distribution										
Own children under 18 years,										
Total	100.0	100.0	100.0	100.0	100.0	100.0	100.0	100.0	100.0	100.0
Biological mother and father	83.7	82.1	81.5	84.7	83.1	83.0	71.5	69.7	63.6	81.1
Biological mother-stepfather	11.3	13.3	14.6	10.3	12.3	13.2	23.2	24.9	31.3	15.3
Stepmother-biological father	1.5	1.6	1.3	1.6	1.7	1.4	1.2	1.3	1.0	0.8
Adoptive mother and father	2.9	1.9	2.1	2.9	1.9	2.1	3.1	2.0	2.6	2.2
Unknown mother or father	0.6	1.1	0.4	0.6	1.0	0.3	0.9	2.0	1.4	0.6

[1]Includes other races not shown separately.   [2]Persons of Hispanic origin may be of any race.

Source: U.S. Bureau of the Census, *Statitical Abstract of the United States: 1993* (113th edition). Washington, DC, 1993, page 62.

A5-2. Living Arrangements of Children Aged 1–17, 1940–1988

	1940	1950	1960	1970	1980	1988
Total Number of children (in thousands)	40,035	46,306	64,782	70,129	64,586	64,496
Percent	100.0	100.0	100.0	100.0	100.0	100.0
Two-Parent Family	84.6	86.1	87.2	82.5	76.6	71.2
Children born after marriage (one or both parents married only once)	75.2	74.5	77.7	72.0	63.0	57.0
Parents married once (intact two-parent family)	69.6	69.8	70.6	65.5	56.8	51.0
Father remarried, mother married once	NA	NA	4.8	4.5	4.6	6.0
Mother remarried, father married once	5.6	4.7	2.3	2.0	1.6	NA
At least one stepchild in family	9.4	11.5	6.0	6.5	8.2	NA
Mother married once	8.2	6.2	2.6	3.0	3.8	NA
Mother remarried	1.2	5.4	3.4	3.5	4.4	NA
Both parents remarried	NA	NA	3.6	4.0	5.5	NA
One-Parent Family	8.8	7.8	8.7	13.6	18.3	23.8
Mother-only family	6.7	6.4	7.7	11.8	16.2	21.0
Mother never married	0.1	0.1	0.3	1.1	3.0	6.7
Mother separated or married spouse absent	2.1	2.7	3.6	4.7	4.4	5.2
Mother divorced	0.9	1.4	1.9	3.5	7.2	7.8
Mother widowed	3.6	2.2	1.9	2.5	1.6	1.3
Father-only family	2.1	1.4	1.0	1.8	2.1	2.8
Father never married	0.1	0.0	0.0	0.1	0.3	0.6
Father separated or married spouse absent	0.6	0.6	0.6	1.0	0.5	0.7
Father divorced	0.1	0.2	0.1	0.3	1.0	1.3
Father widowed	1.3	0.6	0.3	0.4	0.3	0.2
No Parent in Home	6.7	6.0	3.9	4.1	5.1	5.0
Grandparent family	2.0	1.9	1.4	1.5	1.5	NA
Child is married householder or householder's spouse	0.2	0.3	0.3	0.3	0.2	NA
Child is unmarried householder	0.0	0.0	0.0	0.1	0.1	NA
Child is other relative of householder	2.1	1.7	1.0	1.0	1.7	NA
Child not related to householder	1.2	0.8	0.5	0.6	1.1	NA
Child in group quarters	1.2	1.3	0.7	0.6	0.4	NA

Note: Estimates for two-parent families in 1940 and 1950 are derived using marital history information for mothers but not fathers. When both parents remarried, it is not possible to ascertain whether children were born before or after the current marriage, that is, whether any children in the home are stepchildren. NA indicates cannot be estimated from available data.

Source: Hernandez, Donald J. 1993. *America's Children: Resources from Family, Government, and the Economy.* New York: Russell Sage Foundation, page 65. Used with permission of Russell Sage Foundation.

A5-3. Parental Living Arrangements of Children, by Race, 1980 and 1990

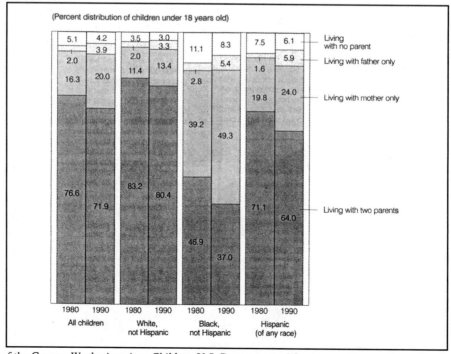

Source: U.S. Bureau of the Census, *We the American Children.* U.S. Department of Commerce, Economics and Statistics Administration. Washington, DC, 1993, page 4.

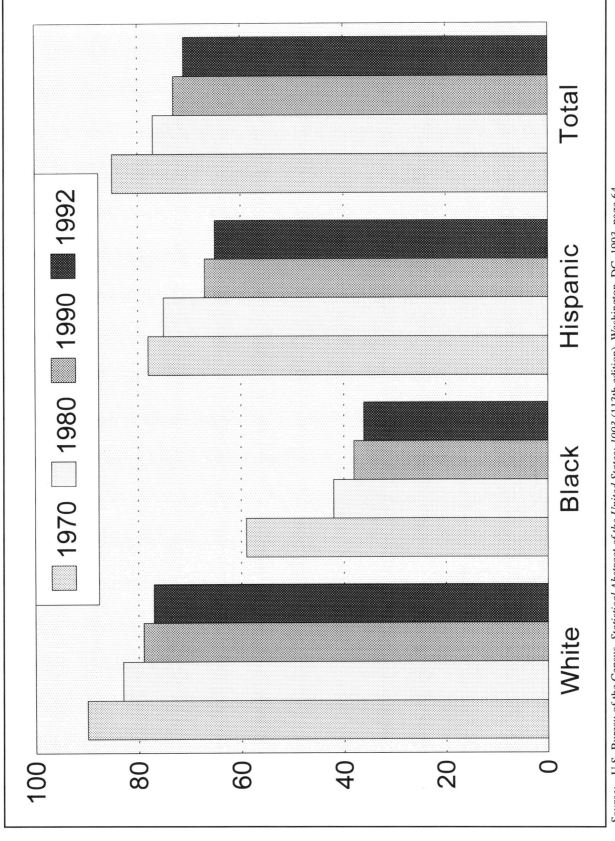

A5-4. Children under 18 Living with Both Parents, by Race, 1970–1992

Source: U.S. Bureau of the Census, *Statistical Abstract of the United States: 1993* (113th edition). Washington, DC, 1993, page 64.

A5-5. Children under 18 Years Old, by Presence of Parents, 1970–1992

Race, Hispanic Origin, and Year	Number (1,000)	Both parents	Percent Living With—Mother only					Father only	Neither parent
			Total	Divorced	Married, spouse absent	Never Married (single)	Widowed		
ALL RACES[1]									
1970	69,162	85	11	3	5	1	2	1	3
1980	63,427	77	18	8	6	3	2	2	4
1985	62,475	74	21	9	5	6	2	3	3
1990	64,137	73	22	8	5	7	2	3	3
1992	65,965	71	23	8	6	8	1	3	3
WHITE									
1970	58,790	90	8	3	3	(Z)	2	1	2
1980	52,242	83	14	7	4	1	2	2	2
1985	50,836	80	16	8	4	2	1	2	2
1990	51,390	79	16	8	4	3	1	3	2
1992	52,493	77	18	8	5	4	1	3	2
BLACK									
1970	9,422	59	30	5	16	4	4	2	10
1980	9,375	42	44	11	16	13	4	2	12
1985	9,479	40	51	11	12	25	3	3	7
1990	10,018	38	51	10	12	27	2	4	8
1992	10,427	36	54	10	12	31	1	3	7
HISPANIC[2]									
1970	4,006	78	(NA)	(NA)	(NA)	(NA)	(NA)	(NA)	(NA)
1980	5,459	75	20	6	8	4	2	2	4
1985	6,057	68	27	7	11	7	2	2	3
1990	7,174	67	27	7	10	8	2	3	3
1992	7,619	65	28	8	9	10	1	4	3

NA not available. Z less than 0.5 percent. [1]Includes other races not shown separately. [2]Hispanic persons may be of any race.

Source: U.S. Bureau of the Census, *Statistical Abstract of the United States: 1993* (113th edition). Washington, DC, 1993, page 64.

A5-6. Grandchildren of the Householder, by Presence of Parents, Race, and Hispanic Origin, 1992, 1980, and 1970

Living Arrangement	1992				1980 Census	1970 Census
	Total	White	Black	Hispanic		
Grandchild of householder (under 18 years)	3,253	1,887	1,208	458	2,306	2,214
Percent of all children under 18	4.9	3.6	11.6	6.0	3.6	3.2
With both parents present	502	428	25	118	310	363
With mother only present	1,740	957	719	220	922	817
With father only present	144	96	40	23	86	78
With neither parent present	867	407	424	97	988	957
Percent	100.0	100.0	100.0	100.0	100.0	100.0
With both parents present	15.4	22.7	2.1	25.8	13.4	16.4
With mother only present	53.5	50.7	59.5	48.0	40.0	36.9
With father only present	4.4	5.1	3.3	5.0	3.7	3.5
With neither parent present	26.7	21.6	35.1	21.2	42.8	43.2

*Persons of Hispanic origin may be of any race.

Source: U.S. Bureau of the Census. *Marital Status and Living Arrangements: March 1992.* Current Population Reports, Series P20, No. 468. U.S. Government Printing Office, Washington, DC, 1992, page xiii.

A5-7. White and Black Children in "Ozzie and Harriet Families" at Ages 0 and 17 for 1920–1980 Birth Cohorts

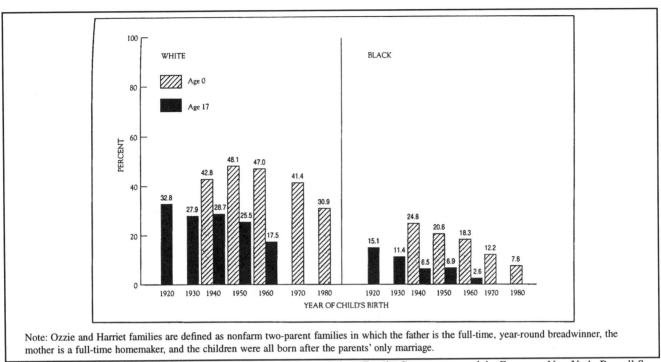

Note: Ozzie and Harriet families are defined as nonfarm two-parent families in which the father is the full-time, year-round breadwinner, the mother is a full-time homemaker, and the children were all born after the parents' only marriage.

Source: Hernandez, Donald J. 1993. *America's Children: Resources from Family, Government, and the Economy.* New York: Russell Sage Foundation, page 123. Used with permission of Russell Sage Foundation.

A5-8. Children Living with a Father Working Full Time and a Mother Not in the Labor Force, 1940–1990

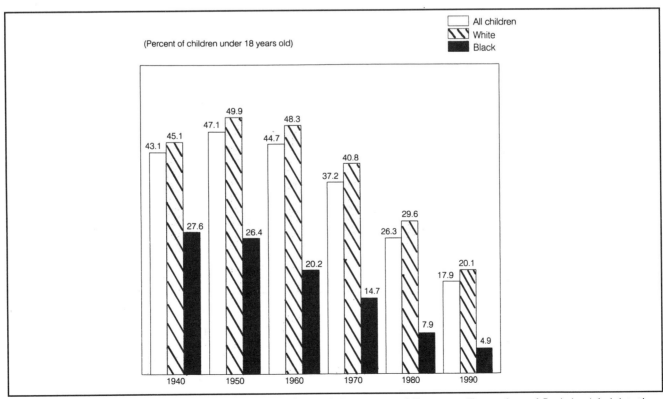

Source: U.S. Bureau of the Census, *We the American Children.* U.S. Department of Commerce, Economics and Statistics Administration. Washington, DC, 1993, page 2.

A5-9. Living Arrangements of Children under 18 Years Old, by Selected Characteristic of Parent, 1992

(Numbers in Thousands)

CHARACTERISTIC OF PARENT	ALL RACES [1]				WHITE				BLACK				HISPANIC [2]			
	Total	Both parents	Mother only	Father only	Total	Both parents	Mother only	Father only	Total	Both parents	Mother only	Father only	Total	Both parents	Mother only	Father only
Children under 18 years old	**64,216**	**46,638**	**15,396**	**2,182**	**51,606**	**40,635**	**9,250**	**1,721**	**9,648**	**3,714**	**5,607**	**327**	**7,382**	**4,935**	**2,168**	**279**
Age:																
15 to 24 years old	3,709	1,345	2,188	176	2,417	1,144	1,139	133	1,163	149	984	31	594	296	274	25
25 to 29 years old	8,486	5,010	3,132	325	6,337	4,328	1,761	249	1,858	527	1,266	65	1,192	731	422	39
30 to 34 years old	14,771	10,559	3,785	427	12,061	9,385	2,331	344	2,105	701	1,353	51	1,853	1,181	605	68
35 to 39 years old	15,733	12,140	3,152	440	13,045	10,739	1,951	355	2,038	905	1,074	59	1,542	1,067	438	38
40 to 44 years old	12,213	9,905	1,915	393	10,080	8,482	1,270	329	1,387	780	558	48	1,189	909	231	49
45 to 54 years old	7,904	6,516	1,090	299	6,609	5,670	712	228	851	481	332	38	833	617	171	46
55 to 64 years old	1,233	1,043	104	87	922	807	64	52	203	138	33	32	159	124	23	12
65 years old and over	186	121	30	36	134	80	22	32	43	34	6	4	19	11	4	4
Educational attainment:																
Less than 9th grade	4,138	2,765	1,182	191	3,504	2,406	929	169	399	173	214	12	2,414	1,663	653	98
9th to 12th grade, no diploma	7,947	4,081	3,548	337	5,471	3,372	1,836	264	2,188	506	1,618	64	1,556	869	651	36
High school graduate [3]	22,858	16,122	5,905	831	17,996	14,055	3,282	659	4,016	1,447	2,431	138	1,911	1,284	556	71
Some college, no degree or associate degree	15,480	11,360	3,594	527	12,712	10,008	2,301	403	2,128	919	1,141	68	1,007	697	260	50
Bachelor's degree	8,652	7,573	857	222	7,442	6,611	652	179	618	440	150	28	301	257	24	20
Graduate or professional degree	5,141	4,757	310	74	4,480	4,184	250	46	299	229	52	18	193	165	23	4
Employment status: [4]																
In the civilian labor force	53,634	42,385	9,345	1,904	44,882	37,376	5,965	1,542	6,442	3,100	3,083	259	5,568	4,313	1,026	229
Employed	49,539	39,819	8,009	1,711	41,890	35,191	5,300	1,398	5,502	2,844	2,441	217	4,911	3,861	850	200
Both parents employed	25,692	25,692	(X)	(X)	22,435	22,435	(X)	(X)	2,107	2,107	(X)	(X)	2,023	2,023	(X)	(X)
Unemployed	4,095	2,566	1,335	193	2,992	2,185	664	143	941	256	642	43	658	452	176	29
Not in the labor force	9,552	3,251	6,046	254	5,961	2,519	3,280	162	3,003	415	2,524	64	1,731	542	1,142	46
Family income:																
Under $5,000	3,789	717	2,901	171	2,113	587	1,439	88	1,526	94	1,387	65	626	167	434	26
$5,000 to $9,999	5,403	1,338	3,850	215	3,223	1,035	2,022	166	1,874	165	1,671	37	1,071	374	660	37
$10,000 to $14,999	4,774	2,431	2,124	219	3,460	1,993	1,294	173	1,069	271	767	33	1,025	648	350	28
$15,000 to $24,999	9,469	6,045	2,904	519	7,289	4,993	1,831	466	1,684	684	956	44	1,657	1,216	368	72
$25,000 to $29,999	4,886	3,783	893	210	4,043	3,226	657	160	621	360	224	38	639	518	84	37
$30,000 to $39,999	9,333	7,714	1,283	336	7,957	6,813	910	234	1,027	623	333	71	972	811	143	18
$40,000 to $49,999	8,149	7,313	634	202	7,173	6,496	496	181	671	546	112	12	587	504	52	30
$50,000 and over	18,414	17,296	808	310	16,348	15,491	602	255	1,176	972	176	27	804	697	77	31
Tenure: [5]																
Owned	39,702	33,703	4,885	1,114	34,612	30,180	3,497	935	3,432	2,104	1,200	128	2,593	2,112	387	94
Rented	24,514	12,935	10,511	1,068	16,994	10,455	5,753	786	6,215	1,609	4,407	199	4,789	2,822	1,781	185

X not applicable. [1]Includes other races, not shown separately. [2]Persons of Hispanic origin may be of any race. [3]Includes equivalency. [4]Excludes children whose parent is in the Armed forces. [5]Refers to the tenure of the householder (who may or may not be the child's parent).

Source: U.S. Bureau of the Census, *Statistical Abstract of the United States: 1993* (113th edition). Washington, DC, 1993, page 63.

A5-10. Ever Lived with 0–1 Parents, by Age 17, 1920–1980

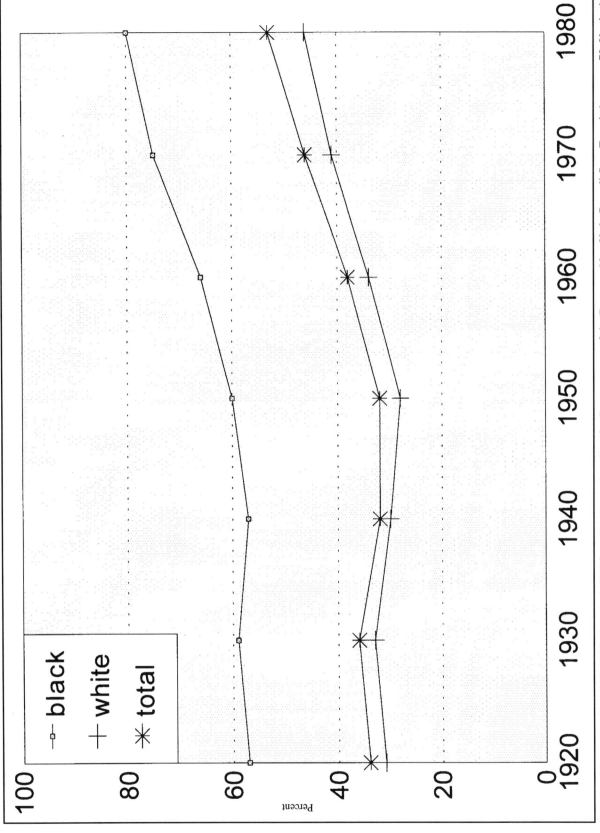

Source: Hernandez, Donald J. 1993. *America's Children: Resources from Family, Government, and the Economy.* New York: Russell Sage Foundation, page 70. Used with permission of Russell Sage Foundation.

A5-11. One-Parent Family Groups, by Race, Hispanic Origin, Sex, and Marital Status of Householder or Reference Person, 1992, 1990, 1980, and 1970 (numbers in thousands)

Subject	1992 Number	1992 Percent	1990 Number	1990 Percent	1980 Number	1980 Percent	1970 Number	1970 Percent	Avg annual change 1990-92	Avg annual change 1980-90	Avg annual change 1970-80
ALL RACES											
One-parent family groups	10,499	100.0	9,749	100.0	6,920	100.0	3,808	100.0	3.7	3.4	6.0
Maintained by mother	9,028	86.0	8,398	86.1	6,230	90.0	3,415	89.7	3.6	3.0	6.0
Never married	3,284	31.3	2,775	28.5	1,063	15.4	248	6.5	8.4	9.6	14.6
Married, spouse absent..	1,947	18.5	1,836	18.8	1,743	25.2	1,377	36.2	2.9	0.5	2.4
Separated...........	1,658	15.8	1,557	16.0	1,483	21.4	962	25.3	3.1	0.5	4.3
Divorced	3,349	31.9	3,194	32.8	2,721	39.3	1,109	29.1	2.4	1.6	9.0
Widowed..............	448	4.3	593	6.1	703	10.2	682	17.9	-14.0	-1.7	0.3
Maintained by father	1,472	14.0	1,351	13.9	690	10.0	393	10.3	4.3	6.7	5.6
Never married	400	3.8	345	3.5	63	0.9	22	0.6	7.4	(B)	(B)
Married, spouse absent*.	308	2.9	217	2.2	181	2.6	247	6.5	17.5	1.8	-3.1
Divorced	664	6.3	700	7.2	340	4.9	(NA)	(NA)	-2.6	7.2	(NA)
Widowed..............	100	1.0	89	0.9	107	1.5	124	3.3	5.8	-1.8	-1.5
WHITE											
One-parent family groups	6,938	100.0	6,389	100.0	4,664	100.0	2,638	100.0	4.1	3.1	5.7
Maintained by mother	5,753	82.9	5,310	83.1	4,122	88.4	2,330	88.3	4.0	2.5	5.7
Never married	1,391	20.0	1,139	17.8	379	8.1	73	2.8	10.0	11.0	16.5
Married, spouse absent..	1,341	19.3	1,206	18.9	1,033	22.1	796	30.2	5.3	1.5	2.6
Separated...........	1,146	16.5	1,015	15.9	840	18.0	477	18.1	6.1	1.9	5.7
Divorced	2,692	38.8	2,553	40.0	2,201	47.2	930	35.3	2.7	1.5	8.6
Widowed..............	328	4.7	411	6.4	511	11.0	531	20.1	-11.3	-2.2	-0.4
Maintained by father	1,186	17.1	1,079	16.9	542	11.6	307	11.6	4.7	6.9	5.7
Never married	292	4.2	253	4.0	32	0.7	18	0.7	7.2	(B)	(B)
Married, spouse absent*.	239	3.4	169	2.6	141	3.0	196	7.4	17.3	1.8	-3.3
Divorced	581	8.4	591	9.3	288	6.2	(NA)	(NA)	-0.9	7.2	(NA)
Widowed..............	73	1.1	65	1.0	82	1.8	93	3.5	(B)	-2.3	-1.3
BLACK											
One-parent family groups	3,216	100.0	3,081	100.0	2,114	100.0	1,148	100.0	2.1	3.8	6.1
Maintained by mother	2,994	93.1	2,860	92.8	1,984	93.9	1,063	92.6	2.3	3.7	6.2
Never married	1,799	55.9	1,572	51.0	665	31.5	173	15.1	6.7	8.6	13.5
Married, spouse absent..	548	17.0	570	18.5	667	31.6	570	49.7	-2.0	-1.6	1.6
Separated...........	482	15.0	502	16.3	616	29.1	479	41.7	-2.0	-2.0	2.5
Divorced	550	17.1	574	18.6	477	22.6	172	15.0	-2.1	1.9	10.2
Widowed..............	97	3.0	144	4.7	174	8.2	148	12.9	-19.8	-1.9	1.6
Maintained by father	222	6.9	221	7.2	129	6.1	85	7.4	0.2	5.4	4.2
Never married	83	2.6	74	2.4	30	1.4	4	0.3	(B)	(B)	(B)
Married, spouse absent*.	45	1.4	38	1.2	37	1.8	50	4.4	(B)	(B)	(B)
Divorced	68	2.1	93	3.0	43	2.0	(NA)	(NA)	-15.7	(B)	(NA)
Widowed..............	25	0.8	18	0.6	19	0.9	30	2.6	(B)	(B)	(B)
HISPANIC+											
One-parent family groups	1,298	100.0	1,140	100.0	568	100.0	(NA)	(NA)	6.5	7.0	(NA)
Maintained by mother	1,112	85.7	1,003	88.0	526	92.6	(NA)	(NA)	5.2	6.5	(NA)
Never married	407	31.4	361	31.7	120	21.1	(NA)	(NA)	6.0	11.0	(NA)
Married, spouse absent..	321	24.7	314	27.5	199	35.0	(NA)	(NA)	1.1	4.6	(NA)
Separated...........	259	20.0	249	21.8	170	29.9	(NA)	(NA)	2.0	3.8	(NA)
Divorced	318	24.5	266	23.3	162	28.5	(NA)	(NA)	8.9	5.0	(NA)
Widowed..............	65	5.0	62	5.4	46	8.1	(NA)	(NA)	14.9	(B)	(NA)
Maintained by father	186	14.3	138	12.1	42	7.4	(NA)	(NA)	(B)	(B)	(NA)
Never married	74	5.7	62	5.4	7	1.2	(NA)	(NA)	(B)	(B)	(NA)
Married, spouse absent*.	41	3.2	26	2.3	13	2.3	(NA)	(NA)	(B)	(B)	(NA)
Divorced	55	4.2	40	3.5	13	2.3	(NA)	(NA)	(B)	(B)	(NA)
Widowed..............	15	1.2	9	0.8	8	1.4	(NA)	(NA)	(B)	(B)	(NA)

*Data for 1970 include divorced fathers; B=base less than 75,000; NA=not available; + may be of any race. A subfamily is a married couple (husband and wife enumerated as members of the same household) with or without never-married children under 18 years old, or one parent with one or more never-married children under 18 years old, living in a household and related to but not including either the householder or the householder's spouse.

Source: Rawlings, Steve W. *Household and Family Characteristics: March 1992.* U.S. Bureau of the Census. Current Population Reports, P20-467. U.S. Government Printing Office, Washington, DC, 1993, page xvi.

A5-12. Percentage of Children in Single-Parent Families, Selected Countries, 1975–1986

Country	1975	1980	1983-86
Canada	10.5	12.8	NA
Norway	8.1	10.9	13.9
Sweden	11.4	13.5	NA
United Kingdom	10.0	12.0	14.0
United States	NA	19.7	23.4
NA - Data not available			

Source: Hobbs, Frank, and Laura Lippman. *Children's Well-Being: An International Comparison.* International Population Reports Series P-95, No. 80. U.S. Department of Commerce, Bureau of the Census. Washington, DC: U.S. Government Printing Office, 1990, page 35.

A5-13. Selected Characteristics of Children under Age 18, by Type of Family Living Arrangement, 1988

Characteristic	Living Arrangement			
	With both biological parents	With formerly married mother only	With never-married mother only	With mother and stepfather
Percent of children whose mothers completed >12 years of schooling	41.4	34.2	18.7	32.7
Percent with annual family income below the poverty level	11.1	40.0	65.9	13.8
Percent of children who had an accident, injury, or poisoning in past year	13.4	17.4	9.1	17.7
Percent of children who ever repeated a grade	11.6	21.5	29.7	21.7
Percent of children who were ever expelled or suspended from school	4.4	10.7	15.3	8.8
Percent of children who were treated for emotional/behavioral problem in past year	2.7	8.8	4.4	6.6
Percent of children with one or more problem behaviors	52.1	68.6	48.9	75.5

Source: *Family Planning Perspectives* 24 (1) 1992, page 42.

A5-14. Household Relationship and Presence of Parents for Persons under 18, by Age, Sex, Race, and Hispanic Origin, March 1992

	Males			Females		
	Under 6	6-11	12-17	Under 6	6-11	12-17
All Races						
In households	99.8	99.9	99.9	99.7	99.9	99.9
Child of householder	89.5	93.1	93.1	89.2	92.6	92.1
Grandchild of householder	7.0	4.1	3.1	6.9	4.2	3.6
Other relative of householder	1.4	1.0	2.0	1.8	1.2	1.7
Nonrelative of householder	1.8	1.6	1.7	1.8	1.7	2.3
Living with both parents	71.5	71.4	70.0	71.5	70.6	68.5
Child of householder	69.6	70.6	69.5	69.7	69.8	67.9
Grandchild of householder	1.4	0.6	0.3	1.1	0.5	0.3
Other relative of householder	0.3	0.1	0.1	0.3	0.2	0.1
Nonrelative of householder	0.1	0.07	0.03	0.1	0.04	—
Living with mother only	23.4	22.7	22.3	23.5	24.4	23.4
Child of householder	17.0	19.4	20.0	16.6	20.4	21.0
Grandchild of householder	4.3	1.7	1.1	4.6	2.3	1.2
Other relative of householder	0.8	0.3	0.3	0.9	0.5	0.2
Nonrelative of householder	1.2	1.2	0.7	1.2	1.1	0.9
Living with father only	3.4	3.5	3.8	3.2	2.4	3.3
Child of householder	2.7	3.1	3.5	2.7	2.2	3.1
Grandchild of householder	0.4	0.2	0.1	0.2	0.05	0.1
Other relative of householder	0.04	0.06	0.009	0.1	0.02	0.02
Nonrelative of householder	0.1	0.1	0.1	0.06	0.09	0.09
Living with neither parent	1.4	2.2	3.6	1.5	2.2	4.5
Grandchild of householder	0.8	1.5	1.4	0.8	1.3	1.8
Other relative of householder	0.2	0.5	1.4	0.4	0.4	1.3
Nonrelative of householder	0.3	0.2	0.7	0.3	0.4	1.2
Foster child	0.2	0.09	0.2	0.2	0.1	0.4
In group quarters	0.1	0.01	0.01	0.2	0.07	0.09
White						
In households	99.9	100	100	99.9	99.9	99.9
Child of householder	91.6	94.3	94.9	91.6	94.8	94.0
Grandchild of householder	5.5	3.2	2.0	5.1	2.7	2.4
Other relative of householder	1.0	0.7	1.3	1.3	0.6	1.1
Nonrelative of householder	1.6	1.6	1.5	1.7	1.6	2.4
Living with both parents	78.7	77.4	76.5	79.5	77.2	74.4
Child of householder	76.7	76.5	76.0	77.5	76.5	73.8
Grandchild of householder	1.5	0.6	0.3	1.3	0.4	0.3
Other relative of householder	0.3	0.1	0.08	0.4	0.2	0.2
Nonrelative of householder	0.1	0.08	0.03	0.2	0.03	—
Living with mother only	16.9	17.4	17.0	16.6	18.8	19.0
Child of householder	12.0	14.6	15.4	11.5	15.8	17.1
Grandchild of householder	3.2	1.3	0.6	3.1	1.4	0.7
Other relative of householder	0.6	0.2	0.1	0.5	0.2	0.1
Nonrelative of householder	1.0	1.2	0.7	1.3	1.2	0.9

A5-14. Household Relationship and Presence of Parents for Persons under 18, by Age, Sex, Race, and Hispanic Origin, March 1992 (continued)

	Males			Females		
	Under 6	6-11	12-17	Under 6	6-11	12-17
Living with father only	3.3	3.5	3.8	2.9	2.6	3.3
Child of householder	2.8	3.1	3.4	2.5	2.4	2.9
Grandchild of householder	0.3	0.1	0.1	0.1	0.05	0.1
Other relative of householder	0.05	0.03	0.1	0.1	0.02	0.02
Nonrelative of householder	0.1	0.1	0.1	0.06	0.1	0.1
Living with neither parent	0.9	1.5	2.5	0.8	1.2	3.1
Grandchild of householder	0.5	1.0	0.8	0.3	0.7	1.1
Other relative of householder	0.1	0.3	1.1	0.2	0.1	0.7
Nonrelative of householder	0.2	0.1	0.5	0.1	0.3	1.2
Foster child	0.1	0.05	0.2	0.1	0.08	0.4
In group quarters	0.02	—	—	0.03	0.02	0.03
Black						
In households	99.2	99.9	99.8	98.9	99.6	99.6
Child of householder	79.2	86.8	84.5	76.2	82.1	82.7
Grandchild of householder	14.0	8.8	8.5	16.5	11.0	9.7
Other relative of householder	3.0	2.4	4.4	3.9	4.1	4.4
Nonrelative of householder	2.8	1.7	2.2	2.1	2.2	2.7
Living with both parents	33.1	39.1	37.8	30.3	36.6	37.3
Child of householder	32.4	38.8	37.4	30.0	36.5	37.1
Grandchild of householder	0.6	0.1	0.06	0.3	—	0.1
Other relative of householder	0.1	0.1	0.3	—	0.05	
Nonrelative of householder	—	—	0.06	—	0.05	—
Living with mother only	58.4	50.9	49.8	59.7	53.9	48.2
Child of householder	44.1	45.0	43.9	43.3	44.2	42.6
Grandchild of householder	10.0	3.9	3.4	12.6	6.4	3.8
Other relative of householder	2.1	0.6	1.4	2.7	2.0	0.5
Nonrelative of householder	1.9	1.2	1.0	0.9	1.1	1.2
Living with father only	3.5	3.6	3.2	3.6	1.5	3.0
Child of householder	2.6	2.8	3.1	2.9	1.4	2.9
Grandchild of householder	0.7	0.5	0.1	0.6	—	0.1
Other relative of householder	—	0.2	—	—	0.05	—
Nonrelative of householder	0.1	—	—	0.05	—	—
Living with neither parent	4.0	6.2	8.8	5.1	7.5	10.9
Grandchild of householder	2.5	4.3	4.8	2.9	4.5	5.5
Other relative of householder	0.8	1.4	2.7	1.1	1.9	3.9
Nonrelative of householder	0.7	0.5	1.2	1.0	1.0	1.4
Foster child	0.6	0.3	0.1	0.7	0.2	0.4
In group quarters	0.7	0.1	0.1	1.0	0.3	0.3

A5-14. Household Relationship and Presence of Parents for Persons under 18, by Age, Sex, Race, and Hispanic Origin, March 1992 (continued)

	Males			Females		
	Under 6	6-11	12-17	Under 6	6-11	12-17
Hispanic*						
In households	99.9	100	100	99.8	99.9	100
Child of householder	85.8	90.1	89.8	84.0	89.9	90.1
Grandchild of householder	9.0	4.8	3.7	8.8	4.8	3.3
Other relative of householder	3.6	2.4	4.7	4.6	2.3	3.9
Nonrelative of householder	1.3	2.6	1.6	2.2	2.7	2.6
Living with both parents	67.1	66.0	63.5	66.0	66.3	57.7
Child of householder	61.4	64.3	62.3	61.1	63.8	57.0
Grandchild of householder	3.4	0.7	0.7	2.3	1.1	0.1
Other relative of householder	1.5	0.7	0.4	1.9	0.9	0.5
Nonrelative of householder	0.6	0.2	0.1	0.5	0.3	—
Living with mother only	27.1	27.2	26.8	28.4	28.9	32.8
Child of householder	20.8	22.8	23.3	20.0	23.8	29.6
Grandchild of householder	4.0	2.0	1.7	5.0	2.5	0.9
Other relative of householder	1.7	0.5	0.8	1.8	0.7	0.9
Nonrelative of householder	0.5	1.7	0.7	1.4	1.6	1.2
Living with father only	4.3	3.4	4.4	3.2	2.7	3.8
Child of householder	3.5	2.9	4.1	2.8	2.3	3.4
Grandchild of householder	0.7	0.1	0.1	0.2	0.2	0.09
Other relative of householder	—	0.07	—	0.1	0.1	—
Nonrelative of householder	—	0.1	0.1	—	0.07	0.2
Living with neither parent	1.3	3.2	5.0	2.0	1.8	5.5
Grandchild of householder	0.8	1.8	1.1	1.1	0.7	2.0
Other relative of householder	0.3	1.0	3.4	0.6	0.3	2.4
Nonrelative of householder	0.2	0.3	0.5	0.2	0.5	1.1
Foster child	—	0.07	—	0.2	0.2	0.2
In group quarters	0.06	—	—	0.1	0.07	0.09

*Persons of Hispanic origin may be of any race.

Source: U.S. Bureau of the Census. *Marital Status and Living Arrangements: March 1992.* Current Population Reports, Series P20, No. 468. U.S. Government Printing Office, Washington, DC, 1992, pages 21–24.

A6. GRANDPARENTS

A6-1. Children Living in the Home of Their Grandparents, by Presence of Parents, Race, and Hispanic Origin, 1970–1992

Living Arrangement	1970 Total	1980 Total	1990 Total	1992 Total[1]	1992 White	1992 Black	1992 Hispanic[2]
Grandchild (under 18 years) of householder							
(number in 1,000)	2,214	2,306	3,155	3,253	1,887	1,208	458
Percent of all children under 18 yrs	3.2	3.6	4.9	4.9	3.6	11.6	6.0
With both parents present (1,000)	363	310	467	502	428	25	118
With mother only present (1,000)	817	922	1,563	1,740	957	719	220
With father only present (1,000)	78	86	191	144	86	40	23
With neither parent present (1,000)	957	988	935	867	407	424	97
Total, percent distribution	100.0	100.0	100.0	100.0	100.0	100.0	100.0
With both parents present	16	13	15	15	23	2	26
With mother only present	37	40	50	53	51	60	48
With father only present	4	4	6	4	5	3	5
With neither parent present	43	43	30	27	22	35	21

[1]Includes other races not shown separately.   [2]Persons of Hispanic origin may be of any race.

Source: U.S. Bureau of the Census, *Statistical Abstract of the United States: 1993* (113th edition). Washington, DC, 1993, page 64.

A6-2. Grandparents in the Homes of Children Aged 0–17, 1940–1980

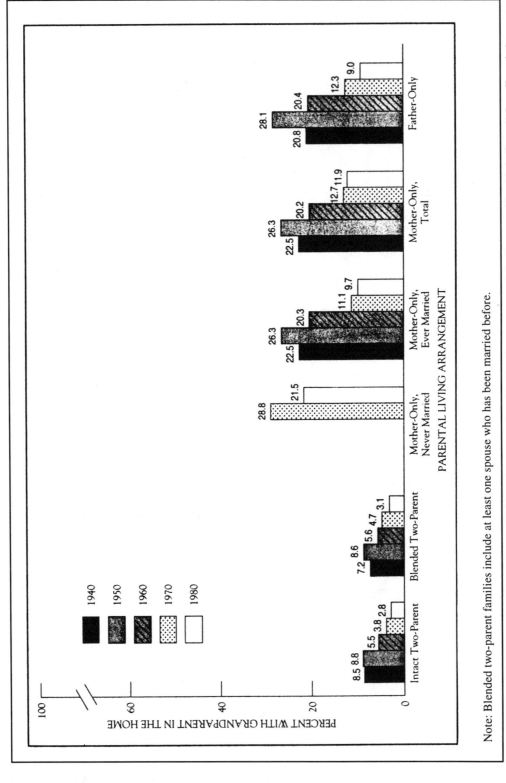

Note: Blended two-parent families include at least one spouse who has been married before.

Source: Hernandez, Donald J. 1993. *America's Children: Resources from Family, Government, and the Economy.* New York: Russell Sage Foundation, page 73. Used with permission of Russell Sage Foundation.

A6-3. Grandparents in the Homes of Children, 1990

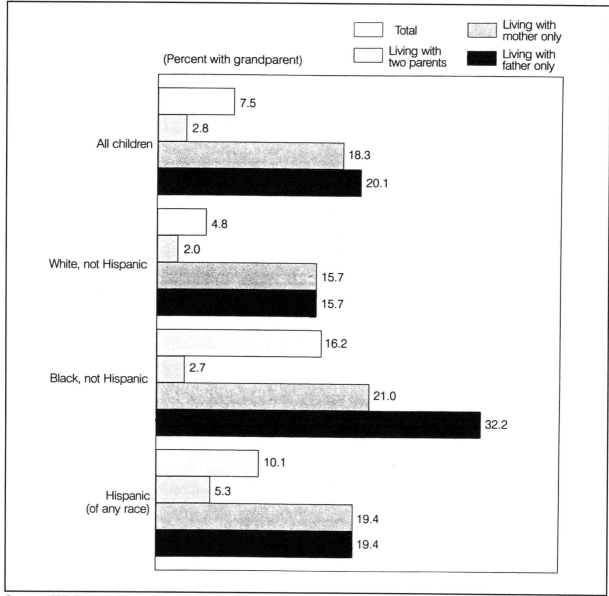

Source: U.S. Bureau of the Census, *We the American Children.* U.S. Department of Commerce, Economics and Statistics Administration. Washington, DC, 1993, page 5.

B.   Health

Recent debates have increased public awareness of health care issues facing our nation. This chapter presents information regarding six major health concerns facing America's youth. First, we examine mortality or death rates. Second, we consider major sources of illness. Third, we discuss reported causes and consequences of abuse as they pertain to children and adolescents. Fourth, we focus on issues related to children's health including birth weight, immunization, and behavior associated with risk factors. Fifth, we present data about medical treatment and health insurance for children and adolescents. Finally, we focus on sexually transmitted diseases that are of particular concern to adolescents.

B1. MORTALITY

A child suffers his or her greatest risk of dying during the first few days following birth. Thereafter, death rates drop sharply, reaching a low in late adolescence and early adulthood. We have made significant improvements in infant (under one year of age) and neonatal (under one month) death rates since 1970, but significant race differences remain. Accidents are the major cause of death among children, and males have a much higher accidental death rate than females. In addition, accidental deaths become much more common as children reach adolescence. Also in adolescence, suicide and HIV infection emerge as leading causes of death, and the homicide rate also increases dramatically.

B2. ILLNESS AND HEALTH PROBLEMS

Infectious diseases are the major cause of most hospitalizations among adolescents. Of all ailments, congenital anomalies generally require the longest hospital stays. Infections are also the primary cause of restricted activity among children, with injuries coming in a close second.

The National Health Interviews conducted in 1988 provide a wealth of information on children's health. Results from this survey indicate that most children are in good health but that a significant percentage have experienced moderate and serious health problems. The frequency of health problems varies by age of the child, gender, race/ethnicity, class background, and mother's marital status. The severity of problem, however, depends more on the type of condition. Chronic conditions have greatly different impacts on limited activity and difficulty of treatment.

Developmental delays and learning disabilities are relatively uncommon. Unfortunately, not all children receive treatment for these conditions, and the probability of treatment varies by social characteristics.

B3. ABUSE

Since child abuse has become recognized as a serious social problem, the number of reported cases has increased dramatically. In 1992, there were more than four reports of child abuse for every 100 children. It is difficult to determine how much of the increase is due to rising incidence of abuse and how much is due to greater awareness by teachers, doctors, and others responsible for the care of children.

Reports of abuse come from a variety of sources, including educators, legal and social service agencies, neighbors, friends, family members, and child care providers. Only about a third of reported cases, however, are ever substantiated. Neglect is the most common form of abuse, constituting nearly half of all cases. Physical abuse and sexual abuse rank second and third.

Younger children appear to be at greater risk of abuse, and a disproportionate number of victims are female. Blacks are also over-represented in abuse statistics. The number and type of reported abuse cases also varies significantly from state to state.

Nearly one-fourth of twelfth-grade girls report that they have been sexually abused sometime in their lives. The figure is much smaller for boys—about 3 percent. Involuntary intercourse is the most common unwanted sexual interaction among sexually experienced women under age 14. Sexual harassment is also a common form of abuse. A large majority of students in grades 8 to 11 report unwanted sexual comments or actions.

B4. RISK FACTORS

Low birth weight is one of the major risk factors associated with infant mortality. In the 1970s and early 1980s some progress was made in increasing average birth weight and reducing the percentage of babies with dangerously low birth weights. This progress did not continue into the last half of the 1980s, however. In fact, there was a slight increase in the percentage of black babies having a low birth weight.

Progress was also made in prenatal care during the 1970s, especially among blacks. This progress stopped, however, in the 1980s. As with low birth weight, there was an increase in the percentage of black babies with inadequate prenatal care.

A majority of children are not up-to-date on immunizations, and black children are less likely to be immunized than white children. A significant proportion of children are also at risk because they do not wear seat belts and because they are subjected to secondary smoke in the household.

B5. MEDICAL TREATMENT AND HEALTH CARE COVERAGE

About 60 percent of all children visited the doctor in 1988, the latest year for which complete statistics are available. The percentage who did visit a doctor was fairly constant by gender, race, and income, although the percentage was somewhat higher in high income households. Children who were not covered by insurance, however, were less likely to visit the doctor. About the same percentage of children see a dentist each year, but dental visits appear to be more influenced by social class, race, and mother's marital status.

Younger children are more likely to be hospitalized than older children, and, until ages of childbearing, males are more likely to be hospitalized than females.

The average hospital stay ranges form five to seven days, depending on the age of the child. Private insurance and governmental funds are the major sources of payment for children's hospital bills.

Approximately 17 percent of children are not covered by health insurance, and the percentage is higher for blacks, Hispanics, single parent households, and low income households. A small fraction go for long periods (over two years) without coverage, but a larger percentage experience some periods of noncoverage. About 70 percent of children are covered by private health insurance.

B6. SEXUALLY TRANSMITTED DISEASES

The increasing incidence of AIDS among young people is of particular concern. Although the absolute number of cases remains small, the rapid increase over the last 10 years is alarming. Gonorrhea is still the most common sexually transmitted disease among adolescents aged 15 to 24. Although rates of gonorrhea are declining, they are still relatively high among adolescents, as are rates of syphilis among those in their late teens and early twenties.

Sexual behavior also puts adolescents at risk. The risk of acquiring a sexually transmitted disease in one act of unprotected intercourse with an infected partner is high, especially for gonorrhea, chlamydia, and genital herpes. Despite this risk and the risk of HIV infection, only about one-fifth of teens have changed their sexual behavior.

A majority of 15- to 19-year-old males report receiving some type of sex education, but the percentage varies by topic. A large majority of teens are aware of the ways people contact AIDS, and a majority favor proposals such as provision of free condoms and counseling centers to prevent the spread of AIDS.

B1. MORTALITY

B1-1. Death Rates, by Age, Sex, and Race, 1970–1991

Sex, Year, and Race	All ages[1]	< 1 yr. old	1-4 yr. old	5-14 yr. old	15-24 yr. old
MALE[2]					
1970	1,090	2,410	93	51	189
1980	977	1,429	73	37	172
1985	949	1,220	59	32	139
1990	918	1,083	52	29	147
1991, prel.[3]	909	1,007	49	29	161
White: 1970	1,087	2,113	84	48	171
1980	983	1,230	66	35	167
1985	964	1,057	53	30	134
1990	931	896	46	26	131
1991, prel.[3]	924	846	43	26	143
Black: 1970	1,187	4,299	151	67	321
1980	1,034	2,587	111	47	209
1985	989	2,220	90	42	174
1990	1,008	2,112	86	41	252
1991, prel. [3]	962	1,899	82	44	277
FEMALE[2]					
1970	808	1,864	75	32	68
1980	785	1,142	55	24	58
1985	809	951	45	21	50
1990	812	856	41	19	49
1991, prel.[3]	802	791	45	19	52
White: 1970	813	1,615	66	30	62
1980	806	963	49	23	56
1985	840	799	40	20	48
1990	847	690	36	18	46
1991, prel.[3]	838	645	37	17	48
Black: 1970	829	3,369	129	44	112
1980	733	2,124	84	31	71
1985	734	1,821	71	29	60
1990	748	1,736	68	28	69
1991, prel.[3]	721	1,546	80	28	77

[1]Includes unknown age [2]Includes other races not shown separately. [3]Includes deaths of nonresidents of the country. Based on a 10-percent sample of deaths.

Source: U.S. Bureau of the Census, *Statistical Abstract of the United States: 1993* (113th edition). Washington, DC, 1993, page 87.

B1-2. Death Rates from Accidents and Violence (per 100,000 Population), by Sex: Youth Aged 15–24, 1970, 1980, and 1990

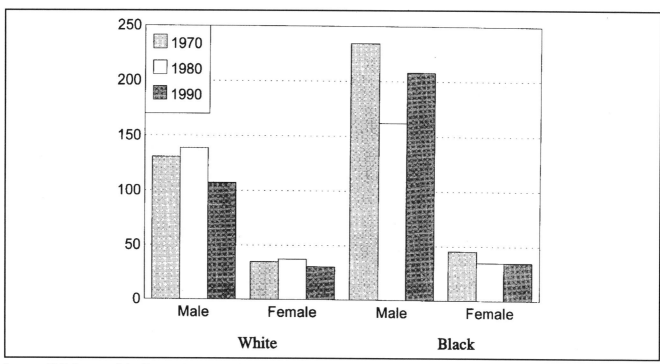

Source: U.S. Bureau of the Census, *Statistical Abstract of the United States: 1993* (113th edition). Washington, DC, 1993, page 89.

B1-3. Suicide Rates, by Sex, Race, and Age (per 100,000 Population), 1970–1990

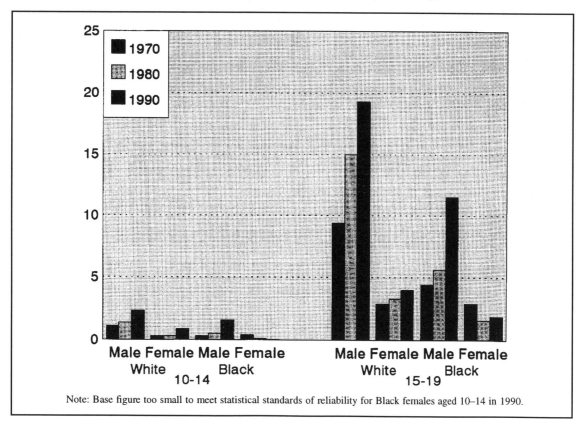

Note: Base figure too small to meet statistical standards of reliability for Black females aged 10–14 in 1990.

Source: U.S. Bureau of the Census, *Statistical Abstract of the United States: 1993* (113th edition). Washington, DC, 1993, page 98.

B2. ILLNESS AND HEALTH PROBLEMS

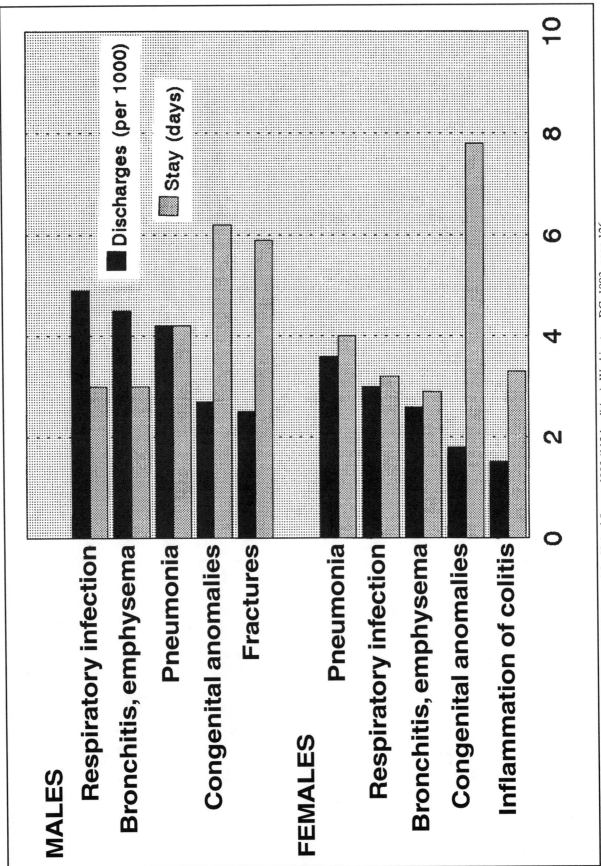

B2-1. Major Causes of Hospitalization and Length of Stay, Children under Age 15, 1991

Source: U.S. Bureau of the Census, *Statistical Abstract of the United States: 1993* (113th edition). Washington, DC, 1993, page 126.

B2-2. Rate of Acute Conditions per 1,000 Population, 1990 (conditions that caused at least one day of restricted activity in the last year)

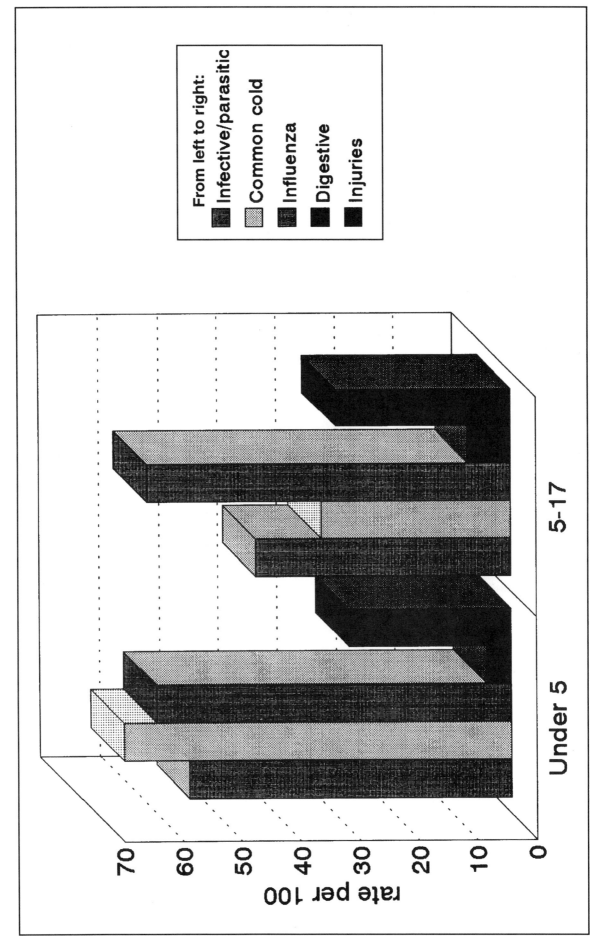

Source: U.S. Bureau of the Census, *Statistical Abstract of the United States: 1993* (113th edition). Washington, DC, 1993, page 135.

B2-3. Children's Health Problems, by Child and Maternal Characteristics, 1988

	Percent accident prone	Percent who have been seriously ill	Among serious-ill, percent so sick they might die	Percent Ever Had repeated tonsilitis	Percent ever had frequent ear infections
Child					
Child's Age:					
<1	3.0	6.3	57.2	0.6	10.3
1-5	9.7	12.9	49.6	6.0	30.6
6-11	10.2	15.1	52.2	14.9	26.9
12-17	7.9	16.2	52.5	19.2	19.7
Child's Gender:					
Female	8.4	13.2	47.9	13.7	23.4
Male	9.4	15.3	54.9	12.0	25.8
Child's Ethnicity:					
White	8.7	15.4	50.6	14.9	27.6
Black	10.2	10.4	55.5	6.5	16.1
Hispanic	9.6	13.9	57.5	10.2	19.9
Other	5.5	8.2	46.0	5.3	13.6
Mother					
Mother's Education:					
< High school	12.0	12.9	56.0	13.0	20.7
High school graduate	9.0	14.5	54.4	13.4	24.6
Some college	8.7	15.9	48.5	14.0	26.6
College graduate	5.9	13.8	42.7	10.0	28.2
Post graduate	4.3	13.8	44.4	11.0	29.0
Mother's Marital Status:					
Married	8.3	14.3	51.5	13.2	25.6
Divorced/separated	11.9	16.2	51.7	14.7	24.2
Widowed	10.9	11.2	61.4	13.3	18.3
Never married	11.2	13.5	53.6	6.2	18.2

Note: Unless otherwise noted, percentages are of all children in the United States.

B2-3. Children's Health Problems, by Child and Maternal Characteristics, 1988 (continued)

	Percent ever had				
	Food/Digest- ive Allergy	Frequent Diarrhea	Diabetes	Sickle Cell Anemia	Anemia
Child					
Child's Age:					
<1	5.8	2.8	0.0	0.2	1.9
1-5	6.3	4.9	0.1	0.2	3.1
6-11	6.6	2.5	0.1	0.1	2.3
12-17	7.1	2.1	0.3	0.2	2.2
Child's Gender:					
Female	6.1	2.5	0.1	0.1	2.6
Male	7.1	3.6	0.2	0.1	2.3
Child's Ethnicity:					
White	7.6	3.1	0.2	0.0	2.4
Black	3.3	2.9	0.0	0.8	2.7
Hispanic	4.4	3.0	0.2	0.1	2.9
Other	6.5	3.2	0.3	0.0	1.3
Mother					
Mother's Education:					
< High school	3.6	3.0	0.3	0.4	3.4
High school graduate	6.5	3.2	0.1	0.1	2.3
Some college	8.5	3.1	0.2	0.1	2.3
College graduate	8.0	2.5	0.2	0.2	2.2
Post graduate	9.3	3.3	0.0	0.0	1.8
Mother's Marital Status:					
Married	7.0	2.9	0.2	0.1	2.2
Divorced/separated	6.4	3.8	0.1	0.3	3.9
Widowed	5.3	2.8	0.0	0.1	1.9
Never married	3.0	4.5	0.1	0.5	4.0

B2-3. Children's Health Problems, by Child and Maternal Characteristics, 1988 (continued)

	Percent ever had					
	Asthma	Mono-nucleosis	Hepatitis	Meningitis	Bladder or uterine infection	Rheumatic Fever
Child						
Child's Age:						
<1	0.8	0.0	0.1	0.1	0.5	0.0
1-5	4.7	0.3	0.2	0.7	2.5	0.1
6-11	7.2	0.9	0.3	0.8	4.9	0.1
12-17	7.6	2.7	0.4	0.6	4.5	0.3
Child's Gender:						
Female	5.0	1.4	0.3	0.5	6.4	0.1
Male	7.4	1.1	0.2	0.8	1.2	0.2
Child's Ethnicity:						
White	5.9	1.6	0.3	0.7	4.5	0.1
Black	8.0	0.4	0.1	0.5	2.0	0.1
Hispanic	5.7	0.6	0.2	1.0	1.8	0.3
Other	6.4	0.4	0.4	0.4	2.4	0.2
Mother						
Mother's Education:						
< High school	6.0	0.5	0.2	0.8	3.3	0.1
High school graduate	6.1	1.4	0.3	0.7	3.8	0.1
Some college	7.3	1.6	0.2	0.7	3.8	0.2
College graduate	5.6	1.4	0.2	0.5	4.7	0.3
Post graduate	5.7	1.7	0.1	0.1	4.1	0.1
Mother's Marital Status:						
Married	5.8	1.3	0.2	0.6	4.0	0.1
Divorced/separated	8.3	1.5	0.6	0.6	3.8	0.2
Widowed	6.8	2.1	0.0	0.8	3.5	0.0
Never married	7.6	0.2	0.2	1.3	1.7	0.3

B2-3. Children's Health Problems, by Child and Maternal Characteristics, 1988 (continued)

	Percent ever had					
	Pneumonia	Hay fever	Respiratory allergy	Deafness	Blindness	Cross eyes
Child						
Child's Age:						
<1	2.7	1.0	1.8	1.0	0.4	0.4
1-5	5.6	3.6	3.9	2.7	0.8	0.9
6-11	7.3	7.0	5.9	4.4	0.8	1.0
12-17	7.7	10.7	6.4	3.8	1.0	1.2
Child's Gender:						
Female	6.0	5.9	4.7	2.9	0.8	1.2
Male	7.3	7.8	5.7	4.1	1.0	0.8
Child's Ethnicity:						
White	7.6	7.9	6.2	4.1	0.9	1.1
Black	4.9	4.0	2.9	1.8	0.5	0.7
Hispanic	3.9	3.8	2.0	2.5	0.9	0.5
Other	3.4	5.9	4.6	2.0	1.1	0.8
Mother						
Mother's Education:						
< High school	5.7	4.1	3.4	3.3	0.9	0.9
High school graduate	6.8	6.2	4.7	3.5	0.8	1.0
Some college	7.8	8.6	6.4	4.3	0.8	1.1
College graduate	6.0	9.5	7.6	3.2	1.0	1.1
Post graduate	7.1	10.4	7.4	3.6	0.8	0.6
Mother's Marital Status:						
Married	6.8	7.0	5.4	3.6	0.8	1.0
Divorced/separated	7.3	7.8	5.3	3.9	1.0	1.0
Widowed	7.1	9.3	8.8	2.9	0.2	4.5
Never married	5.5	2.1	2.4	2.0	0.7	0.6

B2-3. Children's Health Problems, by Child and Maternal Characteristics, 1988 (continued)

	Percent ever had					
	Eczemal skin allergy	Epilepsy	Seizures with fever	Frequent/ severe headaches	Stammering/ stuttering	Bed wetting
Child						
Child's Age:						
<1	3.8	0.4	0.2	0.1	0.0	0.0
1-5	7.1	0.6	1.9	0.6	1.5	0.5
6-11	8.2	0.7	2.2	5.2	2.5	8.6
12-17	8.2	1.4	2.3	8.6	1.9	5.2
Child's Gender:						
Female	7.9	0.9	1.8	4.9	1.2	3.6
Male	7.3	0.8	2.2	4.4	2.6	5.7
Child's Ethnicity:						
White	8.4	0.8	2.0	4.9	1.8	4.9
Black	5.4	0.7	1.9	4.4	2.5	4.3
Hispanic	5.2	1.6	2.4	3.7	2.2	3.9
Other	9.1	0.4	1.5	2.7	1.3	3.0
Mother						
Mother's Education:						
< High school	4.5	1.0	2.3	4.9	2.3	4.3
High school graduate	7.4	0.9	2.0	5.1	2.2	4.7
Some college	9.7	1.0	2.3	5.0	1.5	5.3
College graduate	9.8	0.7	2.0	2.7	1.0	4.0
Post graduate	9.3	0.3	0.8	3.5	1.5	4.9
Mother's Marital Status:						
Married	8.0	0.8	1.9	4.5	1.8	4.7
Divorced/separated	6.9	1.4	3.0	6.2	2.5	5.2
Widowed	6.1	0.7	1.6	8.9	2.5	3.9
Never married	4.9	0.7	1.5	3.3	1.8	2.7

B2-3. Children's Health Problems, by Child and Maternal Characteristics, 1988 (continued)

	Percent ever had				
	Arthritis/ joint disease	Bone disease	Cerebral palsy	Congenital heart disease	Other heart diseases
Child					
Child's Age:					
<1	0.0	0.5	0.4	0.3	1.1
1-5	0.5	0.8	0.3	0.6	1.4
6-11	0.6	1.2	0.2	0.4	1.8
12-17	1.8	3.5	0.2	0.5	2.0
Child's Gender:					
Female	1.0	1.8	0.2	0.6	1.6
Male	0.9	1.8	0.2	0.4	1.8
Child's Ethnicity:					
White	1.0	2.1	0.2	0.6	2.0
Black	0.7	0.7	0.0	0.1	0.9
Hispanic	0.7	1.1	0.4	0.5	1.2
Other	0.5	1.8	0.3	0.0	0.4
Mother					
Mother's Education:					
< High school	0.7	1.0	0.3	0.2	1.7
High school graduate	0.9	1.6	0.2	0.5	1.7
Some college	1.4	2.5	0.2	0.8	1.8
College graduate	0.7	2.5	0.3	0.4	1.7
Post graduate	0.3	2.1	0.2	0.5	2.0
Mother's Marital Status:					
Married	0.9	2.0	0.2	0.5	1.8
Divorced/separated	1.0	1.4	0.2	0.8	1.5
Widowed	1.5	2.7	1.0	0.4	1.0

Source: National Center for Health Statistics. 1992. *The National Health Interview Survey On Child Health, 1988* (Data Set 33-34, B. C. Holmes, A. S. Kaplan, E. L. Lang, and J. J. Card, Archivists [machine-readable data file and documentation]. Washington, DC: Department of Health and Human Services, Producer). Los Altos, CA: Sociometrics Corporation, American Family Data Archive (Producer & Distributor).

B2-4. Impact of Childhood Chronic Conditions on Children's Activity Levels and Use of Medical Services, 1988

Condition	Percent limited in usual activities due to chronic conditions	Average annual bed days due to chronic conditions	Average annual school absence days due to chronic conditions	Percent using medications in last year due to chronic conditions	Percent hospitalized in last year due to chronic conditions	Average annual physician contacts due to chronic conditions
All children with chronic conditions	13.3	2.2	3.1	63.1	3.8	4.7
Impairments						
Musculoskeletal impairments	39.6	1.4*	2.3*	15.4	4.9*	3.1
Deafness and hearing loss	35.5	**	**	27.1	1.8*	2.1
Blindness and vision impairment	19.4	**	**	7.1	1.5*	1.5
Speech defects	33.1	**	**	1.8*	**	4.8*
Cerebral palsy	89.2	1.7*	2.3*	23.5*	12.1*	10.3*
Diseases						
Diabetes	30.0*	3.6*	3.1*	81.7	35.5*	7.9*
Sickle cell disease	15.2*	0.2*	0.2*	22.8*	<0.1	2.2*
Anemia	14.7	0.8*	0.8*	42.7	0.6*	2.3
Asthma	28.6	2.8	4.6	84.9	7.4	4.9
Respiratory allergies	12.3	0.8	1.4	63.4	0.5*	2.8
Eczema and skin allergies	10.5	**	**	66.8	**	1.6
Epilepsy and seizures	58.0	3.0*	3.4*	84.3	19.1*	3.7
Arthritis	24.6	3.3*	3.2*	32.8	5.6*	6.3*
Heart disease	21.6	3.2*	2.2*	15.2	7.9	2.7
Frequent or repeated ear infections	9.1	1.7	2.8	93.2	2.3	4.3
Frequent diarrhea/bowel trouble	16.7	0.9*	1.4	46.0	2.7*	1.9
Digestive allergies	15.7	0.4	1.1	36.0	1.0*	2.8
Frequent or severe headaches	16.9	2.9	3.3	47.5	1.3*	1.6
Other	24.7	2.8	3.4	38.9	8.4	4.5

*Standard error exceeds 30% of estimate value.
**Information on bed days, school absences, and hospitalization was not obtained for these conditions.

Source: American Journal of Public Health 82 (3) 1992, page 369.

B2-5. Subjective Health Status, 1988

	Percent of children rated to have excellent health	Percent of children who have limited activities due to health	Percent of children who spent 1 or more days in bed in past 2 weeks
Age:			
< 1	57.1	1.0	7.1
1-5	53.4	3.2	6.1
6-11	53.0	6.8	7.0
12-17	52.7	7.0	7.7
Child's Gender:			
Male	52.3	6.1	6.4
Female	54.2	4.8	7.6
Child's Ethnicity:			
White	56.7	5.5	7.5
Black	41.1	6.0	4.9
Hispanic	46.5	5.2	6.9
Other	52.2	2.9	4.6
Mother's Education:			
< High school	39.5	6.9	6.2
High school graduate	51.9	5.6	6.8
Some college	59.3	5.1	8.0
College graduate	64.5	3.9	7.1
Post graduate	69.6	4.1	7.2
Mother's Marital Status:			
Married	55.7	4.9	6.8
Divorced/separated	44.7	8.1	8.7
Widowed	38.9	8.8	5.1
Never married	42.2	6.6	5.8

Source: National Center for Health Statistics. 1992. *The National Health Interview Survey On Child Health, 1988* (Data Set 33-34, B. C. Holmes, A. S. Kaplan, E. L. Lang, and J. J. Card, Archivists [machine-readable data file and documentation]. Washington, DC: Department of Health and Human Services, Producer). Los Altos, CA: Sociometrics Corporation, American Family Data Archive (Producer & Distributor).

B2-6. Percent of Children Receiving Treatment and Medication for Delays in Development and Learning Disabilities, 1988

	Delays in Development			Learning Disabilities		
		of those with problems			of those with problems	
	Percent with problem	Percent receiving medication in last 12 mo.	Percent receiving treatment	Percent with problem	Percent receiving medication in last 12 mo.	Percent receiving treatment
Age:						
<1	2.6	9.4	51.9	—	—	—
1-5	4.7	8.0	51.6	1.7	12.1	82.5
6-11	4.1	4.8	53.2	6.8	10.9	78.4
12-17	3.6	3.3	41.8	8.8	5.5	76.9
Child's Gender:						
Male	4.2	5.4	49.2	8.6	8.9	78.9
Female	3.8	5.9	49.6	4.4	6.6	75.6
Child's Ethnicity:						
White	4.5	6.1	48.5	6.8	9.4	81.9
Black	2.1	3.2	42.1	6.6	3.5	61.8
Hispanic	3.4	6.6	50.3	5.8	5.7	73.2
Other	4.9	—	74.6	3.6	—	57.0
Mother's Education:						
< High school	3.3	4.7	51.0	8.7	3.8	64.1
High school graduate	4.3	4.5	44.7	6.8	9.4	81.7
Some college	4.0	7.7	51.0	4.7	10.7	84.8
College graduate	4.3	6.2	50.8	4.4	7.0	82.0
Post graduate	4.9	8.2	74.1	6.6	13.6	83.8
Mother's Marital Status:						
Married	4.0	5.6	49.7	6.2	9.5	76.5
Divorced/separated	4.8	4.5	50.3	7.8	4.1	85.1
Widowed	2.6	—	58.6	7.3	—	92.9
Never Married	3.7	8.7	41.0	7.0	3.4	63.4

Source: National Center for Health Statistics. 1992. *The National Health Interview Survey On Child Health, 1988* (Data Set 33-34, B. C. Holmes, A. S. Kaplan, E. L. Lang, and J. J. Card, Archivists [machine-readable data file and documentation]. Washington, DC: Department of Health and Human Services, Producer). Los Altos, CA: Sociometrics Corporation, American Family Data Archive (Producer & Distributor).

B3. ABUSE

B3-1. Reported Rates of Child Abuse, 1976–1992

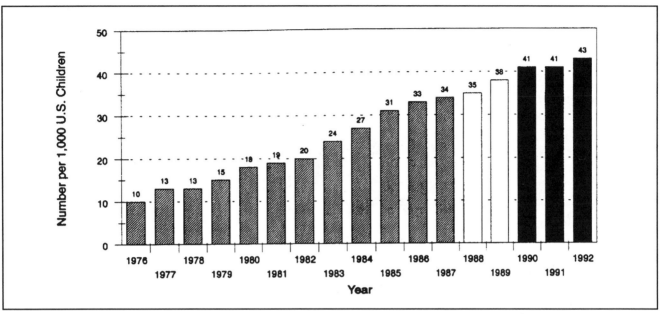

Source: U.S. Department of Health and Human Services, National Center on Child Abuse and Neglect. *Child Maltreatment 1992: Reports From the States to the National Center on Child Abuse and Neglect.* Washington, DC: U.S. Government Printing Office, 1994, page 9.

B3-2. Source of Reports of Child Abuse, 1992

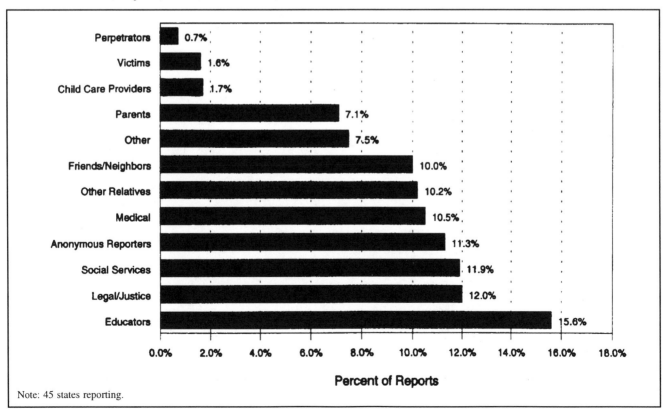

Note: 45 states reporting.

Source: U.S. Department of Health and Human Services, National Center on Child Abuse and Neglect. *Child Maltreatment 1992: Reports From the States to the National Center on Child Abuse and Neglect.* Washington, DC: U.S. Government Printing Office, 1994, page 11.

B3-3. Investigation Dispositions of Reported Cases of Child Abuse, 1992

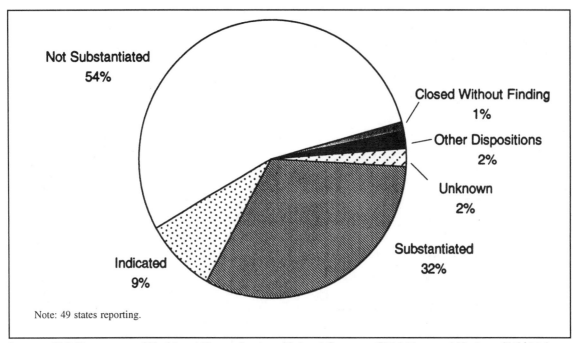

Note: 49 states reporting.

Source: U.S. Department of Health and Human Services, National Center on Child Abuse and Neglect. *Child Maltreatment 1992: Reports From the States to the National Center on Child Abuse and Neglect.* Washington, DC: U.S. Government Printing Office, 1994, page 11.

B3-4. Victims of Child Abuse, by Type of Maltreatment, 1992

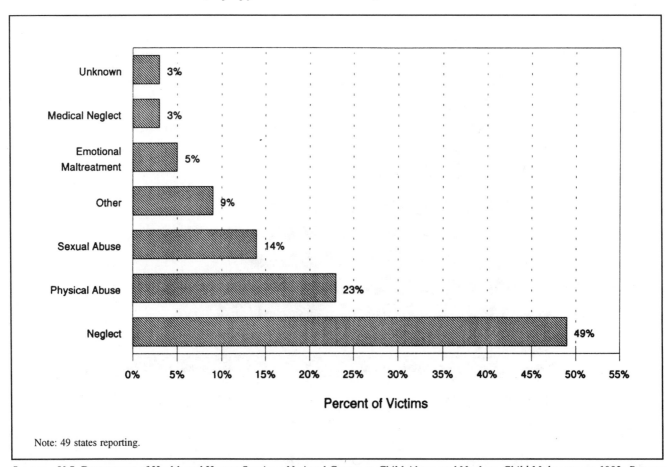

Note: 49 states reporting.

Source: U.S. Department of Health and Human Services, National Center on Child Abuse and Neglect. *Child Maltreatment 1992: Reports From the States to the National Center on Child Abuse and Neglect.* Washington, DC: U.S. Government Printing Office, 1994, page 14.

B3-5. Age of Victims of Child Abuse, 1992

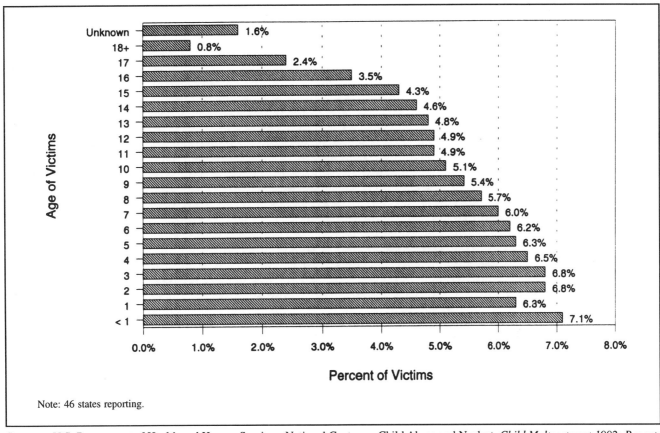

Note: 46 states reporting.

Source: U.S. Department of Health and Human Services, National Center on Child Abuse and Neglect. *Child Maltreatment 1992: Reports From the States to the National Center on Child Abuse and Neglect.* Washington, DC: U.S. Government Printing Office, 1994, page 16.

B3-6. Sex of Victims of Child Abuse, 1992

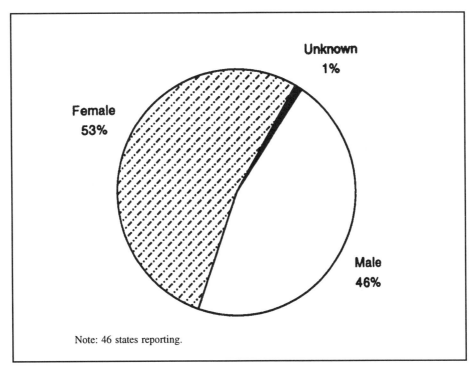

Note: 46 states reporting.

Source: U.S. Department of Health and Human Services, National Center on Child Abuse and Neglect. *Child Maltreatment 1992: Reports From the States to the National Center on Child Abuse and Neglect.* Washington, DC: U.S. Government Printing Office, 1994, page 17.

B3-7. Race/Ethnicity of Victims of Child Abuse, 1992

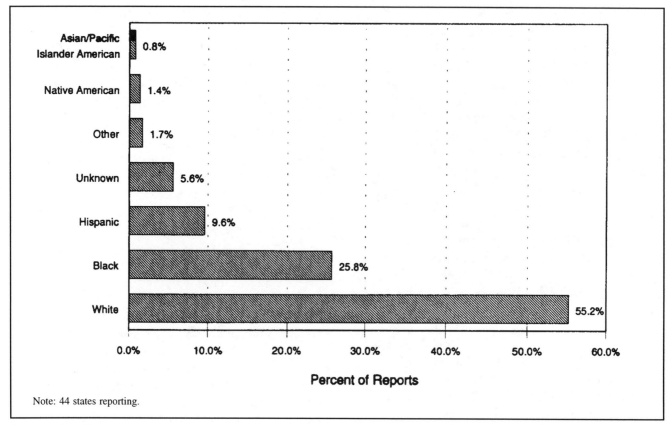

Note: 44 states reporting.

Source: U.S. Department of Health and Human Services, National Center on Child Abuse and Neglect. *Child Maltreatment 1992: Reports From the States to the National Center on Child Abuse and Neglect.* Washington, DC: U.S. Government Printing Office, 1994, page 18.

B3-8. Child Abuse Victim Data, 1992

State/Territory	Physical Abuse	Neglect	Medical Neglect	Sexual Abuse	Emotional Maltreatment	Other	Unknown	Total
Alabama	7,517	12,158		4,594	2,046			26,315
Alaska	2,627	3,204		1,272	129	19		7,251
Arizona	2,230	6,393	569	3,213	617	19,156		32,178
Arkansas	2,628	4,254	301	1,929	341			9,453
California								
Colorado	2,806	4,358	579	2,004	1,095		697	11,539
Connecticut	3,930	11,260		1,066				16,256
Delaware	424	707	78	200	204	513	31	2,157
District of Columbia	424	2,119	998	32		145		3,718
Florida	14,813	42,151	3,223	8,778	4,395	31,322		104,682
Georgia	7,732	27,743	2,405	5,386	2,386	540		46,192
Guam								
Hawaii	893	613	71	297	183	1,364		3,421
Idaho	1,884	3,112	168	1,110		210	96	6,580
Illinios	4,625	25,047	1,876	5,390	498	13,373		50,809
Indiana	7,213	15,822		7,248				30,283
Iowa	2,871	4,084	158	1,422	77	394		8,612
Kansas	761	561	57	861	101			2,735
Kentucky	6,795	15,012		2,610		1,230		25,647
Louisiana	3,991	10,362		1,339	291	123		16,106
Maine	988	1,618		639	1,675			4,920
Maryland								
Massachusetts	6,562	18,307		2,450	2,192	104		29,615
Michigan	5,709	10,828	510	2,570	7,069	285		26,971
Minnesota	4,575	6,460	540	1,375	376	178	2	13,506
Mississippi	2,999	5,622		1,842	246	3		10,712
Missouri	3,320	9,822	601	2,852	329	1,831		18,755
Montana	2,309	3,349		823				6,481
Nebraska	1,671	3,166		729				5,566
Nevada	1,541	4,791	277	405	901	2,574		10,489

Number of Victims by Maltreatment Type

B3-8. Child Abuse Victim Data, 1992 (continued)

State/Territory	Number of Victims by Maltreatment Type							
	Physical Abuse	Neglect	Medical Neglect	Sexual Abuse	Emotional Maltreatment	Other	Unknown	Total
New Hampshire	171	273		292	26			762
New Jersey	6,685	8,214	774	1,618	206			17,499
New Mexico	1,764	4,151		801				6,716
New York	20,696	34,823	4,416	6,951	2,393		22,959	92,238
North Carolina	1,232	25,919	794	1,471	90	40		29,546
North Dakota	1,265	1,786		218		400		3,669
Ohio	14,908	29,638		11,366	5,404	11		61,327
Oklahoma	3,158	5,225	449	1,186	733			10,751
Oregon	2,341	2,932	482	3,092	540	2,247		11,634
Pennsylvania	3,628	414		4,348	167			8,557
Rhode Island	1,627	2,703		601				4,931
South Carolina	2,278	6,229	768	1,860	241	3,806		15,182
South Dakota	555	1,793		542	429			3,319
Tennessee	2,764	4,540	294	2,850	345	676		11,469
Texas	20,132	31,620	2,853	10,747	6,071	2,350		73,773
Utah	2,362	1,906	183	2,501	1,472	2,646		11,070
Vermont	426	364	34	811	32	10		1,677
Virginia	3,694	9,000	485	2,379	1,781	436		17,775
Virgin Islands	42	110	3	37	25	5		222
Washington	12,517	16,780	1,505	6,272	2,791	202	5,870	45,937
West Virginia								
Wisconsin	5,648	6,804		7,213	777			20,442
Wyoming	550	1,295	52	390	252			2,539
National Total	212,281	449,442	25,503	129,982	48,928	86,193	29,655	981,984
No. Reporting	49	49	30	49	39	30	6	49

Source: U.S. Department of Health and Human Services, National Center on Child Abuse and Neglect. *Child Maltreatment 1992: Reports From the States to the National Center on Child Abuse and Neglect.* Washington, DC: U.S. Government Printing Office, 1994, page 42.

B3-9. Percent of Youth Who Report Being Sexually Abused, by Grade, 1990

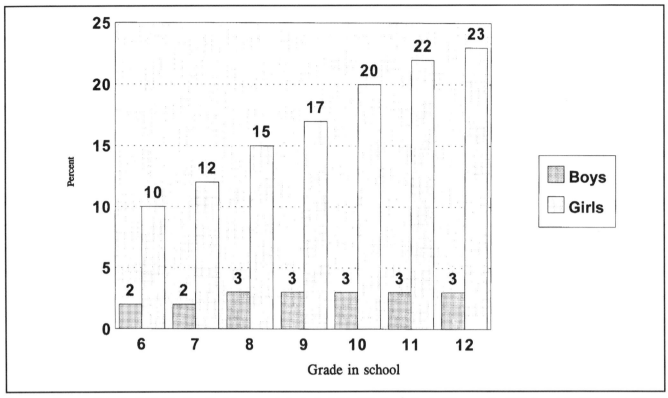

Source: Benson, Peter L. 1993. *The Troubled Journey: A Portrait of 6th-12th Grade Youth.* Minneapolis, MN: Search Institute, page 28.

B3-10. Percent of Sexually Experienced Women Having Involuntary Intercourse, by Age, 1987

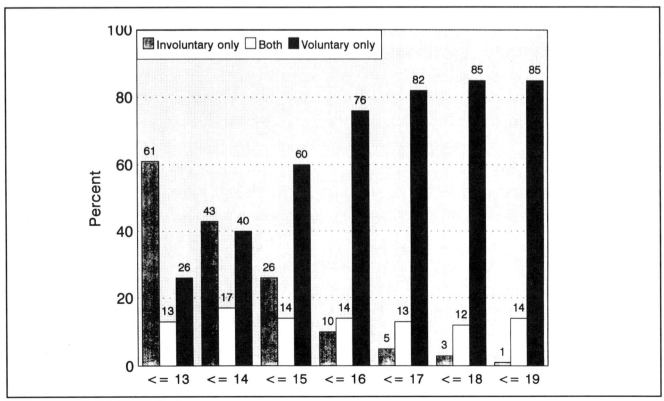

Source: The Alan Guttmacher Institute. 1994. *Sex and America's Teenagers.* New York: The Alan Guttmacher Institute, page 28.

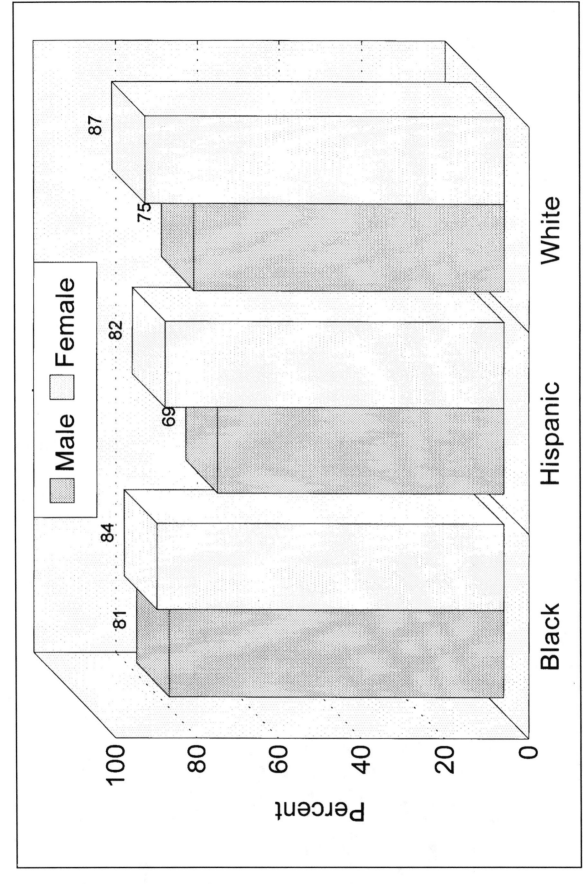

B3-11. Percent of Students in Grades 8–11 Reporting Unwanted Sexual Comments or Actions, by Race, 1993

Source: The Alan Guttmacher Institute. 1994. *Sex and America's Teenagers.* New York: The Alan Guttmacher Institute, page 17.

B4. RISK FACTORS

B4-1. Low Birth Weight and Births to Teenage Mothers and to Unmarried Women, by States, 1980 and 1990

Division and state	Percent of infants with low birth weight[1] 1980	1990	Births to teenage mothers, percent of total 1980	1990	Births to unmarried women, percent of total 1980	1990	Division and state	Percent of births with low birth weight 1980	1990	Births to teenage mothers, percent of total 1980	1990	Births to unmarried women, percent of total 1980	1990
U.S.	6.8	7.0	15.6	12.8	18.4	28.0	VA	7.5	7.2	15.5	11.7	19.2	26.0
							WV	6.7	7.1	20.1	17.8	13.1	25.4
N.E.	6.2	5.9	11.6	8.4	15.5	24.2	NC	7.9	8.0	19.2	16.2	19.0	29.4
ME	6.5	5.1	15.3	10.8	13.9	22.6	SC	8.6	8.7	19.8	17.1	23.0	32.7
NH	5.4	4.9	10.7	7.2	11.0	16.9	GA	8.6	8.7	20.7	16.7	23.2	32.8
VT	5.9	5.3	13.0	8.5	13.7	20.1	FL	7.6	7.4	18.2	13.9	23.0	31.7
MA	6.1	5.9	10.7	8.0	15.7	24.7	E.S.C.	7.8	8.2	21.0	18.4	20.9	30.6
RI	6.3	6.2	12.3	10.5	15.7	26.3	KY	6.8	7.1	21.1	17.5	15.1	23.6
CT	6.7	6.6	11.4	8.2	17.9[2]	26.6[2]	TN	8.0	8.2	19.9	17.6	19.9	30.2
M.A.	7.1	7.3	12.6	9.5	21.3	29.9	AL	7.9	8.4	20.6	18.2	22.2	30.1
NY	7.4	7.6	11.8	9.1	23.8[2]	33.0[2]	MS	8.7	9.6	23.2	21.3	28.0	40.5
NJ	7.2	7.0	12.3	8.4	21.1	24.3	W.S.C.	7.3	7.3	19.1	16.3	15.8	22.2
PA	6.5	7.1	13.9	10.9	17.7	28.6	AR	7.6	8.2	21.6	19.7	20.5	29.4
E.N.C.	6.7	7.1	15.2	13.2	18.0	28.3	LA	8.6	9.2	20.1	17.6	23.4	36.8
OH	6.8	7.1	15.7	13.8	17.8[2]	28.9	OK	6.8	6.6	19.6	16.2	14.0	25.2
IN	6.3	6.6	17.3	14.5	15.5	26.2	TX	6.9	6.9	18.3	15.6	13.3[2]	17.5[2]
IL	7.2	7.6	15.7	13.1	22.5	31.7	Mountain	6.6	6.8	14.3	12.8	12.7	25.1
MI	6.9	7.6	14.0	13.5	16.2[2]	26.2[2]	MT	5.6	6.2	12.4	11.5	12.5[2]	23.7
WI	5.4	5.9	12.3	10.2	13.9	24.2	ID	5.3	5.7	13.1	12.3	7.9	16.7
W.N.C.	5.7	5.9	13.5	11.1	13.1	23.2	WY	7.3	7.4	15.5	13.6	8.2	19.8
MN	5.1	5.1	10.4	8.0	11.4	20.9	CO	8.2	8.0	13.3	11.3	13.0	21.2
IA	5.0	5.4	12.5	10.2	10.3	21.0	NM	7.6	7.4	18.2	16.3	16.1	35.4
MO	6.6	7.1	16.9	14.4	17.6	28.6	AZ	6.2	6.4	16.5	14.2	18.7	32.7
ND	4.9	5.5	10.9	8.6	9.2	18.4	UT	5.2	5.7	11.0	10.3	6.2	13.5
SD	5.1	5.1	13.5	10.8	13.4	22.9	NV	6.6	7.2	15.4	12.6	13.5[2]	25.4[2]
NE	5.6	5.3	12.1	9.8	11.6	20.7	Pacific	5.8	5.7	13.6	11.5	19.6	30.2
KS	5.8	6.2	15.0	12.3	12.3	21.5	WA	5.1	5.3	12.5	10.8	13.6	23.7
S.A.	8.0	7.9	18.3	14.4	22.2	30.9	OR	4.9	5.0	13.3	12.0	14.8	25.7
DE	7.7	7.6	16.7	11.9	24.2	29.0	CA	5.9	5.8	13.9	11.6	21.4[2]	31.6[2]
MD	8.2	7.8	14.8	10.5	25.2[2]	29.6	AK	5.4	4.8	11.8	9.7	15.1	26.2
DC	12.8	15.1	20.7	17.8	56.5	64.9	HI	7.1	7.1	11.5	10.5	17.6	24.8

[1] Less than 2,500 grams (5 pounds-8 ounces). [2] Marital status of mother is inferred.

Note: N.E. stands for New England; M.A. stands for Mid-Atlantic; E.N.C. stands for East North Central; W.N.C. stands for West North Central; S.A. stands for South Atlantic; E.S.C. stands for East South Central; and W.S.C. stands for West South Central.

Source: U.S. Bureau of the Census, *Statistical Abstract of the United States: 1993* (113th edition). Washington, DC, 1993, page 78.

B4-2. Percent of Babies Born to Mothers Who Received Late or No Prenatal Care, 1969–1991

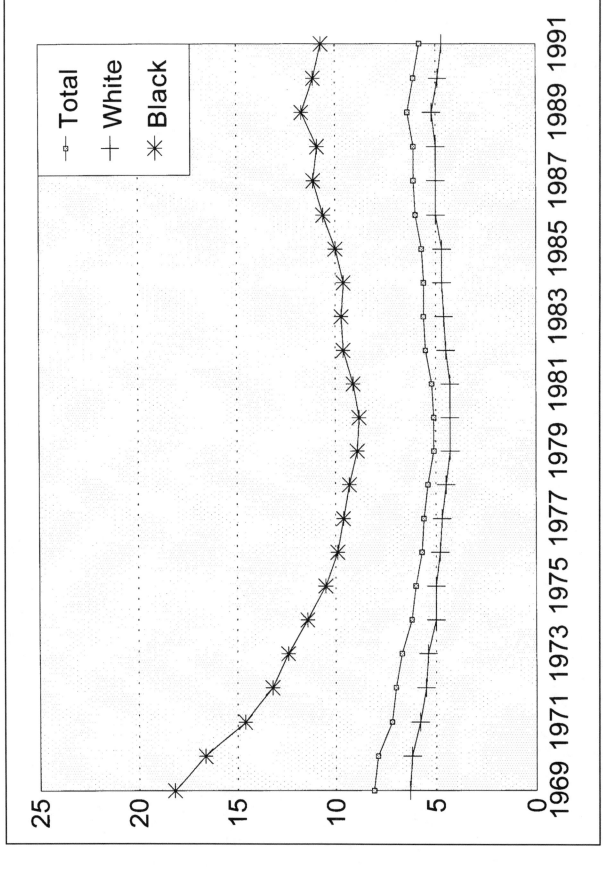

Source: Children's Defense Fund. 1994. *The State of America's Children Yearbook: 1994.* Washington, DC: Children's Defense Fund, page 74.

B4-3. Percent of Children Age 1–4 Who Were Immunized, 1985 and 1991

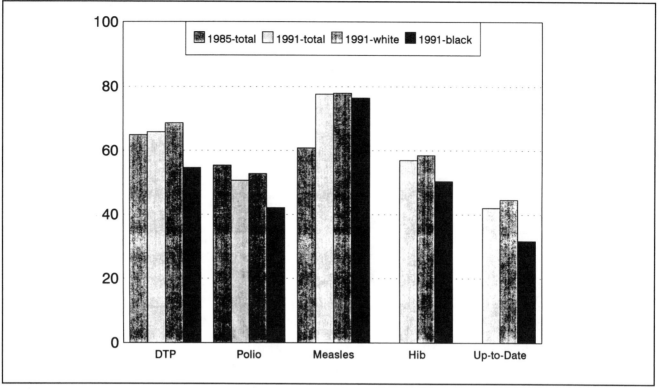

Source: U.S. Bureau of the Census, *Statistical Abstract of the United States: 1993* (113th edition). Washington, DC, 1993, page 133.

B4-4. Factors that Put Children at Risk, 1988

	Percent who do not wear seatbelt all or most of the time	Percent in household where members have smoked	Percent of children who are somewhat clumsy
Age:			
< 1	8.0	39.3	3.5
1-5	8.9	45.2	13.8
6-11	33.8	51.8	13.2
12-17	40.3	56.9	11.6
Child's Gender:			
Male	30.7	50.7	12.4
Female	29.3	50.7	12.2
Child's Ethnicity:			
White	26.4	52.1	12.3
Black	42.1	52.0	14.1
Hispanic	36.3	44.6	11.0
Other	35.9	36.8	9.7
Mother's Education:			
< High school	46.5	63.1	14.3
High school graduate	31.9	54.8	12.6
Some college	21.6	45.6	12.0
College graduate	15.9	31.7	9.4
Post graduate	14.8	26.4	9.8
Mother's Marital Status:			
Married	27.6	48.5	11.6
Divorced/separated	38.1	59.6	15.2
Widowed	46.2	59.2	13.1
Never married	40.5	55.1	15.7

Source: National Center for Health Statistics. 1992. *The National Health Interview Survey On Child Health, 1988* (Data Set 33-34), B. C. Holmes, A. S. Kaplan, E. L. Lang, and J. J. Card, Archivists [machine-readable data file and documentation]. Washington, DC: Department of Health and Human Services, Producer. Los Altos, Ca: Sociometrics Corporation, American Family Data Archive (Producer & Distriburtor).

B5. MEDICAL TREATMENT AND HEALTH CARE COVERAGE

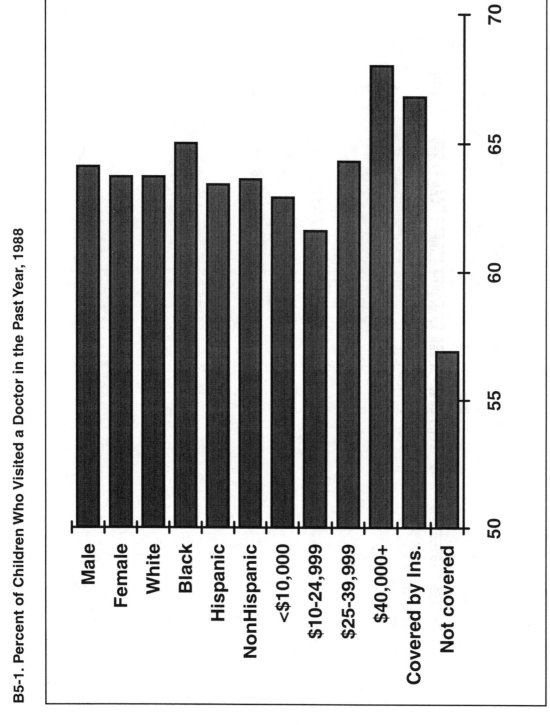

B5-1. Percent of Children Who Visited a Doctor in the Past Year, 1988

Source: U.S. Bureau of the Census, *Statistical Abstract of the United States: 1993* (113th edition). Washington, DC, 1993, page 117.

B5-2. Time Since Child Last Saw the Dentist, by Age, Race, Gender, and Mother's Education and Marital Status, 1988

	Never	More than 1 year	Less than 1 year
Age:			
1-5	39.6	6.9	53.6
6-11	6.6	17.6	75.9
12-17	2.3	23.6	74.2
Child's Gender:			
Male	11.8	18.8	69.5
Female	11.7	16.7	71.7
Child's Ethnicity:			
White	10.3	14.4	75.3
Black	12.5	29.1	58.4
Hispanic	18.4	24.0	57.5
Other	15.3	19.3	65.4
Mother's Education:			
< High school	17.9	27.6	54.4
High school graduate	12.3	18.5	69.1
Some college	8.5	13.3	78.1
College graduate	7.6	8.1	84.3
Post graduate	5.2	7.3	87.5
Mother's Marital Status:			
Married	11.8	16.3	71.9
Divorced/separated	9.5	20.9	69.6
Widowed	8.0	28.7	63.4
Never married	18.6	24.9	56.6

Note: Numbers are percentages of total children under 18.

Source: National Center for Health Statistics. 1992. *The National Health Interview Survey On Child Health, 1988* (Data Set 33-34, B. C. Holmes, A. S. Kaplan, E. L. Lang, and J. J. Card, Archivists [machine-readable data file and documentation]. Washington, DC: Department of Health and Human Services, Producer). Los Altos, CA: Sociometrics Corporation, American Family Data Archive (Producer & Distributor).

B5-3. Hospital Patients per 1,000 Persons, by Gender and Age, 1991

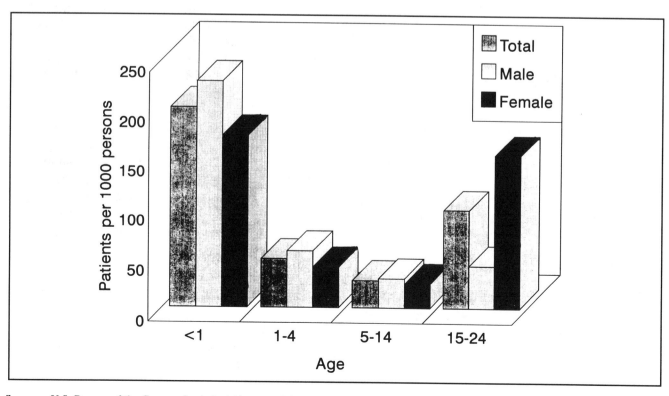

Source: U.S. Bureau of the Census, *Statistical Abstract of the United States: 1993* (113th edition). Washington, DC, 1993, page 125.

B5-4. Average Length of Hospital Stay, by Age, 1991

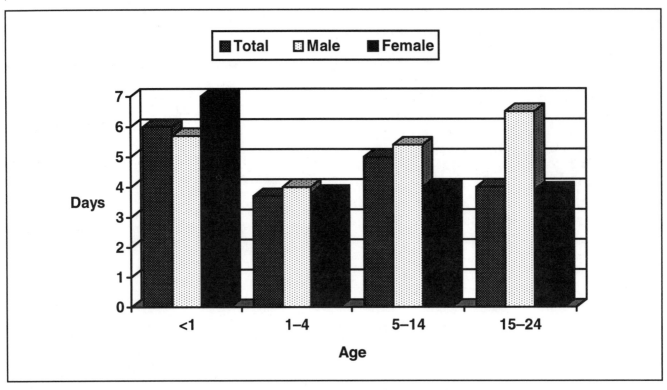

Source: U.S. Bureau of the Census, *Statistical Abstract of the United States: 1993* (113th edition). Washington, DC, 1993, page 125.

B5-5. Principal Source of Hospital Payment, 1991

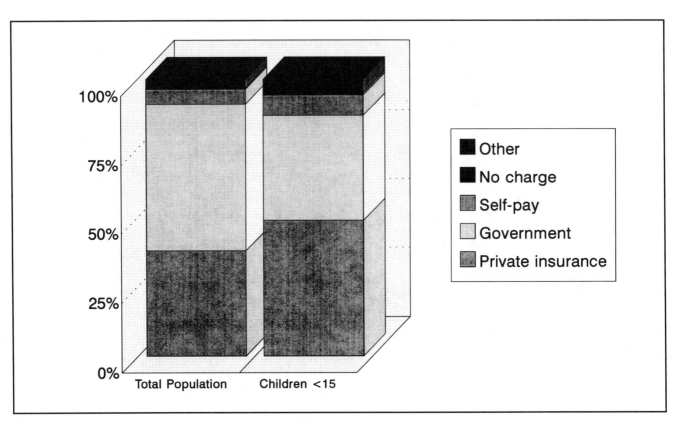

Source: U.S. Bureau of the Census, *Statistical Abstract of the United States: 1993* (113th edition). Washington, DC, 1993, page 128.

B5-6. Children—Health Insurance and Medical Care, 1988

Characteristic	Total	Under 1 year	1 to 4 years	5 to 7 years	8 to 11 years	12 to 14 years	15 to 17 years
All children (1,000)[1]	63,569	3,850	14,536	11,037	13,635	9,872	10,639
PERCENT COVERED BY HEALTH INSURANCE							
All children	83.1	80.1	83.7	83.3	83.8	83.0	82.3
Sex:							
Male	83.5	80.4	83.5	83.7	83.8	84.3	83.1
Female	82.7	79.7	84.0	83.0	83.8	81.4	81.3
Race:							
White	83.7	80.7	84.4	84.3	83.6	83.7	83.5
Black	80.9	81.2	80.5	79.7	84.1	81.7	77.6
Hispanic origin:							
Hispanic	70.0	62.2	75.2	76.3	65.0	68.1	68.3
Non-Hispanic	84.9	82.8	85.2	84.3	86.3	85.1	83.8
Family income:							
Under $10,000	71.8	74.0	75.3	73.9	71.0	69.7	64.4
$10,000 to $24,999	76.1	75.1	76.9	78.2	75.3	73.5	76.6
$25,000 to $39,999	89.8	85.6	90.5	89.4	92.1	90.2	87.4
$40,000 or more	92.4	93.3	93.2	91.7	92.0	93.2	91.6
PERCENT WHO VISITED A DOCTOR FOR HEALTH CARE[2]							
All children	63.9	93.8	81.5	66.0	49.6	54.8	53.9
Sex:							
Male	64.1	94.4	81.3	65.9	49.4	57.6	52.5
Female	63.7	93.1	81.7	66.0	49.9	51.6	55.3
Race:							
White	63.7	95.1	81.4	65.7	47.9	56.0	54.0
Black	65.0	87.6	82.6	66.6	55.7	51.7	55.7
Hispanic origin:							
Hispanic	63.4	93.5	82.3	70.4	49.5	51.9	45.5
Non-Hispanic	63.6	93.5	81.1	65.2	49.5	55.0	54.8
Family income:							
Under $10,000	62.9	87.4	78.9	65.6	49.5	53.5	45.9
$10,000 to $24,999	61.6	96.1	80.4	62.8	43.7	47.9	52.6
$25,000 to $39,999	64.3	94.9	82.5	67.7	47.1	54.3	56.9
$40,000 or more	68.0	97.2	85.8	70.0	56.3	62.5	58.4
Covered by health insurance	66.8	96.1	83.4	68.6	52.6	58.6	57.7
Not covered by health insurance	56.9	91.8	79.3	58.9	39.0	42.1	44.3

[1] Includes other races and unknown income.   [2] For routine health care within the past year.

Source: U.S. Bureau of the Census, *Statistical Abstract of the United States: 1993* (113th edition). Washington, DC, 1993, page 117.

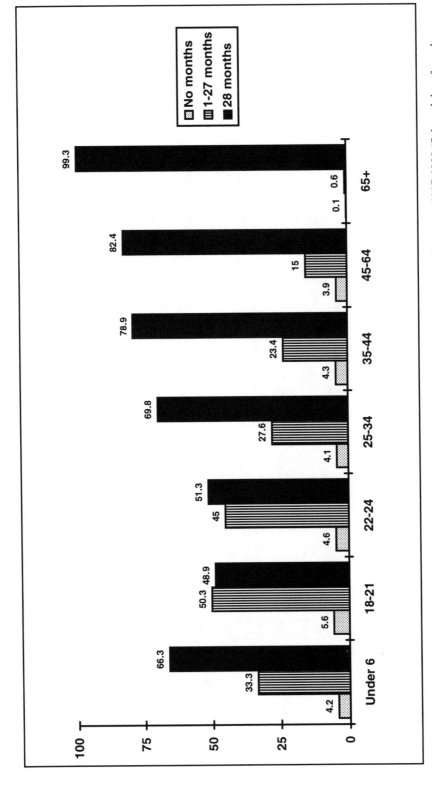

B5-7. Months of Health Insurance Coverage, by Age Group, 1987–1989

Source: U.S. Bureau of the Census. Current Population Reports, Series P-70, No. 29, *Health Insurance Coverage: 1987-1990 (Selected data from the Survey of Income and Program Participation).* U.S. Government Printing Ogffice, Washington, DC, 1992, page 7.

B5-8. Health Insurance Coverage Status—Persons by Sex, Race, and Other Selected Characteristics, Monthly Average October–December 1990

(In thousands)

Characteristics	Total	Percent covered by private or government health insurance						Not covered by private or government health insurance
		Total	Government health insurance			Private health insurance		
			Medicare	Medicaid	CHAMPUS/ VA	Total	Related to employment of self or other	
All persons	248,195	87.1	13.1	8.1	2.7	76.1	61.3	12.9
Sex								
Male........................	120,814	86.0	11.5	6.3	2.1	76.6	63.3	14.0
Female	127,381	88.1	14.5	9.8	3.2	75.7	59.5	11.9
Age								
Less than 16 years..............	58,493	86.2	-	15.5	3.3	70.7	59.0	13.8
16 to 24 years	31,595	78.1	0.2	8.0	2.2	70.0	53.4	21.9
25 to 34 years	43,117	83.0	0.8	6.8	1.5	74.9	67.1	17.0
35 to 44 years	38,174	87.9	1.1	3.8	1.6	82.7	75.3	12.1
45 to 54 years	25,684	88.6	2.4	3.4	2.9	83.8	73.5	11.4
55 to 64 years	21,241	89.5	8.2	5.1	4.9	80.2	64.7	10.5
65 years and over..............	29,892	99.7	97.8	7.4	3.3	77.4	35.1	0.3
Race and Hispanic Origin								
White........................	208,903	88.0	13.9	5.7	2.5	79.5	64.0	12.0
Black........................	30,764	82.0	9.7	23.0	3.1	55.9	46.2	18.0
Hispanic origin[1]	21,180	71.8	6.1	16.9	2.4	53.0	44.8	28.2
Region								
Northeast	49,884	91.7	13.9	7.9	1.1	82.0	67.5	8.3
Midwest......................	62,704	89.9	13.4	7.7	1.4	80.5	64.5	10.1
South........................	84,313	83.2	13.1	8.0	3.9	71.1	56.5	16.8
West	51,294	85.3	11.7	9.0	3.9	73.3	59.5	14.7
Type of Residence								
Inside metropolitan areas	190,599	87.6	12.3	7.8	2.6	77.3	63.4	12.4
Inside central cities..............	75,633	85.0	12.5	12.6	2.7	69.4	56.1	15.0
Outside central cities	114,966	89.3	12.1	4.7	2.6	82.5	68.3	10.7
1 million or more..................	117,994	88.3	12.2	8.0	2.0	78.1	64.2	11.7
Insidecentral cities	45,161	85.1	12.5	13.5	2.0	68.8	55.7	14.9
Outside central cities	72,833	90.2	12.0	4.5	2.0	83.9	69.5	9.8
Under 1 million	72,605	86.5	12.4	7.6	3.7	76.0	62.2	13.5
Inside central cities..............	30,472	84.8	12.5	11.2	3.7	70.4	56.7	15.2
Outside central cities	42,133	87.7	12.3	5.0	3.7	80.0	66.2	12.3
Outside metropolitan areas............	57,596	85.3	15.6	9.0	2.9	72.3	54.4	14.7
Work Disability								
Persons 16 to 64 years:								
With work disability................	19,377	82.0	14.6	19.1	3.2	58.5	46.4	18.0
Retirement or disability income:								
Received.....................	7,955	90.0	34.2	32.2	5.1	47.7	33.7	10.0
Did not receive	11,422	76.5	0.9	10.0	1.8	65.9	55.3	23.5
No work disability	140,434	85.4	0.2	3.7	2.2	80.6	69.9	14.6
Program Recipiency								
Received:								
AFDC or other public assistance.....	10,609	99.3	1.2	98.5	0.6	7.5	3.4	0.7
Federal SSI	4,001	100.0	52.3	100.0	2.1	11.7	4.1	0.0
Public or subsidized housing.........	10,622	83.9	16.8	52.3	2.2	28.4	18.3	16.1
Food stamps	18,066	83.9	8.0	72.6	1.2	13.6	8.0	16.0
Social Security or Railroad Retirement	37,820	96.4	81.7	8.6	3.1	73.9	35.4	3.6
Unemployment Compensation.......	2,501	61.1	1.5	4.2	1.1	56.7	47.5	38.9
VA compensation	2,850	90.8	37.6	4.2	20.5	71.2	51.6	9.2
VA pension.....................	662	89.0	62.2	19.2	33.5	31.6	6.5	11.0
Covered by:								
Medicare......................	32,397	100.0	100.0	8.9	3.1	74.6	34.1	0.0
Medicaid......................	20,104	100.0	14.3	100.0	1.1	11.7	6.1	0.0

[1]Persons of Hispanic origin may be of any race.

Source: U.S. Bureau of the Census. Current Population Reports, Series P-70, No. 29, *Health Insurance Coverage: 1987-1990 (Selected data from the Survey of Income and Program Participation).* U.S. Government Printing Office, Washington, DC, 1992, page 19.

B6. SEXUALLY TRANSMITTED DISEASES

B6-1. Gonorrhea—Age- and Gender-Specific Rates, 1993

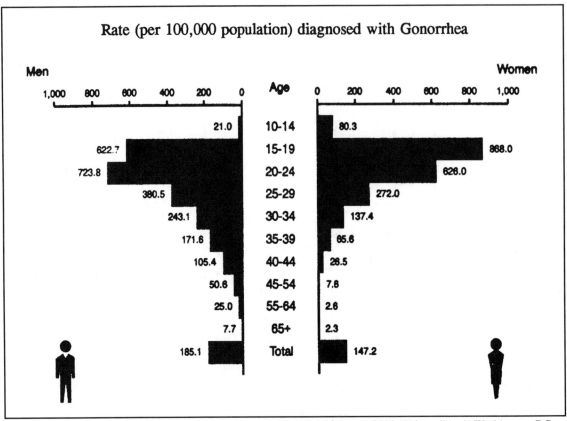

Source: U.S. Bureau of the Census, *Statistical Abstract of the United States: 1993* (113th edition). Washington, DC, 1993, page 134.

B6-2. Gonorrhea—Age-Specific Rates among Women and Men 15–44 Years of Age, 1981–1993

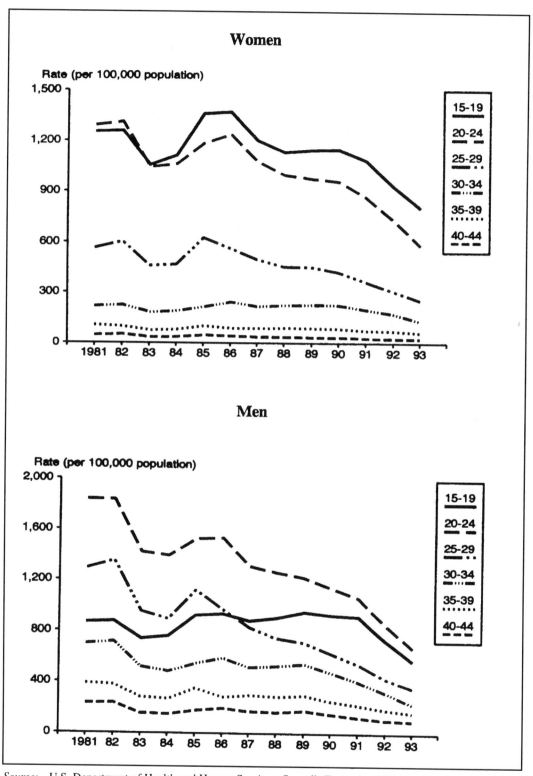

Source: U.S. Department of Health and Human Services, *Sexually Transmitted Disease Surveillance: 1993.* Atlanta, GA: Centers for Disease Control and Prevention, Division of STD/HIV Prevention Surveillance and Information Systems Branch, 1994, p. 13.

B6-3. Primary and Secondary Syphilis—Age- and Gender-Specific Rates, 1993

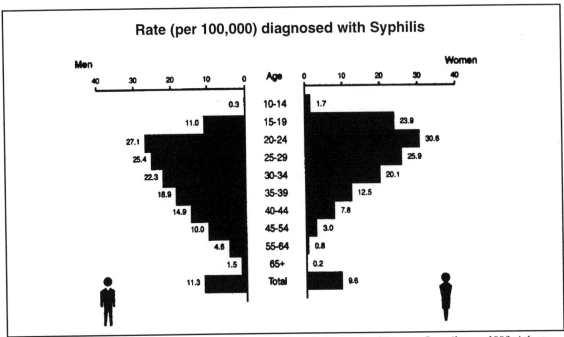

Source: U.S. Department of Health and Human Services, *Sexually Transmitted Disease Surveillance: 1993.* Atlanta, GA: Centers for Disease Control and Prevention, Division of STD/HIV Prevention Surveillance and Information Systems Branch, 1994, p. 43.

B6-4. Estimated Risk of Acquiring a Sexually Transmitted Disease in One Act of Unprotected Intercourse with an Infected Partner, 1993

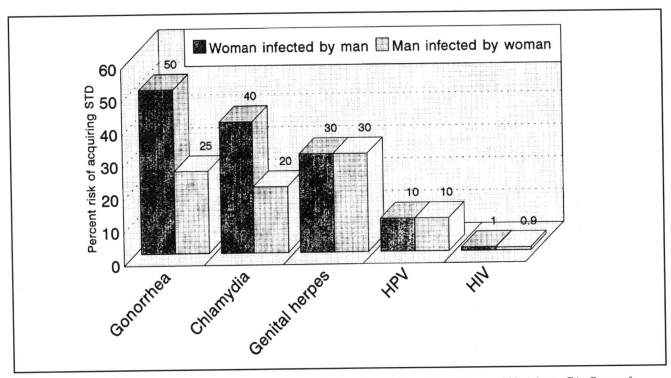

Source: U.S. Department of Health and Human Services, *Sexually Transmitted Disease Surveillance: 1993.* Atlanta, GA: Centers for Disease Control and Prevention, Division of STD/HIV Prevention Surveillance and Information Systems Branch, 1994, p. 22.

B6-5. Fear of Getting AIDS, 1987 and 1991

Survey question: How concerned are you that you, yourself, will get AIDS?		
	1991	1987
Very concerned	34%	28%
Somewhat concerned	29	31
Not very concerned	24	22
Not at all concerned	13	19
Note: Question asked of a sample of 13- to 17-year-olds.		

Source: The Alan Guttmacher Institute. 1994. *Sex and America's Teenagers.* New York: The Alan Guttmacher Institute, page 41.

B6-6. Behavior Changes because of AIDS, 1991

Survey question: As I read off four statements, please tell me which one of the statements best applies to you.				
	Have changed	Considered changing	Have not changed	No need to change
National	23%	11%	11%	55%
Male	22	15	14	49
Female	24	7	7	62
White	19	9	13	59
Non-white	37	18	5	40
Note: Question asked of a sample of 13- to 17-year-olds				

Source: Bezilla, Robert (ed.). 1993. *American's Youth in the 1990s.* Princeton, NJ: The George H. Gallup International Institute, page 52.

B6-7. Percentage of 15- to 19-Year-Old Men Who Received AIDS Education or Sex Education, by Topic, 1988

Topic	Percent (N=1,880)
AIDS	67.2
How to prevent AIDS through safe sex	64.7
Either AIDS topic	72.8
Methods of birth control	75.0
Where to obtain contraceptive methods	58.0
Either birth control topic	78.7
How pregnancy occurs	84.2
The menstrual cycle	73.2
Venereal diseases	81.1
Any biology topic	91.9
How to say no to sex (resistance skills)	58.0
Note: N equals the sample size.	

Source: Bezilla, Robert (ed.). 1993. *American's Youth in the 1990s.* Princeton, NJ: The George H. Gallup International Institute, page 52.

B6-8. Adolescents' Perception of How AIDS Is Caught, 1991

Survey question: Please tell me if the following is a way for people to catch AIDS from someone who has it.		
	November 1991	July 1991
By sharing needles	99%	99%
Intimate heterosexual contact	97	94
Intimate homosexual contact	93	89
Receiving blood transfusions	91	95
Note: Percentages are of those who answered "yes" to the question.		

Source: *Family Planning Perspectives* 24 (3) 1992, page 102.

B6-9. Adolescents' Support for Anti-AIDS Proposals, 1991

Survey question: Please tell me how much you support or oppose each of these issues and causes—support very much, support somewhat, oppose somewhat, or oppose very much. How about providing free condoms to students to help prevent the spread of AIDS? Providing counseling centers where students can be taught not to have sexual relations until after they are married?		
	Percent of Teens Who Very Much or Somewhat Favor Each Proposal	
	Provide free condoms to students	Provide counseling centers
National	**82%**	**65%**
Male	81	64
Female	84	65
Ages 13-15	83	67
Ages 16-17	82	61
White	81	67
Non-white	85	56
Above-average students	83	69
Average and below	80	60
East	85	62
Midwest	89	64
South	83	67
West	69	65
Protestant	84	67
Catholic	86	61

Source: Bezilla, Robert (ed.). 1993. *American's Youth in the 1990s.* Princeton, NJ: The George H. Gallup International Institute, page 55.

C. Parent-Adolescent Relations

"Worry and Distrust of Adults Beset Teenagers" was the headline reporting a national survey of 1,055 teens by the *New York Times* and CBS News (Chira, 1994). According to the survey, substantial numbers of teenagers feel their parents neglect them, especially if both parents work. In addition, teenagers' distrust of their parents restricts any honest communication between them. Communication, trust, family rules, discipline, support, and love are very important ingredients in adolescents' quality of life.

In this chapter, we present information about the frequency and type of interaction between parents and their adolescent children, as well as how the parents and offspring feel about this interaction. Family rules and discipline for violations are discussed, as are how teens perceive their parents and other significant adults, how frequently and under what conditions they argue and disagree, the frequency at which parents assign chores, and whether adolescents are given an allowance. In addition, we reveal the extent to which adolescents feel a part of an extended family and relate to grandparents and other relatives. Finally, we explain the relationship between adopted adolescent children and their parents and compare them to biological families.

C1. INTERACTION BETWEEN PARENTS AND CHILDREN

Over half the mothers in a national survey indicated they have a good time or pleasant experience with their teenager almost every day. Only 10 percent regularly argued or had difficulty with their children. Families spend considerable time together; two-thirds eat dinner together on a regular basis, and nearly all celebrate holidays and birthdays together. Over two-thirds of the parents also indicate they are involved with their children's teachers and school activities. The same number indicate they have read books or pamphlets on how to be a better parent. About a third have attended lectures or support groups that teach parenting skills.

The various surveys of both parents and adolescents reveal a pattern of fairly good communication between them. About half the teenagers indicate their parents talk with them about problems, respect their ideas, and attend events of importance to them. Mothers do somewhat better than fathers, but both are involved in their children's lives. A little more than half of the parents surveyed felt that they spend sufficient time with their older children. The other half wish they spent more time with them. Most teenagers report their parents regularly discuss important topics such as dating, sex, drugs, religious values, and family problems. When asked to identify, in order of importance, topics they would like to discuss more with their parents, teenagers listed school work, family, and religion, respectively.

Most parents and adolescents feel good about the relationship they share, and there is little evidence of the wide-scale generation gap that is so frequently discussed in the media.

C2. PARENTS' SUPPORT, CONTROL, AND DISCIPLINE

Thirty-seven percent of adolescents in 1992 felt their family rules were at about the right level of strictness. Thirty-eight percent indicated their parents were too strict and 24 percent acknowledged they were too lax. When asked a similar question, about half of a sample of teenagers reported they wished their parents would be more strict and keep a closer watch over them.

Three-fourths of the children in one survey reported they have a strong say in the formulation of family rules. Seventy-eight percent of surveyed mothers report that their teenagers keep them informed about their whereabouts. Eighty-five percent of the teens reported their parents know where they are, and seventy percent indicated their parents know what they are doing.

Most families have rules pertaining to a child's behavior. Most teenagers are allowed to be out until 9 p.m. on school nights and midnight on weekends. Only about one out of four parents tries to influence what teenagers watch on TV. In addition, parents reported that they severely discipline their teens most often for drug and alcohol use. Smoking cigarettes, skipping school, sex, talking back, and lying also elicit significant discipline.

C3. ADOLESCENTS' PERCEPTIONS OF PARENTS AND ADULTS

Mothers emerged as the most important person in the lives of adolescent children. Ninety-three percent identified their mother and 79 percent noted their father as being an important adult in their lives. Teachers and coaches were a distant second with only 30 percent of the young people favoring them. Sixty percent of the teens surveyed reported that they look up to, admire, and wish to pattern their life after either their mother or their father. The other 40 percent chose public figures, teachers, or coaches as role models.

C4. PARENT-CHILD CONFLICT

Conflict between parents and their adolescent children occurs fairly infrequently in most families. Less than 10 percent of parents indicated they frequently disagree with their teens about getting along in the family, helping at home, school related issues, dating, staying out late, and sex. These behaviors were a source of occasional disagreement for another 15 to 25 percent. Overall, it appears that most families have a rather modest level of conflict between parents and older children. In a national survey, 43 percent of parents admitted to disciplining their children for serious violations of family rules by spanking them. Verbal insult and crying about a problem with the child were used by 9 and 8 percent of the parents, respectively.

C5. ADOLESCENTS' HOUSEHOLD CHORES AND ALLOWANCE

Eighty-six percent of mothers reported they assign chores to teenagers. Although it appears to be a struggle, parents feel it is important that children take on responsibility for household chores, and the parents follow up to ensure the children complete them. Overall they are reasonably successful. In addition, about half of the mothers in a national survey indicated their teenagers receive an allowance. The average allowance for those teens who receive one is $35 per month.

C6. ADOLESCENTS' INVOLVEMENT WITH EXTENDED FAMILY

In spite of the impression that the United States is a nation of nuclear families, children do maintain ties with extended family members. Nearly half of the teens in a Gallup survey said grandparents, aunts, uncles, and cousins were special adults in their lives, and about a fourth of the teens felt they could go to these relatives for advice.

C7. ADOPTION

In 1994, the Search Institute published results of a major study on adolescents who had been adopted as infants. This study indicates that adopted children have levels of self-esteem at least as high as those in a national random sample of adolescents. Sources of emotional support for adopted adolescents are comparable to non-adopted siblings. Although a significant portion of adopted adolescents see adoption as a part of their identity and wonder about their biological parents, they still report high levels of attachment to and similarity with their legal parents. Adoption appears to work best in homes with two parents who are well educated. Adopted teens report that relationships with parents, emotional support, and communication in the home are comparable to non-adopted children. Measures of well-being, high-risk behavior, and mental health are comparable between adopted samples and national samples, and, in many instances, the adopted sample appears to be better off. Finally, the study did not identify any major differences between transracial and same-race adopted children.

Data from the National Health Interview Survey (NHIS) of 1988 suggests that adoption is more problematic than is reported by the Search Institute. According to NHIS, children with adoptive parents are more likely to exhibit several behavioral problems, including feeling unloved, being high-strung, cheating, arguing, lacking concentration, feeling confused, disobeying, not being sorry after misbehaving, not getting along with others, acting impulsively, feeling inferior, hyperactivity, being stubborn, withdrawing, paranoia, hanging around kids who get into trouble, and being secretive.

C1. INTERACTION BETWEEN PARENTS AND CHILDREN

C1-1. Mother's Report of Experiences with Adolescent during Previous Month, by Mother's Marital Status, Race, and Education, 1987

Survey question: During the past 30 days, how often did you have an especially enjoyable time with (child)? How often during the past 30 days did you argue or have a lot of difficulty dealing with (him/her)? What about your husband/wife/partner? How often did (he/she) have an especially enjoyable time with (child)?

	N	Had a Good Time			Argued or Had Difficulty			Spouse Had a Good Time		
		Never	Some-times*	Almost every day	Never	Some-times*	Almost every day	Never	Some-times*	Almost every day
Marital Status:										
Married	4052	1%	45%	54%	28%	62%	10%	2%	46%	52%
Divorced/separated	425	2	51	47	25	64	11	—	—	—
Cohabiting	211	2	47	51	30	58	12	2	44	54
Never married	189	1	33	70	26	63	11	—	—	—
	4,876									
Race:										
White	3552	1	47	52	24	65	11	2	48	50
Black	552	1	40	59	38	51	11	3	37	60
Hispanic	392	1	34	65	47	44	9	3	34	63
Other	432	2	48	50	35	60	5	2	41	57
	4,928									
Education:										
Less than high school	268	3	43	54	45	46	9	3	33	64
High school	695	2	53	45	34	58	8	1	45	54
Some college	420	1	52	47	31	59	10	1	40	59
College graduate	217	1	56	43	30	58	12	0	40	60
Post graduate	399	1	42	57	26	63	11	1	44	55
	1,999									

*Combined "once," "2 or 3 times," "about once a week," and "about twice a week" into "sometimes."
Note: N indicates sample size. Percents may not add to 100 due to rounding.

Source: National Survey of Families and Households, 1988 [machine-readable data file] James Sweet and Larry Bumpass, principal investigators. Distributed by the Center for Demography and Ecology, University of Wisconsin-Madison, Madison, WI. For a description of this study see James Sweet, Larry Bumpass, and Vaughn Call. *The Design and Content of the National Survey of Families and Households.* Working Paper NSFH-1, Center for Demography and Ecology, University of Wisconsin-Madison, 1988.

C1-2. Adolescents' Report on How Often Family Eats Together during a Typical Week, 1990

Survey question: In a typical week, how often does your whole family living here eat dinner together?	
Number of Times	Percent (N=929)
Always	33%
Usually	30
Sometimes	31
Never	6
Note: N indicates sample size.	

Source: Moore, K. A. 1992. *National Commission on Children: 1990 Survey of Parents and Children.* (Data Set 19, H. M. Daley, E. C. Peterson, E. L. Lang, & J. J. Card, Archivists) [machine-readable data file and documentation]. Washington, DC: Child Trends, Inc. (Producer). Los Altos, CA: Sociometrics Corporation, American Family Data Archive (Producer & Distributor).

C1-3. Parents' Report on How Often Family Eats Together during a Typical Week, 1990

Survey question: In a typical week, for how many nights, out of seven, does your whole family living here eat dinner together?	
Number of Days	Percent (N=1,738)
0	3%
1	5
2	8
3	9
4	8
5	14
6	9
7	44
Note: N indicates sample size.	

Source: Moore, K. A. 1992. *National Commission on Children: 1990 Survey of Parents and Children.* (Data Set 19, H. M. Daley, E. C. Peterson, E. L. Lang, & J. J. Card, Archivists) [machine-readable data file and documentation]. Washington, DC: Child Trends, Inc. (Producer). Los Altos, CA: Sociometrics Corporation, American Family Data Archive (Producer & Distributor).

C1-4. Parents' Feelings about the Amount of Time They Spend with Their Family, 1990

Survey Question: How do you feel about the amount of time you spend with your family?			
	Percent (N=843)		
Parent	Enough Time	Wish More Time	Too Much Time
Biological mother	53%	45%	2%
Mother*	80	19	1
Biological father	44	55	0
Father*	73	27	0
*Includes step parent, adoptive parent, or legal guardian. Note: N indicates sample size.			

Source: Moore, K. A. 1992. *National Commission on Children: 1990 Survey of Parents and Children.* (Data Set 19, H. M. Daley, E. C. Peterson, E. L. Lang, & J. J. Card, Archivists) [machine-readable data file and documentation]. Washington, DC: Child Trends, Inc. (Producer). Los Altos, CA: Sociometrics Corporation, American Family Data Archive (Producer & Distributor).

C1-5. Adolescents' Perceptions of Relationship with Mother and Father, 1990

Survey question: When something is bothering you, are you able to talk it over with (her/him)? Would you say that (she/he) respects your ideas and opinions about the expected things in life? How much does (she/he) make you follow rules? Do you think (she/he) spends enough time with you or do you wish (she/he) spent more time with you? How often does (she/he) miss events or activities that are important to you?

	Percent			
Relationship	Always	Usually	Sometimes	Never
With Mother (N=843):				
Listens when something is bothering you	34%	29%	33%	4%
Respects ideas or opinions about important things in life	52	29	17	2
Makes you follow rules	43	43	11	3
Misses events or activities important to you	9	34	55	2
With Father (N=564):	A Lot	Sometimes	Almost Never	Never
Listens when something is bothering you	26%	27%	39%	8%
Respects ideas or opinions about important things in life	52	28	18	2
Makes you follow rules	49	34	14	3
Misses events or activities important to you	14	43	43	1

Note: Percents may not add to 100 due to rounding. N indicates sample size.

Source: Moore, K. A. 1992. *National Commission on Children: 1990 Survey of Parents and Children.* (Data Set 19, H. M. Daley, E. C. Peterson, E. L. Lang, & J. J. Card, Archivists) [machine-readable data file and documentation]. Washington, DC: Child Trends, Inc. (Producer). Los Altos, CA: Sociometrics Corporation, American Family Data Archive (Producer & Distributor).

C1-6. Adolescents' Perceptions of Discussions with Parents about Various Topics, 1990

Survey question: Now let's talk about the things that you and your parents do together. As I read a list of activities, tell me whether this is something you do together: a) talk about a television show that you watched together; b) have a conversation about something that's worrying you; c) have a conversation about religious values; d) have a conversation about news of what's going on in this country; e) have a conversation about your plans for the future.

	Percent (N=929)			
How often do you talk with parents about	At least once a week	At least once a month	Less often than once a month	Never
TV show you watched together	72%	14%	5%	10%
Something worrying you	53	31	8	8
Religion or values	42	31	11	16
News about this country	65	22	6	7
Plans for the future	50	39	8	4

Note: N indicates sample size.

Source: Moore, K. A. 1992. *National Commission on Children: 1990 Survey of Parents and Children.* (Data Set 19, H. M. Daley, E. C. Peterson, E. L. Lang, & J. J. Card, Archivists) [machine-readable data file and documentation]. Washington, DC: Child Trends, Inc. (Producer). Los Altos, CA: Sociometrics Corporation, American Family Data Archive (Producer & Distributor).

C1-7. Adolescents' Reports of Discussions with Parents about Various Topics, 1990

Survey question: I am going to read a list of some problems (children/teenagers) sometimes ask their parents for help with. For each one, please tell me whether you have ever talked with your parents about it.

Ever Talked with Parents About	Percent (N=929)
Problem of drugs	74%
Problem of dating	59
Problem of boys/girls	59
Problem of sex	58
Problem of school work	95
Problem with friends	73
Problem in your family	75
Problem of religion or values	68

Note: N indicates sample size.

Source: Moore, K. A. 1992. *National Commission on Children: 1990 Survey of Parents and Children.* (Data Set 19, H. M. Daley, E. C. Peterson, E. L. Lang, & J. J. Card, Archivists) [machine-readable data file and documentation]. Washington, DC: Child Trends, Inc. (Producer). Los Altos, CA: Sociometrics Corporation, American Family Data Archive (Producer & Distributor).

C1-8. Topics Adolescents' Desire to Talk in More Depth about with Parents, 1990

Survey question: Now tell me whether you would like to talk more about these same problems with your parents.

Problem	Percent (N=929)
Drugs	49%
Dating	40
Boys/girls	40
Sex	30
School work	66
Friends	48
Family	59
Religion	52

Note: N indicates sample size.

Source: Moore, K. A. 1992. *National Commission on Children: 1990 Survey of Parents and Children.* (Data Set 19, H. M. Daley, E. C. Peterson, E. L. Lang, & J. J. Card, Archivists) [machine-readable data file and documentation]. Washington, DC: Child Trends, Inc. (Producer). Los Altos, CA: Sociometrics Corporation, American Family Data Archive (Producer & Distributor).

C1-9. Adolescents' Report on Relationship with Family, 1992

Survey question: How well would you say you get along with your parents, very well, fairly well, or not at all well?

Characteristic	Get Along with Parents (N=929)		
	Very well	Fairly well	Not at all well
Total National Sample	52%	44%	4%
Sex:			
Males	53	43	4
Females	52	44	4
Race:			
White	51	45	4
Nonwhite	57	40	3
Age:			
13-15 years	54	44	2
16-17 years	50	43	7
Social Class:*			
White-collar family	52	44	4
Blue-collar family	49	46	5

*Primary wage earner in the family occupied a white-collar (such as bank clerk) or blue-collar (such as carpenter) job.
Note: N indicates sample size.

Source: Bezilla, Robert (Ed.). *America's Youth in the 1990s.* Princeton, NJ: The George H. Gallup International Institute, 1993, page 35.

C1-10. Parents' Involvement in School, Church, and Similar Parenting Activities, 1990

Survey question: In the past year have you, yourself, done any of the following things (for any of your children)?

Activity During Past Year	Percent (N=1,546)
School:	
Talked to teacher about child's progress	86%
Attended PTA meeting or other school meeting	75
Attended play, concert, sporting event, or other activity at school	76
Helped with school projects, activities, or field trip at school	55
Worked with youth-group sports team or club	38
Church:	
Led Sunday School class or other religious program	28
Parenting Training:	
Read book or pamphlet about childrearing or parenting	66
Attended class or lecture about childrearing or parenting	32
Participated in parent support or discussion group	30
Neighborhood:	
Participated in regular play group with your child	37

Note: N indicates sample size.

Source: Moore, K. A. 1992. *National Commission on Children: 1990 Survey of Parents and Children.* (Data Set 19, H. M. Daley, E. C. Peterson, E. L. Lang, & J. J. Card, Archivists) [machine-readable data file and documentation]. Washington, DC: Child Trends, Inc. (Producer). Los Altos, CA: Sociometrics Corporation, American Family Data Archive (Producer & Distributor).

C1-11. Adolescents' Report on Family Celebrations for National Holidays, Religious Holidays, Birthdays, and Accomplishments, 1990

Survey question: Some families have special ways of celebrating important occasions, like birthdays and holidays, when people get together and do something special. For each of the occasions I read, please tell me whether your family usually has a special celebration, or doesn't your family do much of anything for this occasion? The first is: a) National holidays like the 4th of July or Thanksgiving; b) religious holidays like Christmas or Passover; c) your birthday; d) you won an award or had some special accomplishment.

Event	Percent Yes (N=929)
National holiday	91%
Religious holiday	97
Birthday	93
Accomplishment or award	79

Note: N indicates sample size.

Source: Moore, K. A. 1992. *National Commission on Children: 1990 Survey of Parents and Children.* (Data Set 19, H. M. Daley, E. C. Peterson, E. L. Lang, & J. J. Card, Archivists) [machine-readable data file and documentation]. Washington, DC: Child Trends, Inc. (Producer). Los Altos, CA: Sociometrics Corporation, American Family Data Archive (Producer & Distributor).

C1-12. High School Seniors' Perceptions of Similarity of Their Ideas with Their Parents, by Sex and Race, 1992

Question: How closely do your ideas agree with your PARENTS' ideas about . . .

	Total (N=2,727)	Sex		Race	
		Males (N=1,270)	Females (N=1,360)	White (N=1,847)	Black (N=3,78)
What you should do with your life:					
Very similar	29.8%	28.3%	30.9%	29.6%	31.6%
Mostly similar	42.8	41.0	44.7	45.0	38.1
Mostly different	10.7	11.4	10.0	10.1	10.3
Very different	8.8	8.5	9.2	8.0	13.2
Don't know	7.8	10.9	5.2	7.4	6.8
How you spend your leisure time:					
Very similar	10.3%	8.1%	11.6%	9.3%	15.3%
Mostly similar	32.2	31.7	32.9	35.9	20.2
Mostly different	25.2	23.9	26.8	25.3	23.1
Very different	25.0	26.5	23.6	22.7	33.2
Don't know	7.3	9.8	5.1	6.8	8.1
How you dress:					
Very similar	25.0%	20.9%	28.8%	25.5%	28.2%
Mostly similar	37.5	36.2	39.2	41.7	25.9
Mostly different	15.4	14.8	15.7	13.8	15.8
Very different	14.9	17.8	12.0	11.8	23.1
Don't know	7.1	10.3	4.4	7.1	7.0
How you spend your money:					
Very similar	10.7%	9.8%	11.3%	9.5%	13.4%
Mostly similar	30.5	27.6	32.9	33.9	18.7
Mostly different	22.9	21.4	24.4	24.4	16.0
Very different	28.3	31.1	25.9	25.3	41.6
Don't know	7.6	10.1	5.5	6.9	10.3

C1-12. High School Seniors' Perceptions of Similarity of Their Ideas with Their Parents, by Sex and Race, 1992 (continued)

	Total (N=2,727)	Sex		Race	
		Males (N=1,270)	Females (N=1,360)	White (N=1,847)	Black (N=3,78)
Things that are okay to do on date:					
Very similar	17.6%	16.3%	19.0%	17.2%	18.5%
Mostly similar	32.5	32.7	32.5	34.4	28.3
Mostly different	18.3	18.6	17.8	19.2	13.9
Very different	17.5	15.6	19.1	17.1	17.7
Don't know	14.1	16.8	11.6	12.1	21.6
Whether it is okay to drink:					
Very similar	29.0%	26.6%	31.3%	26.7%	45.1%
Mostly similar	25.6	24.5	26.5	26.3	17.1
Mostly different	16.1	17.1	15.0	18.3	7.6
Very different	22.7	23.4	22.3	23.1	20.4
Don't know	6.6	8.4	4.9	5.6	9.9
Whether it is okay to use marijuana:					
Very similar	60.7%	55.7%	65.2%	62.2%	63.6%
Mostly similar	10.6	11.5	10.1	12.1	6.3
Mostly different	5.6	6.8	4.5	5.6	4.0
Very different	15.6	16.3	14.7	14.0	16.6
Don't know	7.5	9.7	5.4	6.2	9.5
Whether it is okay to use other drugs:					
Very similar	68.1%	62.6%	73.3%	71.2%	68.0%
Mostly similar	10.2	11.0	9.6	10.2	8.1
Mostly different	2.4	2.4	2.1	2.6	2.3
Very different	11.8	14.0	10.0	10.2	11.7
Don't know	7.5	10.0	5.0	5.8	10.0
What values are important in life:					
Very similar	42.3%	37.8%	45.7%	40.6%	51.6%
Mostly similar	36.1	38.0	35.2	38.6	28.6
Mostly different	10.0	10.9	9.1	10.8	5.9
Very different	6.6	6.5	6.7	5.9	6.6
Don't know	5.0	6.8	3.3	4.1	7.2
The value of education:					
Very similar	63.2%	57.9%	67.8%	62.7%	72.1%
Mostly similar	24.1	26.8	22.2	26.4	14.6
Mostly different	5.1	6.4	3.7	4.6	6.0
Very different	4.1	3.8	4.4	3.4	3.5
Don't know	3.5	5.1	1.8	3.0	3.8
What are appropriate roles for women:					
Very similar	39.7%	29.7%	48.0%	38.7%	50.2%
Mostly similar	32.9	35.7	30.7	34.1	29.2
Mostly different	8.0	9.8	6.7	8.1	4.1
Very different	6.7	6.2	7.0	5.9	5.6
Don't know	12.8	18.6	7.6	13.3	10.9
Conservation and pollution issues:					
Very similar	24.5%	24.6%	24.1%	23.4%	31.1%
Mostly similar	32.8	31.2	34.5	35.9	16.0
Mostly different	10.9	12.1	9.8	12.1	8.1
Very different	5.9	6.3	5.7	4.7	6.9
Don't know	25.8	25.9	25.9	23.9	38.0

C1-12. High School Seniors' Perceptions of Similarity of Their Ideas with Their Parents, by Sex and Race, 1992 (continued)

	Total (N=2,727)	Sex		Race	
		Males (N=1,270)	Females (N=1,360)	White (N=1,847)	Black (N=3,78)
Racial issues:					
Very similar	37.8%	38.9%	37.0%	34.9%	53.1%
Mostly similar	28.0	26.7	28.9	30.2	19.4
Mostly different	10.2	10.4	10.0	10.9	7.1
Very different	9.1	7.9	10.2	9.1	5.8
Don't know	14.9	16.2	13.9	15.0	14.6
Religion:					
Very similar	42.6%	40.5%	44.7%	39.3%	54.8%
Mostly similar	27.2	27.1	27.0	29.7	19.1
Mostly different	9.0	8.5	9.6	10.1	6.9
Very different	8.4	10.4	6.8	8.5	5.3
Don't know	12.7	13.5	12.0	12.4	14.0
Politics:					
Very similar	19.5%	19.9%	19.0%	18.7%	26.1%
Mostly similar	29.9	32.1	28.4	32.5	17.3
Mostly different	9.5	9.5	9.6	10.1	5.9
Very different	8.7	10.3	7.4	8.5	8.1
Don't know	32.4	28.2	35.6	30.3	42.6

Note: N indicates sample size.

Source: Bachman, Jerald G., Lloyd D. Johnston, and Patrick M. O'Malley. 1993. *Monitoring the Future: Questionnaire Responses from the Nation's High School Seniors, 1992.* Ann Arbor, MI: Survey Research Center, Institute for Social Research, The University of Michigan, pages 183–185.

C2.   PARENTS' SUPPORT, CONTROL, AND DISCIPLINE

C2-1. Adolescents' Report of How Strict Their Parents Are with Them, 1985–1992

Survey question: Do you think your parents are too strict with you or not strict enough?

Characteristic	Percent (N=929)		
	Too strict	About right	Too lax
Year:			
1985	29%	41%	28%
1987	34	42	22
1992	38	37	24
Sex:			
Male	34	39	25
Female	42	34	24
Age:			
13-15 years	37	35	27
16-17 years	39	40	21
Race:			
White	35	39	25
Nonwhite	47	30	22
Social Class:*			
White-collar family	35	43	21
Blue-collar family	38	29	32

*Primary wage earner in the family occupied a white- or blue-collar job.
Note: N indicates sample size.

Source: Bezilla, Robert (Ed.) *America's Youth in the 1990s.* Princeton, NJ: The George H. Gallup International Institute, 1993, pages 34 and 37.

C2-2. How Often Adolescents Wished Their Parents Were More Strict or Kept a Closer Watch over Them, 1990

Survey question: How often do you wish your parents were more strict or kept a closer watch over you and your life?	
Wished For More Strictness	Percent (N=929)
A lot	13
Sometimes	39
Hardly ever	47
Never	1
Note: N indicates sample size.	

Source: National Survey of Families and Households, 1988 [machine-readable data file] James Sweet and Larry Bumpass, principal investigators. Distributed by the Center for Demography and Ecology, University of Wisconsin-Madison, Madison, WI. For a description of this study see James Sweet, Larry Bumpass, and Vaughn Call. *The Design and Content of the National Survey of Families and Households.* Working Paper NSFH-1, Center for Demography and Ecology, University of Wisconsin-Madison, 1988.

C2-3. Adolescents' Report of Amount of Influence They Have in Making Family Rules, 1990

Survey question: Many families have rules for how they want their (children/teenagers) to behave. How much say do you have in making up your family's rules?	
Influence	Percent (N=929)
A lot	33%
Some	42
A little	18
No say at all	7
Note: N indicates sample size.	

Source: Moore, K. A. 1992. *National Commission on Children: 1990 Survey of Parents and Children.* (Data Set 19, H. M. Daley, E. C. Peterson, E. L. Lang, & J. J. Card, Archivists) [machine-readable data file and documentation]. Washington, DC: Child Trends, Inc. (Producer). Los Altos, CA: Sociometrics Corporation, American Family Data Archive (Producer & Distributor).

C2-4. Mothers' Report that Adolescents (Age 12–18) Tells Them Their Whereabouts When Gone, by Mother's Marital Status, Race, and Education, 1987

Survey question: When (child) is away from home is (he/she) supposed to let you know where (he/she) is?

Mother	N	All of the time	Most of the time	Some-times*
Marital Status:				
Married	1440	78%	18%	4%
Divorced/separated	201	79	14	7
Cohabiting	47	72	24	4
Never married	26	87	9	4
	1,714			
Race:				
White	1296	77	19	4
Black	186	84	11	5
Hispanic	111	87	10	2
Other	158	70	19	11
	1,750			
Education:				
Less than high school	90	75	21	4
High school graduate	260	75	21	5
Some college	141	84	15	2
College graduate	61	70	18	12
Post graduate	123	68	28	4
	675			

*Sometimes = "Sometimes" and "Hardly ever."
Note: N indicates sample size.

Source: National Survey of Families and Households, 1988 [machine-readable data file] James Sweet and Larry Bumpass, principal investigators. Distributed by the Center for Demography and Ecology, University of Wisconsin-Madison, Madison, WI. For a description of this study see James Sweet, Larry Bumpass, and Vaughn Call. *The Design and Content of the National Survey of Families and Households.* Working Paper NSFH-1, Center for Demography and Ecology, University of Wisconsin-Madison, 1988.

C2-5. Parents' Report that They Know Who Their Adolescent Children Are With and What They Are Doing When Not at Home, 1990

Survey question: About how often do you know who (child) is <u>with</u> when (he/she) is not at home? About how often do you know what (child) is <u>doing</u> when (he/she) is not at home?

How Often	Percent (N=1,306)	
	Who With	What Doing
All of the time	60%	25%
Most of the time	34	58
Some of the time	4	14
Only rarely	2	3

Note: N indicates sample size.

Source: National Survey of Families and Households, 1988 [machine-readable data file] James Sweet and Larry Bumpass, principal investigators. Distributed by the Center for Demography and Ecology, University of Wisconsin-Madison, Madison, WI. For a description of this study see James Sweet, Larry Bumpass, and Vaughn Call. *The Design and Content of the National Survey of Families and Households.* Working Paper NSFH-1, Center for Demography and Ecology, University of Wisconsin-Madison, 1988.

C2-6. Adolescents' Report that Parents Know Who They Are With and What They Are Doing When Not at Home, 1990

Survey question: About how often does your (parent interviewed) know: a) who you are: a) with when you're not at home? b) what you are doing when you're not at home?

How Often	Percent (N=929)	
	Who With	What Doing
All of the time	49%	29%
Most of the time	35	39
Some of the time	10	22
Only rarely	6	10
Note: N indicates sample size.		

Source: Moore, K. A. 1992. *National Commission on Children: 1990 Survey of Parents and Children.* (Data Set 19, H. M. Daley, E. C. Peterson, E. L. Lang, & J. J. Card, Archivists) [machine-readable data file and documentation]. Washington, DC: Child Trends, Inc. (Producer). Los Altos, CA: Sociometrics Corporation, American Family Data Archive (Producer & Distributor).

C2-7. High School Seniors' Report of Their Behavior Being Monitored by Their Parents, by Sex and Race, 1992

Question: How often do your parents (or stepparents or guardians) do the following?

	Total (N=2,727)	Sex		Race	
		Males (N=1,270)	Females (N=1,360)	White (N=1,847)	Black (N=378)
Check if you've done homework:					
Never	35.6%	32.3%	39.1%	37.5%	23.8%
Rarely	27.0	26.7	27.4	27.8	27.5
Sometimes	22.0	22.9	20.6	20.7	27.9
Often	15.4	18.0	12.9	14.0	20.9
Provide help with your homework:					
Never	18.7%	19.2%	18.6%	17.3%	17.1%
Rarely	21.8	20.7	22.7	22.9	17.2
Sometimes	29.3	30.3	27.3	28.4	34.9
Often	30.1	29.8	31.3	31.4	30.9
Require you to do work or chores around the home:					
Never	5.5%	4.9%	6.2%	5.7%	4.0%
Rarely	13.4	15.5	11.6	14.7	7.6
Sometimes	28.6	31.8	25.4	30.6	19.5
Often	52.4	47.9	56.8	49.0	68.8
Limit the amount of time you can spend watching TV:					
Never	66.1%	62.6%	69.2%	67.4%	67.1%
Rarely	17.9	21.2	15.0	19.3	14.3
Sometimes	10.7	10.7	10.9	8.8	12.3
Often	5.3	5.6	4.9	4.4	6.2
Limit time spent with friends on school nights:					
Never	23.8%	27.5%	19.9%	23.5%	23.0%
Rarely	21.4	23.3	19.2	21.9	19.6
Sometimes	26.6	25.9	27.4	27.9	25.6
Often	28.2	23.3	33.5	26.7	31.7
Note: N indicates sample size.					

Source: Bachman, Jerald G., Lloyd D. Johnston, and Patrick M. O'Malley. 1993. *Monitoring the Future: Questionnaire Responses from the Nation's High School Seniors, 1992.* Ann Arbor, MI: Survey Research Center, Institute for Social Research, The University of Michigan, p. 226.

C2-8. High School Seniors' Perceptions of Parental Supervision, by Sex and Race, 1992

Question: The next questions ask how you feel about the amount of supervision that you received from your parents (or guardians) during your high school years.

		Sex		Race	
Amount of Supervision	Total (N=2,736)	Males (N=1,248)	Females (N=1,352)	White (N=1,886)	Black (N=387)
What kinds of parties, dances or events you could go to:					
Far too little supervision	12.7%	15.0%	10.2%	12.2%	14.1%
Too little	8.0	8.8	7.0	6.9	8.7
About right	61.5	59.1	63.8	62.7	60.4
Too much supervision	11.4	10.6	12.4	12.8	6.9
Far too much	6.4	6.6	6.5	5.5	9.9
How late you stayed out on dates:					
Far too little supervision	6.6%	8.9%	4.4%	5.6%	8.4%
Too little	6.6	6.3	6.6	5.6	6.6
About right	57.3	57.9	57.0	58.3	56.8
Too much supervision	18.9	16.6	20.6	20.4	13.7
Far too much	10.7	10.3	11.3	10.1	14.4
The way you dressed:					
Far too little supervision	6.9%	8.2%	5.4%	5.7%	10.2%
Too little	5.4	6.0	4.4	4.3	5.8
About right	76.5	72.9	80.1	79.3	70.4
Too much supervision	7.5	8.4	6.9	7.7	8.3
Far too much	3.7	4.5	3.1	3.1	5.3
How you spent your money:					
Far too little supervision	6.4%	6.9%	6.0%	6.1%	9.0%
Too little	10.7	11.5	9.9	10.1	9.4
About right	60.0	57.1	62.4	63.0	56.3
Too much supervision	16.2	16.5	16.3	14.6	20.6
Far too much	6.6	8.0	5.4	6.2	4.7
How often you went out:					
Far too little supervision	6.6%	7.2%	5.7%	5.9%	8.4%
Too little	6.7	6.6	6.5	4.5	9.9
About right	57.9	60.6	55.7	60.4	55.9
Too much supervision	19.7	16.9	22.5	19.9	16.0
Far too much	9.1	8.6	9.7	9.3	9.8
How much time spent on homework:					
Far too little supervision	8.8%	9.9%	7.7%	7.6%	11.3%
Too little	19.8	21.1	18.4	21.9	14.8
About right	54.1	50.6	57.2	54.2	58.4
Too much supervision	11.0	11.2	11.0	10.7	9.1
Far too much	6.2	7.1	5.6	5.7	6.4
Courses took in school:					
Far too little supervision	6.9%	8.2%	5.7%	5.7%	8.6%
Too little	11.8	11.9	11.4	11.7	11.0
About right	69.6	66.6	72.6	72.5	64.5
Too much supervision	7.3	7.4	7.5	6.5	9.9
Far too much	4.4	6.0	2.9	3.6	6.0
Hours worked during school year:					
Far too little supervision	7.9%	8.8%	7.0%	6.3%	11.3%
Too little	9.1	9.3	9.1	8.4	9.3
About right	69.1	66.9	71.1	72.4	61.0
Too much supervision	9.1	9.3	8.8	8.5	11.0
Far too much	4.9	5.7	4.0	4.4	7.4

C2-8. High School Seniors' Perceptions of Parental Supervision, by Sex and Race, 1992 (continued)

Amount of Supervision	Total (N=2,736)	Sex		Race	
		Males (N=1,248)	Females (N=1,352)	White (N=1,886)	Black (N=387)
How much TV you watched:					
Far too little supervision	11.1%	12.2%	10.2%	9.3%	14.5%
Too little	12.0	13.5	10.9	11.0	13.5
About right	67.0	62.9	70.6	71.4	59.7
Too much supervision	5.7	6.6	4.9	4.9	5.3
Far too much	4.1	4.8	3.4	3.4	7.1
What TV programs you watched:					
Far too little supervision	12.0%	13.7%	10.7%	9.7%	19.2%
Too little	7.6	7.6	7.6	6.3	11.9
About right	70.5	67.8	72.9	74.8	56.6
Too much supervision	6.1	6.2	6.1	5.9	6.8
Far too much	3.7	4.7	2.8	3.2	5.6

Source: Bachman, Jerald G., Lloyd D. Johnston, and Patirck M. O'Malley. 1993. *Monitoring the Future: Questionnaire Responses from the Nation's High School Seniors, 1992.* Ann Arbor, MI: Survey Research Center, Institute for Social Research, The University of Michigan, pages 215–216.

C2-9. Mothers' Report of When 12- to 18-Year-Old Child Is Allowed Home Alone, by Mother's Marital Status, Race, and Education, 1987

Survey question: Would (child) be allowed to be at home alone: (a) in the morning before school; (b) in afternoon after school; (c) all day when there is no school; (d) at night, if you were gone until midnight; (e) overnight, if you went on a trip?

Mother	N	Time of Day				
		Before School*	3-6 p.m.*	All day*	Until Midnight*	All Night*
Marital Status:						
Married	1406	86%	93%	80%	74%	39%
Divorced/separated	191	85	89	83	72	44
Cohabiting	44	87	91	81	72	97
Never married	<u>25</u>	72	76	67	52	33
	1667					
Race:						
White	1262	87	94	82	78	42
Black	180	78	85	76	56	32
Hispanic	106	71	77	66	50	30
Other	<u>152</u>	90	94	87	73	38
	1701					
Education:						
Less than high school	84	75	81	71	58	36
High school graduate	252	88	96	85	76	44
Some college	141	82	92	70	71	37
College graduate	61	87	97	80	87	44
Post graduate	<u>125</u>	90	97	87	81	50
	663					

*Combined "Yes" and "Sometimes, depends."

Note: N indicates sample size.

Source: National Survey of Families and Households, 1988 [machine-readable data file] James Sweet and Larry Bumpass, principal investigators. Distributed by the Center for Demography and Ecology, University of Wisconsin-Madison, Madison, WI. For a description of this study see James Sweet, Larry Bumpass, and Vaughn Call. *The Design and Content of the National Survey of Families and Households.* Working Paper NSFH-1, Center for Demography and Ecology, University of Wisconsin-Madison, 1988.

C2-10. Mothers' Report of Time Child 12- to 18-Years-Old Must Be Home, by Mother's Marital Status, Race, and Education, 1987

Survey question: By what time is (child) supposed to be home on school nights (Friday and Saturday nights)?			
		Average Time	
Mother	N	School Night	Friday or Saturday Night
Marital Status:			
Married	1178	9:00 p.m.	12:00 midnight
Divorced/separated	158	8:30 p.m.	12:00 midnight
Cohabiting	39	9:00 p.m.	1:00 a.m.
Never married	19	8:30 p.m.	11:00 p.m.
	1,394		
Race:			
White	1063	9:00 p.m.	11:00 p.m.
Black	153	8:30 p.m.	12:00 midnight
Hispanic	90	8:00 p.m.	12.00 midnight
Other	117	8:30 p.m.	12:30 a.m.
	1,423		
Education:			
Less than high school	66	8:30 p.m.	11:00 p.m.
High school graduate	213	9:00 p.m.	12:00 midnight
Some college	114	9:00 p.m.	12:30 a.m.
College graduate	48	9:00 p.m.	1:30 a.m.
Post graduate	101	9:00 p.m.	12:30 a.m.
	541		
Note: N indicates sample size.			

Source: National Survey of Families and Households, 1988 [machine-readable data file] James Sweet and Larry Bumpass, principal investigators. Distributed by the Center for Demography and Ecology, University of Wisconsin-Madison, Madison, WI. For a description of this study see James Sweet, Larry Bumpass, and Vaughn Call. *The Design and Content of the National Survey of Families and Households.* Working Paper NSFH-1, Center for Demography and Ecology, University of Wisconsin-Madison, 1988.

C2-11. Mothers' Report of Whether Adolescent (Aged 12–18) Does What Parent Asks, by Mother's Marital Status, Race, and Education, 1987

Survey question: I am going to read some statements that might describe a child's behavior. Please tell me whether each statement has been often true, sometimes true, or has not been true of (child) during past three months: Does what you ask?				
		Frequency		
	N	Never	Sometimes	Often
Marital Status:				
Married	1444	3%	46%	51%
Divorced/Separated	202	5	53	42
Cohabitating	47	1	51	48
Never Married	26	1	39	60
	1,719			
Race:				
White	1298	4	49	47
Black	187	2	39	59
Hispanic	111	3	45	52
Other	158	2	38	60
	1,754			
Education:				
Greater than high school	90	8	47	45
High school	261	3	46	51
Some college	141	2	53	45
College	61	0	36	64
Post graduate	125	2	36	62
	678			
Note: N indicates sample size.				

Source: National Survey of Families and Households, 1988 [machine-readable data file] James Sweet and Larry Bumpass, principal investigators. Distributed by the Center for Demography and Ecology, University of Wisconsin-Madison, Madison, WI. For a description of this study see James Sweet, Larry Bumpass, and Vaughn Call. *The Design and Content of the National Survey of Families and Households.* Working Paper NSFH-1, Center for Demography and Ecology, University of Wisconsin-Madison, 1988.

C2-12. Parents' Report of Restricting Time an Adolescent (Aged 12–18) Can Watch Television, by Mother's Marital Status, Race, and Education, 1987

Survey question: Do you restrict the amount of television that (child) watches?

Mother	N	Yes	Try*	No
Marital Status:				
Married	1444	26%	3%	71%
Divorced/separated	202	23	4	73
Cohabitating	47	23	8	68
Never Married	26	36	6	58
	1,719			
Race:				
White	1300	23	3	74
Black	187	30	5	65
Hispanic	111	36	4	60
Other	158	30	3	74
	1,754			
Education:				
Less than high school	90	22	5	73
High school graduate	261	15	2	83
Some college	141	31	4	65
College graduate	61	25	0	75
Post graduate	125	29	2	69
	678			

* = "Try, but not successful."
Note: N indicates sample size.

Source: National Survey of Families and Households, 1988 [machine-readable data file] James Sweet and Larry Bumpass, principal investigators. Distributed by the Center for Demography and Ecology, University of Wisconsin-Madison, Madison, WI. For a description of this study see James Sweet, Larry Bumpass, and Vaughn Call. *The Design and Content of the National Survey of Families and Households.* Working Paper NSFH-1, Center for Demography and Ecology, University of Wisconsin-Madison, 1988.

C2-13. Parents Restrict Type of Television Programs Adolescents (Aged 12–18) Watch, by Mother's Marital Status, Race, and Education, 1987

Survey question: Do you restrict the types of programs that (he/she) watches?

Mother	N	Yes	Try*	No
Marital Status:				
Married	1444	44%	5%	51%
Divorced/separated	202	23	4	73
Cohabitating	47	35	3	62
Never married	26	43	5	52
	1,713			
Race:				
White	1297	43	5	52
Black	186	44	7	49
Hispanic	110	43	4	54
Other	156	42	4	54
	1,749			
Education:				
Less than high school	88	47	4	49
High school graduate	261	33	5	52
Some college	141	48	4	47
College graduate	61	36	3	51
Post graduate	124	34	5	61
	675			

*"Try, but not successful."
Note: N indicates sample size.

Source: National Survey of Families and Households, 1988 [machine-readable data file] James Sweet and Larry Bumpass, principal investigators. Distributed by the Center for Demography and Ecology, University of Wisconsin-Madison, Madison, WI. For a description of this study see James Sweet, Larry Bumpass, and Vaughn Call. *The Design and Content of the National Survey of Families and Households.* Working Paper NSFH-1, Center for Demography and Ecology, University of Wisconsin-Madison, 1988.

C2-14. Parents' Report that They Help Adolescent Children Avoid Specific Type of Problem, 1990

Survey question: Some problems that (children/teenagers) have are easier than others for *parents* to help solve. For this next list of problems, please tell me if you think *you*, as a parent, can do a lot, some, or not very much to help your child *avoid* this problem.

Activity to Avoid	Percent (N=1,366)		
	A Lot	Some	Not Much
Getting involved with trouble makers	73%	23%	4%
Using drugs	82	15	3
(Girls) getting pregnant	70	25	5
(Boys) getting a girl pregnant	63	28	9
Drinking a lot of alcohol	80	17	3
Getting beat up, attacked, or molested	56	35	9
Doing poorly in school	75	21	4
Being unhappy, feeling badly about self	72	26	2
Not finding good job after school	39	45	16

Note: N indicates sample size.

Source: Moore, K. A. 1992. *National Commission on Children: 1990 Survey of Parents and Children.* (Data Set 19, H. M. Daley, E. C. Peterson, E. L. Lang, & J. J. Card, Archivists) [machine-readable data file and documentation]. Washington, DC: Child Trends, Inc. (Producer). Los Altos, CA: Sociometrics Corporation, American Family Data Archive (Producer & Distributor).

C2-15. Parents' Report that They Discipline Adolescent Children for Various Activities, 1990

Survey question: Parents have different ways of handling their (children/teenagers) when they break the rules or get in trouble. Using a 1 to 5 scale where 1 means to use no discipline at all and 5 means to use severe discipline, how would you handle the following situations if they came up with (child)?

Situation	Amount of Discipline (N=1,131)				
	None 1	2	3	4	Severe 5
If Child:					
Didn't turn in school assignment	7%	18%	39%	19%	18%
Got drunk	3	2	8	17	70
Used drugs	2	1	5	11	81
Late a lot for school	8	7	23	23	40
Had sex	11	10	24	20	35
Smoked cigarettes	6	7	20	21	46
Started a fight	5	9	29	26	32
Wore a strange hairstyle/clothes	40	21	20	9	11
Talked back to you	5	12	26	22	35
Broke an important family rule	5	11	38	28	17

Note: N indicates sample size.

Source: Moore, K. A. 1992. *National Commission on Children: 1990 Survey of Parents and Children.* (Data Set 19, H. M. Daley, E. C. Peterson, E. L. Lang, & J. J. Card, Archivists) [machine-readable data file and documentation]. Washington, DC: Child Trends, Inc. (Producer). Los Altos, CA: Sociometrics Corporation, American Family Data Archive (Producer & Distributor).

C3. ADOLESCENTS' PERCEPTIONS OF PARENTS AND ADULTS

C3-1. Adolescents' Report of Important Adults in Their Lives, 1990

Survey question: Now I want to ask some questions about the important adults in your life, people like your parents, or other relatives, teachers, neighbors, coaches, ministers, and any other adults you know. Who do you think of as the special adults in your own life, the adults who really care about you?	
Adult	Percent (N=929)
Mother	93%
Father	79
Unrelated guardian	0
Teacher or coach	30
Youth group leader	14
Step or foster mother	2
Step or foster father	4
Other adult	9
Note: N indicates sample size.	

Source: Moore, K. A. 1992. *National Commission on Children: 1990 Survey of Parents and Children.* (Data Set 19, H. M. Daley, E. C. Peterson, E. L. Lang, & J. J. Card, Archivists) [machine-readable data file and documentation]. Washington, DC: Child Trends, Inc. (Producer). Los Altos, CA: Sociometrics Corporation, American Family Data Archive (Producer & Distributor).

C3-2. Adolescents' Report of Adults that They Look Up to, Admire, or Would Like to Be Like, 1990

Survey question: And, what adults do you look up to and admire, and maybe would like to be like when you're an adult?	
Adult	Percent (N=929)
Mother	39%
Father	35
Teacher or coach	15
Youth group leader	4
Public figure	20
Step or foster mother	1
Step or foster father	2
Other adult	8
Note: N indicates sample size.	

Source: Moore, K. A. 1992. *National Commission on Children: 1990 Survey of Parents and Children.* (Data Set 19, H. M. Daley, E. C. Peterson, E. L. Lang, & J. J. Card, Archivists) [machine-readable data file and documentation]. Washington, DC: Child Trends, Inc. (Producer). Los Altos, CA: Sociometrics Corporation, American Family Data Archive (Producer & Distributor).

C3-3. High School Seniors' Attitudes about Marriage, by Sex and Race, 1992

Question: How much do you agree or disagree with each statement below?

		Sex		Race	
	Total (N=2,727)	Males (N=1,270)	Females (N=1,360)	White (N=1,847)	Black (N=378)
One sees so few good marriages that one questions it as a way of life:					
Disagree	25.0%	24.6%	25.4%	27.4%	20.2%
Mostly disagree	17.2	16.6	18.0	20.4	12.0
Neither	25.1	29.3	21.4	24.2	24.1
Mostly agree	20.6	17.8	22.5	18.7	26.0
Agree	12.2	11.6	12.6	9.4	17.8
Cohabiting before marriage is good to find out if you really get along:					
Disagree	20.7%	16.8%	25.0%	21.6%	21.5%
Mostly disagree	9.6	9.1	9.9	9.5	7.5
Neither	15.3	15.6	14.5	15.6	13.3
Mostly agree	23.6	26.3	21.5	23.6	21.3
Agree	30.9	32.2	29.1	29.7	36.4
Having a relationship with only one partner is too restrictive:					
Disagree	48.7%	41.2%	56.5%	52.7%	46.9%
Mostly disagree	20.8	20.1	20.7	21.1	16.7
Neither	13.1	15.9	10.7	12.7	12.8
Mostly agree	11.6	14.5	8.7	8.8	15.9
Agree	5.9	8.2	3.4	4.8	7.8
Working takes away from a woman's relationship with her husband:					
Disagree	52.6%	40.7%	63.8%	53.0%	62.9%
Mostly disagree	24.0	26.2	21.9	24.6	16.7
Neither	12.5	18.1	7.3	12.1	9.2
Mostly agree	7.5	10.3	5.0	7.1	6.8
Agree	3.4	4.8	2.0	3.3	4.3
Working gives a wife more of a chance to develop as a person:					
Disagree	3.4%	4.0%	2.6%	2.4%	6.6%
Mostly disagree	3.3	5.2	1.3	2.9	2.6
Neither	11.3	17.4	5.9	11.8	8.5
Mostly agree	27.6	33.3	22.3	28.8	21.7
Agree	54.4	40.1	68.0	54.1	60.5
Being a father is very fulfilling for a man:					
Disagree	3.7%	6.2%	1.3%	3.5%	4.4%
Mostly disagree	3.4	3.7	3.0	3.3	3.5
Neither	20.0	20.5	19.9	23.0	14.1
Mostly agree	28.8	28.8	28.6	31.1	19.9
Agree	44.1	40.7	47.1	39.1	58.2

C3-3. High School Seniors' Attitudes about Marriage, by Sex and Race, 1992 (continued)

	Total (N=2,727)	Sex		Race	
		Males (N=1,270)	Females (N=1,360)	White (N=1,847)	Black (N=378)
Mothers should spend more time with children than they do now:					
Disagree	4.0%	4.7%	3.4%	4.7%	3.0%
Mostly disagree	8.6	9.7	7.6	9.7	6.2
Neither	24.7	29.6	20.3	26.4	19.1
Mostly agree	30.8	30.2	31.6	32.0	24.0
Agree	31.9	25.8	37.1	27.2	47.7
If wife works, husband should share housework more:					
Disagree	6.4%	9.0%	4.0%	5.1%	8.0%
Mostly disagree	5.3	6.3	4.2	5.1	4.0
Neither	16.4	18.4	14.8	16.4	14.9
Mostly agree	31.0	33.9	28.1	32.0	28.0
Agree	40.9	32.4	48.9	41.3	45.1

Note: N indicates sample size.

Source: Bachman, Jerald G., Lloyd D. Johnston, and Patrick M. O'Malley. 1993. *Monitoring the Future: Questionnaire Responses from the Nation's High School Seniors, 1992.* Ann Arbor, MI: Survey Research Center, Institute for Social Research, The University of Michigan, pages 167–168.

C3-4. High School Seniors' Attitudes about Family Life, by Sex and Race, 1992

Question: How much do you agree or disagree with each statement below?

	Total (N=2,727)	Sex		Race	
		Males (N=1,270)	Females (N=1,360)	White (N=1,847)	Black (N=378)
People will be happier if they choose legal marriage rather than staying single or just living with someone:					
Disagree	23.2%	18.1%	28.3%	22.3%	25.3%
Mostly disagree	11.8	10.2	13.5	12.3	11.9
Neither	31.0	35.4	26.5	30.7	30.4
Mostly agree	14.7	16.4	12.8	14.3	13.0
Agree	19.3	19.9	18.9	20.3	19.4
Parents should encourage equal independence in daughters and sons:					
Disagree	4.7%	8.0%	1.4%	3.9%	5.0%
Mostly disagree	5.7	9.4	1.9	5.2	5.3
Neither	9.3	14.9	3.7	8.8	10.8
Mostly agree	20.0	25.8	13.7	20.6	20.2
Agree	60.3	41.9	79.3	61.6	58.7
Being a mother is very fulfilling for a woman:					
Disagree	5.2%	3.6%	6.7%	4.7%	6.8%
Mostly disagree	5.3	4.0	6.5	5.7	2.5
Neither	31.4	46.6	16.7	35.7	17.1
Mostly agree	24.2	21.0	27.0	24.1	24.3
Agree	33.9	24.8	43.0	29.8	49.3
Fathers should spend more time with children:					
Disagree	1.7%	2.5%	1.0%	1.4%	0.4%
Mostly disagree	2.7	3.3	2.0	3.0	0.8
Neither	14.2	16.5	11.5	16.1	7.4
Mostly agree	33.6	34.6	32.4	37.3	18.5
Agree	47.8	43.0	53.1	42.1	72.9
Husband should make all the important decisions:					
Disagree	49.0%	27.6%	70.7%	49.8%	50.7%
Mostly disagree	19.2	21.3	16.4	19.2	17.9
Neither	16.8	26.9	6.4	16.6	15.0
Mostly agree	8.3	12.8	4.0	7.9	10.8
Agree	6.8	11.4	2.4	6.5	5.6

Source: Bachman, Jerald G., Lloyd D. Johnston, and Patrick M. O'Malley. 1993. *Monitoring the Future: Questionnaire Responses from the Nation's High School Seniors, 1992.* Ann Arbor, MI: Survey Research Center, Institute for Social Research, The University of Michigan, pages 196–197.

C4. PARENT-CHILD CONFLICT

C4-1. Parents' Report of Disagreement with 12- to 18-Year-Old Child about Family, Helping at Home, and School, by Mother's Marital Status, Race, and Education, 1987

Survey question: In the last 12 months, how often have you had open disagreements with (child) about each of the following: a) getting along with family members; b) helping around the home; and c) school.

Mother	N	Getting Along with Family			Helping at Home			School		
		Rarely	Occasionally	Frequently	Rarely	Occasionally	Frequently	Rarely	Occasionally	Frequently
Marital Status:										
Married	1439	73%	18%	9%	52%	35%	13%	81%	15%	5%
Divorced/separated	202	70	17	13	48	35	17	71	19	10
Cohabiting	47	77	17	6	52	29	19	80	16	4
Never married	24	76	18	6	63	17	20	80	10	10
	1,713									
Race:										
White	1296	70	19	11	49	37	14	78	16	6
Black	184	83	11	6	56	28	16	84	10	6
Hispanic	111	86	10	4	68	25	8	88	11	2
Other	158	80	14	6	61	28	11	80	15	5
	1,749									
Education:										
Less than high school	89	76	14	11	58	26	16	83	11	7
High school graduate	261	76	17	7	56	35	9	84	14	3
Some college	141	72	22	6	48	38	14	76	19	5
College graduate	60	66	29	6	54	39	6	86	13	1
Post graduate	125	68	23	9	48	38	14	73	23	5
	675									

Note: N indicates sample size.

Source: National Survey of Families and Households, 1988 [machine-readable data file] James Sweet and Larry Bumpass, principal investigators. Distributed by the Center for Demography and Ecology, University of Wisconsin-Madison, Madison, WI. For a description of this study see James Sweet, Larry Bumpass, and Vaughn Call. *The Design and Content of the National Survey of Families and Households.* Working Paper NSFH-1, Center for Demography and Ecology, University of Wisconsin-Madison, 1988.

C4-2. Parents' Report of Disagreement with 12- to 18-Year-Old Child about Their Dress, Friends, and Money, by Mother's Marital Status, Race, and Education, 1987

Survey question: In the last 12 months, how often have you had open disagreements with (child) about each of the following: a) how (he/she) dresses; b) (his/her) friends; and c) money.

Mother	N	How (He/She) Dresses			(His/Her) Friends			Money		
		Rarely	Occasionally	Frequently	Rarely	Occasionally	Frequently	Rarely	Occasionally	Frequently
Marital Status:										
Married	1440	82%	14%	5%	92%	7%	1%	85%	13%	3%
Divorced/separated	202	76	21	3	86	11	3	76	18	6
Cohabiting	47	83	16	2	86	10	4	90	8	3
Never married	24	74	21	5	74	22	3	89	6	5
	1,713									
Race:										
White	1299	82	14	4	92	6	2	83	14	3
Black	183	75	17	8	87	10	3	84	10	6
Hispanic	111	77	18	5	86	12	2	94	5	1
Other	158	83	12	5	96	4	0	80	15	5
	1,751									
Education:										
Less than high school	89	77	14	9	89	7	4	86	8	6
High school graduate	260	90	8	3	93	6	1	88	10	2
Some college	141	81	14	5	91	9	0	87	13	0
College graduate	60	91	8	1	95	5	0	96	5	0
Post graduate	125	83	14	3	94	3	3	82	15	3
	675									

Note: N indicates sample size.

Source: National Survey of Families and Households, 1988 [machine-readable data file] James Sweet and Larry Bumpass, principal investigators. Distributed by the Center for Demography and Ecology, University of Wisconsin-Madison, Madison, WI. For a description of this study see James Sweet, Larry Bumpass, and Vaughn Call. *The Design and Content of the National Survey of Families and Households.* Working Paper NSFH-1, Center for Demography and Ecology, University of Wisconsin-Madison, 1988.

C4-3. Parents' Report of Disagreement with 12- to 18-Year-Old Child about Dating, Staying Out Late, and Sex, by Mother's Marital Status, Race, and Education, 1987

Survey question: Survey question: In last 12 months, how often have you had open disagreements with (child) about each of the following: a) (his/her) boyfriend/girlfriend; b) how late (he/she) stays out at night; c) (his/her) sexual behavior?

Mother	N	Boy/Girl Friend			Staying out Late			Sex		
		Rarely[a]	Occasionally[b]	Frequently[c]	Rarely[a]	Occasionally[b]	Frequently[c]	Rarely[a]	Occasionally[b]	Frequently[c]
Marital Status:										
Married	1440	95%	3%	3%	91%	7%	2%	98%	1%	1%
Divorced/separated	202	89	7	4	80	16	4	99	0	1
Cohabiting	47	92	5	3	75	24	2	97	3	0
Never married	24	85	9	6	75	16	9	95	1	4
	1,713									
Race:										
White	1298	94	3	2	99	89	8	2	98	1
Black	184	90	6	4	84	13	3	96	1	3
Hispanic	111	91	8	1	100	91	8	1	98	1
Other	158	96	2	1	99	92	7	1	99	1
	1,750									
Education:										
Less than high school	88	91	2	7	100	88	4	8	98	1
High school graduate	261	95	3	2	100	89	11	1	98	1
Some college	141	96	2	2	100	90	8	2	99	0
College graduate	60	100	0	0	100	98	3	0	99	1
Post graduate	125	96	3	2	101	92	8	1	97	3
	675									

[a] "Rare" combined "never" and "less than once a month"
[b] "Occasionally" combined "several times a month" and "about once a week"
[c] "Frequently" combined "several times a week" and "almost every day"
Note: N indicates sample size.

Source: National Survey of Families and Households, 1988 [machine-readable data file] James Sweet and Larry Bumpass, principal investigators. Distributed by the Center for Demography and Ecology, University of Wisconsin-Madison, Madison, WI. For a description of this study see James Sweet, Larry Bumpass, and Vaughn Call. *The Design and Content of the National Survey of Families and Households.* Working Paper NSFH-1, Center

C4-4. Parents' Report of Discipline They Used with Their Children during Past Year, 1985

Survey question: Parents and children use many different ways of trying to settle differences between them. I'm going to read a list of some things that you and (your spouse/partner) might have done when you had a problem with this child. I would like you to tell me how often you did it with (him/her) in the last year.

Type of Discipline	Percent (N=2,526)
When Disagreement, Parent <u>Ever</u>:	
Insulted or swore at child	9%
Sulked or refused to talk about issue	3
Stomped out of room or house	5
Cried about a problem with child	8
Did or said something to spite child	3
Threatened to hit or throw item at child	7
Threw or smashed an item	3
Threw something at child	2
Pushed, grabbed, or shoved child	7
Slapped or spanked child	43
Tried to hit child with an object	5
Kicked, bit, or hit child with fist	0.6
Beat up child	0.3
Burned or scalded child	0.2
Threatened child with knife or gun	0.1

Note: N indicates sample size.

Source: Straus, M. A., and R. J. Gelles. 1992. *1985 National Family Violence Survey* (Data Set 32, A. S. Kaplan, E. C. Peterson, E. L. Lang, and J. J. Card, Archivists) [machine-readable data file and documentation]. Durham, NH: Family Research Laboratory, University of New Hampshire, Producer). Los Altos, CA: Sociometrics Corporation, American Family Data Archive (Producer & Distributor).

C5.   ADOLESCENTS' HOUSEHOLD CHORES AND ALLOWANCE

C5-1. Mothers' Report of 12- to 18-Year-Old Child's Chores, by Mother's Marital Status, Race, and Education, 1987

Survey question: Does (he/she) have regular chores to do around the house? How often do you remind (child) to do (his/her) chores? Is (he/she) required to complete (his/her) chores before playing, watching TV, or going out? Does (child) get (his/her) chores done?

Mother	N	Have Chores	Remind Child about Chores			Child Gets Chores Done			Chores Done Before Pleasure
			Most of the Time[a]	Some of the Time	Rarely/ Never	All of the Time	Most of the Time	Some of the Time[b]	
Marital Status:									
Married	1444	86%	41%	45%	15%	25%	54%	21%	49%
Divorced/separated	202	85	45	40	15	20	48	32	52
Cohabiting	47	91	40	46	14	27	53	20	50
Never married	26	82	36	47	16	49	36	15	72
	1,719								
Race:									
White	1300	86	42	44	14	22	55	23	46
Black	187	92	38	48	14	30	46	24	65
Hispanic	111	86	38	41	21	40	45	15	61
Other	157	83	40	46	14	25	54	21	55
	1,756								
Education:									
Less than high school	90	92	51	28	21	32	34	34	50
High school graduate	261	88	33	52	15	26	57	17	43
Some college	141	85	45	43	12	17	60	23	43
College graduate	61	63	37	41	22	24	76	0	50
Post graduate	125	87	39	50	11	18	57	25	36
	679								

[a] "Most of the time" combined "All" and "most of the time"
[b] "Some of the time" combined "some of the time," "rarely," and "never."
Note: N indicates sample size

Source: National Survey of Families and Households, 1988 [machine-readable data file] James Sweet and Larry Bumpass, principal investigators. Distributed by the Center for Demography and Ecology, University of Wisconsin-Madison, Madison, WI. For a description of this study see James Sweet, Larry Bumpass, and Vaughn Call. *The Design and Content of the National Survey of Families and Households.* Working Paper NSFH-1, Center for Demography and Ecology, University of Wisconsin-Madison, 1988.

C5-2. Mothers' Report of Adolescent Children (Aged 12–18) Carrying Out Responsibilities, by Mother's Marital Status, Race, and Education, 1987

Survey question: I am going to read some statements that might describe a child's behavior. Please tell me whether each statement has been true of (child) during the past three months: (Child) carries out assigned responsibilities.

Mother	N	Never	Sometimes	Often
		Frequency		
Marital Status:				
Married	1444	51%	43%	6%
Divorced/separated	202	48	44	9
Cohabiting	47	53	43	4
Never married	26	49	44	7
	1,718			
Race:				
White	1298	49	45	6
Black	187	54	39	7
Hispanic	111	62	36	2
Other	158	60	34	6
	1,755			
Education:				
Less than high school	90	47	41	12
High school graduate	261	52	46	3
Some college	141	37	56	7
College graduate	61	61	38	1
Post graduate	25	57	36	8
	664			

Note: N indicates sample size.

Source: National Survey of Families and Households, 1988 [machine-readable data file] James Sweet and Larry Bumpass, principal investigators. Distributed by the Center for Demography and Ecology, University of Wisconsin-Madison, Madison, WI. For a description of this study see James Sweet, Larry Bumpass, and Vaughn Call. *The Design and Content of the National Survey of Families and Households.* Working Paper NSFH-1, Center for Demography and Ecology, University of Wisconsin-Madison, 1988.

C5-3. Parents' Perception of Number of Hours per Week Older Children Do Household Chores, 1990

Survey question: About how many hours per week, if any, does (child) spend doing chores around the house like doing dishes or taking out the trash, or babysitting for younger children in your household?

Hours	Percent (N=1,738)
0	8%
1-2	28
3-5	29
6-10	24
11-20	7
21 and more	2
Don't know	2

Note: N indicates sample size.

Source: Moore, K. A. 1992. *National Commission on Children: 1990 Survey of Parents and Children.* (Data Set 19, H. M. Daley, E. C. Peterson, E. L. Lang, & J. J. Card, Archivists) [machine-readable data file and documentation]. Washington, DC: Child Trends, Inc. (Producer). Los Altos, CA: Sociometrics Corporation, American Family Data Archive (Producer & Distributor).

C5-4. Mothers' Report of Allowance Paid to 12- to 18-Year-Old Children, by Mother's Marital Status, Race, and Education, 1987

Survey question: Does (child) receive an allowance? How much is (his/her) allowance? Does this allowance pay (him/her) for work that (he/she) regularly does around the house? Is (he/she) paid for extra jobs done around the house? In a typical month, how much is (he/she) usually paid for work around the house (in addition to allowance)?

Mother	N	Receive allowance	Average $/month	Allowance for work	Paid extra jobs	Average pay for extra jobs
Marital Status:						
Married	1444	48%	$35	54%	34%	$17
Divorced/separated	202	42	43	49	27	17
Cohabiting	47	60	49	59	31	15
Never married	26	52	31	40	25	17
	1,719					
Race:						
White	1300	46	35	59	37	17
Black	187	58	41	29	18	20
Hispanic	111	46	38	31	14	16
Other	158	49	41	57	25	21
	1,756					
Education:						
Less than high school	90	44	36	35	16	21
High school graduate	261	44	38	68	35	20
Some college	141	53	32	60	34	15
College graduate	61	63	43	46	58	13
Post graduate	125	52	38	44	41	17
	678					

Note: N indicates sample size.

Source: National Survey of Families and Households, 1988 [machine-readable data file] James Sweet and Larry Bumpass, principal investigators. Distributed by the Center for Demography and Ecology, University of Wisconsin-Madison, Madison, WI. For a description of this study see James Sweet, Larry Bumpass, and Vaughn Call. *The Design and Content of the National Survey of Families and Households.* Working Paper NSFH-1, Center for Demography and Ecology, University of Wisconsin-Madison, 1988.

C5-5. Mothers' Report of Their 12- to 18-Year-Old Child's Expenditures of Their Money, by Mother's Marital Status, Race, and Education, 1987

Survey question: Families have different expectations concerning what child should do with the money they earn. Do you require that (child) use some of (his/her) earnings: a) to pay for regular expenses such as clothes and haircuts; b) to save for future educational expenses; c) to save for special purchases; d) to help pay for day-to-day family expenses?

Mother	N	Percent Yes			
		Pays for Clothes/Haircuts	Saves for Education	Saves for Special Purchases	Helps Pay Family Expenses
Marital Status:					
Married	909	44%	36%	80%	5%
Divorced/separated	120	54	28	81	14
Cohabiting	27	47	23	74	16
Never married	10	69	28	84	6
	1,066				
Race:					
White	895	43	34	81	5
Black	67	64	37	75	13
Hispanic	32	54	33	73	23
Other	88	53	44	77	6
	1,081				
Education:					
< High school	38	39	30	91	10
High school grad	182	43	29	79	3
Some college	84	42	42	80	2
College graduate	39	29	31	73	7
Post graduate	91	48	44	85	6
	435				

N indicates sample size.

Source: National Survey of Families and Households, 1988 [machine-readable data file] James Sweet and Larry Bumpass, principal investigators. Distributed by the Center for Demography and Ecology, University of Wisconsin-Madison, Madison, WI. For a description of this study see James Sweet, Larry Bumpass, and Vaughn Call. *The Design and Content of the National Survey of Families and Households.* Working Paper NSFH-1, Center for Demography and Ecology, University of Wisconsin-Madison, 1988.

C6.   ADOLESCENTS' INVOLVEMENT WITH EXTENDED FAMILY

C6-1. Adolescents' Perceptions of Relations with Extended Family Members, 1990

Survey question: Composite of several different questions.	
Relationship	Percent (N=929)
Grandparent is a special adult in the adolescent's life	44%
Aunt, uncle, cousin is a special adult in the adolescent's life	46
Admire grandparent	11
Admire aunt, uncle, cousin, or other relative	20
Think grandparent has let you down	3
Think aunt, uncle, or cousin has let you down	12
N indicates sample size.	

Source: Moore, K. A. 1992. *National Commission on Children: 1990 Survey of Parents and Children.* (Data Set 19, H. M. Daley, E. C. Peterson, E. L. Lang, & J. J. Card, Archivists) [machine-readable data file and documentation]. Washington, DC: Child Trends, Inc. (Producer). Los Altos, CA: Sociometrics Corporation, American Family Data Archive (Producer & Distributor).

C6-2. Extended Family Members Who Help Parents Deal with Problems Associated with Their Children, 1990

Survey question: If you needed advice about a problem you were having with (child) because you were concerned about how (he/she) was feeling or behaving, who do you feel you could turn to for help?	
Parent's Source of Help	Percent (N=1,738)
Grandparents	23%
Other relatives	22
Friend or neighbor	18
Teacher or principal	25
Child-care worker	1
Minister, priest, rabbi	35
Counselor	26
Health professional	14
Child's friends' parents	2
Other person	14
No one	4
N indicates sample size.	

Source: Moore, K. A. 1992. *National Commission on Children: 1990 Survey of Parents and Children.* (Data Set 19, H. M. Daley, E. C. Peterson, E. L. Lang, & J. J. Card, Archivists) [machine-readable data file and documentation]. Washington, DC: Child Trends, Inc. (Producer). Los Altos, CA: Sociometrics Corporation, American Family Data Archive (Producer & Distributor).

C7.   ADOPTION

C7-1. Behavior Problems of Adopted and Biological Children, Aged 12–17, 1988

How often child. . .	Percent Often or Sometimes True	
	Both parents biological (N=2,874)	Both parents adoptive (N=70)
Has sudden changes in mood or feelings	45.4%	50.0%
Feels or complains that no one loves them	16.2	32.9
Is rather high strung, tense, or nervous	26.3	34.3
Cheats or tells lies	16.7	34.3
Is too fearful or anxious	20.2	22.9
Argues too much	43.7	44.3
Has difficulty concentrating or paying attention	22.4	35.7
Is easily confused, seems to be in a fog	9.3	22.9
Bullies, or is cruel or mean to others	9.0	12.9
Is disobedient at home	20.8	37.1
Is disobedient at school	10.3	20.0
Does not seem to feel sorry after misbehaving	13.3	34.3
Has trouble getting along with other children	6.9	20.0
Has trouble getting along with teachers	9.3	17.1
Is impulsive, or acts without thinking	31.5	44.3
Feels worthless or inferior	13.5	29.0
Is not liked by other children	4.9	15.7
Has difficulty getting mind off certain thoughts, has obsessions	15.5	28.6
Is restless or overly active, cannot sit still	22.1	37.1
Is stubborn, sullen, or irritable	35.4	47.1
Has a very strong temper and loses it easily	24.1	31.4
Is unhappy, sad, or depressed	14.4	28.6
Is withdrawn, does not get involved with others	6.8	17.6
Feels others are out to get him or her	5.4	12.9
Hangs around with kids who get into trouble	8.0	18.6
Is secretive, keeps things to [himself/herself]	28.7	47.1
Worries too much	29.9	28.6

N indicates sample size.

Source: Holmes, B. C., A. S. Kaplan, E. L. Lang, and J. J. Card. 1991. *National Health Interview Survey on Children, 1988: A User's Guide to the Machine-Readable Files and Documentation* (Data Set 33-34). Los Altos, CA: Sociometrics Corporation, American Family Data Archive, pages 110–111.

C7-2. Indicators of Adjustment of Biological and Adoptive Children, Aged 12–17, 1988

Indicators of Adjustment	Both parents biological (N=2,874)	Both parents adoptive (N=70)
Percent of children with 1 or more behavior problems - often true	25.4%	47.1%
Percent of children with 1 or more behavior problems - sometimes true	76.5	85.7
Percent of children who have ever had emotional/behavioral problems	4.6	18.8
Percent of children who have seen psychiatrist/counselor for emotional/behavioral problems	5.5	10.4
Percent of children who have repeated any grades for any reason	14.3	25.0
Percent ever suspended/expelled from school	8.0	5.8

N indicates sample size.

Source: Holmes, B. C., A. S. Kaplan, E. L. Lang, and J. J. Card. 1991. *National Health Interview Survey on Children, 1988: A User's Guide to the Machine-readable Files and Documentation* (Data Set 33-34). Los Altos, CA: Sociometrics Corporation, American Family Data Archive.

C7-3. Family Dynamics, Adopted Adolescents and Non-Adopted Siblings Compared, 1993

DOMAIN	INDICATORS	ADOPTED (% agree)			NON-ADOPTED (% agree)
		Boys	Girls	Total	
CHILD-PARENT RELATIONSHIPS	I get along well with my parents.[1]	77%	72%	74%	86%
	My mother accepts me as I am.[1]	85%	81%	83%	90%
	My father accepts me as I am.[1]	83%	79%	81%	82%
WARMTH	There is a lot of love in my family.[1]	79%	78%	78%	76%
	My parents give me help and support when I need it.[1]	81%	83%	82%	91%
	My parents often tell me they love me.[1]	81%	84%	83%	80%
COMMUNICATION	I have lots of good conversations with my parents.[1]	66%	64%	65%	71%
	My parents are easy to talk with.[1]	63%	58%	60%	59%
PARENTS AS RESOURCES	If you had an important question about drugs, alcohol, or some other serious issue, would you talk to your parents about it?[2]	52%	51%	52%	56%
EXTENDED FAMILY	My relatives make me feel like I'm really part of the family.[3]	91%	91%	92%	75%

[1] Percent refers to sum of agree and strongly agree.
[2] Percent refers to sum of yes and probably.
[3] Percent refers to sum of often true and always true.

Source: Benson, P. L., Anu R. Sharma, and Eugene C. Roehlkepartain. 1994. *Growing Up Adopted: A Portrait of Adolescents and Their Families.* Minneapolis, MN: Search Institute, page 47. For further information contact: Search Institute, Thresher Square West, Suite 210, 700 South Third Street, Minneapolis, MN 55415; (612) 376-8955.

C7-4. Sixteen Indicators of Well-Being for Adopted Youth, Their Non-Adopted Siblings, and a Comparison Sample of Adolescents, 1993

DIMENSION OF WELL-BEING	INDICATORS OF WELL-BEING	PERCENT WITH EACH INDICATOR		
		Adopted Youth	Non-Adopted Siblings	Sample of Adolescents[1]
SCHOOL	1. B average or better	62%	82%	53%
	2. Has high achievement motivation	72%	80%	71%
	3. Aspires to pursue post-high school education	94%	94%	90%
CONNECTED-NESS	4. Has 3 or more good friends	83%	77%	78%
	5. Has access to 2 or more non-parent adults for advice and support	71%	61%	72%
CARING	6. Places high personal value on helping other people	71%	48%	48%
	7. Spends 1 hour or more a week helping others	44%	51%	37%
OPTIMISM	8. Expects to be happy 10 years from now	74%	82%	68%
	9. Expects to be successful when an adult	83%	84%	79%
SELF-CONCEPT	10. Has high self-esteem	55%	70%	45%
SOCIAL COMPETENCY	11. Has friendship-making skills	83%	75%	74%
	12. Has assertiveness skills	89%	86%	82%
	13. Has decision-making skills	74%	79%	69%
SUPPORT	14. Experiences high level of parental support	82%	91%	68%
	15. Experiences high level of support at school	58%	54%	46%
ANXIETY	16. Reports little or no anxiety	54%	54%	42%

[1] Based on analysis of 51,098 6th-12th grade, non-adopted public school students in Colorado, Illinois, Minnesota, and Wisconsin.

Source: Benson, P. L., Anu R. Sharma, and Eugene C. Roehlkepartain. 1994. *Growing Up Adopted: A Portrait of Adolescents and Their Families.* Minneapolis, MN: Search Institute, page 67. For further information contact: Search Institute, Thresher Square West, Suite 210, 700 South Third Street, Minneapolis, MN 55415; (612) 376-8955.

C7-5. Percent of Adopted Adolescents Reporting High-Risk Behavior, 1993

AT-RISK DOMAIN	AT-RISK INDICATOR	ADOPTED ADOLESCENTS		PUBLIC SCHOOL SAMPLE	
		Age 12-15	Age 16-18	Age 12-15	Age 16-18
ALCOHOL	1. Frequent alcohol use (6+, last 30 days)	2%	15%	5%	15%
	2. Binge drinking (1+, last 2 weeks)	8%	25%	15%	31%
TOBACCO	3. Daily cigarette use	6%	23%	9%	20%
	4. Frequent chewing tobacco use (20+)	1%	6%	2%	7%
ILLICIT DRUGS	5. Frequent use of illicit drugs (6+, last year)	2%	14%	5%	13%
SEXUALITY	6. Sexually active (2+, in lifetime)	5%	41%	12%	42%
	7. Non-use of contraceptives[1]	41%	40%	47%	41%
DEPRESSION/ SUICIDE	8. Depression	6%	9%	13%	15%
	9. Attempted suicide	11%	17%	11%	14%
ANTI-SOCIAL BEHAVIOR	10. Vandalism (2+, last year)	6%	7%	10%	12%
	11. Group fighting (2+, last year)	9%	9%	12%	11%
	12. Police trouble (2+, last year)	3%	10%	7%	12%
	13. Theft (2+, last year)	8%	11%	12%	14%
	14. Weapon use (2+, last year)	1%	<1%	2%	2%
SCHOOL PROBLEMS	15. School absenteeism (2+ days, last month)	4%	14%	8%	15%
	16. Desire to drop out	1%	1%	1%	1%
VEHICLE SAFETY	17. Driving and drinking (2+, last year)	<1%	14%	2%	19%
	18. Riding and drinking (2+, last year)	6%	25%	23%	34%
	19. Seat belt non-use	23%	30%	37%	39%
OTHER	20. Bulimia (1+ per week)	<1%	2%	1%	2%

[1] Refers to percentage of sexually active youth who do not always use contraceptives.

Source: Benson, P. L., Anu R. Sharma, and Eugene C. Roehlkepartain. 1994. *Growing Up Adopted: A Portrait of Adolescents and Their Families.* Minneapolis, MN: Search Institute, page 72. For further information contact: Search Institute, Thresher Square West, Suite 210, 700 South Third Street, Minneapolis, MN 55415; (612) 376-8955.

C7-6. Assessment of Mental Health, Achenbach's Youth Self-Report, Comparing Adopted Adolescents with National Norms, 1993

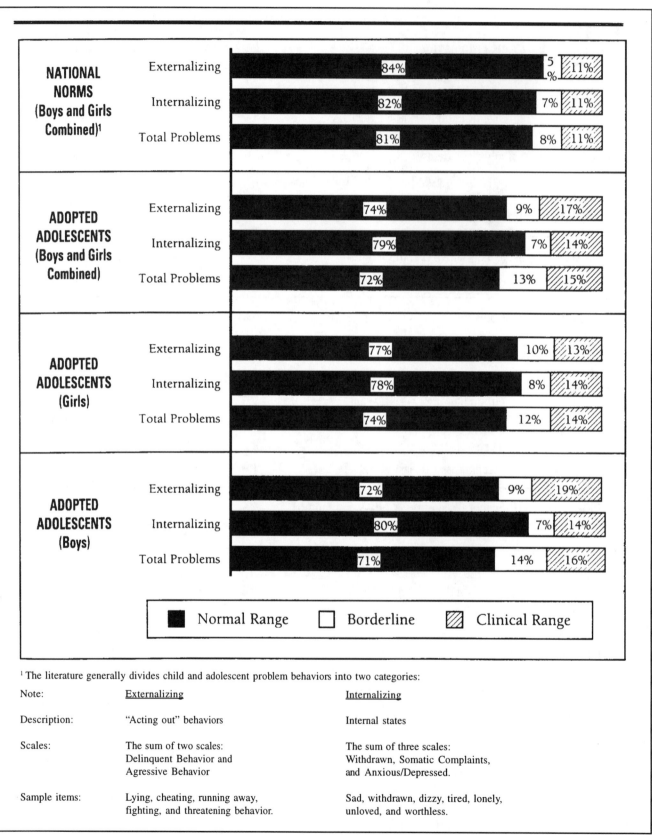

[1] The literature generally divides child and adolescent problem behaviors into two categories:

Note:	Externalizing	Internalizing
Description:	"Acting out" behaviors	Internal states
Scales:	The sum of two scales: Delinquent Behavior and Agressive Behavior	The sum of three scales: Withdrawn, Somatic Complaints, and Anxious/Depressed.
Sample items:	Lying, cheating, running away, fighting, and threatening behavior.	Sad, withdrawn, dizzy, tired, lonely, unloved, and worthless.

Source: Benson, P. L., Anu R. Sharma, and Eugene C. Roehlkepartain. 1994. *Growing Up Adopted: A Portrait of Adolescents and Their Families.* Minneapolis, MN: Search Institute, page 79. For further information contact: Search Institute, Thresher Square West, Suite 210, 700 South Third Street, Minneapolis, MN 55415; (612) 376-8955.

C7-7. Percent of Adopted Adolescents with High Self-Esteem, 1993

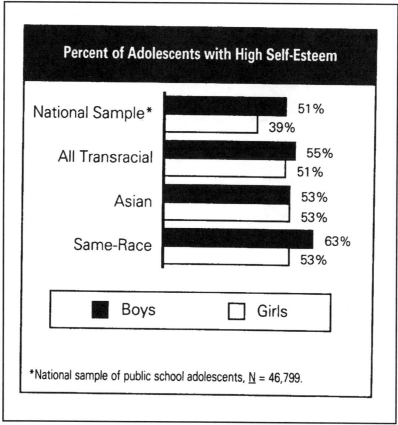

Source: Benson, P. L., Anu R. Sharma, and Eugene C. Roehlkepartain. 1994. *Growing Up Adopted: A Portrait of Adolescents and Their Families.* Minneapolis, MN: Search Institute, page 98. For further information contact: Search Institute, Thresher Square West, Suite 210, 700 South Third Street, Minneapolis, MN 55415; (612) 376-8955.

C7-8. Percent of Adopted Adolescents Reporting They Are Very or Somewhat Similar to Their Parents on the Following Factors, 1993

Similar to	Adopted	Non-Adopted Siblings
Father's		
Interests	63%	70%
Physical appearance	26	59
Personality	49	54
Values	52	68
Mother's		
Interests	52	56
Physical appearance	24	52
Personality	45	55
Values	55	62

Source: Benson, P. L., Anu R. Sharma, and Eugene C. Roehlkepartain. 1994. *Growing Up Adopted: A Portrait of Adolescents and Their Families.* Minneapolis, MN: Search Institute, page 40. For further information contact: Search Institute, Thresher Square West, Suite 210, 700 South Third Street, Minneapolis, MN 55415; (612) 376-8955.

C7-9. Family Demographics: Adopted Adolescent and National Samples Compared, 1993

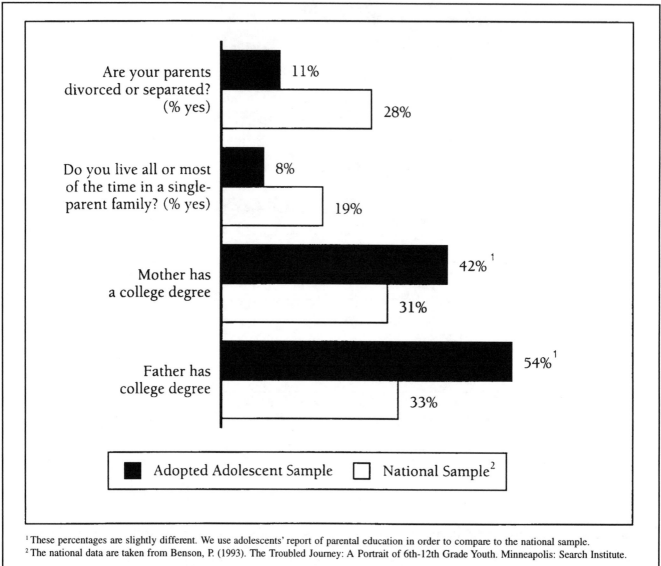

Are your parents divorced or separated? (% yes)
- 11%
- 28%

Do you live all or most of the time in a single-parent family? (% yes)
- 8%
- 19%

Mother has a college degree
- 42%[1]
- 31%

Father has college degree
- 54%[1]
- 33%

■ Adopted Adolescent Sample   □ National Sample[2]

[1] These percentages are slightly different. We use adolescents' report of parental education in order to compare to the national sample.
[2] The national data are taken from Benson, P. (1993). The Troubled Journey: A Portrait of 6th-12th Grade Youth. Minneapolis: Search Institute.

Source: Benson, P. L., Anu R. Sharma, and Eugene C. Roehlkepartain. 1994. *Growing Up Adopted: A Portrait of Adolescents and Their Families.* Minneapolis, MN: Search Institute, page 45. For further information contact: Search Institute, Thresher Square West, Suite 210, 700 South Third Street, Minneapolis, MN 55415; (612) 376-8955.

C7-10. Percent of Adopted Adolescents Reporting High Attachment to Both, One, or Neither Parent, by Age and Gender, 1993

	Percent with High Attachment			
	To both parents	To father only	To mother only	To neither parent
All	54%	12%	18%	16%
Gender				
Boys	53	13	20	15
Girls	55	11	16	17
Age				
12-15	61	13	16	9
16-18	45	11	20	25

Source: Benson, P. L., Anu R. Sharma, and Eugene C. Roehlkepartain. 1994. *Growing Up Adopted: A Portrait of Adolescents and Their Families.* Minneapolis, MN: Search Institute, page 35. For further information contact: Search Institute, Thresher Square West, Suite 210, 700 South Third Street, Minneapolis, MN 55415; (612) 376-8955.

C7-11. Adolescents' Interest in Adoption History, 1993

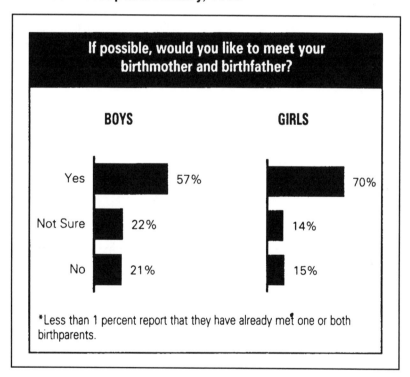

Source: Benson, P. L., Anu R. Sharma, and Eugene C. Roehlkepartain. 1994. *Growing Up Adopted: A Portrait of Adolescents and Their Families.* Minneapolis, MN: Search Institute, page 26. For further information contact: Search Institute, Thresher Square West, Suite 210, 700 South Third Street, Minneapolis, MN 55415; (612) 376-8955.

C7-12. Adopted Adolescents' Thoughts on Their Own Adoption, 1993

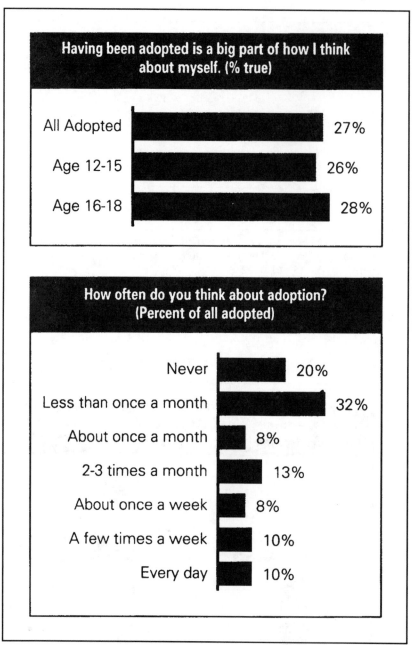

Source: Benson, P. L., Anu R. Sharma, and Eugene C. Roehlkepartain. 1994. *Growing Up Adopted: A Portrait of Adolescents and Their Families.* Minneapolis, MN: Search Institute, page 22. For further information contact: Search Institute, Thresher Square West, Suite 210, 700 South Third Street, Minneapolis, MN 55415; (612) 376-8955.

C7-13. Sources of Support as Experienced by Adopted Adolescents and Their Non-Adopted Siblings, 1993

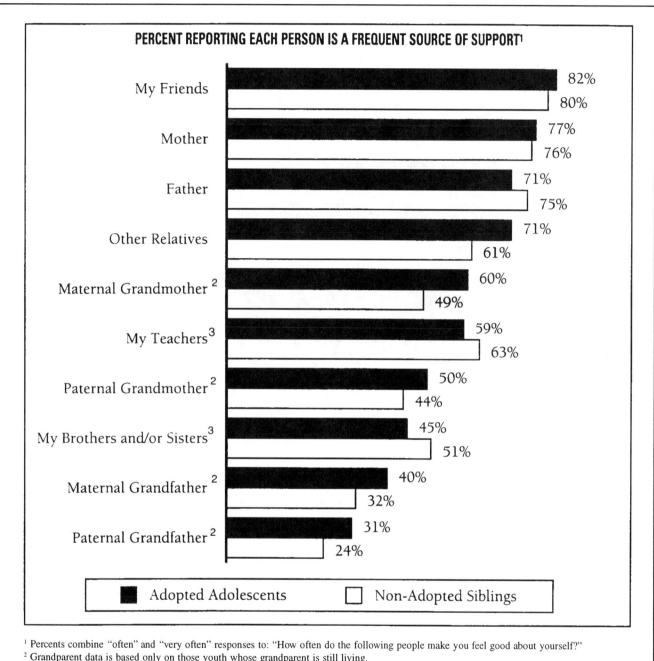

PERCENT REPORTING EACH PERSON IS A FREQUENT SOURCE OF SUPPORT[1]

	Adopted Adolescents	Non-Adopted Siblings
My Friends	82%	80%
Mother	77%	76%
Father	71%	75%
Other Relatives	71%	61%
Maternal Grandmother [2]	60%	49%
My Teachers [3]	59%	63%
Paternal Grandmother [2]	50%	44%
My Brothers and/or Sisters [3]	45%	51%
Maternal Grandfather [2]	40%	32%
Paternal Grandfather [2]	31%	24%

[1] Percents combine "often" and "very often" responses to: "How often do the following people make you feel good about yourself?"
[2] Grandparent data is based only on those youth whose grandparent is still living.
[3] Brother/sister data is based only on those youth who have one or more siblings.

Source: Benson, P. L., Anu R. Sharma, and Eugene C. Roehlkepartain. 1994. *Growing Up Adopted: A Portrait of Adolescents and Their Families.* Minneapolis, MN: Search Institute, page 21. For further information contact: Search Institute, Thresher Square West, Suite 210, 700 South Third Street, Minneapolis, MN 55415; (612) 376-8955.

C7-14. Self-Esteem of Adopted Adolescents, by Age and Gender, with Comparisons to a National Sample, 1993

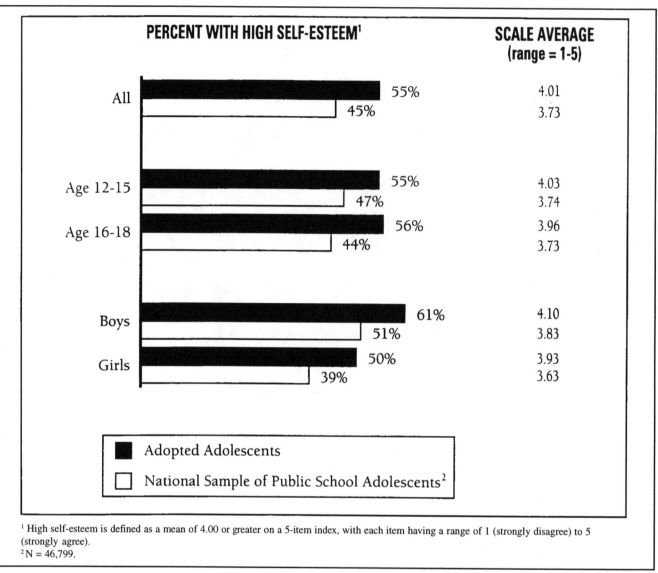

---

[1] High self-esteem is defined as a mean of 4.00 or greater on a 5-item index, with each item having a range of 1 (strongly disagree) to 5 (strongly agree).
[2] N = 46,799.

Source: Benson, P. L., Anu R. Sharma, and Eugene C. Roehlkepartain. 1994. *Growing Up Adopted: A Portrait of Adolescents and Their Families.* Minneapolis, MN: Search Institute, page 19. For further information contact: Search Institute, Thresher Square West, Suite 210, 700 South Third Street, Minneapolis, MN 55415; (612) 376-8955.

C7-15. Adoptions, by Relationship of Petitioner, 1960–1986

TOTAL ADOPTIONS

YEAR	Total	Related petitioners	Unrelated petitioners by type of agency making placement			
			Total	Public agency	Private agency	Independent
1960.........	107,000	49,200	57,800	13,300	20,800	23,700
1965.........	142,000	65,300	76,700	20,700	32,200	23,800
1970.........	175,000	85,800	89,200	29,500	40,100	19,600
1975.........	129,000	81,300	47,700	18,600	18,100	11,000
1982.........	141,861	91,141	50,720	19,428	14,549	16,743
1986.........	104,088	52,931	51,157	20,064	15,053	16,040

FOREIGN ADOPTIONS

Year	Number	Country of origin of adoptee	Number
1980.........	5,139	1991, total	9,008
1985.........	9,286	Romania	2,552
1987.........	10,097	Korea	1,817
1988.........	9,120	Peru	722
1989.........	7,948	Columbia	527
1990.........	7,088	India	448

Source: U.S. Bureau of the Census, *Statistical Abstract of the United States: 1992* (112th edition). Washington, DC, 1992, page 373.

D. Education

Parents, educational leaders, politicians, and the general public have for the past decade expressed considerable concern about the educational achievement of American students. Reports such as *A Nation at Risk* have challenged contemporary educational policies and practices and have called for major reform. In this chapter, we examine enrollment of children between five and 17 years of age in public and private schools. The number of students who drop out of school before completing high school is also reviewed. A lack of homework has been cited as one reason why educational achievement of American students is not keeping pace with that of children in other countries. We present information about how many hours students spend doing homework. Students' attitudes and feelings about school are discussed, and a variety of test results are presented to reveal academic achievement. The educational aspirations of parents and students is reviewed, as is student participation in extracurricular activities. Violence and discipline in public schools have been identified as serious problems by the general public, and we present information about the frequency of such behavior. Finally, we review the number of high school graduates who continue their formal education.

D1. ENROLLMENT AND ENVIRONMENT

All states have mandatory attendance policies, rules specifying curriculum content, and regulations about who is qualified to teach. Such policies have been rather successful, as over 98 percent of children in this country between the ages of five and 17 attend either public or private elementary, middle, or secondary schools. A substantial majority of American children, 85 percent, attend public schools.

Rising taxes and taxpayer revolts have focused attention on public school funding. One way to stretch the educational dollar is to increase the number of students in classes. Although there was considerable variability between states in 1990, the national average pupil/teacher ratio was 17.3. Delaware had the lowest ratio, 13.2, while Utah with its high fertility had a ratio of 24.9 students per each teacher. The number of days American students attend school each year is lower than in most other industrialized nations. But American students attend school longer each day than do students of other nations, so that the total number of classroom hours each year is above the average for those nations.

D2. DROPOUTS

The 1960s War on Poverty focused much of its attention on education as a means to eradicate poverty. Educational research during this period found that nearly one out of four students who entered the ninth grade didn't stay to graduate from high school. After reforms were put into place, the national dropout rate had declined to 16 percent in 1972 and has decreased a little more during the past 20 years to 14 percent in 1991. Minority students have significantly higher dropout rates than do white students. The rate is 16.9 percent for African Americans and 35.9 percent for Hispanic Americans, compared to only 10.7 percent for white Americans. Also, children with more siblings near their age have dropped out more frequently than children with fewer siblings. It is suspected that this, at least in part, is a function of social class as children in poor families tend to have more brothers and sisters. Among children who don't drop out, attendance is rather high, and few miss more than just an occasional day.

D3. HOMEWORK

During the early 1980s, national test scores of high school juniors and seniors dropped somewhat, and considerable concern was expressed by parents, school officials, and the general public about whether educational performance was declining. *A Nation at Risk* singled out a lack of homework as one reason why American students were not doing as well as in the past. In 1990, nearly 30 percent of 13-year-old students reported that they did less than an hour of homework each day. Forty-two percent claimed one hour, 20 percent claimed two hours, and less than 10 percent said they did more than two hours of homework. Seventeen-year-old students, mostly seniors, reported that they did a little more homework. In addition, more than two-thirds of the 13-year-olds and half of the 17-year-olds admitted they watched at least three hours of television each day. The rule seems to be one hour of homework to three hours of television. Most mothers, over 90 percent, acknowledged that their children have homework to do. Only half of the students reported they get their homework done all of the time, while 40 percent claimed they do it most of the time. About half of the mothers reported that they rarely or never remind their children to do their homework.

D4. FEELINGS ABOUT SCHOOL

A majority, around 80 percent, of students in junior and senior high school enjoy their educational experience. Caring teachers supportive principals, extracurricular activities, friends, and interesting curricular material all contribute to students' positive feelings about school.

D5. ACADEMIC ACHIEVEMENT

The Scholastic Aptitude Test (SAT) and the American College Test (ACT) are the two tests used to assess the level of performance of high school juniors and seniors. Generally, those students who desire post-secondary education take one of them. Thus the scores are somewhat higher than they would be if all students were tested. As the proportion of high school graduates who have gone on to post-secondary training increases, the number who have taken the ACT or the SAT also increases. Although there has been some fluctuation in the test scores during the past 25 years, overall, the academic achievement of graduating students has remained fairly constant. Additional tests of achievement in reading, science, history, and other subjects reveal that a majority of students in American schools are doing well.

On the other hand, international comparisons between 13-year-old students living in six industrial nations reveals that students in the United States have the lowest levels of achievement. One reason for this apparent poor performance is that math and science are introduced earlier in other school systems and American students generally close the gap in high school.

In 1990, about half of high school sophomores were enrolled in a "general education" program, while 41 percent were in a "college preparation" program. Only 8 percent were enrolled in a "vocational" program. The number of students seeking a college education has increased considerably during the past 10 years while the number in vocational programs has declined.

D6. EDUCATIONAL ASPIRATIONS

A large majority of high school students, 92 percent, report it is "very likely" that they will graduate. Another 6 percent feel it is "somewhat likely," and only 2 percent are concerned they will not finish high school. A few more young women than young men claim they will graduate, 94 percent versus 90 percent.

Seventy-five percent of the students surveyed and 79 percent of their parents aspire to college graduation. In another study, 86 percent of the high school students indicated they planned on attending college at least part-time. Students in secondary schools feel that additional education is important, and most plan on attending college.

D7. EXTRACURRICULAR ACTIVITIES

Extracurricular activities are an important part of the junior and high school experience. Nearly half of all students reported they participate in sports, 17 percent participate in band, 16 percent in choir, 14 percent in drama, and 10 percent in student newspapers or yearbooks.

D8. DISCIPLINE AND VIOLENCE

Violence in schools has become a major concern for students, their parents, and school administrators. In some communities, a substantial proportion of high school students carry weapons, primarily guns, while at school. About a fourth of the students in several surveys reported that disturbances and fighting were "very big problems" in their schools. These students fear for their safety. Fifteen percent of the students surveyed indicated that money had been stolen from them during the past year. Fourteen percent reported their property had been vandalized, and 7 percent had been physically assaulted.

Most students reported that discipline in their schools is either "very strict" or "somewhat strict" as school administrators work to reduce violence in schools. Some communities have resorted to assigning a police officer to a junior or senior high school.

D9. POST-SECONDARY EDUCATION

The percentage of high school graduates enrolling in college has steadily increased during the past 30 years. In 1960, 24 percent of white and 19 percent of black high school graduates enrolled in college. In 1990, the percents rose to 40 percent for whites and 34 percent for blacks. Although the gaps have closed, men still attend college a little more often than women, and whites more than blacks. There is also concern because progress in blacks' college enrollment has slowed in recent years.

D1.   ENROLLMENT AND ENVIRONMENT

D1-1. Percent of School-Age Population (Ages 5–17) Enrolled in Public and Nonpublic Schools in the U.S., 1920–1990

Year	Percent of Young People
1920	83%
1930	90
1940	94
1950	92
1960	95
1970	98
1980	97
1990	98

Source: U.S. Bureau of the Census, *Statistical Abstract of the United States: 1992* (112th edition). Washington, DC, 1992, page 142.

D1-2. School Enrollment in Public and Private Secondary Schools and Colleges, 1965–1990

Year	Secondary (in thousands)		Colleges (in thousands)	
	Public	Private	Public	Private
1965	15,465	1,400	3,970	1,951
1970	18,402	1,311	6,428	2,153
1975	19,164	1,300	8,835	2,350
1980	16,681	1,339	9,457	2,640
1985	15,193	1,362	9,479	2,768
1990	15,412	1,129	10,741	2,910
1995 projected	16,049	1,252	12,186	3,448
2000 projected	17,252	1,356	12,457	3,536

Source: U.S. Bureau of the Census, *Statistical Abstract of the United States: 1992* (112th edition). Washington, DC, 1992, page 147.

D1-3. Percent of Population Enrolled in School, by Age and Race, 1960–1980

Age	1960 Total	1970 Nonwhites	1980 Total	1980 Black	Total	Black	Total	Black
7-13	98%	96%	99%	99%	99%	99%	100%	100%
14-15	94	90	98	98	98	98	99	99
10-17	81	73	90	86	89	91	93	92
18-19	42	38	48	40	46	46	57	55
20-21	21	16	32	23	31	23	40	28
22-24	10	8	15	8	16	14	21	20

Source: U.S. Bureau of the Census, *Statistical Abstract of the United States: 1986* (106th edition). Washington, DC, 1985, page 131; 1992, 142.

D1-4. Secondary School Enrollment, by State, 1990

State	Grades 9 - 12 Enrollment (1,000)	Enrollment Rate[1]	State	Grades 9 - 12 Enrollment (1,000)	Enrollment Rate[1]
U.S. Total	11,336	91.3	Missouri	227	86.0
Alabama	195	93.3	Montana	42	93.8
Alaska	29	97.3	Nebraska	76	88.7
Arizona	161	93.3	Nevada	51	98.7
Arkansas	123	95.9	New Hampshire	46	89.1
California	1,336	92.8	New Jersey	306	86.1
Colorado	154	94.6	New Mexico	94	94.3
Connecticut	122	90.2	New York	770	86.6
Deleware	27	87.4	North Carolina	304	94.8
Washington, DC	19	100.0	North Dakota	33	92.8
Florida	492	92.6	Ohio	514	88.0
Georgia	303	93.6	Oklahoma	154	95.1
Hawaii	49	87.6	Oregon	134	93.0
Idaho	61	96.9	Pennsylvania	496	83.6
Illinois	512	86.9	Rhode Island	37	87.3
Indiana	279	90.4	South Carolina	170	93.8
Iowa	139	92.1	South Dakota	34	89.7
Kansas	117	92.6	Tennessee	226	93.5
Kentucky	177	90.5	Texas	872	98.4
Lousiana	199	88.2	Utah	122	98.0
Maine	60	96.5	Vermont	25	93.9
Maryland	188	89.1	Virginia	270	94.2
Massachusetts	230	88.8	Washington	227	94.0
Michigan	436	90.2	West Virginia	98	95.7
Minnesota	211	91.3	Wisconsin	232	86.0
Mississippi	131	91.3	Wyoming	27	97.3

[1] Percent of persons 5-17 years old. Based on enumerated resident population as of April 1, 1980, and 1990.

Source: U.S. Bureau of the Census, *Statistical Abstract of the United States: 1992* (112th edition). Washington, DC, 1992, page 159.

D1-5. Pupil-Teacher Ratios in Public Elementary and Secondary Schools, by State, Fall 1986–Fall 1991

State	Pupil-Teacher Ratio Fall 1986	Pupil-Teacher Ratio Fall 1990	Pupil-Teacher Ratio Fall 1991
United States	**17.7**	**17.2**	**17.3**
Alabama	19.8	19.9	17.8
Alaska	16.7	17.0	16.7
Arizona	18.4	19.4	19.3
Arkansas	17.5	16.8	17.0
California	23.0	22.8	22.8
Colorado	18.2	17.8	17.9
Connecticut	13.7	13.5	14.0
Delaware	16.0	16.7	16.8
District of Columbia	14.3	13.6	13.2
Florida	17.5	17.2	17.6

D1-5. Pupil-Teacher Ratios in Public Elementary and Secondary Schools, by State, Fall 1986–Fall 1991 *(continued)*

State	Pupil-Teacher Ratio Fall 1986	Pupil-Teacher Ratio Fall 1990	Pupil-Teacher Ratio Fall 1991
Georgia	18.9	18.3	18.5
Hawaii	22.6	18.9	18.5
Idaho	20.4	19.6	19.4
Illinois	17.4	16.7	16.8
Indiana	18.3	17.4	17.5
Iowa	15.5	15.6	15.7
Kansas	15.4	15.0	15.2
Kentucky	18.6	17.3	17.2
Louisiana	18.5	17.3	16.6
Maine	15.5	13.9	14.0
Maryland	17.1	16.8	16.9
Massachusetts	14.4	15.4	15.1
Michigan	19.2	19.8	19.2
Minnesota	17.4	17.4	17.2
Mississippi	19.0	17.9	17.9
Missouri	16.4	15.6	15.8
Montana	15.6	15.9	15.8
Nebraska	15.1	14.6	14.7
Nevada	20.4	19.4	18.6
New Hampshire	15.9	16.2	15.5
New Jersey	14.7	13.6	13.8
New Mexico	19.0	18.1	17.6
New York	15.4	14.7	15.4
North Carolina	18.7	16.9	16.8
North Dakota	15.3	15.5	15.3
Ohio	18.1	17.2	17.3
Oklahoma	16.9	15.6	15.6
Oregon	18.3	18.0	18.6
Pennsylvani	16.3	16.6	16.8
Rhode Island	15.1	14.6	14.6
South Carolina	17.3	16.8	16.9
South Dakota	15.6	15.2	14.8
Tennessee	19.9	19.2	19.4
Texas	17.2	15.4	15.8
Utah	24.6	25.0	24.9
Vermont	—	13.2	13.8
Virginia	16.8	15.7	15.7
Washington	20.5	20.1	20.2
West Virginia	15.3	15.0	15.3
Wisconsin	16.3	16.2	15.7
Wyoming	14.0	14.5	15.6

— Not available

Source: Snyder, T. D., and C. M. Hoffman. 1993. *Digest of Education Statistics.* Washington, DC: National Center for Education Statistics, page 76.

D1-6. Catholic Secondary Schools, 1960–1991

Item	1960	1970	1980	1990	1991
Secondary schools	2,392	1,981	1,516	1,296	1,269
Pupils enrolled	880,000	1,008,000	837,000	592,000	587,000
Teachers, total	44,000	54,000	49,000	40,000	44,000
Religious	33,000	28,000	14,000	6,000	7,000
Lay	11,000	26,000	35,000	34,000	37,000

Source: U.S. Bureau of the Census, *Statistical Abstract of the United States: 1992* (112th edition). Washington, DC, 1992, page 167.

D1–7. Youth 12- to 21-Years Old with Disabilities, by Age and Educational Environment, 1989

Environment	Total	12-17 years old	18-21 years old
(Numbers in thousands)			
Total	1,960.5	1,734.1	226.4
Regular class	367.2	335.1	32.1
Resource room		779.7	79.3
Separate class		487.5	71.3
Separate school facility:			
Public		63.1	26.0
Private		26.1	7.1
Separate residential facility:			
Public		12.9	5.3
Private		7.2	2.1
Correctional facility		NA	NA
Home/hospital		22.5	3.2

Source: U.S. Bureau of the Census, *Statistical Abstract of the United States: 1992* (112th edition). Washington, DC, 1992, page 167.

D1-8. Instructional Use of Computers in Secondary Schools, 1989

Item	Unit	
ALL SCHOOLS		
Computers used for instruction	1,000	895
Schools using computers	Percent	98
Schools with 15 or more computers	Percent	68
SCHOOLS USING COMPUTERS FOR INSTRUCTION		
Mean number of computers	Number	45
Median	Number	31
Students per computer, median	Number	14
Percent of all instructional computers in:		
Classrooms	Percent	32
Computer labs	Percent	55
Other locations	Percent	13
Percent of all instructional computers used:		
Usually every day	Percent	77
Less than every week for instruction or not used at all	Percent	9
Median hours of use per week (in rooms with greatest number of computers)	Number	22
Percent of all student computer use:		
Learning math	Percent	8
Word processing (how to use)	Percent	15
Keyboarding (how to)	Percent	12
Learning English	Percent	8
Programming	Percent	12
Recreational use	Percent	5
Tools, e.g. spreadsheets	Percent	11
Learning science	Percent	6
Learning social studies	Percent	3
Business education (other than keyboarding or word processing instruction	Percent	10
Industrial arts	Percent	5
Fine arts	Percent	2
Learning foreign languages	Percent	2
Other	Percent	1

Source: U.S. Bureau of the Census, *Statistical Abstract of the United States: 1992* (112th edition). Washington, DC, 1992, page 165.

D1–9. Instructional Time in the Classroom of 13-Year-Olds, by Country, School Year 1990–91

Larger Countries	Average days per year	Average hours per day	Average hours per year
Canada	188	5.1	953
England	192	5.0	960
France	174	6.2	1,073
Germany	210	4.6	966
Italy	204	4.8	983
Japan	220	4.0	875
Korea	222	4.4	977
Taiwan	222	5.3	1,177
United States	178	5.6	1,003

Source: U.S. Department of Education, National Center for Education Statistics, *The Condition of Education,* 1993. Washington, DC, page 128.

D2. DROPOUTS

D2-1. High School Dropout Rate for 19- to 20-Year-Olds, by Race, 1972–1991

| Year | Dropout Rate/Percent of Students | | | |
	Total	White	Black	Hispanic
1972	16.1%	13.1%	26.8%	38.0%
1973	15.3	12.2	25.8	39.6
1974	16.4	13.8	24.8	32.6
1975	16.2	13.5	26.4	31.7
1976	15.9	13.2	24.1	34.8
1977	15.7	13.3	22.0	34.6
1978	16.0	12.8	24.9	38.1
1979	16.7	13.8	26.7	35.2
1980	16.4	12.7	23.5	44.1
1981	15.8	12.9	21.1	36.1
1982	16.3	13.4	23.0	34.9
1983	15.2	12.2	21.3	34.1
1984	15.0	12.8	18.1	30.6
1985	13.6	11.1	18.7	28.8
1986	12.9	10.2	17.6	28.3
1987	13.9	11.4	15.5	30.2
1988	14.9	10.8	20.2	40.9
1989	15.1	11.6	18.6	34.2
1990	13.6	10.4	15.6	34.0
1991	14.3	10.7	16.9	35.9

Source: U.S. Department of Education, National Center for Education Statistics, *The Condition of Education,* 1993. Washington, DC, page 58.

D2-2. High School Dropout Rate of 14- to 24-Year-Olds, by Age and Race, 1968–1990

| Age* | 1968 | | 1970 | | 1980 | | 1990 | |
	White	Black	White	Black	White	Black	White	Black
16-24 years	**11.9%**	**21.6%**	**10.8%**	**22.2%**	**11.3%**	**16.0%**	**10.5%**	**11.3%**
16-17 years	4.5	7.0	7.3	12.8	9.2	6.9	5.9	7.4
18-21 years	15.6	28.6	14.3	30.5	14.7	23.0	13.9	16.6
22-24 years	20.1	40.5	16.3	37.8	14.0	24.0	14.6	14.0
*Age at time of survey.								

Source: U.S. Bureau of the Census, *Statistical Abstract of the United States: 1992* (112th edition). Washington, DC, 1992, page 161.

D2-3. Tenth Graders' Attendance Patterns, by Sex, Race, and Social Class, 1990

Attendance Patterns	All 10th graders	Sex		Race/ethnicity			Socioeconomic Status[1]		
		Male	Female	White	Black	Hispanic	Low	Middle	High
Number of days missed first half of current school year									
None	14.3%	17.1%	11.6%	13.0%	21.2%	12.5%	13.1%	15.0%	14.9%
1 or 2 days	23.2	24.9	21.5	22.8	27.2	20.6	20.0	23.0	26.6
3 or 4 days	27.7	27.1	28.3	28.8	24.5	25.0	25.3	27.6	29.5
5 or more days	34.8	30.9	38.7	35.4	27.1	41.9	41.6	34.3	29.0
Number of times late first half of current school year									
None	25.2	25.4	24.9	27.8	17.8	17.8	23.9	25.7	26.6
1 or 2 days	38.2	38.1	38.3	38.0	41.1	36.7	37.4	38.6	38.2
3 or more days	36.7	36.6	36.8	34.2	41.1	45.5	38.7	35.7	35.2
Cut classes									
Never or almost never	84.8	83.5	86.2	85.8	86.5	75.8	82.3	84.5	89.0
At least sometimes	15.2	16.5	13.8	14.2	13.5	24.2	17.7	15.5	11.0

[1] Parents' education, occupational status, and income are used to compute socioeconomic status. The respondents were divided into three groups based on their socioeconomic status.

Source: Snyder, T. D., and C. M. Hoffman. 1993. *Digest of Education Statistics.* Washington, DC: National Center for Education Statistics, page 143.

D3. HOMEWORK

D3-1. Percentage of 13-Year-Olds Who Spent Given Amounts of Time Doing Homework Each Day, by Sex, School Type, and Parents' Highest Level of Education, 1990

Characteristics	Time Spent on Homework					
	Had none	Did not do	½ hour	1 hour	2 hours	Greater than 2 hours
Total	**4.8**	**4.4**	**20.1**	**42.0**	**19.0**	**9.8**
Sex:						
Male	6.1	6.1	23.4	41.0	16.0	7.5
Female	3.5	2.7	16.9	42.9	22.0	12.0
School Type:						
Public	5.2	4.7	20.9	42.3	17.8	9.1
Private	1.1	1.4	13.4	39.0	29.6	15.6
Parents' highest level of education:						
Less than high school	8.7	7.0	23.9	37.2	13.0	10.2
High school graduate	5.2	5.6	23.0	41.0	17.1	8.0
Some college	3.3	3.8	20.4	45.2	19.2	8.1
College graduate	3.6	2.8	17.4	43.8	21.5	11.0

Note: Percentages may not add to 100 due to rounding.

Source: U.S., Department of Education, National Center for Education Statistics, *The Condition of Education,* 1993. Washington, DC, page 351.

D3-2. Percentage of 17-Year-Olds Who Spent Given Amounts of Time Doing Homework Each Day, by Sex, School Type, and Parents' Highest Level of Education, 1990

Characteristics	Time Spent on Homework					
	Had none	Did not do	½ hour	1 hour	2 hours	Greater than 2 hours
Total	**6.4%**	**8.4%**	**19.2%**	**33.2%**	**19.7%**	**13.1%**
Sex:						
Male	7.6	12.4	22.6	34.1	15.3	8.0
Female	5.4	4.7	15.9	32.4	23.8	17.9
School Type:						
Public	6.8	8.6	19.6	33.4	19.2	12.3
Private	—	—	—	—	—	—
Parents' highest level of education:						
Less than high school	12.6	12.5	19.4	31.1	14.8	9.6
High school graduate	10.3	7.1	21.1	34.5	17.4	9.5
Some college	5.9	8.5	20.6	33.2	20.2	11.6
College graduate	2.5	7.8	17.4	33.0	22.3	17.0

Note: Percentages may not add to 100 due to rounding.

— Not Available

Source: U.S. Department of Education, National Center for Education Statistics, *The Condition of Education,* 1993. Washington, DC, page 352.

D3-3. Percentage of Students Who Reported Doing at Least One Hour of Homework Each Day, by Age, Sex, School Type, and Parents' Highest Level of Education, 1978–1990

Year	Total	Sex		School Type		Parents' highest Level of Education			
		Male	Female	Public	Private	Less than high school	Graduated high school	More than high school	Graduated college
13-year-olds:									
1982	39.6%	35.2%	44.0%	37.9%	53.3%	33.8%	35.4%	39.5%	47.0%
1986	74.1	70.8	77.3	73.8	—	68.7	73.4	75.4	76.7
1990	70.8	64.5	76.9	69.2	84.2	60.4	66.1	72.5	76.3
17-year-olds:									
1978	32.5	26.8	37.7	31.6	47.9	26.0	28.3	32.2	40.3
1982	37.4	31.4	43.1	36.2	51.1	29.0	33.7	38.7	45.2
1986	66.8	58.4	74.8	66.0	—	62.6	64.6	63.7	71.9
1990	66.0	57.4	74.1	64.9	—	55.5	61.5	65.0	72.3

— Not available

Source: U.S. Department of Education, National Center for Education Statistics, *The Condition of Education,* 1993. Washington, DC, page 122.

D3-4. Percentage of 13-Year-Old Students Who Spent Given Amounts of Time Doing Homework Each Day, by Country, 1991

Country	No homework	1 hour or less	2 or more hours
Canada	7.5%	65.1%	27.0%
China	2.9	51.7	43.7
England	1.6	64.3	33.4
France	0.5	43.8	55.4
Hungary	0.3	41.5	58.1
Ireland	1.4	35.1	63.3
Israel	0.5	48.8	50.3
Italy	0.1	19.1	79.1
Jordan	3.5	40.3	56.1
Korea	3.0	56.1	40.9
Mozambique	2.3	55.5	41.9
Portugal	5.2	64.8	29.7
Scotland	15.9	70.0	13.6
Slovenia	0.7	70.2	28.2
Soviet Union	0.5	47.1	52.4
Spain	1.2	33.3	64.4
Switzerland	0.6	78.7	20.4
Taiwan	4.2	54.9	40.8
United States	9.7	60.9	29.4

Note: Percentages may not add to 100 due to rounding.

Source: U.S. Department of Education, National Center for Education Statistics, *The Condition of Education,* 1993. Washington, DC, page 356.

D3-5. Mother's Report of 12- to 18-Year-Old Child's Homework, by Mother's Marital Status, Race, and Education, 1987–88 School Year

Mother	N	Have Homework	Remind to Do			Gets Homework Done			Homework Done Before Pleasure
			Most of Time*	Some of Time**	Rarely/ Never	All of Time	Most of Time	Some of Time**	
Marital Status:									
Married	1331	94%	25%	25%	50%	52%	38%	10%	58%
Divorced/separated	182	91	30	28	42	42	43	13	60
Cohabiting	42	94	21	35	44	56	30	14	74
Never married	25	94	21	24	55	51	38	11	82
	1,578								
Race:									
White	1197	93	27	26	47	49	39	12	59
Black	172	95	22	26	52	57	35	9	77
Hispanic	102	93	22	23	55	54	38	8	74
Other	139	93	17	21	62	53	37	10	68
	1,609								
Education:									
< High school	83	90	35	18	47	61	32	7	72
High school graduate	248	96	23	31	46	50	39	11	56
Some college	135	96	37	25	38	38	51	11	54
College graduate	55	99	21	8	71	63	33	4	26
Post graduate	112	96	20	28	52	51	39	10	47
	633								

* = "All" and "most of the time."
** = "yes" and "sometimes, depends."
Note: N indicates sample size.

Source: National Survey of Families and Households, 1988 [machine-readable data file] James Sweet and Larry Bumpass, principal investigators. Distributed by the Center for Demography and Ecology, University of Wisconsin-Madison, Madison, WI. For a description of this study see James Sweet, Larry Bumpass, and Vaughn Call. *The Design and Content of the National Survey of Families and Households.* Working Paper NSFH-1, Center for Demography and Ecology, University of Wisconsin-Madison, 1988.

D3-6. Percentage of Students Who Reported Watching at Least Three Hours of Television Each Day, by Age, Sex, School Type, and Parents' Highest Level of Education, 1978–1990

| | | Sex | | School Type | | Parents' highest Level of Education | | | |
| | | | | | | Less than high school | Graduated high school | More than high school | Graduated college |
Year	Total	Male	Female	Public	Private				
13-year-olds:									
1982	55.4%	58.0%	52.8%	56.3%	48.0%	62.7%	59.7%	52.9%	46.8%
1986	74.7	75.4	74.0	75.1	—	79.7	74.2	79.8	66.6
1990	69.0	70.5	67.3	70.0	59.4	75.3	66.7	68.7	62.8
17-year-olds:									
1978	31.2	32.9	29.6	31.8	22.0	39.1	34.8	30.5	23.8
1982	36.0	39.0	33.1	36.7	27.5	44.8	41.0	32.2	28.1
1986	55.4	56.7	54.1	56.7	—	70.8	64.0	55.0	44.9
1990	49.4	53.1	45.8	50.6	—	61.5	55.5	52.0	40.1
—Not available									

Source: U.S. Department of Education, National Center for Education Statistics, *The Condition of Education,* 1993. Washington, DC, page 122.

D4. FEELINGS ABOUT SCHOOL

D4-1. Feelings of Children Aged 10 to 17 about Their School, 1990

Feeling	Percent (N=913)
Like it a lot	44%
Like it somewhat	40
Like it a little	14
Don't like it at all	2
Note: N indicates sample size. Percentages may not add to 100 due to rounding.	

Source: Moore, K. A. 1992. *National Commission on Children: 1990 Survey of Parents and Children.* (Data Set 19, H. M. Daley, E. C. Peterson, E. L. Lang, & J. J. Card, Archivists) [machine-readable data file and documentation]. Washington, DC: Child Trends, Inc. (Producer). Los Altos, CA: Sociometrics Corporation, American Family Data Archive (Producer & Distributor).

D4-2. Opinions of Children Aged 10 to 17 about Their School, 1990

| | Evaluation | | |
Characteristic	True	Not true	Don't Know
My teacher knows me well	81%	19%	0%
Principal cares about students	93	5	2
Kids with good grades are respected	80	19	1
Parents talk to teacher	65	34	1
Kids get away with almost anything	18	82	0
Lots of kids use drugs	19	76	5
Lots of kids drink a lot of alcohol	34	63	4
I feel safe at school	87	13	0
Sample: (N=929), percentages may not add to 100 due to rounding.			

Source: Moore, K. A. 1992. *National Commission on Children: 1990 Survey of Parents and Children.* (Data Set 19, H. M. Daley, E. C. Peterson, E. L. Lang, & J. J. Card, Archivists) [machine-readable data file and documentation]. Washington, DC: Child Trends, Inc. (Producer). Los Altos, CA: Sociometrics Corporation, American Family Data Archive (Producer & Distributor).

D4-3. Parents' Evaluation of Public Schools, 1990

Characteristic	Evaluation* A	B	C, D, or F	Don't know
Teachers care about students	43%	40%	15%	2%
Teacher's skills	43	42	12	3
Principal is effective leader	47	32	14	7
Maintains order and discipline	50	34	14	2
Help student learn right from wrong	47	33	18	3
Safety for students	52	30	17	1
Inform parents of student progress	59	26	13	2
Facilitating parents' input about school	35	32	30	4

Sample: (N=1417), percentages may not add to 100 due to rounding.
*An "A" grade means the parents have a very positive evaluation; "B" equals good evaluation; "C" equals mediocre evaluation, and "D" or "F" are negative evaluations.

Source: Moore, K. A. 1992. *National Commission on Children: 1990 Survey of Parents and Children.* (Data Set 19, H. M. Daley, E. C. Peterson, E. L. Lang, & J. J. Card, Archivists) [machine-readable data file and documentation]. Washington, DC: Child Trends, Inc. (Producer). Los Altos, CA: Sociometrics Corporation, American Family Data Archive (Producer & Distributor).

D4-4. Adolescents' Educational Values, by Sex, Age, Race, and Social Class, 1991

Survey question: Now, I'm going to read a list of statements. For each of them, tell me whether you agree very much, agree somewhat, disagree somewhat, or disagree very much. If you neither agree nor disagree with a statement, you can tell me that.

Student Characteristic	Percent Agreeing with Educational Value Want to reach top of chosen career	Main purpose of education is to get a good job	Knowledge is important for its own sake
National	78%	55%	46%
Sex:			
Male	79	52	41
Female	78	58	51
Age:			
13-15 years	80	61	42
16-17 years	75	48	50
Race:			
White	77	53	44
Nonwhite	83	64	52
Above-average students	82	50	50
Average and below	74	62	40
Social class:*			
White-collar background	83	50	46
Blue-collar background	72	60	45

*Primary wage earner in the family occupied a white- or blue-collar job.

Source: Bezilla, Robert (ed.). 1993. *American's Youth in the 1990s.* Princeton, NJ: The George H. Gallup International Institute, page 145.

D4-5. Tenth-Graders Who Agree or Strongly Agree with Statements on Why They Go to School, 1990

Reason for going to school	All 10th graders	Sex		Race/ethnicity			Socioeconomic Status		
		Male	Female	White	Black	Hispanic	Low	Middle	High
Think subjects are interesting	71.0%	70.1%	71.9%	68.8%	79.1%	74.5%	72.8%	68.7%	74.9%
Get a feeling of satisfaction	76.9	74.2	79.6	74.8	85.8	81.3	78.2	75.3	79.1
Nothing else to do	30.3	33.4	27.3	30.1	29.0	31.1	33.2	30.8	26.5
Need education to get a job	96.6	95.3	97.8	96.5	96.7	96.8	95.4	96.5	97.7
To meet friends	82.7	83.0	82.4	85.5	66.1	80.1	76.8	82.5	87.4
Play on a team or belong to a club	53.6	58.4	49.0	55.3	49.3	45.3	40.4	54.3	64.1
Teachers care and expect student to succeed	74.0	72.6	75.4	72.4	81.6	76.0	75.2	72.8	75.5

Source: Snyder, T. D., and C. M. Hoffman. 1993. *Digest of Education Statistics.* Washington, DC: National Center for Education Statistics, page 143.

D5. ACADEMIC ACHIEVEMENT

D5-1. Scholastic Aptitute Test (SAT) and American College Test (ACT) Scores from 1967–1990

	SAT		ACT				
	Verbal	Math	Composite	English	Math	Reading	Reasoning
1967	466	492	19.9	18.5	20.0	19.7	20.8
1970	460	488	18.6	17.7	17.6	17.4	21.1
1975	434	472	18.5	17.9	17.4	17.2	21.1
1980	424	466	18.5	17.8	17.3	17.2	21.0
1985	431	475	18.6	18.1	17.2	17.4	21.2
1990	424	476	20.6	20.5	19.9	21.2*	20.7*
1992	423	476	20.6	20.2	20.0	21.1	20.7

*1991 (1990 not available)

Source: U.S. Bureau of the Census, *Statistical Abstract of the United States: 1993* (113th edition). Washington, DC, 1993, page 170.

D5-2. Scholastic Aptitude Test (SAT) Score Averages, by State, 1991–92 School Year

State	Verbal	Mathematical	Percent of graduates taking SAT
United States	423	476	42
Alabama	476	520	8
Alaska	433	475	42
Arizona	440	493	27
Arkansas	474	516	6
California	416	484	46
Colorado	453	507	29
Connecticut	430	470	79
Delaware	432	463	66
District of Columbia	405	437	73
Florida	416	468	50
Georgia	398	444	65
Hawaii	402	477	56
Idaho	460	503	17
Illinois	473	537	15
Indiana	409	459	58
Iowa	512	584	5
Kansas	487	546	10
Kentucky	470	518	11
Louisiana	471	520	9
Maine	422	460	66
Maryland	431	476	66
Massachusetts	428	474	80
Michigan	464	523	11
Minnesota	492	561	10
Mississippi	478	526	4
Missouri	574	529	11
Montana	465	523	24
Nebraska	478	540	11
Nevada	434	488	27
New Hampshire	440	483	76
New Jersey	420	471	75
New Mexico	475	521	12
New York	416	466	75
North Carolina	405	450	57
North Dakota	501	567	6
Ohio	450	501	23
Oklahoma	480	527	9
Oregon	439	486	55
Pennsylvania	418	459	68
Rhode Island	421	460	70
South Carolina	394	437	59
South Dakota	490	550	6
Tennessee	484	529	13
Texas	410	466	44
Utah	496	545	5
Vermont	429	468	69
Virginia	425	468	63
Washington	432	484	50
West Virginia	440	484	17
Wisconsin	481	548	11
Wyoming	462	516	13

Source: Snyder, T. D., and C. M. Hoffman. 1993. *Digest of Education Statistics.* Washington, DC: National Center for Education Statistics, page 129.

D5-3. Student Proficiency in Reading, by Age, Sex, Race, and Parental Education, 1970-71 School Year to 1989-90 School Year

Selected Characteristics of Students	13-year-olds			17-year-olds		
	1970-71	1979-80	1989-90	1970-71	1979-80	1989-90
Total	**255.2***	**258.5**	**256.8**	**285.2**	**285.5**	**290.2**
Sex:						
Male	249.6	254.3	250.5	278.9	281.8	284.0
Female	260.8	262.6	263.1	291.3	289.2	296.5
Race/ethnicity:						
White	260.9	264.4	262.3	291.4	292.8	296.6
Black	222.4	232.8	241.5	238.7	243.1	267.3
Hispanic	—	237.2	237.8	—	261.4	274.8
Parental Education:						
Not high school graduate	238.4	238.5	240.8	261.3	262.1	269.7
Graduated high school	255.5	253.5	251.3	283.0	277.5	282.9
Post high school	270.2	270.9	266.9	302.2	298.9	299.9

*Numbers represent proficiency in reading. The larger the number, the more proficient the students' reading.

Source: Snyder, T. D., and C. M. Hoffman. 1993. *Digest of Education Statistics.* Washington, DC: National Center for Education Statistics, page 113.

D5-4. Writing Performance of 8th- and 12th-Graders, by Sex, Race, and Parental Education, 1989-90 School Year

Selected characteristics of students	8th-Graders	12th-Graders
All students	**197.8***	**211.5**
Sex:		
Male	186.8	199.8
Female	208.3	223.7
Race/ethnicity:		
White	202.3	216.9
Black	182.1	193.7
Hispanic	189.0	197.6
Parental Education:		
Less than high school	191.7	190.2
High school graduate	195.1	204.8
Some college	206.9	215.1
College graduate	203.4	221.3

* Numbers represent writing performance. The larger the number, the stronger the writing performance.

Source: Snyder, T. D., and C. M. Hoffman. 1993. *Digest of Education Statistics.* Washington, DC: National Center for Education Statistics, page 116.

D5-5. Student Proficiency in Geography and U.S. History, by Sex, Race, and Parental Education, 1988

Characteristic	Geography Scores 12th-graders	History Scores 8th-graders	12th-graders
United States	**293.1***	**263.9**	**295.0**
Sex:			
Male	301.2	266.2	298.5
Female	285.7	261.6	291.8
Race:			
White	301.1	270.4	301.1
Black	258.4	246.0	274.4
Hispanic	271.8	244.3	273.9
Parents' Level of Education:			
Not high school diploma	267.0	244.9	274.2
Graduated high school	283.5	256.2	285.3
Some college	294.2	269.1	296.8
Graduated college	305.3	274.9	306.0

*Numbers represent proficiency in geography and history. The larger the number, the more proficient the students are in geography and history.

Source: Snyder, T. D., and C. M. Hoffman. 1993. *Digest of Education Statistics.* Washington, DC: National Center for Education Statistics, page 117.

D5-6. Percent of Students at or above Selected History Proficiency Levels, by Age, Sex, and Race/Ethnicity, 1988

Characteristics	8th Graders				12th Graders			
	Simple historical facts	Beginning historical information and interpretation	Basic historical terms and historical facts	Interprets historical information and ideas	Simple historical facts	Beginning historical information and interpretation	Basic historical terms and relationships	Interprets historical information and ideas
All students	96.0%	67.7	12.7%	0.1%	99.4%	88.9%	45.9%	4.6%
Male	95.6	69.2	15.7	0.2	99.2	88.3	50.8	6.5
Female	96.5	66.2	9.8	—	99.6	89.4	41.4	2.8
White	97.4	75.9	15.7	0.1	99.6	92.7	52.8	5.5
Black	93.2	44.9	3.5	—	99.0	77.3	21.2	0.5
Hispanic*	91.2	43.8	4.1	—	98.4	76.1	23.2	1.4

*Persons of Hispanic origin maybe of any race
—Not available

Source: Snyder, T. D., and C. M. Hoffman. 1993. *Digest of Education Statistics.* Washington, DC: National Center for Education Statistics, page 118.

D5-7. Mathematics Proficiency, by Age, Sex, and Race/Ethnicity, 1977–78 School Year to 1989–90 School Year

Selected characteristics of students	13-year-olds		17-year-olds	
	1977–78	1989–90	1987–78	1989–90
All students	**264.1***	**270.4**	**300.4**	**304.6**
Sex:				
Male	263.6	271.2	303.8	306.3
Female	264.7	269.6	297.1	302.9
Race/ethnicity:				
White	271.6	276.3	305.9	309.5
Black	229.6	249.1	268.4	288.5
Hispanic	238.0	254.6	276.3	283.5

*Numbers represent proficiency in mathematics. The larger the number, the more proficient the students' mathematical ability.

Source: Snyder, T. D., and C. M. Hoffman. 1993. *Digest of Education Statistics.* Washington, DC: National Center for Education Statistics, page 119.

D5-8. Thirteen-Year-Old Students' Proficiency Scores on Mathematics, by Country, 1991

Larger Countries	Average Proficiency Score*		
	Total	Male	Female
Taiwan	545	546	544
Korea	542	546	537
Soviet Union	533	533	532
France	519	523	515
Canada	513	515	512
Spain	495	498	492
United States	494	494	494

*Numbers represent proficiency in mathematics. The larger the number, the more proficient the students' mathematics.

Source: U.S. Department of Education, National Center for Education Statistics, *The Condition of Education,* 1993. Washington, DC, page 48.

D5-9. Proficiency Scores on Science Assessment of 13-Year-Old Students, by Country, 1991

Larger Counries	Total	Male	Female
Korea	571	580	559
Taiwan	564	567	560
Soviet Union	541	546	535
Canada	533	539	527
France	532	540	524
Spain	525	531	519
United States	521	530	513

*Numbers represent proficiency in science. The larger the number, the more proficient the students' sciences.

Source: U.S. Department of Education, National Center for Educatin Statistics, *The Condition of Education,* 1993. Washington, DC, page 50.

D5-10. Percent of High School Sophomores in General, College Preparatory, and Vocational Programs, by Race/Ethnicity, Test Performance, Social Class, and Type of School, 1980 and 1990

Student characteristics	General		College prep or academic		Vocational	
	1980	1990	1980	1990	1980	1990
All Sophomores	46.0%	50.8%	33.1%	41.3%	21.0%	7.9%
Race/ethnicity:						
White	47.4	51.7	35.0	42.0	17.6	6.3
Black	39.0	42.9	26.9	40.9	34.1	6.2
Hispanic	46.1	55.0	24.6	35.1	29.2	9.9
Asian	37.1	42.3	48.8	49.2	14.1	8.5
American Indian	51.6	58.5	19.8	22.9	28.7	8.6
Test performance quartile:						
Lowest test quartile	50.1	61.0	12.8	19.6	37.0	9.4
Second test quartile	54.1	61.1	22.4	29.2	23.5	9.7
Third test quartile	48.1	50.2	37.0	44.4	14.9	5.4
Highest test quartile	32.4	35.4	60.9	62.7	6.7	1.9
Socioeconomic status:						
Low quartile[1]	51.5	57.2	19.0	27.7	29.5	15.2
Middle 2 quartiles	47.8	51.7	31.0	40.9	22.2	7.5
High quartile	36.8	43.1	53.8	54.9	9.4	2.0
Type of school:						
Public	47.3	52.2	30.2	39.1	22.6	8.7
Catholic	32.3	35.9	61.9	62.7	5.8	1.6
Other private	36.9	43.9	57.6	55.6	5.5	0.5
Region:						
Northeast	33.2	41.2	44.7	50.6	22.1	8.2
North Central	44.8	56.7	31.8	36.9	23.4	6.4
South	51.5	48.6	27.1	41.6	21.4	9.8
West	52.2	56.1	32.3	37.6	15.5	6.3

[1] A quartile is one-fourth of the respondents. Thus the "lowest test quartile" is the fourth of the respondents with the lowest scores on the achievement test.

Source: Snyder, T. D., and C. M. Hoffman. 1993. *Digest of Education Statistics.* Washington, DC: National Center for Education Statistics, page 131.

D5-11. Tenth Graders' Attitudes about Academic Classes, by Sex, Race, and Social Class, 1990

Percent of 10th graders who answered, "a few times a week" or more often

Class subject and opinion	All 10th graders	Sex		Race/ethnicity			Socioeconomic Status		
		Male	Female	White	Black	Hispanic	Low	Middle	High
Mathematics class:									
Understood the material	60.8%	60.4%	61.3%	59.5%	68.5%	60.7%	61.1%	60.2%	62.0%
Try very hard	80.2	75.9	84.6	79.0	84.9	81.8	81.7	80.4	79.6
Feel challenged	74.4	71.8	77.1	73.7	77.7	75.1	73.3	74.1	77.3
English class:									
Understood the material	50.9	50.2	51.5	49.0	59.7	52.0	51.7	49.7	52.4
Try very hard	79.3	75.5	83.2	77.7	84.8	82.5	82.3	79.2	77.4
Feel challenged	59.8	57.8	61.9	56.7	72.6	66.0	65.3	58.4	58.2
History class:									
Understood the material	32.5	34.0	31.0	31.7	32.6	36.7	33.5	31.7	33.0
Try very hard	53.5	53.4	53.7	52.9	54.4	55.4	55.4	53.1	53.1
Feel challenged	42.1	42.4	41.9	40.5	48.0	45.1	46.2	40.8	41.3
Science class:									
Understood the material	48.3	49.0	47.6	47.4	53.0	47.6	47.0	47.3	51.1
Try very hard	72.8	69.5	76.0	72.8	73.5	70.4	71.3	72.7	75.3
Feel challenged	66.6	65.0	68.1	66.1	69.9	63.9	62.9	66.2	71.2

Source: Snyder, T. D., and C. M. Hoffman. 1993. *Digest of Education Statistics.* Washington, DC: National Center for Education Statistics, page 135.

D6. EDUCATIONAL ASPIRATIONS

D6-1. Adolescents' Expectations of High School Graduation, by Sex, Age, Race, and Social Class, 1992

Survey question: How likely is it that you will graduate from high school—very likely, somewhat likely, not too likely, or not at all likely?

Student Characteristic	Expectation of Graduation			
	Very likely	Somewhat likely	Not too likely	Not at all likely
National	**92%**	**6%**	**1%**	**1%**
Sex:				
Male	90	7	*	1
Female	94	5	1	1
Age:				
11-13 years	92	8	—	—
14-15 years	92	6	1	1
16-17 years	94	4	1	1
Race:				
White	92	5	1	1
Nonwhite	93	7	—	*
Black	92	8	—	*
Hispanic†	87	12	2	—
Social class:**				
White-collar background	94	6	*	*
Blue-collar background	92	6	1	1

* Less than one-half of 1 percent.
** Primary wage earner in the family occupied a white- or blue-collar job.
† Persons of Hispanic origin may be of any race.

Source: Bezilla, Robert (ed.). 1993. *American's Youth in the 1990s.* Princeton, NJ: The George H. Gallup International Institute, page 85.

D6-2. High School Students' Educational Aspirations, 1990

Desired Education	Parents' desire for children (N=1,417)	Students' desire for themselves (N=923)
Graduate from high school	6%	10%
Some college	14	15
Graduate from college	44	44
Further training after college	34	30
Other	1	1

Note: N indicates sample size. Percentages may not add to 100 due to rounding.

Source: Moore, K. A. 1992. *National Commission on Children: 1990 Survey of Parents and Children.* (Data Set 19, H. M. Daley, E. C. Peterson, E. L. Lang, & J. J. Card, Archivists) [machine-readable data file and documentation]. Washington, DC: Child Trends, Inc. (Producer). Los Altos, CA: Sociometrics Corporation, American Family Data Archive (Producer & Distributor).

D6-3. Adolescents' Post-High School Plans, by Sex, Age, Race, and Social Class, 1992

Survey question: What are you likely to do after high school—Attend college full time? Find a job and go to college part time? Join the armed services? Work full time?

Student Characteristic	Percent				
	College full-time	College part-time	Armed services	Work full time	No response
National	68%	18%	5%	5%	4%
Sex:					
Male	66	17	7	5	5
Female	70	19	3	5	3
Age:					
12-13 years	70	17	4	3	6
14-15 years	71	17	4	4	4
16-17 years	63	19	6	7	5
Race:					
White	68	18	5	5	4
Nonwhite	67	18	5	5	5
Black	68	15	6	6	5
Hispanic	46	28	8	9	9
Social class:*					
White-collar background	74	15	4	2	5
Blue-collar background	63	20	6	7	4

*Primary wage earner in the family occupied a white- or blue-collar job.
Note: Percentages may noty add to 100 due to rounding.

Source: Bezilla, Robert (ed.). 1993. *American's Youth in the 1990s.* Princeton, NJ: The George H. Gallup International Institute, page 86.

D7. EXTRACURRICULAR ACTIVITIES

D7-1. Participation of 10th-Graders in Extracurricular Activities, by Sex, Race, and Social Class, 1990

Extracurricular activities	Percent who participated in extracurricular activities								
	Total	Sex		Race/ethnicity			Socioeconomic Status		
		Male	Female	White	Black	Hispanic	Low	Middle	High
Athletics:									
Baseball/softball	15.6%	19.2%	12.1%	16.0%	13.7%	15.7%	14.0%	16.8%	15.2%
Basketball	19.9	24.3	15.4	18.2	30.9	16.6	18.4	20.8	19.8
Football	15.9	28.9	2.9	14.7	22.6	16.0	15.5	16.5	15.2
Soccer	7.6	9.1	6.1	7.9	4.0	8.5	4.6	6.8	11.6
Swim team	3.9	3.9	3.9	4.1	2.8	3.3	2.3	3.3	6.2
Other team sport	14.2	11.1	17.2	14.5	11.3	13.5	11.0	14.5	17.1
Individual sports	23.2	27.7	18.7	23.9	21.9	17.9	16.7	21.8	31.9
Performing arts:									
Cheerleading	5.9	1.7	10.0	5.3	9.9	5.2	5.3	6.2	6.2
Drill team	4.5	1.2	7.7	3.6	9.4	5.2	5.1	4.8	3.5
School band or orchestra	20.9	15.0	26.8	21.7	22.3	14.1	17.4	21.4	23.6
School play or musical	11.0	8.4	13.6	11.0	12.1	9.3	9.3	10.8	13.0
School government/clubs:									
Student government	7.3	5.5	9.1	7.3	7.4	5.9	4.0	7.0	10.8
Academic honor society	7.7	6.6	8.7	7.3	8.1	7.5	5.0	7.1	11.3
School yearbook/newspaper	8.8	6.8	10.8	8.5	10.5	7.3	7.7	8.2	11.1
School service clubs	11.5	7.8	15.2	11.7	10.4	9.9	6.6	11.1	16.8
School academic clubs	30.7	26.7	33.5	31.1	25.1	26.7	24.7	30.9	34.3
School hobby clubs	7.3	7.6	6.7	7.4	5.2	6.4	5.6	6.8	9.4
School FTA, FHA, & FFA	11.7	11.1	12.6	12.3	13.8	8.0	17.9	12.0	6.6

Source: Snyder, T. D., and C. M. Hoffman. 1993. *Digest of Education Statistics.* Washington, DC: National Center for Education Statistics, page 137.

D7-2. High School Seniors' Participation during Past Year in School Activities, by Sex and Race, 1992

Question: To what extent have you participated in the following school activities during this school year?

	Total (N=2,727)	Sex		Race	
		Males (N=1,270)	Females (N=1,360)	White (N=1,847)	Black (N=378)
School newspaper or yearbook:					
Not at all	73.2%	78.7%	67.7%	72.6%	76.1%
Slight	10.5	10.4	10.8	10.6	10.4
Moderate	4.9	3.7	5.9	4.9	6.0
Considerable	4.5	2.9	6.0	4.5	2.5
Great extent	6.9	4.4	9.6	7.4	5.0
Music or other performing arts:					
Not at all	58.0%	66.3%	50.3%	59.5%	50.2%
Slight	9.5	7.4	11.2	8.3	12.2
Moderate	8.3	8.0	8.8	8.2	7.5
Considerable	7.2	6.4	8.2	7.2	7.6
Great extent	17.0	11.9	21.6	16.8	22.6
Athletic teams:					
Not at all	44.0%	36.6%	50.7%	42.8%	51.4%
Slight	9.7	9.8	9.9	9.2	10.9
Moderate	9.1	9.8	8.4	9.2	6.4
Considerable	12.3	14.2	11.0	13.1	7.9
Great extent	24.9	29.5	20.0	25.7	23.4
Academic clubs (e.g., science, math, language):					
Not at all	66.1%	69.6%	62.3%	68.1%	63.5%
Slight	11.1	11.9	10.7	10.9	10.4
Moderate	9.3	8.4	10.2	8.9	9.3
Considerable	7.0	4.7	8.9	6.7	7.2
Great extent	6.5	5.3	7.9	5.4	9.6
Student council or government:					
Not at all	76.2%	79.6%	72.6%	76.8%	70.5%
Slight	7.2	6.8	7.6	7.6	6.1
Moderate	5.6	4.9	6.5	5.6	7.1
Considerable	4.9	4.4	5.3	4.5	5.4
Great extent	6.1	4.3	7.9	5.6	10.9
Other school clubs or activities:					
Not at all	31.3%	37.9%	24.3%	30.6%	28.6%
Slight	12.9	15.5	10.9	14.4	9.7
Moderate	20.0	19.9	20.5	22.2	14.4
Considerable	16.2	13.8	18.2	15.7	16.5
Great extent	19.6	12.9	26.0	17.1	30.9

Note: Percentages may not add to 100 due to rounding.

Source: Bachman, Jerald G., Lloyd D. Johnston, and Patrick M. O'Malley. 1993. *Monitoring the Future: Questionnaire Responses from the Nation's High School Seniors, 1992.* Ann Arbor, MI: Survey Research Center, Institute for Social Research, The University of Michigan, pages 226–227.

D7-3. High School Seniors' Perception of School, by Sex and Race, 1992

Question: Now, thinking back over the past year in school, how often did you. . .

	Total (N=2,727)	Sex		Race	
		Males (N=1,270)	Females (N=1,360)	White (N=1,847)	Black (N=378)
Enjoy being in school:					
Never	3.9%	4.0%	3.8%	4.2%	3.2%
Seldom	15.7	15.7	15.1	17.2	10.2
Sometimes	42.1	43.8	41.3	43.8	44.2
Often	29.0	28.9	29.0	27.2	29.0
Almost always	9.3	7.6	10.7	7.6	13.3
Hate being in school:					
Never	5.8%	5.4%	5.8%	3.8%	11.3%
Seldom	26.3	25.7	26.4	25.8	27.5
Sometimes	38.8	39.4	38.3	38.9	39.4
Often	21.2	21.9	21.4	23.1	15.3
Almost always	7.9	7.6	8.0	8.4	6.5
Try to do your best work in school:					
Never	0.9%	1.0%	0.7%	0.9%	--
Seldom	8.3	11.8	5.0	9.4	4.1
Sometimes	29.5	33.1	25.4	30.9	24.1
Often	34.6	34.3	35.6	35.2	33.8
Almost always	26.7	19.8	33.4	23.7	38.0
Find school work too hard to understand:					
Never	13.3%	17.1%	10.2%	14.4%	11.8%
Seldom	42.4	43.3	42.2	44.0	43.0
Sometimes	34.6	30.9	37.5	32.2	36.6
Often	8.7	8.2	9.1	8.4	8.1
Almost always	0.9	0.5	1.0	0.9	0.6
Fool around in class:					
Never	9.1%	5.5%	12.4%	6.9%	14.5%
Seldom	28.3	22.6	33.5	27.1	32.2
Sometimes	34.7	34.5	35.1	36.1	33.6
Often	19.8	25.5	14.1	22.0	12.3
Almost always	8.1	11.8	4.7	7.9	7.4
Fail to complete or turn in assignments:					
Never	20.4%	14.4%	26.3%	21.0%	19.3%
Seldom	44.1	42.3	45.7	45.6	44.1
Sometimes	25.2	29.9	20.5	23.4	28.1
Often	8.7	11.4	6.3	8.4	7.3
Almost always	1.6	2.0	1.3	1.6	1.1
Get good grades (like As or Bs):					
Never	2.8%	4.4%	0.8%	2.7%	1.0%
Seldom	11.4	14.7	8.6	10.2	10.6
Sometimes	27.3	31.1	23.0	23.1	39.6
Often	27.0	25.1	29.0	27.1	30.0
Almost always	31.6	24.8	38.7	36.9	18.8

D7-3. High School Seniors' Perception of School, by Sex and Race, 1992 (continued)

		Sex		Race	
How often did you . . .	Total (N=2,727)	Males (N=1,270)	Females (N=1,360)	White (N=1,847)	Black (N=378)
Get sent to the office, or have to stay after school for misbehaving:					
Never	68.0%	57.3%	79.2%	69.6%	65.4%
Seldom	22.6	28.6	16.3	21.4	25.3
Sometimes	6.6	9.5	3.5	6.0	7.7
Often	2.2	3.7	0.7	2.3	1.0
Almost always	0.6	0.9	0.3	0.6	0.7
Skip school:					
Never	43.4%	37.2%	49.5%	43.7%	48.6%
Seldom	25.3	26.4	24.8	24.6	24.3
Sometimes	19.6	22.1	16.5	19.2	18.8
Often	9.4	11.2	7.5	10.1	6.7
Almost always	2.3	3.0	1.7	2.3	1.5

Note: Percentages may not add to 100 due to rounding.
— Not Available

Source: Bachman, Jerald G., Lloyd D. Johnston, and Patrick M. O'Malley. 1993. *Monitoring the Future: Questionnaire Responses from the Nation's High School Seniors, 1992.* Ann Arbor, MI: Survey Research Center, Institute for Social Research, The University of Michigan, pages 223–224.

D7-4. Years of High School Seniors' Participation in School Activities, by Sex and Race, 1992

Question: During how many years (if any) have you participated in each of the following types of organized activities or groups?

		Sex		Race	
	Total (N=2,727)	Males (N=1,270)	Females (N=1,360)	White (N=1,847)	Black (N=378)
School newspaper or yearbook:					
None	69.7%	77.1%	62.2%	68.6%	74.5%
A year or less	21.5	16.8	26.4	21.9	22.0
2-3 years	7.4	5.0	9.8	7.8	2.4
4-5 years	1.1	0.9	1.3	1.4	0.6
6 or more	0.3	0.1	0.3	0.2	0.4
Music or other performing arts in school:					
None	43.1	51.0	35.4	42.0	40.9
A year or less	17.3	17.8	17.4	16.8	19.3
2-3 years	17.7	14.5	20.6	18.0	16.7
4-5 years	8.9	6.5	10.7	8.5	8.9
6 or more	13.0	10.1	15.9	14.7	14.1
Music or other performing arts outside of school:					
None	57.7	63.5	52.1	56.9	51.9
A year or less	12.9	11.9	13.5	12.4	14.0
2-3 years	12.2	11.6	13.1	13.7	11.3
4-5 years	5.3	4.8	5.9	5.4	5.2
6 or more	11.9	8.2	15.4	11.6	17.6
School athletic teams:					
None	31.6	25.6	36.8	28.3	45.4
A year or less	13.1	11.8	14.5	12.2	15.3
2-3 years	21.2	23.3	19.4	20.9	16.3
4-5 years	14.3	14.0	14.7	14.7	11.6
6 or more	19.8	25.2	14.6	23.9	11.4
Organized sports outside of school:					
None	41.7	29.6	53.2	37.1	58.6
A year or less	11.5	10.5	12.5	10.9	10.1
2-3 years	15.2	16.6	13.6	15.4	14.3
4-5 years	9.4	12.0	6.7	10.7	4.6
6 or more	22.2	31.2	14.0	25.9	12.5
Academic clubs:					
None	63.4	68.1	58.5	63.0	65.1
A year or less	15.5	15.9	15.2	14.9	16.8
2-3 years	13.2	9.4	17.0	13.8	11.9
4-5 years	5.9	4.5	7.2	5.9	5.1
6 or more	2.1	2.2	2.1	2.5	1.2
Other school clubs or activities:					
None	33.5	43.2	23.1	32.1	33.5
A year or less	20.5	20.6	20.9	19.8	21.9
2-3 years	25.2	21.2	29.3	25.8	25.1
4-5 years	15.2	11.0	19.4	15.9	15.0
6 or more	5.6	4.0	7.2	6.4	4.5

D7-4. Years of High School Seniors' Participation in School Activities, by Sex and Race, 1992 (continued)

Question: During how many years (if any) have you participated in each of the following types of organized activities or groups?

	Total (N=2,727)	Sex		Race	
		Males (N=1,270)	Females (N=1,360)	White (N=1,847)	Black (N=378)
Student council or government:					
None	72.4%	77.2%	67.5%	72.2%	68.1%
A year or less	13.9	12.7	15.4	13.6	16.1
2-3 years	8.6	5.8	11.4	8.7	11.2
4-5 years	4.0	3.2	4.7	4.4	3.3
6 or more	1.1	1.2	1.0	1.0	1.3
Vocational clubs (4-H, Future Farmers, Future Teachers, etc.):					
None	67.6	71.6	63.9	68.3	60.1
A year or less	13.7	10.4	16.7	12.0	20.8
2-3 years	11.5	10.9	12.0	12.1	13.2
4-5 years	4.9	5.3	4.6	5.0	3.2
6 or more	2.3	1.7	2.9	2.6	2.7
Hobby clubs (photography, model building, etc.):					
None	67.9	66.1	69.1	68.6	66.8
A year or less	15.2	15.2	15.5	15.0	15.9
2-3 years	9.3	9.7	8.9	8.7	9.7
4-5 years	3.5	3.8	3.5	3.4	3.4
6 or more	4.1	5.2	3.1	4.3	4.2
Scouting (including Cubs, Brownies, etc.):					
None	55.6	58.1	52.5	50.2	67.4
A year or less	13.7	13.3	14.3	14.0	11.3
2-3 years	20.1	17.6	22.6	22.8	15.9
4-5 years	5.9	4.4	7.3	6.8	3.7
6 or more	4.8	6.6	3.2	6.1	1.7
Boys Clubs/Girls Clubs:					
None	83.1	82.5	83.6	85.3	73.0
A year or less	7.8	7.3	8.2	7.2	9.6
2-3 years	5.7	6.1	5.5	5.0	9.2
4-5 years	1.7	1.9	1.7	1.2	4.7
6 or more	1.6	2.2	1.0	1.3	3.5
Other community youth organizations:					
None	58.8	64.3	53.4	59.8	51.4
A year or less	16.1	14.2	18.4	15.9	17.6
2-3 years	14.7	12.9	16.0	14.1	17.3
4-5 years	5.7	4.8	6.7	5.7	7.7
6 or more	4.7	3.8	5.6	4.4	6.1
Church youth groups:					
None	41.8	44.4	38.9	40.7	39.4
A year or less	16.1	16.2	15.9	14.5	17.8
2-3 years	17.7	16.0	19.6	19.4	14.1
4-5 years	8.8	8.9	8.9	10.0	6.8
6 or more	15.6	14.5	16.7	15.4	22.0

Note: Percentages may not add to 100 due to rounding.

Source: Bachman, Jerald G., Lloyd D. Johnston, and Patrick M. O'Malley. 1993. *Monitoring the Future: Questionnaire Responses from the Nation's High School Seniors, 1992.* Ann Arbor, MI: Survey Research Center, Institute for Social Research, The University of Michigan, pages 223–224.

D7-5. Part-Time Employment of High School Seniors, by Sex and Race, 1992

Question: During how many years (if any) have you participated in a regular part-time job (during the school year)?

Regular part-time job during school year:	Total (N=2,727)	Sex		Race	
		Males (N=1,270)	Females (N=1,360)	White (N=1,847)	Black (N=378)
None	21.8%	20.9%	22.3%	18.6%	32.8%
A year or less	24.7	23.3	26.6	22.7	28.1
2-3 years	36.0	35.3	36.1	39.9	26.9
4-5 years	12.0	13.0	11.4	12.9	10.4
6 or more	5.5	7.4	3.6	5.8	1.9

Note: Percentages may not add to 100 due to rounding.

Source: Bachman, Jerald G., Lloyd D. Johnston, and Patrick M. O'Malley. 1993. *Monitoring the Future: Questionnaire Responses from the Nation's High School Seniors, 1992.* Ann Arbor, MI: Survey Research Center, Institute for Social Research, The University of Michigan, page 229.

D7-6. Characteristics Associated with Being Looked up to in High School, by Sex and Race, 1992

Question: How important is each of the following for being looked up to or having high status in your high school?

	Right family	Student leader	Nice car	Good grades	Good athlete	Know a lot	Plan on college
Total (N=2,316)							
No importance	17%	8%	16%	6%	9%	12%	9%
Little importance	20	17	23	15	11	26	15
Moderate importance	31	34	30	34	28	35	28
Great importance	18	27	18	24	30	18	24
Very great importance	15	14	14	21	22	10	25
Males (N=1,077)							
No importance	17%	9%	14%	5%	6%	12%	9%
Little importance	21	17	21	17	9	23	15
Moderate importance	29	34	31	37	27	37	32
Great importance	17	26	18	23	33	19	22
Very great importance	16	14	16	19	24	10	22
Females (N=1,193)							
No importance	16%	7%	17%	6%	11%	12%	8%
Little importance	19	17	24	15	13	28	14
Moderate importance	33	33	30	32	29	33	25
Great importance	18	28	18	26	27	17	26
Very great importance	14	14	11	22	21	9	27
Whites (N=1,660)							
No importance	14%	7%	12%	6%	7%	12%	10%
Little importance	21	18	23	17	10	28	15
Moderate importance	34	34	32	38	28	37	31
Great importance	18	28	20	23	33	16	25
Very great importance	14	13	12	16	22	6	20
Blacks (N=289)							
No importance	20%	11%	26%	4%	11%	7%	5%
Little importance	18	14	19	5	12	18	10
Moderate importance	20	30	21	21	25	29	17
Great importance	16	20	13	24	22	22	26
Very great importance	27	25	21	46	29	25	43

Note: Percentages may not add to 100 due to rounding.

Source: Bachman, Jerald G., Lloyd D. Johnston, and Patrick M. O'Malley. 1993. *Monitoring the Future: Questionnaire Responses from the Nation's High School Seniors, 1992.* Ann Arbor, MI: Survey Research Center, Institute for Social Research, The University of Michigan, page 151–152.

D8. DISCIPLINE AND VIOLENCE

D8-1. Students' Perception of School Discipline, by Sex, Age, Race, and Social Class, 1992

Survey question: Do you feel that discipline in your school is very strict, somewhat strict, not very strict, or not at all strict?

	Perceptions			
Student Characteristic	Very strict	Somewhat strict	Not very strict	Not at all strict
National	**32%**	**52%**	**11%**	**5%**
Sex:				
Male	29	56	8	7
Female	34	48	14	4
Age:				
13-15 years	28	54	13	5
16-17 years	37	50	8	6
Race:				
White	30	53	12	4
Non-white	35	48	5	13
Social class:				
White-collar background	27	57	12	4
Blue-collar background	36	47	10	7

Note: Percentages may not add to 100 due to rounding.

Source: Bezilla, Robert (ed.). 1993. *American's Youth in the 1990s.* Princeton, NJ: The George H. Gallup International Institute, page 71.

D8-2. Discipline Experiences of High School Seniors, by Sex and Race, 1992

Question: Have you ever had to repeat a grade in school? Did you ever attend summer school to make up for poor grades or to keep from being held back? Have you ever been suspended or expelled from school?

	Total (N=2,727)	Sex		Race	
		Males (N=1,270)	Females (N=1,360)	White (N=1,847)	Black (N=378)
Repeat a grade in school:					
No	85.5%	82.6%	88.9%	88.7%	77.4%
Yes, one time	13.6	16.6	10.4	10.6	21.1
Yes, two or more times	0.9	0.8	0.6	0.7	1.6
Attend summer school:					
No	76.4%	73.4%	80.3%	82.1%	59.4%
Yes, one summer	17.8	19.8	15.1	14.1	29.9
Yes, two summers	4.5	5.4	3.4	3.0	8.7
Yes, three or more summers	1.3	1.3	1.2	0.8	2.0
Been suspended or expelled from school:					
No	77.4%	10.7%	85.3%	82.2%	59.7%
Yes, one time	13.7	17.1	10.6	10.5	27.5
Yes, two or more times	8.9	12.8	4.2	7.3	12.8

Note: N indicates sample size. Percentages may not add to 100 due to rounding.

Source: Bachman, Jerald G., Lloyd D. Johnston, and Patrick M. O'Malley. 1993. *Monitoring the Future: Questionnaire Responses from the Nation's High School Seniors, 1992.* Ann Arbor, MI: Survey Research Center, Institute for Social Research, The University of Michigan, page 230.

D8-3. Students' Perception of Cheating in School, by Sex, Age, Race, and Social Class, 1992

Survey question: At your school, how common is cheating on tests or exams? Would you say there is a great deal, a fair amount, or not very much cheating? Have you, yourself, ever cheated on a test or exam?

Student Characteristic	Perception of Cheating			
	Great deal	Fair amount	Not very much	Have cheated
National	21%	34%	44%	46%
Sex:				
Male	20	33	46	49
Female	22	34	43	43
Age:				
13-15 years	19	31	49	39
16-17 years	24	38	37	57
Race:				
White	22	35	42	47
Non-white	16	29	55	44
Social class:				
White-collar background	19	39	42	47
Blue-collar background	21	31	46	45

Note: Percentages may not add to 100 due to rounding.

Source: Bezilla, Robert (ed.). 1993. *American's Youth in the 1990s.* Princeton, NJ: The George H. Gallup International Institute, page 73.

D8-4. Students' Perception of School Disturbances and Violence, by Sex, Age, Race, and Social Class, 1992

Survey question: How big a problem would you say each of the following is in your school—very big, fairly big, or not big at all: Students creating disturbances which disrupt classroom work? Fighting? Theft of personal property? Vandalism, the destruction of personal or school property? Students bringing weapons such as guns or knives to school?

Student Characteristics	"Very Big Problem" in School				
	Disturbances	Fighting	Theft	Vandalism	Weapons
National	30%	23%	14%	14%	9%
Sex:					
Male	30	23	12	13	12
Female	29	24	16	15	6
Age:					
13-15 years	32	24	10	12	8
16-17 years	27	22	19	17	11
Race:					
White	28	20	14	12	8
Non-white	37	33	12	20	13
Social class:					
White-collar background	25	16	14	11	6
Blue-collar background	35	32	16	17	12

Source: Bezilla, Robert (ed.). 1993. *American's Youth in the 1990s.* Princeton, NJ: The George H. Gallup International Institute, page 76.

D8-5. Students' Victimization at School, by Sex, Age, Race, and Social Class, 1992

Survey question: When you are at school, do you ever fear for your physical safety, or not? During the past 12 months have any of the following happened to you at school: Have you been physically assaulted or beaten up? Have you had money stolen? Have you had your personal property damaged or stolen?

	Victimization			
Student Characteristic	Fear for safety	Physical assault	Money stolen	Property vandalized
National	24%	7%	15%	14%
Sex:				
Male	23	9	10	17
Female	25	5	19	10
Age:				
13-15 years	28	8	16	14
16-17 years	19	4	13	13
Race:				
White	23	7	15	14
Non-white	30	6	14	12
Social class:				
White-collar background	21	4	14	12
Blue-collar background	27	8	16	17

Source: Bezilla, Robert (ed.). 1993. *American's Youth in the 1990s.* Princeton, NJ: The George H. Gallup International Institute, page 77.

D8-6. Tenth Graders' Attitudes about School Climate, by Sex, Race, and Social Class, 1992

Statements about school climate	Percent who "strongly agree" or "agree" with statement								
	Total	Sex		Race/ethnicity			Socioeconomic Status		
		Male	Female	White	Black	Hispanic	Low	Middle	High
Students get along well with teachers	74.9%	74.7%	75.2%	77.0%	62.8%	73.3%	68.6%	74.3%	82.7%
There is real school spirit	70.4	71.7	69.2	71.7	67.5	67.1	69.7	71.1	70.5
Rules for behavior are strict	63.8	65.5	62.1	64.4	62.3	63.7	65.1	62.2	65.8
Discipline is fair	70.2	69.3	71.0	70.4	65.1	72.5	66.0	69.6	74.7
Other students often disrupt class	70.7	71.6	69.8	69.9	76.3	69.1	74.0	72.2	64.3
Teaching is good	81.9	80.6	83.2	81.1	83.1	84.9	82.5	80.3	84.9
Teachers are interested in students	76.0	74.8	77.1	75.6	76.0	77.3	74.5	74.5	80.6
Teachers praise my effort when I work hard	57.2	56.1	58.2	54.4	64.6	64.6	60.9	55.4	57.9
I often feel "put down" by my teachers	16.0	16.0	16.0	16.2	16.3	15.7	17.2	16.3	13.7
Teachers listen to what I have to say	70.1	68.1	72.0	68.8	74.8	73.4	71.0	68.3	73.5
I don't feel safe at this school	8.0	8.8	7.3	6.7	12.8	10.8	10.8	8.1	5.1
Disruptions by other students interfere with my learning.	39.9	38.5	41.3	36.7	51.1	44.6	44.6	41.3	32.0
Misbehaving students often get away with it	52.7	55.8	49.7	53.4	45.5	53.8	50.7	52.2	55.0

Source: Snyder, T. D., and C. M. Hoffman. 1993. *Digest of Education Statistics.* Washington, DC: National Center for Education Statistics, page 136.

D8-7. Students' Report of Being Victims of Violence at School, 1977 and 1992.

Survey question: When you are at school, do you ever fear for your physical safety or not? During the past 12 months have any of the following happened to you at school: Have you been physically assaulted or beaten up? Have you had money stolen? Have you had your personal property damaged or stolen?

	Year	
Violent Behavior	1992	1977
Been physically assaulted	7%	4%
Had money stolen	15	12
Had property stolen	NA	24
Had property vandalized	14	11
Ever feared for physical safety	24	18

NA = Not available

Source: Bezilla, Robert (ed.). 1993. *American's Youth in the 1990s.* Princeton, NJ: The George H. Gallup International Institute, page 10.

D9. POST-SECONDARY EDUCATION

D9-1. Enrollment Status of Persons 18- to 21-Years-Old, by Race, Hispanic Origin, and Sex, 1975 and 1991

	Total Persons 18 to 21 Years Old (1,000)		PERCENT DISTRIBUTION									
			Enrolled in high school		High school graduates							
					Total		In college		Not in college		Not high school graduates	
Characteristic	1975	1991	1975	1991	1975	1991	1975	1991	1975	1991	1975	1991
Total	15,693	13,906	5.7	8.2	78.0	77.7	33.5	42.2	44.5	35.5	16.3	14.1
White	13,448	11,187	4.7	6.9	80.6	79.1	34.6	44.1	46.0	35.0	14.7	13.9
Black	1,997	2,138	12.5	14.2	60.4	69.3	24.9	28.3	35.6	41.0	27.0	16.6
Hispanic	899	1,637	12.0	13.4	57.2	51.6	24.4	23.9	32.8	27.7	30.8	35.1
Male	7,584	6,772	7.4	10.5	76.6	75.0	35.4	40.1	41.3	34.9	15.9	14.6
White	6,545	5,459	6.2	8.9	79.7	76.1	36.9	41.4	42.8	34.7	14.1	15.0
Black	911	1,026	15.9	18.9	55.0	66.3	23.9	26.8	31.1	39.5	29.0	14.7
Hispanic	416	826	17.3	13.9	54.6	45.3	25.2	17.8	29.3	27.5	27.9	41.0
Female	8,109	7,134	4.2	6.0	79.2	80.3	31.8	44.2	47.4	36.1	16.6	13.6
White	6,903	5,728	3.2	5.0	81.4	82.1	32.4	46.8	49.0	35.3	15.3	12.8
Black	1,085	1,112	9.7	9.6	65.0	71.9	25.8	29.7	39.2	42.3	25.4	18.4
Hispanic	484	812	7.6	12.8	59.3	58.1	23.6	30.0	35.7	28.1	33.1	29.1

Source: U.S. Bureau of the Census, *Statistical Abstract of the United States: 1993* (113th edition). Washington, DC, 1993, page 169.

D9-2. Enrollment in Institutions of Higher Learning, by Sex, Age, and Attendance Status, 1983 and 1988; and Projections, 1991, 1998, and 2003

(in thousands) Sex and Age	1983 Total	1983 Part-time	1988 Total	1988 Part-time	1991, proj. Total	1991, proj. Part-time	1998, proj. Total	1998, proj. Part-time	2003, proj. Total	2003, proj. Part-time
Total	12,465	5,204	13,055	5,619	14,169	6,137	15,167	6,625	16,124	6,796
Male	6,024	2,264	6,002	2,340	6,412	2,522	6,794	2,725	7,386	2,879
14 to 17 years old	102	16	55	5	79	12	117	14	142	15
18 to 19 years old	1,256	158	1,290	132	1,352	141	1,458	170	1,580	189
20 to 21 years old	1,241	205	1,243	216	1,366	257	1,355	292	1,587	350
22 to 24 years old	1,158	382	1,106	378	1,123	358	1,176	352	1,372	420
Female	6,441	2,940	7,053	3,278	7,757	3,615	8,373	3,900	8,738	3,819
14 to 17 years old	142	16	115	17	93	15	108	17	113	18
18 to 19 years old	1,496	179	1,536	195	1,445	178	1,632	216	1,787	243
20 to 21 years old	1,125	204	1,278	218	1,377	258	1,416	265	1,631	298
22 to 24 years old	884	378	932	403	1,103	445	1,110	438	1,259	502

Source: U.S. Bureau of the Census, *Statistical Abstract of the United States: 1993* (113th edition). Washington, DC, 1993, page 173.

D9-3. College Freshmen, Summary Characteristics, 1970–1992

Characteristics of College Freshmen	1970	1980	1990	1992
Sex:				
Male	55%	49%	46%	46%
Female	45	51	54	54
Applied to four or more colleges	15	26	36	33
Average grade in high school:				
A- to A+	16	21	23	26
B- to B+	58	60	58	57
C to C+	27	19	19	17
D	1	1	0	0
Political orientation:				
Liberal	34	20	23	24
Middle of the road	45	60	55	53
Conservative	17	17	20	19
Probable field of study:				
Arts and humanities	16	9	9	8
Biological sciences	4	4	4	5
Business	16	24	21	16
Education	11	7	10	10
Engineering	9	12	8	9
Physical science	2	3	2	2
Social science	14	7	10	9
Professional	NA	15	15	20
Technical	4	6	4	3
Data processing/computer programming	NA	2	1	1
Other	NA	NA	16	17
Communications	NA	2	2	2
Computer science	NA	1	2	1
Recipient of financial aid:				
Pell grant	NA	33	23	23
Supplemental educational opportunity grant	NA	8	7	6
State scholarship or grant	NA	16	16	14
College grant	NA	13	22	24
Federal guaranteed student loan	NA	21	23	23
Perkins loan	NA	9	8	8
College loan	NA	4	6	6
College work-study grant	NA	15	10	12

NA = Not available.

Source: U.S. Bureau of the Census, *Statistical Abstract of the United States: 1993* (113th edition). Washington, DC, 1993, page 180.

D9-4. Participation in Adult Education of 17- to 34-Year-Olds Not in Secondary School, 1990–1991

			PARTICIPANTS IN ADULT EDUCATION					
	Adult popu- lation (1,000)	Number taking adult ed. courses (1,000)	Reason for taking course (percent)					
Characteristic			Percent of total	Personal/ social	Advance on the job	Train for a new job	Improve basic skills	Complete degree or diploma
Total	181,800	57,391	32	30	60	9	1	13
Age:								
17 to 24 yrs	21,688	7,125	33	30	38	18	4	29
25 to 34 yrs	47,244	17,530	37	25	63	12	1	14

Source: U.S. Bureau of the Census, *Statistical Abstract of the United States: 1993* (113th edition). Washington, DC, 1993, page 187.

D9-5. Employment Status of High School Graduates Not Enrolled in College, and of School Dropouts, 16- to 24-Years Old, by Sex and Race, 1980–1991

Employment Status, Sex, and Race	GRADUATES			DROPOUTS		
	1980	1990	1991	1980	1990	1991
(in 1,000s)						
Civilian population	11,622	8,370	7,804	5,254	3,800	3,884
In labor force	9,795	7,107	6,444	3,549	2,506	2,464
Percent of population	84.3	84.9	82.6	67.5	66.0	63.4
Employed	8,567	6,279	5,641	2,651	1,993	1,849
Percent of labor force	87.5	88.3	87.5	74.7	79.5	75.0
Male	4,462	3,435	3,123	1,780	1,304	1,288
Female	4,105	2,845	2,518	871	689	561
White	7,638	5,334	4,724	2,310	1,761	1,631
Black	817	794	766	305	178	167
Unemployed	1,228	828	803	898	513	614
Percent of labor force	12.5	11.7	12.5	25.3	20.5	24.9
Male	695	438	441	548	301	362
Female	532	400	362	350	212	253
White	924	526	506	636	361	447
Black	289	279	273	239	136	153
Not in labor force	1,827	1,262	1,360	1,705	1,294	1,420
Percent of population	15.7	15.1	17.4	32.5	34.1	36.6

Source: U.S. Bureau of the Census, *Statistical Abstract of the United States: 1993* (113th edition). Washington, DC, 1993, page 169.

E. Economic Conditions

Several important economic trends are having an impact on adolescents, including the feminization of poverty, the widening gap between rich and poor, declining wages for many entry-level positions, and rising rates of female labor force participation. Some trends, such as growing numbers of single parents, place adolescents at greater risk of economic hardship, while others, such as increasing educational attainment and rising age at marriage, may be beneficial to adolescents. The economic well-being of adolescents is of particular concern because economic deprivation may have long term implications. This chapter reviews several aspects of adolescents' economic conditions, including family income, poverty and dependency, parental employment patterns, parental education, adolescent employment, and the costs of raising children.

E1. FAMILY AND HOUSEHOLD INCOME

Income can be measured in dollar amounts or relative to the poverty level. Family income depends on how many wage earners there are. Family incomes are much higher on average if both husband and wife are working and are much lower in female-headed households. In the early 1990s, the average real value of family income declined for most types of families. In 1992, about one-third of the women who gave birth lived in families with incomes under $20,000 and one-fourth lived in families with incomes above $50,000. It is also interesting to note that the percentage of adolescents who lived in "middle class comfort" grew during the economic boom of the 1950s and 60s but declined during the 1980s. The data on family income also clearly show that departure of the father through divorce or desertion severely lowers family income.

Income tends to be much higher in white families than in either black or Hispanic families. Most white teenagers live in higher income households, but only about a third of black and Hispanic teens are relatively well-off. Minority status and living in a single-parent family appear to expose adolescents to a higher likelihood of economic hardship.

In 1992, 42 percent of teens said their families were better off than they were one year ago, while 33 percent said they were worse off. Males tend to be more opti-

mistic than females about their future financial situation. Republicans and church-attenders also appear to be relatively better off economically speaking. In contrast, residents in the East were more likely than those in other regions to feel they were worse off.

E2. POVERTY AND OTHER RISK FACTORS

The poverty level is calculated from the estimated costs of providing a basic standard of living, according to family size. For example, the poverty threshold for a family of four was $13,926 in 1991. Families falling below that estimate are "in poverty." Corresponding to trends in income, the percentage of children in poverty declined in the 1960s but has increased since the early 1970s. The youngest children (under age six) are more likely to live in poor families than are all children under 18. Many children who are currently poor have spent a majority of their lives in poverty.

Several factors are associated with a higher risk of poverty. Black and Hispanic adolescents are more likely to be poor than white adolescents. Poor children are more likely to live in single-parent families. Families with many children are also more likely to be poor. Poverty rates are also associated with parental employment. Less than 1 percent of children in dual, full-time employed families live in poverty. Comparatively, nearly half of children in families where the mother works part-time and the father is absent live in poverty.

Various family characteristics other than parental employment also create a disadvantage for adolescents, including size, low educational attainment, farm origin, and single-parent status. The percent of adolescents experiencing these characteristics, however, has been declining.

Housing and neighborhood characteristics can also affect adolescents. Over one-fourth of children live in neighborhoods that have at least one symptom of distress, including an increasing number of unemployed, high school dropouts, single-parent families, welfare recipients, or families in poverty. Blacks and Hispanics are over-represented in severely distressed neighborhoods.

Also, adolescents in the United States experience a higher poverty rate than do adolescents in most other industrialized nations. Yet fewer poor children receive financial support from the U.S. government in the form of transfer payments.

E3. CHILD SUPPORT AND WELFARE

In 1990, 58 percent of women with children and absent fathers were awarded child support. Of the women who were awarded child support, only 26 percent received full payment, and 12 percent received none. Although child support was an important issue in the 1980s, there has been little progress in increasing the likelihood that women will receive payment. Child support received, however, tends to be higher for divorced women than for never married women, for whites than for minorities, for the more educated than for the less educated, and for women with incomes above the poverty level. Not surprisingly, women who do receive awarded support have significantly higher incomes than women who do not receive payments or who were not awarded child support.

By 1988, roughly one-third of white children and one-half of black children who were nearly poor or below the poverty level were either mainly or fully dependent on welfare. These percentages have increased sharply since 1959. In addition, the race gap in welfare dependency increased in the 1960s and 1970s but has remained relatively stable since.

E4. PARENTAL EMPLOYMENT

Although paternal employment in general is one of the major influences on an adolescent's economic circumstances, maternal employment seems to be the single most influential factor. Maternal employment has increased steadily for at least three decades and is projected to increase even further. Moreover, the magnitude of the increase has been as great for mothers with children under six years of age as for other mothers. By 1992, nearly two-thirds of women who gave birth that year were employed. Although mothers of children under age one are less likely to work, trends in employment are similar.

Although father's employment patterns have not changed as much as have the mother's, some changes are evident. Fewer children have employed fathers in the home, and when the father is in the home, he most likely works full time. In addition, white fathers are more likely to be working full time that either black or Hispanic fathers.

E5. PARENTAL EDUCATION

Nearly 50 percent of adolescents now live in families where at least one parent has had college experience, and only 20 percent of adolescents live in homes where the parent(s) has not completed high school. Parents' educational attainment is lower in single-parent families than in two-parent families, and lower in minority families than in white families. Even so, educational attainment of both mothers and fathers has improved steadily during this century. Despite this improvement, 21 percent of the mothers who gave birth in 1992 did not have a high school degree, and fewer than half had attended college.

E6. ADOLESCENT LABOR FORCE PARTICIPATION

Before age 14 almost all teens are enrolled in school, but at age 15 some begin working; a few even drop out of school in order to work. A majority of 20- to 24-year-olds work and do not attend school, and 13 percent are neither in school or working.

Adolescent labor force participation rates increased between 1970 and 1980 but declined somewhat thereafter. Male adolescents are more likely to work than females, and they make slightly higher wages. Also, nearly all married adolescent males are in the labor force. Many adolescents work regular daytime hours, but about 30 percent have evening, night, rotating, or other work arrangements.

Only 7 percent of 13- to 17-year-olds are depended on to work and earn money "a great deal," but a majority are expected to earn some money on their own. Fourteen percent of 13- to 17-year-olds do not have a social security card, but 62 percent have a savings account, 19 percent have a checking account, and 4 percent have a credit card.

E7. COSTS OF RAISING CHILDREN

The amount of money parents spend on children depends on family size, family income, and marital status of the parent(s). Based on estimates in 1993, it would cost approximately $100,000 to raise a child through age 17. For a child born in 1993 to a middle income family, however, the estimated cost of raising the child through age 17 is $213,140. Housing is the single greatest cost of raising children, followed by food, transportation, clothing, health care, education, and child care. Single parents spend more on housing than do dual parents, but spend less on other items; thus, overall, they spend a little less on children.

E1. FAMILY AND HOUSEHOLD INCOME

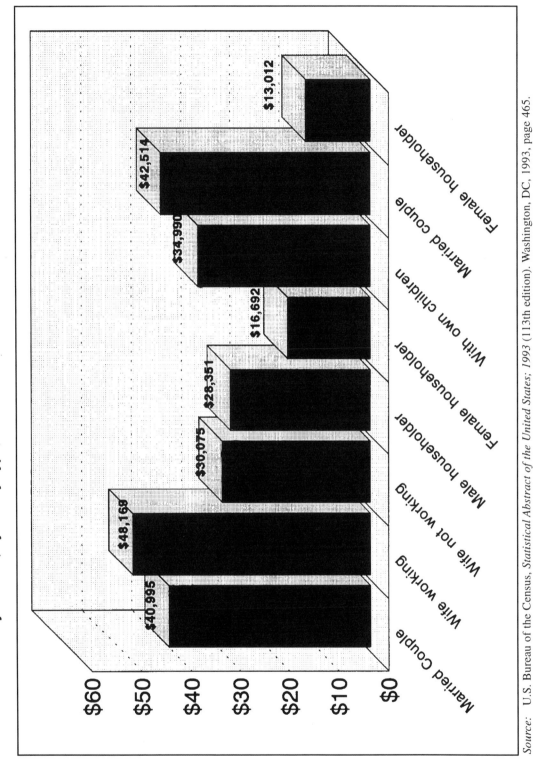

E1-1. Median Family Income, by Family Type, 1991

Source: U.S. Bureau of the Census, *Statistical Abstract of the United States; 1993* (113th edition). Washington, DC, 1993, page 465.

E1-2. Percent with Comfortable, Prosperous, or High Family Income for Children, by Parental Amount of Work and Living Arrangements, 1990

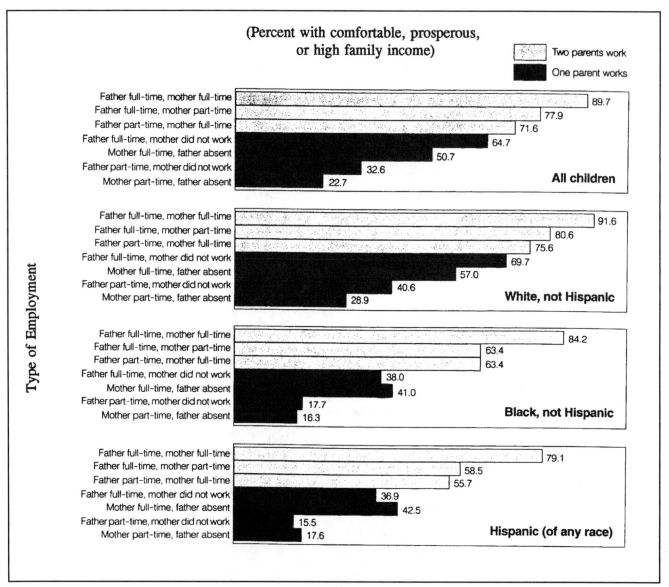

Source: U.S. Bureau of the Census, *We the American children.* U.S. Department of Commerce, Economics and Statistics Administration. Washington, DC, 1993, page 15.

E1-3. Median Money Income of Families and Unrelated Individuals, in Current and Constant (1991) Dollars, 1970–1991

Item	1970	1980	1984	1985	1986	1987	1988	1989	1990	1991
CURRENT DOLLARS										
Families:										
Married-couple families	10,516	23,141	29,612	31,100	32,805	34,879	36,389	38,547	39,895	40,995
Wife in paid labor force	12,276	26,879	34,668	36,431	38,346	40,751	42,709	45,266	46,777	48,169
Wife not in paid labor force	9,304	18,972	23,582	24,556	25,803	26,640	27,220	28,747	30,265	30,075
Male householder, no wife present	9,012	17,519	23,325	22,622	24,962	25,208	26,827	27,847	29,046	28,351
Female householder, no husband present	5,093	10,408	12,803	13,660	13,647	14,683	15,346	16,442	16,932	16,692
Unrelated individuals:										
Male	4,540	10,939	13,566	14,921	15,281	16,082	16,976	17,860	17,927	18,069
Female	2,483	6,668	9,501	9,865	10,142	11,029	11,881	12,390	12,450	12,731
CONSTANT (1991) DOLLARS										
Families:										
Married-couple families	34,680	38,297	38,818	39,366	40,767	41,818	41,895	42,340	41,574	40,995
Wife in paid labor force	40,484	44,483	45,445	46,114	47,653	48,858	49,171	49,720	48,745	48,169
Wife not in paid labor force	30,683	31,397	30,913	31,083	32,065	31,940	91,339	31,575	31,539	30,075
Male householder, no wife present	29,720	28,993	30,576	28,635	31,020	30,223	30,886	30,587	30,268	28,351
Female householder, no husband present	16,796	17,224	16,783	17,291	16,959	17,604	17,668	18,060	17,645	16,692
Unrelated individuals:										
Male	14,972	18,103	17,783	18,887	18,990	19,281	19,545	19,617	18,681	18,069
Female	8,188	11,035	12,455	12,487	12,603	13,223	13,679	13,609	12,974	12,731

Source: U.S. Bureau of the Census, *Statistical Abstract of the United States: 1993* (113th edition). Washington, DC, 1993, page 465.

E1-4. Relative Income Levels and Official Poverty Rates, Children and Adults, 1939–1988

Relative Economic Age, and Family Status	1939	1949	1959	1969	1979	1988
Relative Poverty:						
Children aged 0-17	37.9%	26.9%	24.4%	22.7%	23.8%	27.0%
Adults aged 18 and over	29.2	23.4	18.9	17.9	17.0	16.6
Parents aged 18 and over	27.9	18.0	16.1	14.6	15.9	18.3
Potential parents aged 18-44	28.1	24.5	17.3	15.1	16.4	14.2
Post-parental adults aged 45-64	25.5	22.0	16.8	14.0	12.4	12.7
Post-parental adults aged 65+	42.8	41.7	34.3	37.0	27.1	22.7
Post-parental adults aged 65+ adjusted for housing cost	39.3	NA	27.6	29.6	19.8	15.9
Total population	31.7	24.5	20.9	19.6	18.9	19.3
Near-Poor Frugality:						
Children aged 0-17	11.6	15.2	18.1	19.0	15.4	14.4
Adults aged 18 and over	10.8	10.7	13.0	13.4	12.3	12.0
Parents aged 18 and over	12.3	12.6	15.3	16.2	13.7	13.2
Potential parents aged 18-44	9.3	9.5	9.5	10.6	9.8	9.9
Post-parental adults aged 45-64	9.9	8.3	9.2	8.6	8.5	8.6
Post-parental adults aged 65+	12.1	12.1	16.4	16.8	19.2	17.7
Middle-Class Comfort						
Children aged 0-17	27.5	39.3	42.1	42.8	42.4	36.5
Adults aged 18 and over	25.2	32.3	37.5	38.2	37.5	33.7
Parents aged 18 and over	30.1	43.0	46.6	47.4	45.5	38.8
Potential parents aged 18-44	24.5	26.3	32.5	35.5	35.1	31.0
Post-parental adults aged 45-64	22.3	25.3	29.6	31.8	30.7	28.7
Post-parental adults aged 65+	18.9	23.8	27.4	26.2	32.6	34.6

E1-4. Relative Income Levels and Official Poverty Rates, Children and Adults, 1939–1988 (continued)

Relative Economic Circumstances, Age, and Family Status	1939	1949	1959	1969	1979	1988
Luxury:						
Children aged 0-17	23.0%	18.6%	15.3%	15.4%	18.4%	22.1%
Adults aged 18 and over	34.9	33.6	30.6	30.5	33.2	37.8
Parents aged 18 and over	29.7	26.4	22.1	21.9	24.9	29.7
Potential parents aged 18-44	38.1	39.6	40.8	38.9	38.7	44.9
Post-parental adults aged 45-64	42.3	44.4	44.4	45.6	48.5	50.0
Post-parental adults aged 65+	26.2	22.4	22.0	20.0	21.2	25.0
Official Poverty:						
Children aged 0-17	71.8	47.6	25.8	16.1	16.3	19.7
Adults aged 18 and over	57.7	37.8	20.1	12.9	10.7	10.8
Total population	61.8	40.8	22.2	14.0	12.3	13.1
Total (in thousands):						
Children aged 0-17	29,647	44,340	64,121	69,434	63,816	63,747
Adults aged 18 and over	67,889	100,717	111,888	128,408	157,122	179,783
Parents aged 18 and over	25,503	38,819	50,474	53,566	56,207	59,543
Potential parents aged 18-44	26,009	27,995	21,253	26,677	43,657	53,990
Post-parental adults aged 45-64	12,243	22,400	24,966	29,139	33,277	37,382
Post-parental adults aged 65+	4,134	11,504	15,195	19,026	23,981	28,868

Specifically, a family's income level is "relatively poor" if it is less than one-half as large as the median family income; "near-poor" if it is above the relative poverty level but less than three-fourths as large as the median; "middle-class comfort" if it is above the near-poor level but less than 50 percent more than the median; or "luxurious" if it is at least 50 percent more than the median.

Source: Hernandez, Donald J. 1993. *America's Children: Resources from Family, Government, and the Economy.* New York: Russell Sage Foundation, pages 246–47.

E1-5. Distribution of White and Black Children, by Relative Income Levels, 1939–1988

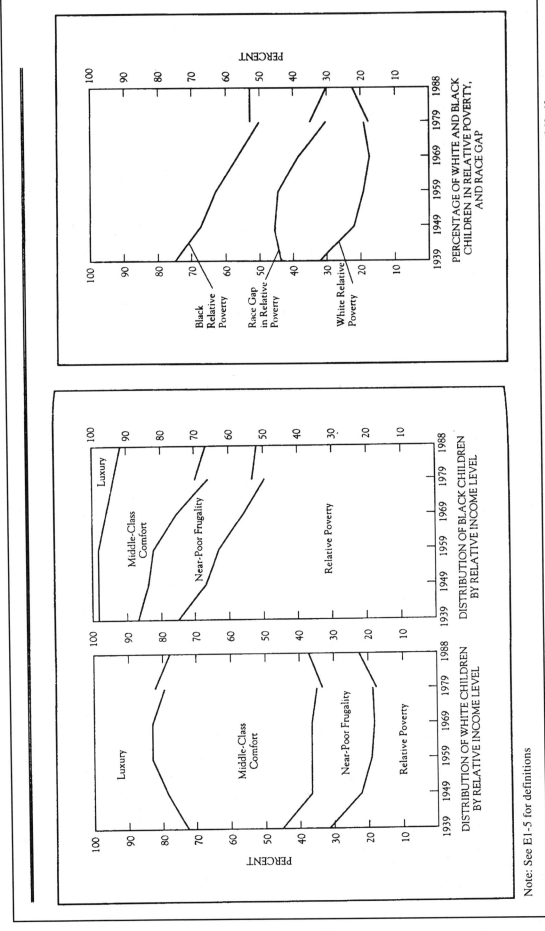

Note: See E1-5 for definitions

Source: Hernandez, Donald J. 1993. *America's Children: Resources from Family, Government, and the Economy*. New York: Russell Sage Foundation, pages 262–63.

E1-6. Family Income of Women Who Had a Birth, 1992

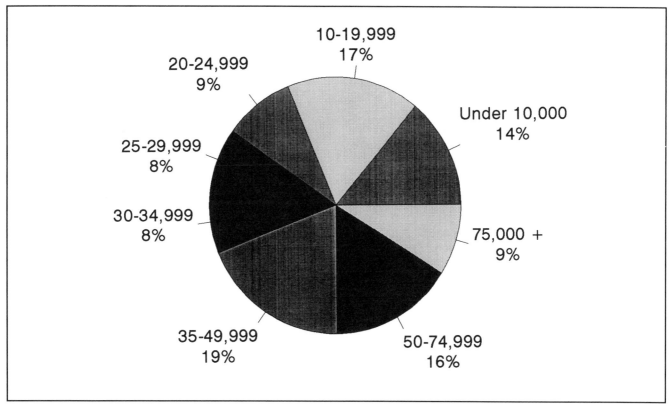

Source: Bachu, Amara. 1993. *Fertility of American Women: June 1992, U.S. Bureau of the Census, Current Population Reports, P20-470.* U.S. Government Printing Office, Washington, DC, page ix.

E1-7. Ratio of Income of Children in One- or No-Parent Situations to Income of Children Who Live with Two Parents throughout the Panel, at the First and Eighth Interviews, 1983–1986

| Income | Always two parents present | Mother always present | | | Father always present | Neither parent present |
		Father leaves	Mother only	"Father" enters		
Mean family income:						
First interview	$2,834	0.828	0.400	0.411	0.859	0.570
Eighth interview	$3,060	0.593	0.384	0.819	0.758	0.479
Mean household income:						
First interview	$2,847	0.829	0.420	0.504	0.881	0.652
Eighth interview	$3,073	0.593	0.406	0.788	0.767	0.529
Mean per capita income:						
First interview	$649	0.817	0.470	0.609	0.954	0.689
Eighth interview	$689	0.704	0.476	0.858	0.886	0.643
Mean income/needs ratio:						
First interview	2.83	0.819	0.427	0.483	0.900	0.598
Eighth interview	3.06	0.671	0.424	0.860	0.834	0.561
Percent with income/needs ratio less than 1.00:						
First interview	12.1	1.754	4.630	3.953	1.689	3.277
Eighth interview	9.7	3.184	5.491	1.873	1.362	3.925
Number (in thousands)	36,867	2,884	8,390	1,402	1,372	948

Source: U.S. Bureau of the Census, Current Population Reports, Series P-70, No. 23, *Family Disruption and Economic Hardship: The Short-Run Picture for Children.* U.S. Government Printing Office, Washington, DC, 1991, page 5.

E1-8. Changes in Income among Children Who Lived with Both Parents at the Beginning of the Panel and Whose Father Left in Subsequent Months, 1983–1986

Subject	Prior to loss	At time of loss	After loss of father from household			
			Time 1	Time 2	Time 3	Time 4
ALL CHILDREN						
Average monthly income:						
Family income	$2,435	$1,746	$1,543	$1,548	$1,739	$1,711
Household income	$2,461	$1,749	$1,546	$1,645	$1,781	$1,687
Per capita income	$549	$449	$436	$447	$468	$456
Income/needs ratio	2.43	1.91	1.79	1.77	1.94	1.96
Percent in poverty	18.8	30.3	35.5	30.9	29.3	30.7
Ratio of income to income prior to loss:						
Family income	1.000	0.717	0.634	0.636	0.714	0.703
Household income	1.000	0.711	0.628	0.669	0.724	0.685
Per capita income	1.000	0.817	0.795	0.814	0.852	0.831
Income/needs ratio	1.000	0.787	0.737	0.729	0.801	0.805
Percent in poverty	1.000	1.617	1.892	1.646	1.564	1.635
Number (in thousands)	2,884	2,884	2,522	2,194	1,804	1,454
CHILDREN WHOSE MOTHER DOES NOT REMARRY/RECONCILE						
Average monthly income:						
Family income	$2,416	$1,735	$1,452	$1,364	$1,424	$1,432
Household income	$2,450	$1,732	$1,451	$1,459	$1,465	$1,395
Per capita income	$540	$445	$424	$409	$409	$399
Income/needs ratio	2.39	1.90	1.73	1.60	1.67	1.71
Percent in poverty	18.5	30.7	37.6	32.9	35.6	35.3
Ratio of income to income prior to loss:						
Family income	1.000	0.718	0.601	0.565	0.589	0.593
Household income	1.000	0.707	0.592	0.596	0.598	0.570
Per capita income	1.000	0.825	0.785	0.757	0.757	0.739
Income/needs ratio	1.000	0.796	0.723	0.670	0.699	0.714
Percent in poverty	1.000	1.660	2.029	1.780	1.922	1.905
Number (in thousands)	2,225	2,225	1,863	1,589	1,301	1,036

Source: U.S. Bureau of the Census, Current Population Reports, Series P-70, No. 23, *Family Disruption and Economic Hardship: The Short-Run Picture for Children.* U.S. Government Printing Office, Washington, DC, 1991, page 10.

E1-9. Family Income Level for Children, by Race, 1989 and 1990 (percent distribution)

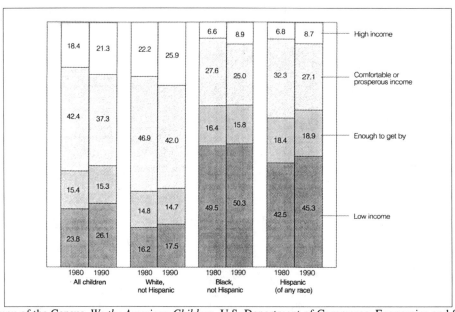

Source: U.S. Bureau of the Census, *We the American Children.* U.S. Department of Commerce, Economics and Statistics Administration. Washington, DC, 1993, page 12.

E1-10. Economic Status of Teens Aged 15–19, by Race, 1992

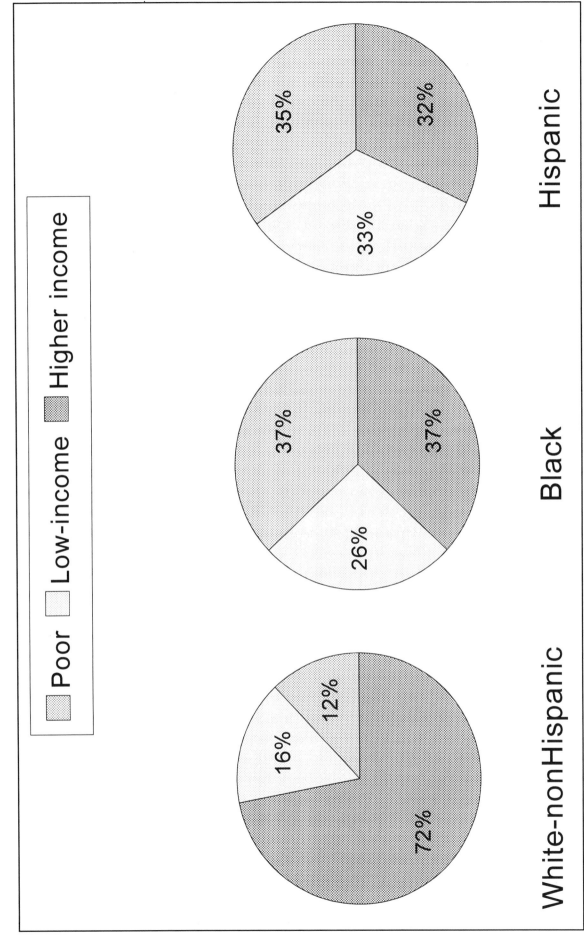

Source: The Alan Guttmacher Institute. 1994. *Sex and America's Teenagers.* New York: The Alan Guttmacher Institute, page 12.

E1-11. Family Income Level for Children, by Parental Living Arrangements, 1990

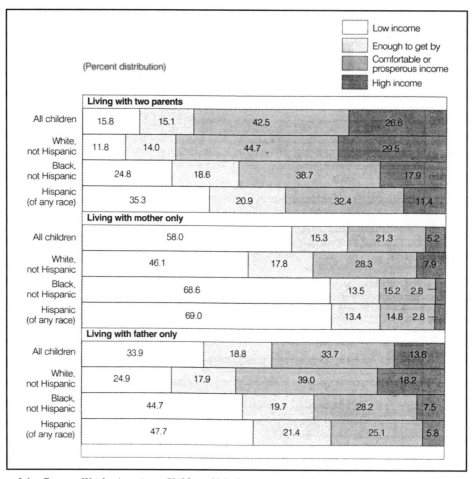

Source: U.S. Bureau of the Census, *We the American Children.* U.S. Department of Commerce, Economics and Statistics Administration. Washington, DC, 1993, page 13.

E1-12. Changes in Financial Situation, by Sex, Age, Race, and Social Class, 1992

Survey question: We are interested in how people's financial situation may have changed. Would you say that your family is financially better off now than you were a year ago, or is financially worse off now?			
	Change		
Characteristic	Better	Same	Worse
National	42%	20%	33%
Sex:			
Male	45	23	27
Female	38	18	39
Age:			
13-15 years	43	20	30
16-17 years	41	20	37
Race:			
White	40	24	31
Non-white	46	10	41
Social class:			
White-collar background	41	22	34
Blue-collar background	40	16	38

Source: Bezilla, Robert (ed.). 1993. *American's Youth in the 1990s.* Princeton, NJ: The George H. Gallup International Institute, page 263.

E2. POVERTY AND OTHER RISK FACTORS

E2-1. Children Poverty Rates, 1959–1991

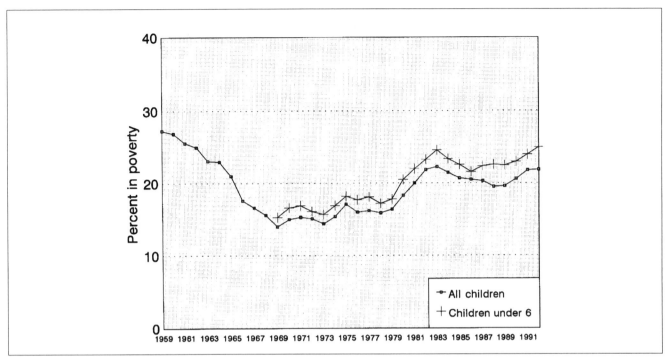

Source: Children's Defense Fund. 1994. *The State of America's Children Yearbook: 1994.* Washington, DC: Children's Defense Fund, page 73.

E2-2. Distribution of Children, by Percent of Life in Poverty, 1986

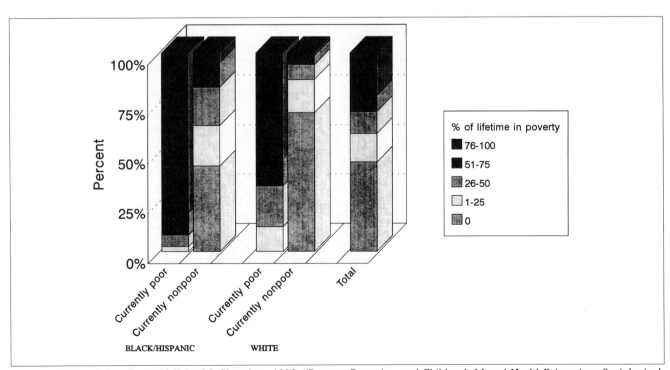

Source: McLeod, Jane D., and Michael J. Shanahan. 1993. "Poverty, Parenting, and Children's Mental Health." *American Sociological Review* 58:351–366.

E2-3. Percent of Children in Single-Parent Families, by Poverty Status and Ethnicity, 1991

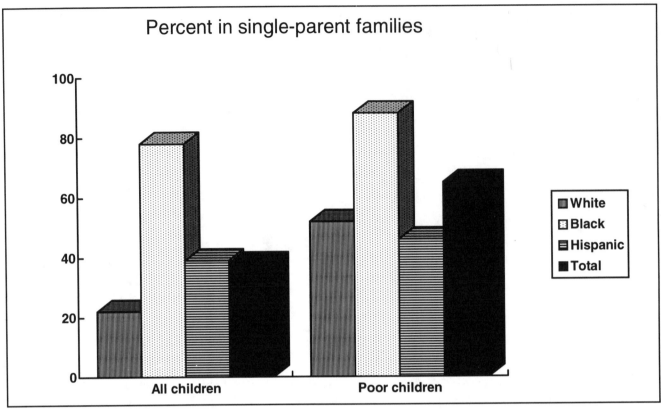

Source: U.S. Bureau of the Census, *Statistical Abstract of the United States: 1993* (113th edition). Washington, DC, 1993, page 470.

E2-4. Distribution of All Children and of Children below Poverty Level, Six Years Old, by Family Type and Race, 1991

Race and Family Type	All Children		Children Below Poverty Level		
	Number (millions)	Percent	Number (millions)	Percent	Poverty rate
All races:					
All family types 22.9	100.0	5.3	100.0	23.0
Married-couple 17.2	74.7	2.1	39.5	12.1
Single-parent 5.8	25.2	3.2	60.4	55.0
Mother-only 5.1	22.4	3.0	57.5	59.0
White, non-Hispanic:					
All family types 15.7	100.0	2.2	100.0	14.2
Married-couple 13.1	83.7	1.1	51.1	8.6
Single-parent.......................................2.5	16.3	1.1	49.0	42.7
Mother-only1 ....2.1	13.7	1.1	45.7	47.3
Black, non-Hispanic:					
All family types 3.5	100.0	1.8	100.0	49.5
Married-couple 1.3	35.5	0.3	14.5	20.2
Single-parent.......................................2.3	64.5	0.3	85.5	65.7
Mother-only 2.2	60.8	1.4	80.3	67.9
Hispanic:2					
All family types 2.8	100.0	1.1	100.0	40.1
Married-couple 2.0	72.0	0.6	53.6	29.9
Single-parent.......................................0.7	28.0	0.6	46.4	66.4
Mother-only 0.7	24.6	0.4	36.8	70.4

[1] Includes father-only, relative-only, and nonrelative-only families.
[2] Persons of Hispanic origin may be of any race.

Source: U.S. Bureau of the Census, *Statistical Abstract of the United States: 1993* (113th edition). Washington, DC, 1993, page 470.

E2-5. Percent of Families below Poverty, by Family Size and Race, 1991

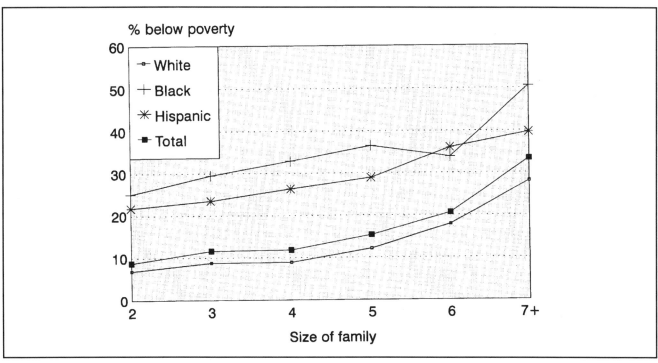

Source: U.S. Bureau of the Census, *Statistical Abstract of the United States: 1993* (113th edition). Washington, DC, 1993, page 472.

E2-6. Poverty Rates for Children, by Parental Living Arrangements and Race, 1980 and 1990

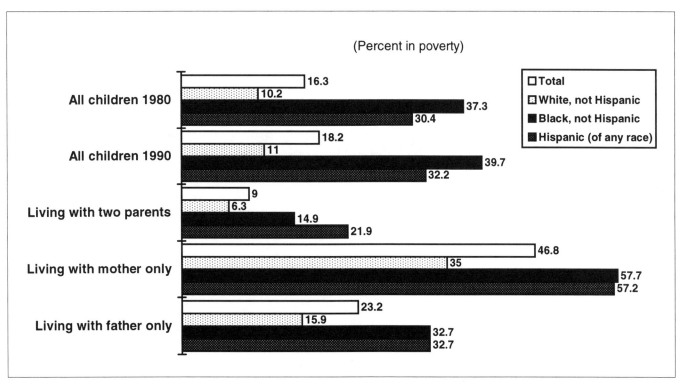

Source: U.S. Bureau of the Census, *We the American Children.* U.S. Department of Commerce, Economics and Statistics Administration. Washington, DC, 1993, page 14.

E2-7. Poverty Rates for Children, by Parental Amount of Work, Living Arrangements, and Race, 1990

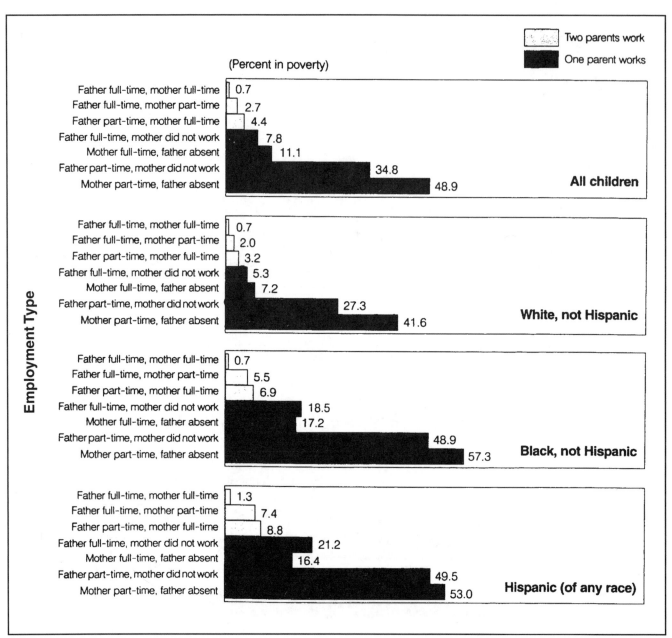

Source: U.S. Bureau of the Census, *We the American Children.* U.S. Department of Commerce, Economics and Statistics Administration. Washington, DC, 1993, page 17.

E2-8. Indicators of the Economic Status of Children, Selected Countries, 1980

Country	Year	Earnings of poor families with children (before taxes and transfers) as percentage of U.S. poverty line		Government transfers to families with children (before taxes and transfers) in 1979 U.S. dollars (thousands)		Poverty rate for children		Poverty rate for families with children		Percent of pre-tax and transfer poor who receive transfers
		All families	Single parent	Means tested	Social insurance	All families	Single parent	All families	Single parent	All families
Australia	1981	21	11	2,397	369	16.9	65.0	15.0	61.4	99
Canada	1981	36	16	1,383	1,498	9.6	38.7	8.6	35.3	99
Germany, Fed. Rep.	1981	45	15	328	2,726	8.2	35.1	6.9	31.9	100
Sweden	1981	48	39	2,357	4,028	5.1	8.6	4.4	7.5	100
United Kingdom	1979	48	17	1,239	1,971	10.7	38.6	8.5	36.8	99
United States	1979	33	21	1,660	692	17.1	51.0	13.8	42.9	73

Note: Poverty is defined as the percentage of people who have adjusted disposable income below the U.S. poverty line ($5,763 for a family of 3 in 1979) converted into national currencies using the purchasing power parities developed by the Organization for Economic Co-operation and Development (OECD). The definition of adjusted disposable income includes all forms of cash income (earnings, property income, and all cash transfers including the value of food stamps in the United States and housing allowances in the United Kingdom and Sweden) and it subtracts income and payroll taxes. This definition differs slightly from the definition of income used in the official United States calculation of poverty rates. In 1979, the U.S. Bureau of the Census estimated that 16.0 percent of United States children were in families with income below the poverty line.

Source: Hobbs, Frank, and Laura Lippman. 1990. *Children's Well-Being: An International Comparison.* International Population Reports Series P-95, no. 80. U.S. Department of Commerce, Bureau of the Census. Washington, DC: U.S. Government Printing Office, page 36.

E2-9. Disadvantaged White and Black Children Born between the 1920s and 1960s, by Family Origins

	1920s	1930s	1940s	1950s	1960s
White children (in thousands)	11,384	9,992	14,987	19,251	18,302
Black children (in thousands)	1,102	1,127	1,638	2,638	2,984
Percent with at least 1 disadvantage:					
5 siblings or more and mother completed less than 4 years of high school:					
White	37.4	29.8	20.1	16.5	10.6
Black	52.5	58.2	53.6	48.4	32.4
5 siblings or more and mother completed less than 4 years of high school or not in intact two-parent family:					
White	54.0	48.3	39.1	38.6	40.6
Black	78.0	81.6	78.8	81.9	78.8
5 siblings or more and mother completed less than 4 years of high school or farm origin:					
White	50.1	41.0			
Black	66.2	66.8			
5 siblings or more and mother completed less than 4 years of high school or not in intact two-parent family, or farm origin:					
White	63.8	57.0			
Black	86.0	86.2			
Percent living on farm:					
White	27.1	21.2	11.8	6.0	3.6
Black	40.5	34.2	14.9	3.2	0.3
Percent with multiple disadvantages:					
5 siblings or more and mother completed less than 4 years of high school and not in intact two-parent family:					
White	8.5	8.0	6.3	5.9	5.9
Black	20.5	25.6	26.1	28.2	22.6
5 siblings or more and mother completed less than 4 years of high school and farm origin:					
White	14.6	10.0			
Black	26.9	25.6			

Disadvantages include each of the five factors described in the table.

Source: Hernandez, Donald J. 1993. *America's Children: Resources from Family, Government, and the Economy.* New York: Russell Sage Foundation, page 216.

E2-10. Percent of Children Living with Parents in Owner-Occupied Housing, by Race, 1992

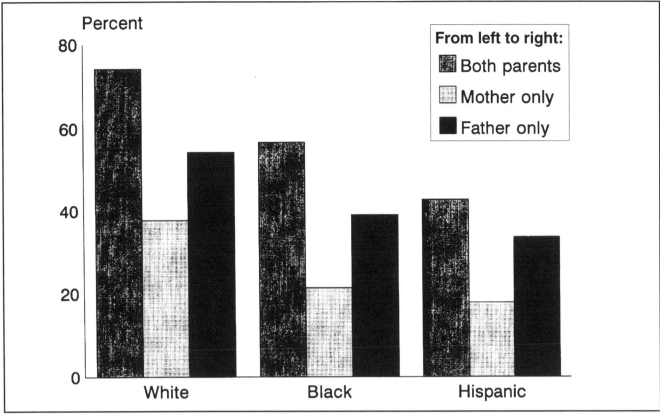

Source: O'Hare, William P. 1994. "3.9 Million U.S. Children in Distressed Neighborhoods," *Population Today* 22 (9) Population Reference Bureau, Inc., page 5.

E2-11. Census Tracts/BNAs and Children, Number of Characteristics at Distress Level, 1990

Number of Characteristics at Distress Level	Census Tracts/BNAs		Children	
	Number	Percent	Number (in millions)	Percent
None	41,163	69	45.4	73
1	8,328	14	7.8	12
2	3,470	6	3.0	5
3	2,479	4	2.5	4
4	2,733	5	2.7	4
5	1,152	2	1.1	2
Total	59,325	100	62.6	100

Note: Numbers may not add to totals due to rounding. Distress levels include: (1) more than 47 percent of adult men worked fewer than 26 weeks the previous year; (2) more than 23 percent of 16- to 19-year-olds are not enrolled in school; (3) more than 40 percent of families are single-parent, female-headed families; (4) more than 17 percent of families receive public assistance payments; (5) more than 28 percent of families are poor.

Source: O'Hare, William P. 1994. "3.9 Million U.S. Children in Distressed Neighborhoods," *Population Today* 22 (9) Population Refernce Bureau, Inc., page 5.

E2-12. Race/Ethnicity of Children in Severely Distressed Neighborhoods, 1990

Type of Neighborhood	Number of children	Race/ethnicity of children (percent)			
		White	Black	Asian	Hispanic*
In all neighborhoods	62,601,000	75	15	3	12
In severely distressed neighborhoods	3,858,000	20	64	2	20
Below poverty level in severely distressed neighborhoods	2,224,000	16	68	2	20

*Hispanics may be of any race.

Note: Severely distressed neighborhoods have at least four out of the following characteristics: 1) 47 percent of adult men unemployed; 2) more than 23 percent of 16- to 19-year-olds not enrolled in school; 3) more than 40 percent single-parent families; 4) more than 17 percent of families receiving public assistance; and 5) more than 28 percent of families are poor.

Source: O'Hare, William P. 1994. "3.9 Million U.S. Children in Distressed Neighborhoods," *Population Today* 22 (9) Population Reference Bureau, Inc., page 5.

E3. CHILD SUPPORT AND WELFARE

E3-1. Child Support Award Status of Women with Children from an Absent Father, Spring 1990

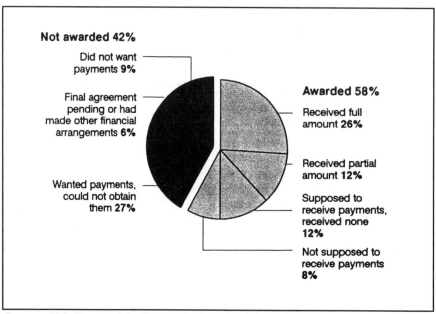

Source: U.S. Bureau of the Census, *Statistical Brief.* October 1991.

E3-2. Percentage of Women Who Are Supposed to Receive and Who Do Receive Child Support, 1981–1989

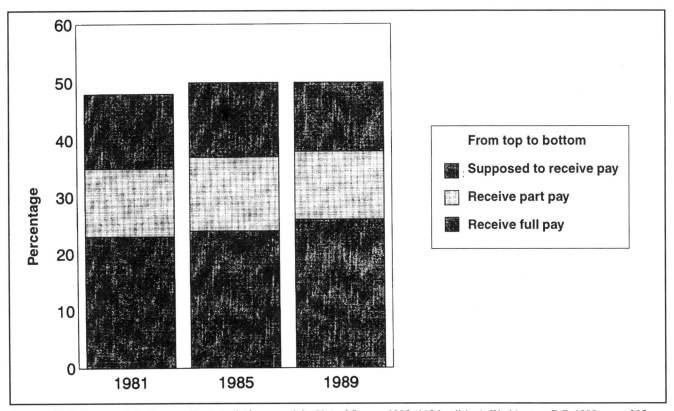

Source: U.S. Bureau of the Census, *Statistical Abstract of the United States: 1993* (113th edition). Washington, DC, 1993, page 385.

E3-3. Child Support—Award and Recipiency Status of Women, 1981–1989

Award and Recipiency Status	Number (1,000)			Percent distribution		
	1981	1985	1989	1981	1985	1989
ALL WOMEN						
Total	8,387	8,808	9,955	100	100	100
Payments awarded	4,969	5,396	5,748	59	61	58
Supposed to receive payments	4,043	4,381	4,953	48	50	50
Not supposed to receive payments	926	1,015	795	11	12	8
Payments not awarded	3,417	3,411	4,207	41	39	42
Supposed to receive payments	4,043	4,381	4,953	100	100	100
Actually received payments	2,902	3,243	3,725	72	74	75
Received full amount	1,888	2,112	2,546	47	48	51
Received partial amount	1,014	1,131	1,179	25	26	24
Did not receive payments	1,140	1,138	1,228	28	26	25
WOMEN BELOW THE POVERTY LEVEL						
Total	2,566	2,797	3,206	100	100	100
Payments awarded	1,018	1,130	1,387	40	40	43
Supposed to receive payments	806	905	1,190	31	32	37
Not supposed to receive payments	212	225	197	8	8	6
Payments not awarded	1,547	1,668	1,819	60	60	57
Supposed to receive payments	806	905	1,190	100	100	100
Actually received payments	495	595	813	61	66	68
Received full amount	NA	NA	NA	NA	NA	NA
Received partial amount	NA	NA	NA	NA	NA	NA
Did not receive payments	311	310	377	39	34	32

NA not available.

Source: U.S. Bureau of the Census, *Statistical Abstract of the United States: 1993* (113th edition). Washington, DC, 1993, page 385.

E3-4. Women's Incomes Who Were Awarded and Received Child Support, 1989

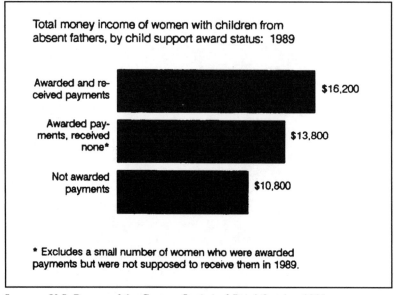

Total money income of women with children from absent fathers, by child support award status: 1989

Awarded and received payments — $16,200
Awarded payments, received none* — $13,800
Not awarded payments — $10,800

* Excludes a small number of women who were awarded payments but were not supposed to receive them in 1989.

Source: U.S. Bureau of the Census, *Statistical Brief.* October 1991.

E3-5. Child Support and Alimony, Selected Characteristics of Women, 1989

Recipiency Status of Women	Unit	Total¹	18-29 years	30-39 years	40 yrs and over	White	Black	Hispanic²	Divorced	Never Married³	Married	Separated
			AGE			RACE			CURRENT MARITAL STATUS			
CHILD SUPPORT												
All women, total	1,000	9,955	3,086	4,175	2,566	6,905	2,770	1,112	3,056	2,531	2,950	1,352
Payments awarded	1,000	5,748	1,408	2,685	1,632	4,661	955	452	2,347	1,999	704	648
Percent of total	Percent	58	46	64	64	68	35	41	77	79	24	48
Supposed to receive child support in 1989	1,000	4,953	1,208	2,413	1,309	4,048	791	364	2,123	1,685	583	527
% received payment	Percent	75	76	74	76	77	70	70	77	72	73	80
Mean child support	Dollars	2,995	1,981	3,032	3,903	3,132	2,263	2,965	3,322	2,931	1,888	3,060
% of total income	Percent	19	20	18	19	19	16	20	17	20	20	21
Women with incomes below the poverty level in 1989	1,000	3,206	1,531	1,189	434	1,763	1,314	536	820	176	1,590	612
Payments awarded	1,000	1,387	608	568	195	962	384	177	577	127	389	288
Percent of total	Percent	43	40	48	45	55	29	33	70	72	25	47
Supposed to receive child support in 1989	1,000	1,190	507	500	168	827	325	148	525	106	334	221
% received payment	Percent	68	68	67	72	68	70	64	66	67	69	74
Mean child support	Dollars	1,889	1,515	2,167	2,316	1,972	1,674	1,824	2,112	2,275	1,553	1,717
% of total income	Percent	37	33	36	56	39	32	37	38	52	34	35
ALIMONY												
All women, total	1,000	20,610	2,464	6,093	12,051	17,245	2,863	1,499	8,888	7,738	X	2,790
Number awarded payments	1,000	3,189	184	610	2,394	2,801	305	171	1,472	1,170	X	316
% of total	Percent	16	8	10	20	16	11	11	17	15	X	11
Supposed to receive payments	1,000	922	85	267	569	787	98	63	567	170	X	164
Women with incomes below the poverty level in 1989	1,000	3,692	726	1,206	1,758	2,640	931	477	1,860	420	X	1,147
Number awarded payments	1,000	429	60	96	273	340	76	31	223	55	X	110
% of total	Percent	12	8	8	16	13	8	6	12	13	X	10
Supposed to receive payments	1,000	178	43	56	79	149	26	21	112	11	X	54

X not applicable ¹ Includes other items, not shown separately. ² Hispanic women may be of any race. ³ Remarried women whose previous marriage ended in divorce.

Source: U.S. Bureau of the Census, *Statistical Abstract of the United States: 1993* (113th edition). Washington, DC, 1993, page 385.

E3-6. White and Black Poor Children in Self-Supporting and Welfare-Dependent Families, 1939–1988.

	1959		1969		Census 1979		CPS* 1979		CPS* 1988	
	White	Black	White	Black	White	Black	White	Black	White	Black
Relatively Poor Children: Percent by Family Work and Welfare Status										
Total Number (1,000s)	9,980	4,884	9,890	5,048	9,899	4,526	9,395	4,900	11,756	5,096
Fully self-supporting	72.3	65.0	73.1	53.5	65.9	42.6	59.3	30.5	60.0	35.0
Mainly self-supporting	16.4	19.0	11.0	18.2	12.8	17.8	13.4	21.7	12.9	14.8
Mainly welfare-dependent	5.3	8.5	7.3	11.1	8.4	12.5	14.1	21.4	12.9	22.0
Fully welfare-dependent	6.1	7.4	8.6	17.2	12.9	27.1	13.2	26.4	14.1	28.1
Total	100.0	100.0	100.0	100.0	100.0	100.0	100.0	100.0	100.0	100.0
Officially Poor Children:										
Total Number (1,000s)	10,683	5,031	6,352	3,998	6,252	3,377	6,191	3,762	7,983	4,226
Fully self-supporting	72.6	65.1	68.6	51.0	59.6	35.2	52.3	24.8	51.9	29.1
Mainly self-supporting	17.9	19.6	9.8	16.7	11.0	16.1	12.0	17.9	12.3	13.3
Mainly welfare-dependent	4.9	8.0	8.8	11.7	10.2	13.9	16.8	24.1	15.8	24.2
Fully welfare-dependent	4.7	7.4	12.8	20.6	19.2	34.8	18.9	33.2	20.0	33.4
Total	100.0	100.0	100.0	100.0	100.0	100.0	100.0	100.0	100.0	100.0

*CPS is the Current Population Survey.

Note: Officially poor is below the poverty level, relatively poor is below 125 percent of the poverty level.

Source:　Hernandez, Donald J. 1993. *America's Children: Resources from Family, Government, and the Economy.* New York: Russell Sage Foundation, page 304.

E4. PARENTAL EMPLOYMENT

E4-1. Percent of Children Aged 0–17 in Farm Families, Father-as-Breadwinner Families, Dual-Earner Families, and One-Parent Families, 1790–1989

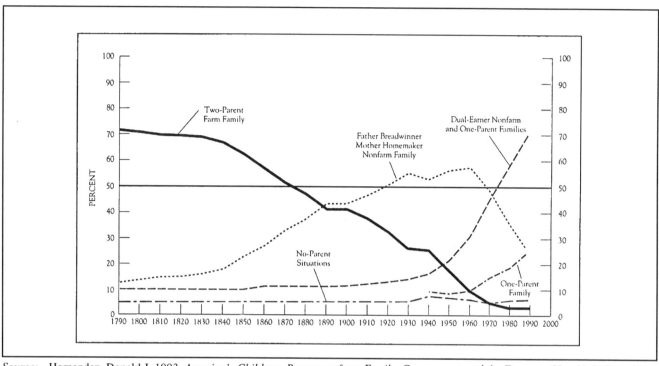

Source: Hernandez, Donald J. 1993. *America's Children: Resources from Family, Government, and the Economy.* New York: Russell Sage Foundation, page 103.

E4-2. Actual and Projected Percentage of Children under 18 with a Mother in the Labor Force, 1970–1995

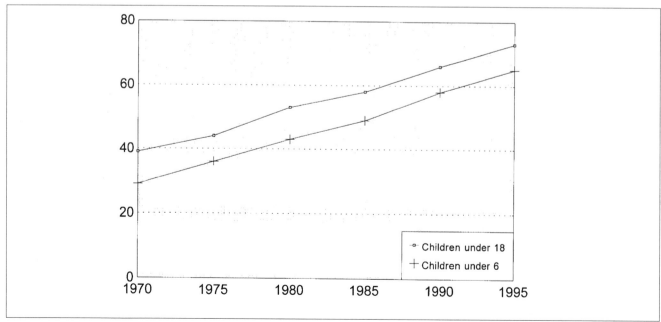

Source: Hofferth, Sandra L. and Deborah A. Phillips. 1987. "Child Care in the United States, 1970 to 1995." *Journal of Marriage and the Family* 49 (August) page 560.

E4-3. Employment of Women Who Had a Birth, 1992

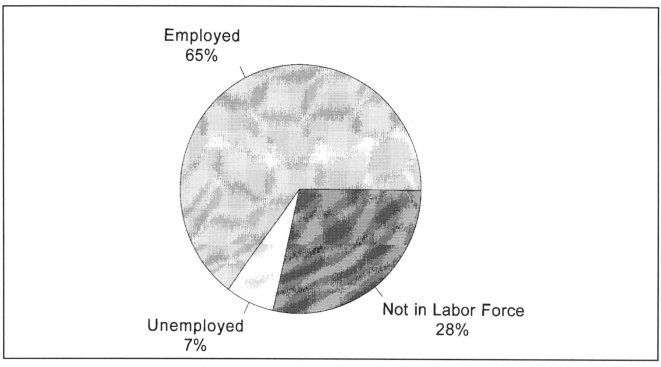

Source: Bachu, Amara. 1993. *Fertility of American Women: June 1992, U.S. Bureau of the Census, Current Population Reports, P20-470.* U.S. Government Printing Office, Washington, DC, page ix.

E4-4. Percent of Mothers (with Children Aged 17) Employed, by Race of Mother, 1940–1980

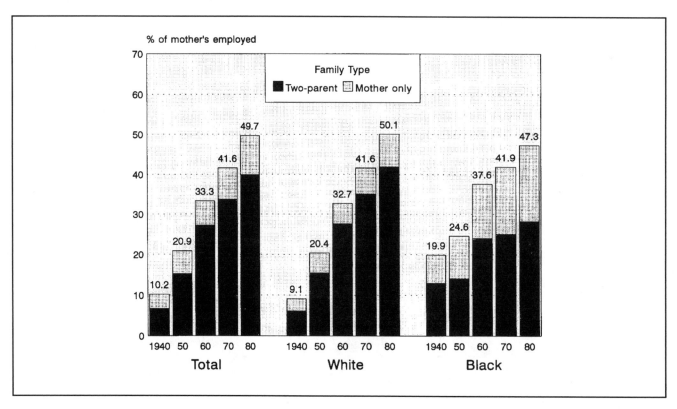

Source: Hernandez, Donald J. 1993. *America's Children: Resources from Family, Government, and the Economy.* New York: Russell Sage Foundation, pages 124–125.

E4-5. Mothers' Employment and Parental Living Arrangements for Children, 1980 and 1990

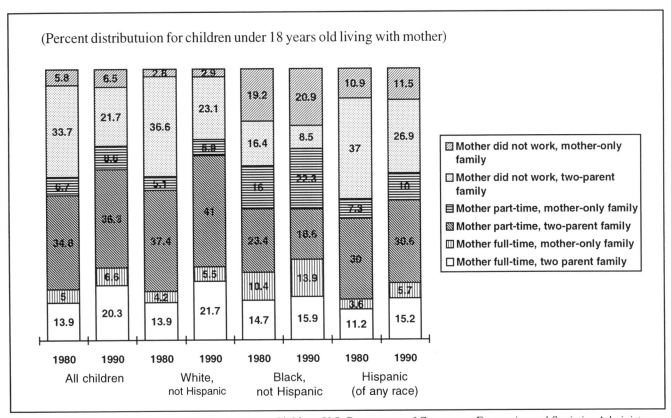

(Percent distributuion for children under 18 years old living with mother)

Legend:
- ▨ Mother did not work, mother-only family
- ▢ Mother did not work, two-parent family
- ▤ Mother part-time, mother-only family
- ▧ Mother part-time, two-parent family
- ▥ Mother full-time, mother-only family
- ▢ Mother full-time, two parent family

Categories (x-axis):
- All children — 1980, 1990
- White, not Hispanic — 1980, 1990
- Black, not Hispanic — 1980, 1990
- Hispanic (of any race) — 1980, 1990

Source: U.S. Bureau of the Census, *We the American Children.* U.S. Department of Commerce, Economics and Statistics Administration. Washington, DC, 1993, page 9.

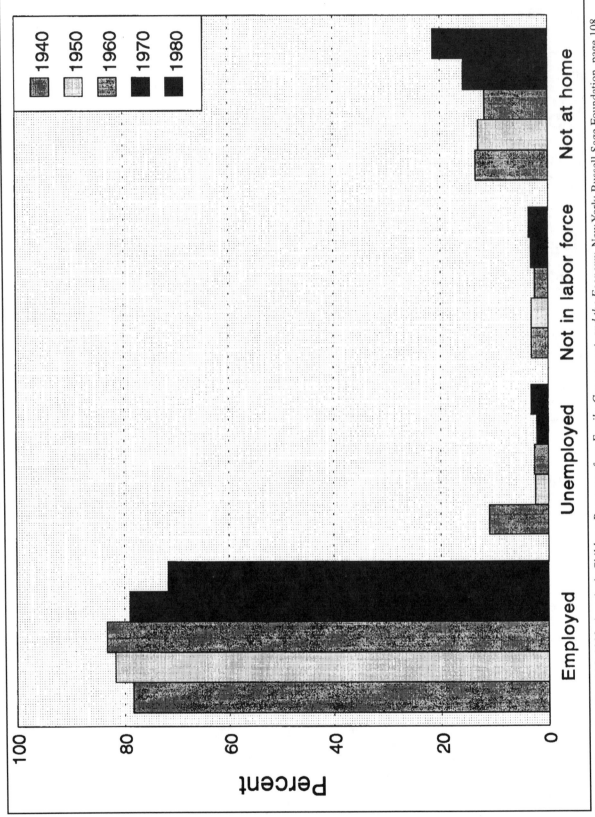

E4-6. Fathers' Labor Force Status of Children Aged 0–17, 1940–1980

Source: Hernandez, Donald J. 1993. *America's Children: Resources from Family, Government, and the Economy.* New York: Russell Sage Foundation, page 108.

E4-7. Fathers' Employment and Parental Living Arrangements for Children, 1980 and 1990

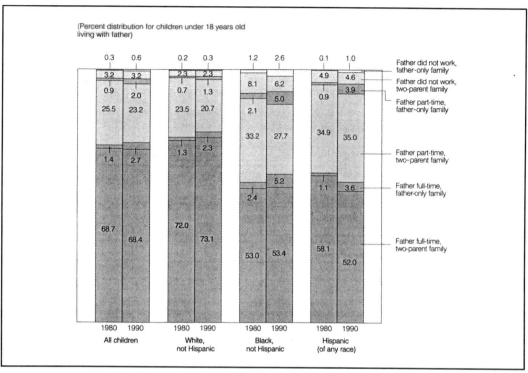

Source: U.S. Bureau of the Census, *We the American Children.* U.S. Department of Commerce, Economics and Statistics Administration. Washington, DC, 1993, page 8.

E4-8. Fathers' and Mothers' Employment and Parental Living Arrangements for Children, 1980 and 1990

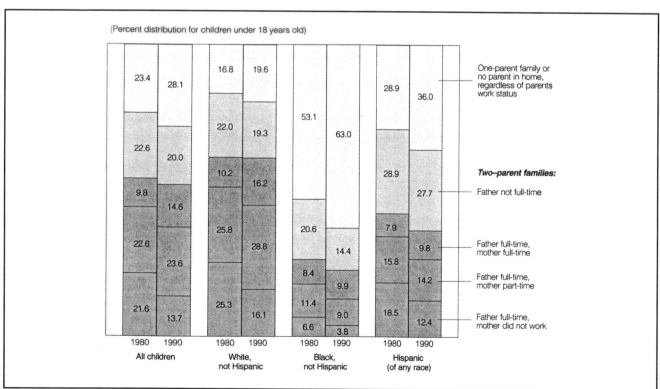

Source: U.S. Bureau of the Census, *We the American Children.* U.S. Department of Commerce, Economics and Statistics Administration. Washington, DC, 1993, page 10.

E5. PARENTAL EDUCATION

E5-1. Education of Parent for Children under 18, by Living Arrangements, 1992

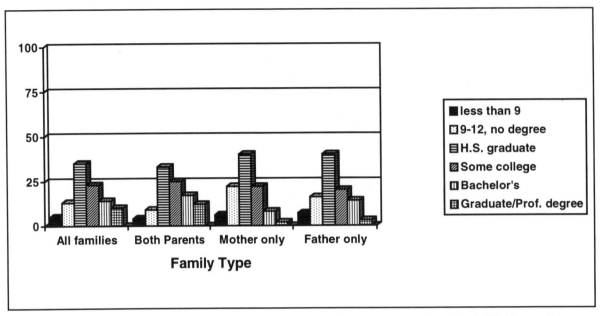

Source: U.S. Bureau of the Census, *Statistical Abstract of the United States: 1993* (113th edition). Washington, DC, 1993, page 63.

E5-2. Education of Parent for Children under 18 In Married-Couple Households, by Race, 1992

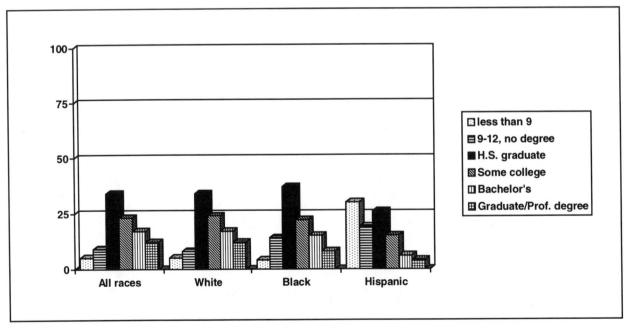

Source: U.S. Bureau of the Census, *Statistical Abstract of the United States: 1993* (113th edition). Washington, DC, 1993, page 63.

E5-3. Distribution of Children Born between the 1920s and 1980s, by Father's and Mother's Educational Attainments

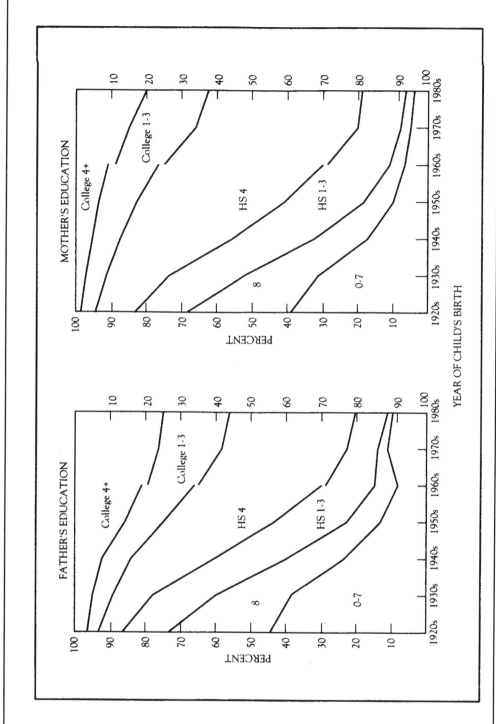

Source: Hernandez, Donald J. 1993. *America's Children: Resources from Family, Government, and the Economy.* New York: Russell Sage Foundation, page 196.

E5-4. Mothers' Educational Attainment, 1980 and 1990

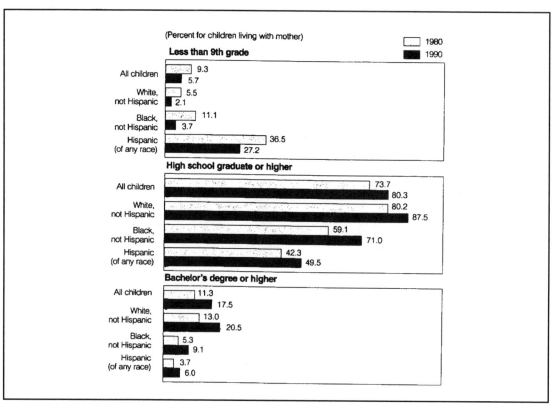

Source: U.S. Bureau of the Census, *We the American Children.* U.S. Department of Commerce, Economics and Statistics Administration. Washington, DC, 1993, page 7.

E5-5. Education of Women Who Had a Birth, 1992

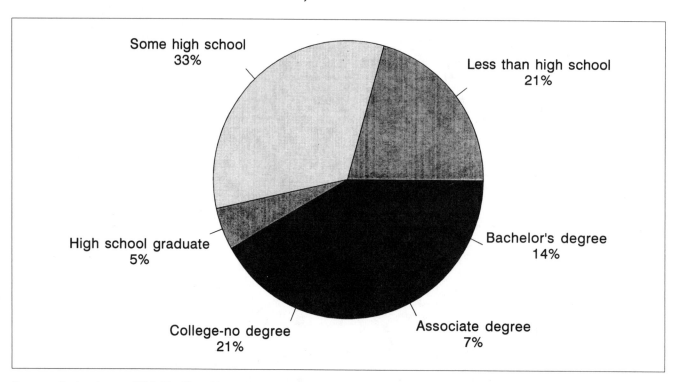

Source: Bachu, Amara. 1993. *Fertility of American Women: June 1992, U.S. Bureau of the Census, Current Population Reports, P20-470.* U.S. Government Printing Office, Washington, DC, page ix.

E6. ADOLESCENT LABOR FORCE PARTICIPATION

E6-1. Activity of Persons Aged 10–24, 1992

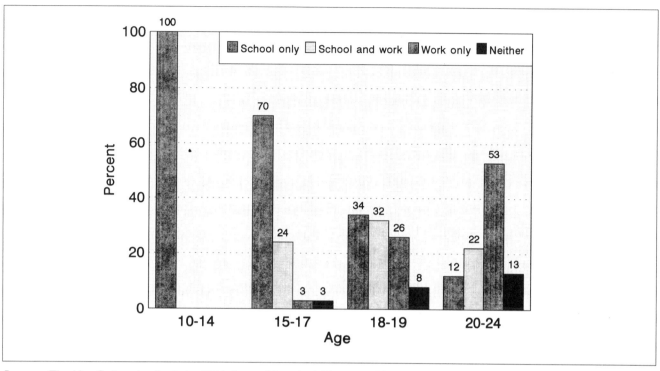

Source: The Alan Guttmacher Institute. 1994. *Sex and America's Teenagers.* New York: The Alan Guttmacher Institute, page 16.

E6-2. Labor Force Participation Rate of Adolescents, 1970–1992

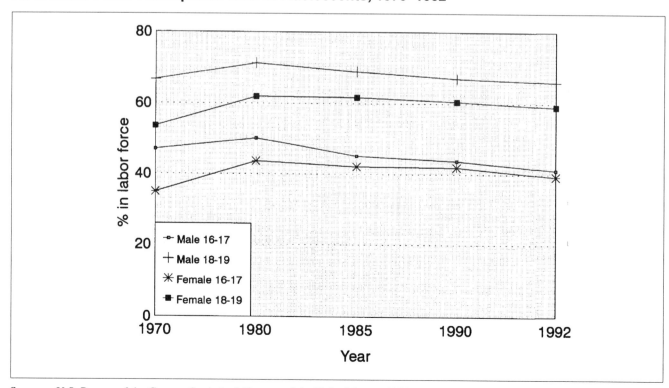

Source: U.S. Bureau of the Census, *Statistical Abstract of the United States: 1993* (113th edition). Washington, DC, 1993, page 393.

E6-3. Labor Force Participation Rate, Ages 16–19, 1960–1992

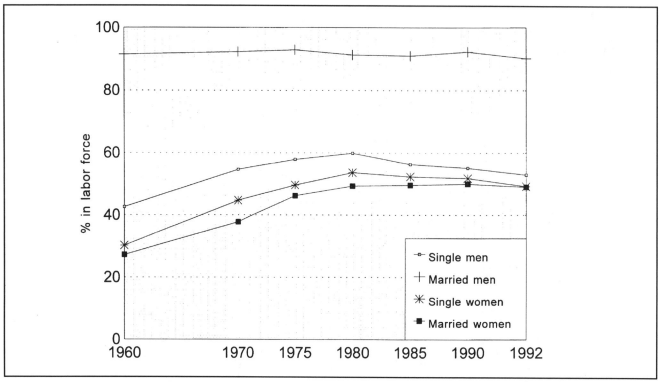

Source: U.S. Bureau of the Census, *Statistical Abstract of the United States: 1993* (113th edition). Washington, DC, 1993, page 399.

E6-4. Median Hourly Earnings for Workers Aged 16–19, by Sex, 1992

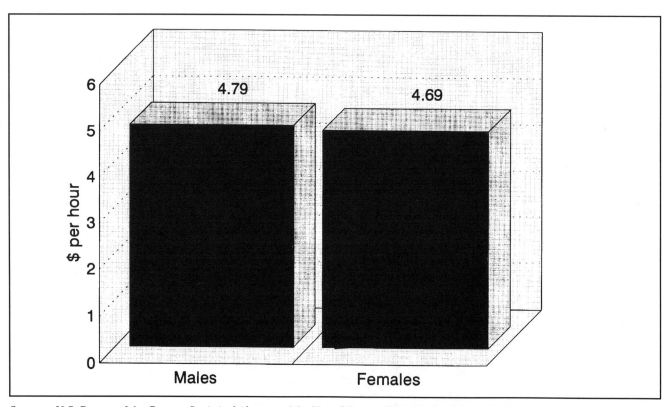

Source: U.S. Bureau of the Census, *Statistical Abstract of the United States: 1993* (113th edition). Washington, DC, 1993, page 429.

E6-5. Work Schedules of 16- to 19-Year-Olds Compared to the Total Work Force, 1991

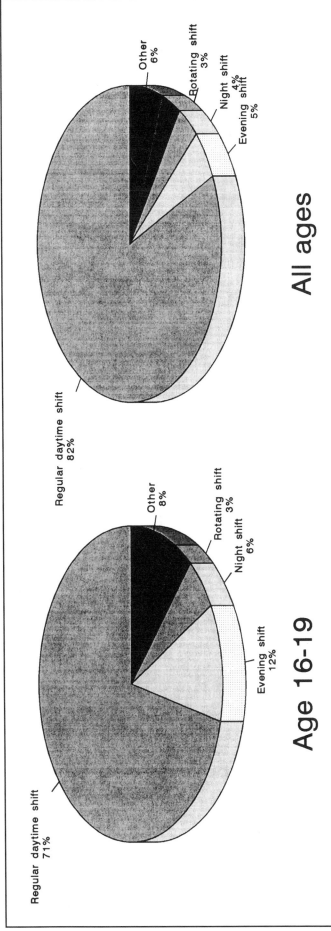

All ages

Regular daytime shift
82%

Other
6%

Rotating shift
3%

Night shift
4%

Evening shift
5%

Age 16-19

Regular daytime shift
71%

Other
8%

Rotating shift
3%

Night shift
6%

Evening shift
12%

Source: U.S. Bureau of the Census, *Statistical Abstract of the United States: 1993* (113th edition). Washington, DC, 1993, page 404.

E6-6. Contribution of Adolescents to Family Finances by Sex, Age, Race, and Social Class, 1992

Survey question: How much does your family depend upon you to work and earn money—a great deal, a fair amount, a little, or not at all?

Characteristic	Great deal	Fair amount	Little	Not at all
National	**7%**	**21%**	**25%**	**46%**
Sex:				
Male	7	23	26	44
Female	6	19	24	50
Age:				
13-15 years	6	22	25	46
16-17 years	8	18	26	48
Race:				
White	5	19	27	47
Non-white	11	24	18	47
Social class:				
White-collar background	5	19	26	50
Blue-collar background	9	23	25	43

Source: Bezilla, Robert (ed.). 1993. *American's Youth in the 1990s.* Princeton, NJ: The George H. Gallup International Institute, page 266.

E6-7. Possession of Economic Documents, by Sex, Age, Race, and Social Class, 1992

Survey question: Which, if any, of the following do you, yourself, how have—Social security card? Savings account? Checking account? Credit card?

Characteristic	Social security card	Savings account	Checking account	Credit card
National	**86%**	**62%**	**19%**	**4%**
Sex:				
Male	84	63	18	2
Female	87	62	21	6
Age:				
13-15 years	78	57	12	3
16-17 years	97	70	29	6
Race:				
White	85	68	21	4
Non-white	88	39	12	4
Social class:				
White-collar background	84	73	22	5
Blue-collar background	88	54	19	4

Source: Bezilla, Robert (ed.). 1993. *American's Youth in the 1990s.* Princeton, NJ: The George H. Gallup International Institute, page 268.

E6-8. Employment Experience of High School Seniors, by Sex and Race, 1992

	Total (N=2,727)	Sex		Race	
		Males (N=1,270)	Females (N=1,360)	White (N=1,847)	Black (N=378)
Employment experience:					
I have a paid job now	56.1%	55.3%	56.5%	61.5%	39.8%
No paid job now, but I had one during the past three months	12.8	14.0	11.9	12.0	11.0
No paid job in the past three months	21.3	21.9	20.6	19.7	30.9
Never had a paid job	9.8	8.8	11.0	6.8	18.4
Type of work:					
Have not worked for pay	0.7%	0.8%	0.6%	0.4%	2.0%
Lawn work	1.4	2.6	0.4	1.3	2.0
Fast food worker	16.6	16.2	16.5	15.0	27.6
Waiter or waitress	7.6	5.4	9.9	8.8	1.0
Newspaper route	0.4	0.6	0.3	0.4	1.0
Babysitting or childcare	6.7	1.1	12.0	6.6	8.6
Farm or agricultural work	4.0	7.3	0.9	4.1	0.2
Store clerk\salesperson	26.0	24.1	27.8	26.8	22.9
Office or clerical	10.3	4.2	16.1	9.5	11.7
Odd jobs	2.7	3.8	1.6	2.6	2.2
Other	23.6	33.9	14.0	24.6	20.9
Job satisfaction:					
Completely dissatisfied	6.6%	7.2%	5.9%	6.2%	8.6%
Quite dissatisfied	8.5	9.0	8.2	8.8	7.8
Somewhat dissatisfied	9.2	10.5	8.2	9.9	5.7
Neither/mixed feelings	14.4	14.1	14.7	12.6	17.8
Somewhat satisfied	23.7	24.5	22.7	22.3	32.6
Quite satisfied	27.4	25.5	29.8	29.3	22.1
Completely satisfied	10.1	9.3	10.4	10.8	5.4
Hours per week on job:					
5 or less hours	8.6%	6.7%	10.4%	7.8%	13.8%
6 to 10 hours	13.1	12.7	13.5	13.1	12.0
11 to 15 hours	17.7	14.9	19.6	17.5	19.4
16 to 20 hours	23.5	23.0	24.2	25.0	20.5
21 to 25 hours	16.1	16.6	15.7	16.0	15.4
26 to 30 hours	10.4	11.5	9.3	10.4	9.6
31 to 35 hours	4.2	5.5	3.1	4.2	6.2
36 or more hours	6.5	9.1	4.2	6.1	3.0
Preferred work hours during school year:					
None	5.9%	6.4%	5.5%	6.3%	3.0%
5 or less hours	3.5	2.5	4.5	2.7	4.6
6-10	10.4	9.1	12.1	11.1	8.2
11-15	12.0	11.2	13.4	14.8	4.4
16-20	19.1	18.6	19.9	21.0	14.3
21-25	14.0	13.9	14.2	14.2	15.2
26-30	9.5	10.5	9.1	9.8	10.2
31 or more hours	11.5	13.9	9.4	9.5	16.4
Don't know, can't say	14.2	14.0	11.8	10.5	23.7

E6-8. Employment Experience of High School Seniors, by Sex and Race, 1992 (continued)

	Total (N=2,727)	Sex		Race	
		Males (N=1,270)	Females (N=1,360)	White (N=1,847)	Black (N=378)
Hours parents prefer kids to work:					
None	11.2%	9.2%	13.2%	11.8%	6.5%
5 or less hours	4.7	3.9	5.7	4.3	4.9
6-10	10.5	9.3	12.0	11.6	9.0
11-15	12.2	11.3	13.4	13.8	6.9
16-20	15.9	15.9	16.0	17.3	11.6
21-25	8.2	8.9	7.7	8.0	11.2
26-30	5.2	5.2	5.4	5.1	4.8
31 or more hours	7.6	11.1	4.4	6.6	10.5
Don't know, can't say	24.6	25.2	22.2	21.5	34.7

N= Sample size

Source: Bachman, Jerald G., Lloyd D. Johnston, and Patrick M. O'Malley. 1993. *Monitoring the Future: Questionnaire Responses from the Nation's High School Seniors, 1992.* Ann Arbor, MI: Survey Research Center, Institute for Social Research, The University of Michigan, pages 173–174.

E6-9. Characteristics of Jobs Held by High School Seniors, by Sex and Race, 1992

	Total (N=2,727)	Sex		Race	
		Males (N=1,270)	Females (N=1,360)	White (N=1,847)	Black (N=378)
TO WHAT EXTENT DOES THIS JOB. . .					
Use your skills and abilities:					
Not at all	21.9%	25.0%	18.7%	21.9%	28.5%
A little	27.0	25.8	28.5	27.6	25.7
Some extent	25.8	24.2	27.2	26.7	22.3
Considerable extent	14.0	12.4	15.5	12.6	10.8
A great extent	11.3	12.7	10.1	11.3	12.6
Interfere with family life:					
Not at all	48.0%	47.2%	48.7%	44.9%	65.0%
A little	22.4	21.8	23.0	24.1	13.0
Some extent	16.3	16.2	16.0	17.3	11.9
Considerable extent	6.9	7.9	6.3	6.8	5.8
A great extent	6.5	6.9	6.0	7.0	4.4
TO WHAT EXTENT IS THIS JOB. . .					
An interesting job to do:					
Not at all	21.0%	22.3%	19.8%	22.0%	18.4%
A little	22.0	24.3	20.1	21.7	21.5
Some extent	26.0	24.2	27.2	25.7	27.0
Considerable extent	17.2	15.1	19.3	16.0	18.5
A great extent	13.9	14.1	13.6	14.6	14.7
One I'd be happy doing the rest of my life:					
Not at all	66.5%	64.2%	68.5%	67.0%	69.8%
A little	12.1	11.3	12.9	12.9	6.3
Some extent	10.2	11.5	8.8	9.6	11.5
Considerable extent	5.2	6.7	3.9	4.7	6.9
A great extent	6.0	6.3	5.9	5.9	5.5

E6-9. Characteristics of Jobs Held by High School Seniors, by Sex and Race, 1992 (continued)

	Total (N=2,727)	Sex		Race	
		Males (N=1,270)	Females (N=1,360)	White (N=1,847)	Black (N=378)
Type of work you expect for rest of life:					
Not at all	75.6%	72.6%	78.5%	77.2%	75.1%
A little	8.5	8.4	8.6	7.8	11.4
Some extent	6.9	8.3	5.4	6.9	6.0
Considerable extent	4.2	6.0	2.5	3.6	3.9
A great extent	4.8	4.6	4.9	4.5	3.6
A stepping-stone toward desired work:					
Not at all	56.9%	52.8%	60.5%	56.7%	60.6%
A little	15.7	14.6	16.7	16.9	11.2
Some extent	10.4	12.9	8.1	9.9	11.3
Considerable extent	8.3	10.0	6.6	7.7	10.0
A great extent	8.7	9.7	8.1	8.7	6.9
Kind of work people do just for money:					
Not at all	19.3%	18.5%	19.7%	19.5%	18.0%
A little	18.1	17.1	19.2	17.6	17.7
Some extent	18.2	19.5	17.2	18.7	13.7
Considerable extent	16.5	16.6	16.9	16.9	13.3
A great extent	27.9	28.3	27.0	27.3	37.3

N = Sample Size

Source: Bachman, Jerald G., Lloyd D. Johnston, and Patrick M. O'Malley. 1993. *Monitoring the Future: Questionnaire Responses from the Nation's High School Seniors, 1992.* Ann Arbor, MI: Survey Research Center, Institute for Social Research, The University of Michigan, pages 175–176.

E6-10. Feelings of Job Security for High School Seniors with a Job, by Sex and Race, 1992

	Total (N=2,727)	Sex		Race	
		Males (N=1,270)	Females (N=1,360)	White (N=1,847)	Black (N=378)
I can keep working:					
Never	6.5%	7.9%	4.6%	5.1%	15.6%
Seldom	5.1	5.5	4.9	5.3	4.0
Sometimes	15.8	14.7	16.3	14.0	19.3
Often	27.6	30.0	26.0	29.2	18.7
Always	45.1	42.0	48.2	46.4	42.5
I worry about losing my job:					
Never	57.1%	53.7%	60.1%	60.2%	48.7%
Seldom	24.7	24.5	25.6	24.5	27.4
Sometimes	12.1	14.1	9.6	10.4	14.9
Often	3.8	4.7	3.1	3.4	5.2
Always	2.3	3.0	1.8	1.4	3.8

N = Sample Size

Source: Bachman, Jerald G., Lloyd D. Johnston, and Patrick M. O'Malley. 1993. *Monitoring the Future: Questionnaire Responses from the Nation's High School Seniors, 1992.* Ann Arbor, MI: Survey Research Center, Institute for Social Research, The University of Michigan, p. 208.

E6-11. High School Seniors' Perceptions of Factors that May Prevent Them from Obtaining Work They Desire, by Sex and Race, 1992

Question: To what extent do you think the things listed below will prevent you from getting the kind of work you would like to have?

Factor	Total (N=2,727)	Sex		Race	
		Males (N=1,270)	Females (N=1,360)	White (N=1,847)	Black (N=378)
Your religion:					
Not at all	88.1%	86.4%	90.6%	90.7%	82.0%
Somewhat	5.5	5.9	5.1	5.1	6.6
A lot	1.6	1.9	1.1	1.0	2.8
Don't know	4.7	5.7	3.2	3.3	8.6
Your sex:					
Not at all	72.0%	86.2%	59.2%	72.9%	66.2%
Somewhat	21.1	9.4	32.3	21.8	23.9
A lot	4.4	2.4	6.0	3.3	5.8
Don't know	2.4	1.9	2.6	1.9	4.1
Your race:					
Not at all	77.4%	75.9%	79.5%	89.5%	37.0%
Somewhat	13.3	13.9	12.6	6.6	33.8
A lot	6.1	6.6	5.4	1.9	22.3
Don't know	3.1	3.6	2.5	2.0	7.0
Your family background:					
Not at all	84.2%	82.2%	87.0%	88.2%	79.6%
Somewhat	9.8	11.0	8.6	7.9	11.3
A lot	2.3	2.6	1.9	1.5	4.0
Don't know	3.6	4.1	2.6	2.4	5.1

E6-11. High School Seniors' Perceptions of Factors that May Prevent Them from Obtaining Work They Desire, by Sex and Race, 1992 (continued)

		Sex		Race	
	Total	Males	Females	White	Black
Factor	(N=2,727)	(N=1,270)	(N=1,360)	(N=1847)	(N=378)
Your political views:					
Not at all	79.2%	78.0%	80.6%	82.3%	69.9%
Somewhat	11.2	12.1	10.7	10.5	14.8
A lot	2.7	3.5	1.9	2.1	3.1
Don't know	6.9	6.4	6.9	5.1	12.3
Your education:					
Not at all	43.5%	42.5%	44.5%	44.4%	44.1%
Somewhat	21.1	22.4	19.8	21.4	17.2
A lot	31.6	31.4	32.3	30.6	34.3
Don't know	3.8	3.8	3.4	3.6	4.4
Lack of vocational training:					
Not at all	51.8%	50.2%	53.1%	54.5%	49.3%
Somewhat	24.5	26.5	23.2	22.9	25.0
A lot	14.3	14.2	14.4	13.4	16.2
Don't know	9.5	9.0	9.4	9.2	9.5
Lack of ability:					
Not at all	55.5%	55.7%	54.8%	56.5%	54.0%
Somewhat	14.8	15.1	14.4	14.3	14.1
A lot	26.0	25.0	27.5	25.3	30.1
Don't know	3.7	4.1	3.3	3.9	1.8
Not knowing the right people:					
Not at all	45.8%	44.0%	47.5%	45.3%	44.6%
Somewhat	36.5	37.5	36.0	37.6	38.4
A lot	10.2	11.8	9.0	10.1	9.4
Don't know	7.5	6.7	7.5	7.1	7.7
Not wanting to work hard:					
Not at all	56.5%	55.3%	57.4%	58.2%	55.0%
Somewhat	9.3	9.5	8.8	8.6	8.2
A lot	32.1	33.0	32.0	31.3	35.0
Don't know	2.2	2.1	1.9	2.0	1.8
Not wanting to conform:					
Not at all	47.0%	44.2%	49.1%	47.2%	48.0%
Somewhat	22.7	24.4	21.6	24.2	17.2
A lot	18.6	20.5	17.6	17.7	21.5
Don't know	11.7	10.9	11.8	11.0	13.3

N = Sample Size

Source: Bachman, Jerald G., Lloyd D. Johnston, and Patrick M. O'Malley. 1993. *Monitoring the Future: Questionnaire Responses from the Nation's High School Seniors, 1992.* Ann Arbor, MI: Survey Research Center, Institute for Social Research, The University of Michigan, pp. 166–167.

E6-12. High School Seniors' Attitudes about Selected Characteristics of Work, by Sex and Race, 1992

Question: Different people may look for different things in their work. Below is a list of some of these things. Please read each one, then indicate how important this thing is for you.

		Sex		Race	
Job Characteristics	Total (N=2,727)	Males (N=1,270)	Females (N=1,360)	White (N=1,847)	Black (N=378)
Interesting:					
Not important	0.5%	0.7%	0.4%	0.1%	1.8%
A little important	1.4	1.3	0.9	0.8	3.4
Pretty important	11.1	12.4	9.4	10.8	11.4
Very important	87.0	85.6	89.3	88.3	83.5
Use skills and abilities:					
Not important	0.5%	1.0%	0.1%	0.4%	0.6%
A little important	2.8	3.0	2.6	3.2	2.5
Pretty important	22.4	25.8	19.5	23.8	16.1
Very important	74.3	70.3	77.8	72.6	80.7
No pretentions:					
Not important	4.2%	5.7%	2.7%	3.2%	5.9%
A little important	4.5	6.2	2.7	4.3	5.4
Pretty important	17.2	21.4	12.7	18.0	11.5
Very important	74.1	66.7	81.9	74.5	77.1
Reasonably secure future:					
Not important	1.0%	1.4%	0.5%	1.1%	0.3%
A little important	4.6	5.3	3.6	5.0	2.4
Pretty important	26.1	28.4	24.2	28.8	18.6
Very important	68.4	64.9	71.7	65.0	78.7
Advancement:					
Not important	1.6%	1.9%	1.4%	1.9%	0.2%
A little important	8.0	6.6	9.4	9.0	4.3
Pretty important	28.8	28.3	29.2	33.0	19.0
Very important	61.6	63.1	59.9	56.2	76.4
See results:					
Not important	1.3%	2.2%	0.5%	1.3%	1.0%
A little important	6.9	7.4	6.1	7.4	6.2
Pretty Important	34.8	38.2	32.1	37.8	22.5
Very important	57.0	52.2	61.3	53.5	70.3
Earn good deal of money:					
Not important	2.6%	2.6%	2.6%	3.4%	0.3%
A little important	9.5	8.9	10.6	11.7	2.3
Pretty important	31.9	28.6	35.5	35.5	20.5
Very important	55.9	59.9	51.3	49.5	76.9
Skills will not go out of date:					
Not important	4.9%	5.2%	4.4%	5.2%	3.4%
A little important	12.0	11.1	12.8	13.6	9.0
Pretty important	27.7	28.4	26.7	29.9	17.6
Very important	55.5	55.3	56.2	51.4	69.9

E6-12. High School Seniors' Attitudes about Selected Characteristics of Work, by Sex and Race, 1992 (continued)

		Sex		Race	
Job Characteristics	Total (N=2,727)	Males (N=1,270)	Females (N=1,360)	White (N=1,847)	Black (N=378)
Opportunity to help:					
Not important	3.1%	5.5%	0.7%	3.4%	1.2%
A little important	12.9	17.9	7.8	14.7	5.0
Pretty important	32.3	39.4	26.0	32.9	35.2
Very important	51.7	37.2	65.5	48.9	58.6
Learn new skills:					
Not important	1.4%	2.1%	0.8%	1.6%	1.0%
A little important	11.7	13.4	10.1	13.6	5.8
Pretty important	38.4	38.9	38.9	41.9	29.2
Very important	48.4	45.6	50.3	42.8	63.9
Worthwhile to society:					
Not important	3.7%	5.6%	2.0%	3.8%	2.7%
A little important	13.6	17.5	9.9	14.2	9.7
Pretty important	34.5	35.6	33.1	34.1	34.4
Very important	48.2	41.3	55.1	47.9	53.2
Chance to make friends:					
Not important	4.1%	4.5%	3.3%	3.2%	7.3%
A little important	12.7	14.2	11.1	11.8	16.4
Pretty important	35.3	38.4	32.2	36.0	37.5
Very important	48.0	43.0	53.4	49.0	38.9
Respect:					
Not important	5.6%	6.9%	4.7%	6.2%	3.5%
A little important	14.7	16.3	13.3	16.4	10.8
Pretty important	33.0	33.1	33.0	35.3	24.6
Very important	46.6	43.7	48.9	42.0	61.2
Roots in a community:					
Not important	8.3%	8.8%	7.8%	8.7%	7.0%
A little important	16.1	17.0	15.2	17.4	15.4
Pretty important	32.6	33.7	31.5	32.9	29.2
Very important	43.1	40.6	45.5	41.1	48.3
Creativity:					
Not important	4.7%	4.1%	5.3%	5.2%	3.7%
A little important	18.6	19.4	18.0	20.5	14.2
Pretty important	34.9	34.6	35.2	34.0	34.8
Very important	41.9	41.9	41.5	40.2	47.3
Make decisions:					
Not important	4.0%	4.5%	3.4%	4.6%	2.7%
A little important	16.1	16.6	15.8	16.6	12.8
Pretty important	40.8	39.8	41.9	41.8	38.1
Very important	39.1	39.1	38.9	37.0	46.4
Time for other things:					
Not important	2.3%	2.9%	1.9%	2.4%	1.9%
A little important	19.1	16.3	21.7	20.5	17.3
Pretty important	39.9	38.7	40.5	42.1	35.1
Very important	38.6	42.1	35.9	35.0	45.7

E6-12. High School Seniors' Attitudes about Selected Characteristics of Work, by Sex and Race, 1992 (continued)

	Total (N=2,727)	Sex		Race	
		Males (N=1,270)	Females (N=1,360)	White (N=1,847)	Black (N=378)
Contact with people:					
Not important	10.5%	14.3%	6.7%	10.7%	12.3%
A little important	21.0	25.0	16.5	21.0	25.8
Pretty important	34.0	34.4	34.1	32.3	32.8
Very important	34.5	26.3	42.7	35.9	29.1
High status:					
Not important	9.1%	9.3%	9.3%	10.8%	4.5%
A little important	25.5	23.9	27.2	29.1	15.7
Pretty important	35.0	34.5	35.4	34.4	34.4
Very important	30.3	32.3	28.1	25.7	45.4
Free of supervision:					
Not important	7.9%	7.5%	8.4%	7.6%	11.9%
A little important	25.6	22.6	28.7	26.9	21.8
Pretty important	36.7	38.4	34.6	38.0	31.1
Very important	29.8	31.5	28.3	27.5	35.2
More than two weeks vacation:					
Not important	18.3%	15.0%	21.5%	19.4%	22.0%
A little important	33.8	29.6	37.8	35.0	31.3
Pretty important	24.2	25.8	22.4	23.8	21.3
Very important	23.8	29.6	18.4	21.9	25.4
Difficult and challenging problems:					
Not important	16.0%	17.1%	15.4%	15.6%	17.6%
A little important	35.0	33.4	36.9	37.9	27.8
Pretty important	33.4	33.0	33.4	32.1	35.3
Very important	15.6	16.5	14.3	14.4	19.4
Easy pace, work slowly:					
Not important	23.9%	22.0%	25.9%	26.0%	23.4%
A little important	36.1	35.3	36.7	37.8	33.0
Pretty important	27.0	27.7	26.2	24.9	26.0
Very important	13.1	15.0	11.2	11.4	17.6

N = Sample Size

Source: Bachman, Jerald G., Lloyd D. Johnston, and Patrick M. O'Malley. 1993. *Monitoring the Future: Questionnaire Responses from the Nation's High School Seniors, 1992.* Ann Arbor, MI: Survey Research Center, Institute for Social Research, The University of Michigan, pp. 161–164.

E6-13. Financial Concerns of High School Seniors, by Sex and Race, 1992

	Total (N=2,727)	Sex		Race	
		Males (N=1,270)	Females (N=1,360)	White (N=1,847)	Black (N=378)
Have enough money:					
Never	13.0%	11.0%	14.9%	10.7%	23.8%
Seldom	21.8	22.7	21.0	22.0	21.7
Sometimes	33.0	32.4	33.4	32.4	30.0
Often	22.3	23.9	21.0	24.1	16.1
Always	9.9	10.0	9.7	10.7	8.5
Concerned about bills:					
Never	28.8%	27.4%	30.7%	27.3%	42.9%
Seldom	24.0	23.7	23.9	25.0	20.4
Sometimes	25.3	25.6	24.7	26.8	17.2
Often	14.7	16.0	13.5	15.0	12.0
Always	7.2	7.3	7.2	5.9	7.5
Worry about having a job in a few months:					
Never	38.8%	37.3%	40.5%	41.3%	35.4%
Seldom	23.2	24.4	22.1	23.9	18.5
Sometimes	19.4	19.4	19.5	19.6	18.2
Often	11.2	10.5	11.3	10.1	11.7
Always	7.4	8.4	6.6	5.0	16.2
I feel I could get a new job:					
Never	13.3%	11.2%	15.2%	11.9%	23.2%
Seldom	22.9	20.5	24.8	22.2	23.4
Sometimes	32.0	31.3	33.0	32.1	28.4
Often	20.0	22.3	17.9	22.3	13.4
Always	11.8	14.6	9.2	11.5	11.7

N = Sample Size

Source: Bachman, Jerald G., Lloyd D. Johnston, and Patrick M. O'Malley. 1993. *Monitoring the Future: Questionnaire Responses from the Nation's High School Seniors, 1992.* Ann Arbor, MI: Survey Research Center, Institute for Social Research, The University of Michigan, pp. 207–208.

E6-14. Type of Work High School Seniors Perceive They Will Be Engaged in When They Are 30 Years of Age, by Sex and Race, 1992

Question: What kind of work do you think you will be doing when you are 30 years old?

	Total (N=2,736)	Sex		Race	
		Males (N=1,248)	Females (N=1,352)	White (N=1,886)	Black (N-381)
Laborer (car washer, sanitary worker, farm laborer)	0.3%	0.5%	—	0.3%	—
Service worker (cook, waiter, barber, janitor, gas station attendant, practical nurse, beautician)	2.0	1.3	2.6%	2.0	1.8%
Operative or semi-skilled worker (garage worker, taxicab, bus or truck driver, assembly line worker, welder)	1.2	2.2	0.3	1.5	0.6
Sales clerk in a retail store (shoe salesperson, department store clerk, drug store clerk)	0.5	0.6	0.4	0.3	0.7
Clerical or office worker (bank teller, bookkeeper, secretary, typist, postal clerk or carrier, ticket agent)	5.2	0.7	9.1	4.8	7.7
Protective service (police officer, fireman, detective)	4.9	8.0	2.0	4.7	4.6
Military service	3.1	5.1	1.2	2.9	4.8
Craftsman or skilled worker (carpenter, electrician, brick layer, mechanic, machinist, tool and die maker, telephone installer)	6.1	11.9	0.8	6.0	5.0
Farm owner, farm manager	**1.1**	**1.7**	**0.6**	**1.1**	—
Owner of small business (restaurant owner, shop owner)	4.3	5.2	3.5	4.4	4.1
Sales representative (insurance agent, real estate broker, bond salesman)	2.2	3.3	1.0	1.8	2.3
Manager or administrator (office manager, sales manager, school administrator, government official)	7.4	6.7	8.2	7.3	10.1
Professional without doctoral degree (registered nurse, librarian, engineer, architect, social worker, technician, accountant, actor, artist, musician)	33.8	29.2	38.2	34.3	35.1
Professional with doctoral degree or equivalent (lawyer, physician, dentist, scientist, college professor)	20.2	16.5	23.7	20.8	18.6
Full-time homemaker or housewife	0.9	—	1.8	1.2	—
Don't know	6.7	6.9	6.7	6.7	4.7

— too few cases
n = Sample Size

Source: Bachman, Jerald G., Lloyd D. Johnston, and Patrick M. O'Malley. 1993. *Monitoring the Future: Questionnaire Responses from the Nation's High School Seniors, 1992.* Ann Arbor, MI: Survey Research Center, Institute for Social Research, The University of Michigan, p. 165.

E6-15. What High School Seniors Have Done with Money They Have Earned during the Past Year, by Sex and Race, 1992

Question: Please think about all the money you earned during the past year, including last summer. About how much of your past year's earnings have gone into:

	Total (N=2727)	Sex		Race	
		Males (N=1270)	Females (N=1360)	White (N=1847)	Black (N=378)
Savings for future education:					
None	53.1%	53.2%	52.6%	51.7%	57.7%
A little (1-20%)	19.9	22.5	17.8	20.8	16.0
Some (21-40%)	11.1	10.1	11.8	11.7	9.3
About half (41-60%)	6.3	5.1	7.4	6.0	7.2
Most (61-80%)	5.5	4.8	6.4	5.7	6.4
Almost all (81-99%)	3.1	3.1	3.2	3.5	0.7
All	1.1	1.3	0.9	0.7	2.7
Savings/payments for car:					
None	42.9%	36.2%	49.3%	37.8%	68.5%
A little (1-20%)	17.0	18.4	15.7	19.0	8.0
Some (21-40%)	15.4	17.9	13.1	16.3	12.2
About half (41-60%)	10.5	12.6	8.4	11.1	4.8
Most (61-80%)	8.0	7.9	8.0	9.5	3.6
Almost all (81-99%)	4.1	4.6	3.7	4.5	1.1
All	2.0	2.3	1.8	1.8	1.8
Long-range purposes:					
None	48.5%	46.9%	49.9%	46.8%	55.6%
A little (1-20%)	23.5	25.9	21.6	24.6	17.5
Some (21-40%)	13.3	13.2	13.5	13.4	13.8
About half (41-60%)	6.1	6.2	5.8	6.7	4.9
Most (61-80%)	4.4	4.5	4.1	4.6	3.8
Almost all (81-99%)	2.9	1.8	3.9	2.7	2.4
All	1.3	1.5	1.2	1.2	2.1
Spending on own needs:					
None	7.1%	7.7%	6.3%	5.1%	15.4%
A little (1-20%)	18.8	18.9	18.0	19.5	13.3
Some (21-40%)	18.3	17.6	19.1	19.2	13.4
About half (41-60%)	16.7	19.5	14.4	17.3	11.1
Most (61-80%)	15.6	15.5	15.6	16.4	14.3
Almost all (81-99%)	14.1	11.7	16.6	13.7	19.9
All	9.4	9.0	10.0	8.8	12.7
Family living expenses:					
None	57.3%	59.2%	56.4%	63.4%	41.3%
A little (1-20%)	23.0	23.3	22.4	23.0	23.9
Some (21-40%)	9.9	9.7	9.2	7.2	17.3
About half (41-60%)	4.0	3.0	4.9	2.6	5.5
Most (61-80%)	2.0	1.7	2.3	1.3	3.9
Almost all (81-99%)	2.1	1.4	2.7	1.4	4.9
All	1.8	1.7	2.1	1.1	3.3

N = Sample size

Source: Bachman, Jerald G., Lloyd D. Johnston, and Patrick M. O'Malley. 1993. *Monitoring the Future: Questionnaire Responses from the Nation's High School Seniors, 1992.* Ann Arbor, MI: Survey Research Center, Institute for Social Research, The University of Michigan, pp. 208–209.

E7.   COSTS OF RAISING CHILDREN

E7-1. Estimated Annual Expenditures on Children by Husband-Wife Families with One, Two, and Three Children, 1993*

Age of child	Age of older child	Annual Expenditure
One-child household:		
0-2 years		$8,660
3-5 years		9,100
6-8 years		9,400
9-11 years		8,790
12-14 years		9,310
15-17 years		10,460
Two-child household:		
0-2 years	16	$15,170
3-5 years	16	15,520
6-8 years	16	15,760
9-11 years	16	15,280
12-14 years	16	15,690
15 years	16	16,600
Three-child household:		
0-2 years	16	$17,600
3-5 years	16	17,870
6-8 years	16	18,060
9-11 years	16	17,680
12 years	16	18,000

*Estimates are for families in the overall United States with 1993 before-tax incomes between $32,000 and $54,100.

Source: U.S. Department of Agriculture. 1994. *Expenditures on a Child by Families, 1993.* Agricultural Research Service, Family Economics Research Group, page 8.

E7-2. A Comparison of Estimated Expenditures on a Child by Single-Parent and Husband-Wife Families, 1993

Age of Child	Single-Parent Households	Husband-Wife Households
0-2 years	$4,310	$4,960
3-5 years	4,970	5,260
6-8 years	5,710	5,520
9-11 years	4,980	5,070
12-14 years	5,350	5,500
15-17 years	6,400	6,260
Total	$95,160	$97,710

Note: Estimates are for the younger child in a two-child family in the overall United States with 1993 before-tax income less than $32,000

Source: U.S. Department of Agriculture. 1994. *Expenditures on a Child by Families, 1993.* Agricultural Research Service, Family Economics Research Group, page 9.

E7-3. Estimated Annual Expenditures on a Child Born in 1993, by Income Group, 1993–2010*

Year	Age	Income Group Lowest	Middle	Highest
1993	<1	$4,960	$6,870	$10,210
1994	1	5,260	7,280	10,820
1995	2	5,570	7,720	11,470
1996	3	6,260	8,600	12,660
1997	4	6,640	9,120	13,420
1998	5	7,040	9,660	14,230
1999	6	7,830	10,580	15,250
2000	7	8,300	11,220	16,160
2001	8	8,800	11,890	17,130
2002	9	8,570	11,790	17,230
2003	10	9,080	12,500	18,270
2004	11	9,620	13,250	19,360
2005	12	11,070	14,870	21,490
2006	13	11,730	15,760	22,780
2007	14	12,430	16,710	24,150
2008	15	15,000	19,890	28,260
2009	16	15,900	21,080	29,950
2010	17	16,860	22,350	31,750
Total		$170,920	$231,140	$334,590

*Estimates are for the younger child in a husband-wife family with two children for the overall United States.
Note: Adjusted for inflation.

Source: U.S. Department of Agriculture. 1994. *Expenditures on a Child by Families, 1993.* Agricultural Research Service, Family Economics Research Group, page 14.

E7-4. Estimated Annual Expenditures on a Child by Husband-Wife Families, 1993

Age of Child	Total	Housing	Food	Transportation	Clothing	Health Care	Child Care and Education	Other
Income: Less than $32,000 (Average income = $20,000)								
0-2	$4,960	$1,870	$730	$720	$380	$330	$530	$400
3-5	5,260	1,910	830	740	380	330	600	470
6-8	5,520	1,830	1,040	960	450	370	290	580
9-11	5,070	1,490	1,240	810	450	410	180	490
12-14	5,500	1,530	1,220	1,010	720	380	110	530
15-17	6,260	1,550	1,490	1,270	730	460	220	540
Total	97,710	30,540	19,650	16,530	9,330	6,840	5,790	9,030
Income: $32,000 to $54,100 (Average income = $42,600)								
0-2	$6,870	$2,560	$870	$1,080	$450	$410	$840	$660
3-5	7,220	2,600	1,020	1,100	440	400	930	730
6-8	7,460	2,520	1,270	1,320	530	470	510	840
9-11	6,980	2,190	1,500	1,170	520	510	340	750
12-14	7,390	2,220	1,490	1,370	830	470	220	790
15-17	8,300	2,250	1,750	1,650	850	560	440	800
Total	132,660	43,020	23,700	23,070	10,860	8,460	9,840	13,710
Income: More than $54,100 (Average income = $79,400)								
0-2	$10,210	$4,050	$1,200	$1,330	$600	$480	$1,320	$1,230
3-5	10,630	4,090	1,370	1,360	600	480	1,430	1,300
6-8	10,750	4,010	1,620	1,580	700	560	870	1,410
9-11	10,200	3,670	1,870	1,430	690	600	620	1,320
12-14	10,680	3,710	1,890	1,630	1,090	570	430	1,360
15-17	11,790	3,730	2,140	1,920	1,110	660	860	1,370
Total	192,780	69,780	30,270	27,750	14,370	10,050	16,590	23,970

Source: U.S. Department of Agriculture. 1994. *Expenditures on a Child by Families, 1993.* Agricultural Research Service, Family Economics Research Group, page 16.

E7-5. Estimated Annual Expenditures on a Child by Single Parent Families, 1993

Age of Child	Total	Housing	Food	Transpor- tation	Clothing	Health Care	Child Care and Education	Other
Income: Less than $32,000 (Average income = $13,700)								
0-2	$4,310	$1,570	$830	$690	$450	$190	$380	$200
3-5	4,970	1,870	860	760	430	270	490	290
6-8	5,710	2,090	1,060	630	550	390	530	460
9-11	4,980	1,910	1,170	580	530	420	120	250
12-14	5,350	1,830	1,200	670	750	420	160	320
15-17	6,400	2,130	1,420	820	1,010	530	150	340
Total	95,160	34,200	19,620	12,450	11,160	6,660	5,490	5,580
Income: $32,000 or more (Average income = $47,900)								
0-2	$9,600	$3,630	$1,350	$1,570	$600	$330	$950	$1,170
3-5	10,370	3,920	1,420	1,630	570	440	1,140	1,250
6-8	11,320	4,140	1,730	1,500	720	600	1,200	1,430
9-11	10,310	3,960	1,930	1,450	690	650	420	1,210
12-14	10,860	3,890	1,940	1,550	960	640	600	1,280
15-17	11,850	4,180	2,150	1,590	1,260	790	580	1,300
Total	192,930	71,160	31,560	27,870	14,400	10,350	14,670	22,920

Source: U.S. Department of Agriculture. 1994. *Expenditures on a Child by Families, 19934.* Agricultural Research Service, Family Economics Research Group, page 22.

F.   Quality of Life

Adolescence is generally considered a difficult time for young people. Physical maturity, radical changes in hormonal levels, and a desire to break away from their parents and establish their own identity creates stress and anxiety in many teenagers. Friendships and acceptance by peers becomes of paramount importance. The pressures of this difficult stage in life sometimes manifest themselves in emotional problems such as depression and eating disorders. In this chapter, we present information about teenagers' feelings of happiness, satisfaction with life, and self-esteem. Information about emotional problems is also given, as well as data about suicide. Finally, we report what adolescents have indicated are the problems and challenges they perceive they face.

F1. HAPPINESS AND SELF-ESTEEM

As mentioned above, a number of pressures, including acceptance by peers and participation in the dating game, generate anxiety in teenagers. In spite of these challenges, most teens, 86 percent, are satisfied with the way things are going in their personal lives. Also, nearly 70 percent of mothers of children of all ages feel that things are going "very well" for their children. Mothers reported that their children in general are happy, keep themselves busy, and explore their social environment. In addition, both fathers and mothers agree their children have reasonable feelings of self-esteem.

F2. DEPRESSION AND MENTAL ILLNESS

Parents reported that a rather small number of their children, less than 10 percent, have ever had an emotional or behavior problem that lasted three months or longer. They also indicated that a majority of these troubled children received treatment. About one-third of a national sample of parents reported their children in junior and senior high school had missed school during the past 12 months because of an emotional illness.

In general, teenagers reported they are happy and only occasionally feel sad, blue, nervous, or lonely. Also, boredom and tiredness appear to bother adolescents somewhat more often than other children. Thirty-one percent reported that they are "often" bored or worn out.

F3. SUICIDE

In many communities across the country, teenage suicide has emerged as a serious problem. Once it appears, a contagion effect often occurs and other teens imitate a friend or classmate. The Gallup Organization interviewed a national sample of 1,152 adolescents about their involvement in suicide thought and behavior. Over half the adolescents had discussed suicide, with others, while a third had thought about committing it. Fifteen percent of these young men and women reported they had come very close to attempting suicide, and 6 percent had actually made an effort. Three percent of those who attempted suicide required medical attention to save their lives.

Twelve percent of the 1,152 teenagers also revealed that a family member had attempted suicide, and 5 percent reported that that family member had succeeded. Observed rates reported in the Health Chapter indicate that this is an exaggeration. Surprisingly, 60 percent of teenagers claimed they personally knew someone who attempted suicide and 36 percent claimed they knew someone who succeeded. Unfortunately, most teenagers didn't know whether their community has a suicide prevention program. Only 21 percent were aware of hot lines, shelters, support groups, or clinics.

F4. FRIENDSHIPS

Most parents rate their children's friendships as either "excellent" or "good." Only a few parents, 1 or 2 percent, reported that someone was out to get their child or their child hung out with troublemakers. Overall, parents rate their children's friendships as supportive and exerting a good influence. In addition, parents feel their children have adequate social skills to make and keep friends.

Not surprisingly, friends were identified as the most important influence in teenagers' lives, followed by family and school. Music and television were also noted as exerting a "great deal of influence" on 41 and 32 percent (respectively) of the young people surveyed. Religion was admitted to be a strong influence by only 13 percent. When asked to identify the most influential person in their own life, teens chose their mother most often, followed by their fathers and then both parents. Surprisingly, only 13 percent noted friends as the most influential persons in their lives.

F5. CHALLENGES AND PROBLEMS

In 1992, 40 percent of a sample of teenagers identified drug abuse as the biggest problem facing young people in general, while 15 percent tabbed peer pressures to participate in forbidden activities to be the top threat. When asked to identify the single greatest problem they *personally* faced, teenagers reported the greatest problem they face was their grades (33 percent) followed by their career uncertainties (25 percent). In other words, the problems adolescents attribute to young people in general are way down the list of problems they themselves are coping with.

F1. HAPPINESS AND SELF-ESTEEM

F1-1. Adolescents' Report of Their Satisfaction with Their Life, by Sex, Age, Race, and Social Class, 1979–1992

Survey question: In general, are you satisfied or dissatisfied with the way things are going in your own personal life?	
Characteristics	Percent Satisfied
Year:	
1979	87%
1983	82
1987	87
1992	86
Sex:	
Male	88
Female	85
Age:	
13-15 years	88
16-17 years	83
Race:	
White	86
Non-white	86
Social Class:*	
White-collar family	89
Blue-collar family	85
*Primary wage earner in the family occupied a white- or blue-collar job.	

Source: Bezilla, Robert (ed.). 1993. *American's Youth in the 1990s.* Princeton, NJ: The George H. Gallup International Institute, 28–29.

F1-2. High School Seniors' Feelings of Life Satisfaction, by Sex and Race, 1992

Question: How satisfied are you with your life as a whole these days?					
		Sex		Race	
	Total (N=2,727)	Males (N=1,270)	Females (N=1,360)	White (N=1,847)	Black (N=378)
Completely dissatisfied	1.8%	1.9%	1.8%	1.8%	1.2%
Quite dissatisfied	7.2	8.1	6.3	7.7	4.4
Somewhat dissatisfied	7.9	7.3	8.1	6.8	12.4
Neither, or mixed feelings	15.3	14.7	15.6	14.4	13.2
Somewhat satisfied	25.6	25.6	25.8	24.3	27.9
Quite satisfied	35.0	35.3	35.3	37.6	32.1
Completely satisfied	7.2	7.0	7.2	7.3	8.7

Note: N indicates sample size. Percentages may not add to 100 due to rounding.

Source: Bachman, Jerald G., Lloyd D. Johnston, and Patrick M. O'Malley. 1993. *Monitoring the Future: Questionnaire Responses from the Nation's High School Seniors, 1992.* Ann Arbor, MI: Survey Research Center, Institute for Social Research, The University of Michigan, page 199.

F1-3. High School Seniors' Feelings of Self-Esteem, by Sex and Race, 1992

Question: Do you agree or disagree with each of the following?

Statement	Total (N=2,727)	Sex		Race	
		Males (N=1,270)	Females (N=1,360)	White (N=1,847)	Black (N=378)
I take a positive attitude toward myself:					
Disagree	3.3%	2.1%	4.2%	3.0%	2.3%
Mostly disagree	6.9	4.9	9.1	7.3	6.1
Neither	7.9	7.6	8.0	8.2	3.6
Mostly agree	45.5	44.1	46.8	49.6	28.6
Agree	36.4	41.3	31.9	31.9	59.5
I am a person of worth:					
Disagree	2.3%	2.4%	2.2%	2.3%	2.4%
Mostly disagree	4.6	3.6	5.2	4.7	3.7
Neither	11.1	12.0	10.0	11.2	6.5
Mostly agree	40.8	40.7	41.3	43.3	30.6
Agree	41.1	41.3	41.2	38.4	56.8
I do as well as others:					
Disagree	1.4%	1.3%	1.3%	1.3%	2.4%
Mostly disagree	2.9	3.0	2.8	2.9	1.6
Neither	5.8	6.4	5.0	6.3	4.6
Mostly agree	42.0	39.3	44.5	44.2	33.1
Agree	47.9	50.0	46.3	45.3	58.4
I am satisfied with myself:					
Disagree	3.6%	2.4%	4.7%	3.2%	5.3%
Mostly disagree	7.2	6.5	8.0	7.3	5.3
Neither	8.8	9.4	8.1	8.9	6.3
Mostly agree	39.8	38.2	41.6	41.7	32.4
Agree	40.5	43.5	37.6	39.0	50.6
I feel lonely:					
Disagree	19.9%	22.8%	17.6%	19.5%	24.1%
Mostly disagree	27.6	26.7	28.0	30.6	15.5
Neither	19.7	21.4	17.6	19.9	20.9
Mostly agree	20.8	18.7	22.9	21.1	18.9
Agree	12.0	10.4	13.8	8.9	20.6
I don't have much to be proud of:					
Disagree	42.7%	43.0%	42.5%	42.0%	56.2%
Mostly disagree	29.4	29.9	29.2	31.9	17.7
Neither	12.0	13.2	10.6	12.4	8.0
Mostly agree	12.1	10.4	13.7	11.0	12.3
Agree	3.9	3.5	4.0	2.8	5.8

Note: N indicates sample size. Percentages may not add to 100 due to rounding.

Source: Bachman, Jerald G., Lloyd D. Johnston, and Patrick M. O'Malley. 1993. *Monitoring the Future: Questionnaire Responses from the Nation's High School Seniors, 1992.* Ann Arbor, MI: Survey Research Center, Institute for Social Research, The University of Michigan, pp. 203–205.

F1-4. Mother's Report of Children's Quality of Life, by Mother's Marital Status, Race, and Education, 1987

Survey question: All things considered, is (child's) life going:

Mother's Characteristic	N	Very well	Fairly well	Not so well/ not well at all
			Percent	
Mother's Marital Status:				
Married	4,065	70%	28%	2%
Divorced/separated	426	40	45	6
Cohabiting	214	59	39	2
Never married	191	67	32	2
Mother's Race:				
White	3,567	69	30	1
Black	556	67	30	3
Hispanic*	393	70	28	2
Other	434	67	31	2
Mother's Education:				
Less than high school	269	63	34	3
High school	696	65	32	3
Some college	421	73	26	1
College graduate	219	72	27	1
Post graduate	400	73	25	2

*May be of any race.
Note: N indicates sample size. Percentages may not add to 100 due to rounding.

Source: National Survey of Families and Households, 1988 [machine-readable data file] James Sweet and Larry Bumpass, principal investigators. Distributed by the Center for Demography and Ecology, University of Wisconsin-Madison, Madison, WI. For a description of this study see James Sweet, Larry Bumpass, and Vaughn Call. *The Design and Content of the National Survey of Families and Households.* Working Paper NSFH-1, Center for Demography and Ecology, University of Wisconsin-Madison, 1988.

F1-5. Parents' Report of Children's Feelings of Self-Esteem, by Mother's Marital Status and Education, 1987

Survey question: I am going to read some statements that might describe a child's behavior. Please tell me whether each statement has been often true, sometimes true, or has not been true of (child) during the past three months: a) feels worthless; b) is unhappy, sad, or depressed.

	N	Feels Worthless Often	Some-times	Never	Is Unhappy, Sad, or Depressed Often	Some-times	Never
Child							
Age:							
1-5	952	0%	11%	89%	1%	6%	93%
6-11	5,490	1	14	85	1	12	87
12-17	5,261	2	18	80	3	14	83
	11,703						
Sex:							
Male	5,955	1	16	83	2	13	85
Female	5,748	1	16	83	2	12	86
	11,703						
Race:							
White	8,405	1	16	83	2	13	85
Black	1,652	1	14	85	1	9	90
Hispanic*	1,280	2	16	82	2	11	87
Other	366	3	18	79	0	8	92
	11,703						
Mother							
Marital Status:							
Married	9,124	1	14	85	1	12	87
Divorced/separated	1,665	2	22	76	3	14	83
Widowed	197	6	24	70	4	13	83
Never married	494	2	19	79	2	12	86
	11,479						
Education:							
Less than high school	2,326	2	18	80	2	10	88
High school graduate	5,040	1	16	83	2	12	86
Some college	2,323	1	15	84	1	14	85
College graduate	1,061	1	12	87	1	13	86
Post graduate	717	1	14	85	1	14	85
	11,467						

*May be of any race.
Note: N indicates sample size. Percentages may not add to 100 due to rounding.

Source: Holmes, B. C., A. S. Kaplan, E. L. Lang, and J. J. Card. 1991. *National Health Interview Survey on Children, 1988: A User's Guide to the Machine-readable Files and Documentation* (Data Set 33-34). Los Altos, CA: Sociometrics Corporation, American Family Data Archive.

F1-6. Mothers' Report on How Often Their Adolescent Is Cheerful and Happy, by Mother's Marital Status, Race, and Education, 1987

Survey question: I am going to read some statements that might describe a child's behavior. Please tell me whether each statement has been often true, sometimes true, or has not been true of (child) during the past three months: a) is cheerful and happy.

| Mother's Characteristic | N | Is cheerful and happy | | |
		Never	Some-times	Often
Marital Status:				
Married	1444	1%	26%	73%
Divorced/separated	202	3	28	69
Cohabiting	47	2	26	72
Never married	25	3	30	67
	1,194			
Race:				
White	1298	1	27	72
Black	187	1	25	74
Hispanic*	111	0	33	67
Other	158	3	25	72
	1,197			
Education:				
Less than high school	90	5	33	62
High school graduate	261	1	28	71
Some college	141	0	22	78
College graduate	61	0	25	75
Post graduate	125	0	27	73
	678			

*May be of any race.
Note: N indicates sample size. Percentages may not add to 100 due to rounding.

Source: National Survey of Families and Households, 1988 [machine-readable data file] James Sweet and Larry Bumpass, principal investigators. Distributed by the Center for Demography and Ecology, University of Wisconsin-Madison, Madison, WI. For a description of this study see James Sweet, Larry Bumpass, and Vaughn Call. *The Design and Content of the National Survey of Families and Households.* Working Paper NSFH-1, Center for Demography and Ecology, University of Wisconsin-Madison, 1988.

F1-7. Mothers' Report of Their Adolescent's Willingness to Try New Things, by Mother's Marital Status, Race, and Education, 1987

Survey question: I am going to read some statements that might describe a child's behavior. Please tell me whether each statement has been often true, sometimes true, or has not been true of (child) during the past three months: a) is willing to try new things.

| Mother's Characteristic | N | Is Willing to Try New Things | | |
		Never	Sometimes	Often
Marital Status:				
Married	1426	3%	43%	54%
Divorced/separated	200	6	43	51
Cohabitating	47	0	54	46
Never Married	24	3	26	71
	1,697			
Race:				
White	1284	4	43	53
Black	182	4	36	60
Hispanic*	111	2	54	44
Other	156	2	41	57
	1,733			
Education:				
Less than high school	89	1	45	54
High school graduate	257	3	50	47
Some college	141	2	51	48
College graduate	61	4	32	64
Post graduate	126	2	47	51
	674			

*May be of any race.
Note: N indicates sample size. Percentages may not add to 100 due to rounding.

Source: National Survey of Families and Households, 1988 [machine-readable data file] James Sweet and Larry Bumpass, principal investigators. Distributed by the Center for Demography and Ecology, University of Wisconsin-Madison, Madison, WI. For a description of this study see James Sweet, Larry Bumpass, and Vaughn Call. *The Design and Content of the National Survey of Families and Households.* Working Paper NSFH-1, Center for Demography and Ecology, University of Wisconsin-Madison, 1988.

F2. DEPRESSION AND MENTAL ILLNESS

F2-1. Parents' Report of Children's Emotional and Behavioral Problems, by Child's Age, Sex, and Race, and Mother's Marital Status and Education, 1987

Survey question: Has (child) ever had an emotional or behavioral problem that lasted three months or longer? Has (child) received treatment or counseling for the (condition)? During the past 12 months has (child) been taking any medications for the (condition)? Has (child) ever seen a psychiatrist, psychologist, doctor, or counselor about any emotional or behavioral problem?

	Ever had emotional problem		Received treatment		Taken medicine		Seen psychiatrist/ counselor	
	N	% Yes	N	% Yes	N	% Yes	N	% Yes
Child								
Age:								
1-5 years	2,813	3%	80	38%	77	10%	2,584	1%
6-11 years	5,541	6	304	64	301	10	4,789	5
12-17 years	5,289	8	397	75	393	5	4,402	9
	13,643		781		771		11,776	
Sex:								
Male	6,913	7	465	65	462	8	5,779	7
Female	6,730	5	316	69	309	7	5,997	5
	13,643		781		771		11,776	
Race:								
White	9,766	7	597	69	591	7	8,325	7
Black	1,877	5	77	68	76	8	1,680	4
Hispanic*	1,556	6	85	49	84	13	1,368	5
Other	445	5	21	59	20	10	402	3
	13,643		781		771		11,776	
Mother								
Marital Status:								
Married	10,653	5	511	65	506	8	9,293	5
Divorced	1,877	10	178	74	173	5	1,547	11
Widowed	205	12	21	56	21	11	164	6
Never married	652	8	46	52	46	16	558	4
	13,388		757		747		11,563	
Education:								
Less than high school	2,680	7	173	57	170	11	2,275	5
High school graduate	5,845	6	335	63	332	7	5,032	5
Some college	2,742	7	167	73	165	4	2,386	8
College graduate	1,283	3	41	89	41	13	1,153	6
Post graduate	826	5	40	85	37	10	709	6
	13,376		756		746		11,555	

*May be of any race. N indicates sample size.

Source: Holmes, B. C., A. S. Kaplan, E. L. Lang, and J. J. Card. 1991. *National Health Interview Survey on Children, 1988: A User's Guide to the Machine-readable Files and Documentation* (Data Set 33-34). Los Altos, CA: Sociometrics Corporation, American Family Data Archive.

F2-2. Parents' Report of Children's Emotional Problems Interfering with School, by Mother's Marital Status, Race, and Education, 1987

Survey questions: Has (child) ever had an emotional or behavioral problem that lasted three months or longer? During the past 12 months, did the (condition) cause (child) to: a) miss any time from school? b) attend special classes, or a special school, or get special help at school?

	Missed school because of emotional problems		Went to a special class	
	N	% Yes	N	% Yes
Child				
Age:				
1-5 years	54	9%	54	13%
6-11 years	302	13	303	26
12-17 years	380	32	378	26
	736		735	
Sex:				
Male	441	22	441	26
Female	295	24	294	23
	736		735	
Race:				
White	566	21	564	24
Black	73	38	74	32
Hispanic*	77	16	78	28
Other	20	35	20	3
	736		735	
Mother				
Marital status:				
Married	481	20	479	25
Divorced	168	26	168	27
Widowed	21	29	21	25
Never married	44	39	44	19
	714		712	
Education:				
Less than high school	160	31	159	28
High school graduate	314	18	311	23
Some college	162	23	163	24
College graduate	37	22	38	21
Post graduate	39	29	40	32
	712		711	

*May be of any race. N indicates sample size.

Source: Holmes, B. C., A. S. Kaplan, E. L. Lang, and J. J. Card. 1991. *National Health Interview Survey on Children, 1988: A User's Guide to the Machine-readable Files and Documentation* (Data Set 33-34). Los Altos, CA: Sociometrics Corporation, American Family Data Archive.

F2-3. Mothers' Report of Adolescent Being Unhappy, Sad, or Depressed, by Mother's Marital Status, Race, and Education, 1987

Survey question: I am going to read some statements that might describe a child's behavior. Please tell me whether each statement has been often true, sometimes true, or has not been true of (child) during the past three months: a) is unhappy, sad, or depressed.

Mother's Characteristics	N	Is Unhappy, Sad, or Depressed		
		Never	Sometimes	Often
Marital status:				
Married	1442	54%	41%	5%
Divorced/separated	202	47	43	10
Cohabiting	47	57	33	10
Never married	26	54	42	4
	1,717			
Race:				
White	1298	50	44	6
Black	188	63	32	5
Hispanic*	111	65	31	4
Other	156	59	31	11
	1,753			
Education:				
Less than high school	90	54	37	9
High school graduate	261	56	40	4
Some college	141	50	41	9
College graduate	61	66	33	1
Post graduate	126	48	50	2
	680			

*May be of any race. N indicates sample size.

Source: National Survey of Families and Households, 1988 [machine-readable data file] James Sweet and Larry Bumpass, principal investigators. Distributed by the Center for Demography and Ecology, University of Wisconsin-Madison, Madison, WI. For a description of this study see James Sweet, Larry Bumpass, and Vaughn Call. *The Design and Content of the National Survey of Families and Households.* Working Paper NSFH-1, Center for Demography and Ecology, University of Wisconsin-Madison, 1988.

F2-4. Mothers' Report of Their Adolescent Being Fearful and Anxious, by Mother's Marital Status, Race, and Education, 1987

Survey question: I am going to read some statements that might describe a child's behavior. Please tell me whether each statement has been often true, sometimes true, or has not been true of (child) during the past three months: a) is fearful and anxious.

Mother's Characteristics	N	Is Fearful and Anxious		
		Never	Sometimes	Often
Marital Status:				
Married	1441	59%	35%	6%
Divorced/separated	202	56	35	9
Cohabitating	47	64	30	6
Never married	75	38	45	16
	1,716			
Race:				
White	1298	56	37	7
Black	187	55	34	11
Hispanic*	110	73	21	6
Other	158	65	32	3
	1,753			
Education:				
Less than high school	89	55	36	9
High school graduate	261	59	32	9
Some college	141	55	39	6
College graduate	61	72	25	2
Post graduate	125	62	36	2
	677			

*May be of any race. N indicates sample size.

Source: National Survey of Families and Households, 1988 [machine-readable data file] James Sweet and Larry Bumpass, principal investigators. Distributed by the Center for Demography and Ecology, University of Wisconsin-Madison, Madison, WI. For a description of this study see James Sweet, Larry Bumpass, and Vaughn Call. *The Design and Content of the National Survey of Families and Households.* Working Paper NSFH-1, Center for Demography and Ecology, University of Wisconsin-Madison, 1988.

F2-5. Mothers' Report that Their Adolescent Loses Their Temper Easily, by Mother's Marital Status, Race, and Education, 1987

Survey question: I am going to read some statements that might describe a child's behavior. Please tell me whether each statement has been often true, sometimes true, or has not been true of (child) during the past three months: a) loses temper easily.

Mother's Characteristics	N	Loses Temper Easily		
		Never	Sometimes	Often
Marital Status:				
Married	1441	40%	42%	18%
Divorced/separated	201	31	42	27
Cohabitating	47	45	42	23
Never married	<u>26</u>	38	39	13
	1,715			
Race:				
White	1295	38	42	20
Black	187	48	35	17
Hispanic*	111	46	38	16
Other	<u>158</u>	39	45	16
	1,751			
Education:				
Less than high school	90	44	32	24
High school graduatte	260	43	40	17
Some college	141	41	45	14
College graduate	61	40	48	12
Post graduate	<u>125</u>	35	50	15
	677			

*May be of any race. N indicates sample size.

Source: National Survey of Families and Households, 1988 [machine-readable data file] James Sweet and Larry Bumpass, principal investigators. Distributed by the Center for Demography and Ecology, University of Wisconsin-Madison, Madison, WI. For a description of this study see James Sweet, Larry Bumpass, and Vaughn Call. *The Design and Content of the National Survey of Families and Households.* Working Paper NSFH-1, Center for Demography and Ecology, University of Wisconsin-Madison, 1988.

F2-6. Adolescents' Report of Symptoms of Emotional Distress, 1990

Survey question: People have many different moods and sometimes feel differently from day to day. As I read some descriptions of different feelings, please tell me how often you have days when you feel this way:

How often do you feel:	Percent (N=929)			
	Often	Sometimes	Ever	Never
Sad or blue	13%	42%	43%	2%
Nervous, tense, or on edge	14	46	36	4
Happy	76	21	4	0
Bored	29	48	21	2
Lonely	11	36	45	8
Tired or worn out	31	47	20	2
Excited about something	55	39	6	0
Too busy to get everything done	33	44	21	2
Pressured by parent	12	31	49	8

N indicates sample size. Percentages may not add to 100 due to rounding.

Source: Moore, K. A. 1992. *National Commission on Children: 1990 Survey of Parents and Children.* (Data Set 19, H. M. Daley, E. C. Peterson, E. L. Lang, & J. J. Card, Archivists) [machine-readable data file and documentation]. Washington, DC: Child Trends, Inc. (Producer). Los Altos, CA: Sociometrics Corporation, American Family Data Archive (Producer & Distributor).

F3.   SUICIDE

F3-1. Adolescent Suicide Rates, by Sex and Race, 1970–1990

Age, Race, and Sex	Rate per 100,000 Youth		
	1970	1980	1990
Age 10 to 14			
White			
Female	0.3	0.3	0.9
Male	1.1	1.4	2.3
Black			
Female	0.4	0.1	—
Male	0.3	0.5	1.6
Age 15 to 19			
White			
Female	2.9	3.3	4.0
Male	9.4	15.5	19.3
Black			
Female	2.9	1.6	1.9
Male	4.7	5.6	11.5
Age 20 to 24			
White			
Female	5.7	5.9	4.4
Male	19.3	27.8	26.8
Black			
Female	4.9	3.1	2.6
Male	18.7	20.0	19.0

Source: U.S. Bureau of the Census, *Statistical Abstract of the United States; 1993* (113th edition). Washington, DC, 1993, page 99.

F3-2. Self-Reported Suicidal Behaviors of High School Seniors, 1991

Survey Question: Have you ever: 1) Discussed the topic of suicide with others? 2) Talked or thought about committing suicide? 3) Come very close to trying to commit suicide? 4) Tried to commit suicide? 5) What factors led you to discuss or think about suicide? 6) How did you deal with the situation?

(N=1152)	N	% Yes
Suicidal Behavior		
Discussed the topic of suicide with others	601	52%
Talked or thought about committing suicide	405	35
Come very close to trying to commit suicide	169	15
Tried to commit suicide	70	6
If came close or tried suicide: Factors responsible		
Family problems/problems at home	84	47%
Depression	42	23
Problems with friends/peer pressure/social relations	37	22 ·
Low self-esteem/feeling worthless	33	18
Boy/girl relationships	29	16
Felt like no one cared	24	13
School problems	16	9
Personal problems	14	8
Grades in school	14	8
Life in general	11	6
Drug/alcohol abuse	9	5
Other (Each 3% or less)	61	36
No answer	6	3
If came close or tried suicide: Coping strategies		
Talked to a friend	44	25%
Thought about it	22	12
Just forgot about it	13	7
Talked to a counselor	11	6
Thought about good things in life	9	5
Talked about it	7	4
Talked to a family member	7	4
Other (Each 3% or less)	52	29
Don't know	2	1
None	2	1
No answer	10	6

*May exceed number of respondents or 100 percent because respondents were allowed to select more than one response. Note: N indicates sample size

Source: The George H. Gallup International Institute. 1991. *The Gallup Survey on Teenage Suicide.* Princeton, NJ: The George H. Gallup International Institute, page 75.

F3-3. High School Students Reporting Suicidal Thoughts and Behaviors during Previous 12 Months, by Sex, 1991

Survey question: Students were asked whether they had thought seriously about attempting suicide during the 12 months preceeding the survey, whether they had made a specific plan to attempt suicide, whether they had actually attempted suicide and whether the suicide attempt(s) resulted in an injury or poisioning that had to be treated by a doctor or nurse.

Behavior	Total	Male	Female
Had suicidal thoughts	29%	21%	37%
Made specific suicidal plans	19	13	25
Made one or more suicidal attempts	7	4	11
Made suicide attempt requiring medical attention	3	1	2

Source: K. Maguire, A. L. Pastore, and T. J. Flanagan (eds.). 1993. *Sourcebook of Criminal Justice Statistics 1992.* U.S. Department of Justice, Bureau of Justice Statistics. Washington, DC: U.S. Government Printing Office.

F3-4. Suicidal Behavior of Family Members as Reported by High School Seniors, 1991

Survey Question: In your family has anyone: 1) Talked about committing suicide? 2) Tried to commit suicide? 3) Succeeded at committing suicide?

(N=1152)	% yes
Family Member Suicidal Behavior	
Talked about committing suicide	20%
Tried to commit suicide	12
Succeeded at committing suicide	5

N indicates sample size.

Source: The George H. Gallup International Institute. 1991. *The Gallup Survey on Teenage Suicide.* Princeton, NY: The George H. Gallup International Institute, page 70.

F3-5. Adolescents' Estimates of Other Adolescents' Thinking about Committing Suicide and the Reasons for Such Thoughts, 1991

Survey question: Based on your feelings and what other teenagers have said, do you feel most, some, a few, or virtually no teenagers have thought about committing suicide? Which one of the following reasons do you think causes teenagers to think about committing suicide? (List) of the possible reasons mentioned, which is the major or number one reason? Which do you feel is the second most frequent reason?

	N	Most	Some	Few	Virtually None
Estimate of teens who have thought of suicide	1,152	27%	35%	23%	15%

Reasons teens think about committing suicide	Primary Reason	Secondary Reason
Problems with growing up	22%	13%
Drug use	20	14
Peer pressure	16	14
Getting along with parents	14	16
Involvement with satanic cults	7	6
AIDS	3	4
Alcohol abuse	3	9
School Problems	3	6
Teen pregnancy	3	4
Other (each, less than 2% of teens)	8	11
Don't know	2	3

N indicates sample size.

Source: The George H. Gallup International Institute. 1991. *The Gallup Survey on Teenage Suicide.* Princeton, NY: The George H. Gallup International Institute, page 95.

F3-6. Adolescents' Report They Personally Know an Adolescent Who Attempted Suicide, 1991

Survey Question: Do you personally know of any teenagers who have tried to commit suicide? Did they actually commit suicide? Was this a relative, a close friend or an acquaintance? Did this person appear to be very religious, somewhat religious, not very religious, or not at all religious? Looking back, were there any signs that this person might attempt suicide? What were the signs?

	N	Percent
Personally know teen who attempted suicide?		
Yes	692	60
No	453	39
No answer	7	1
Successfully committed suicide?		
Yes	178	36
No	509	74
No answer	5	1
Teenage attempter tried to get help?		
Yes	113	16
No	328	47
Don't know	241	35
No answer	10	1
Relationship of attempter to respondent?		
Relative	30	4
Close friend	231	33
Acquaintance	295	43
No answer	136	20
Religiosity of teen who attempted suicide?		
Very religious	26	4
Somewhat religious	205	30
Not very religious	283	41
Not at all religious	163	23
Don't know/no answer	16	2
Were there any signs of potential suicide?		
Yes	362	52
No	157	23
Don't know	168	24
No answer	5	1
What were the signs?		
Depressed	330	91
Having personal problems for a long time	297	82
Being mixed up	272	75
Feeling worthless	269	74
Not getting along with parents	260	72
Sudden change in attitude/behavior	231	64
Getting mad/angry very easily	206	57
Talking or writing about wanting to die	196	54
Keeping to self/withdrawing from friends	185	51
Getting into trouble at school	169	47
Grades getting worse	157	43
Acting wild	154	43
Dating problems	133	37
Using alcohol	129	36
Staying out late a lot	115	32
Using other drugs	109	30
Giving away personal possessions	60	17
Excessive fear of some things	49	14
Shoplifting	37	10
Satanic involvement	24	7
Overly concerned about school grades	22	6
Other	49	14
None/don't know/no answer	3	1
	3,456*	

Note: N indicates sample size. Percents may not add to 100 due to rounding.

* Sample size is greater than 362 and percent is greater than 100 because respondents were allowed to identify more than one sign.

Source: The George H. Gallup International Institute. 1991. *The Gallup Survey on Teenage Suicide.* Princeton, NY: The George H. Gallup International Institute, pages 60–62.

F3-7. High School Seniors' Perceptions of Community Teenage Suicide Prevention, 1991

	Number	Percent
Community prevention of teen suicide	(1152)	
Yes	247	21
No	368	32
Don't know	506	44
No answer	31	3
Type of community prevention (if yes)	(247)	
Hot lines	129	52
Counseling	41	17
Programs/seminar/meetings	41	17
Support groups	22	9
Clubs/organizations in the community	16	6
Advertisements	14	6
Shelter/place for kids to go	13	5
Clinics/rehabilitation/help centers	12	5
Awareness/education classes	9	4
Extracurricular activities/youth centers	9	4
Other (each 2% or less)	47	19
No answer	4	2

Source: The George H. Gallup International Institute. 1991. *The Gallup Survey on Teenage Suicide.* Princeton, NY: The George H. Gallup International Institute, p. 37.

F4.   FRIENDSHIPS

F4-1. Friendships Reported by High School Seniors, by Sex and Race, 1992

		Sex		Race	
	Total (N=2,727)	Males (N=1,270)	Females (N=1,360)	White (N=1,847)	Black (N=378)
I have good friends:					
Disagree	5.6%	4.9%	6.1%	4.9%	6.5%
Mostly disagree	6.4	5.5	6.9	6.3	5.0
Neither	7.2	8.3	5.4	6.7	11.3
Mostly agree	33.7	35.7	32.6	34.4	29.0
Agree	47.1	45.5	48.9	47.8	48.2
There is usually someone I can talk to:					
Disagree	3.4%	4.1%	2.8%	2.7%	4.9%
Mostly disagree	4.1	5.6	2.7	4.1	3.1
Neither	5.8	8.1	3.1	5.5	5.5
Mostly agree	25.6	28.0	23.7	26.0	21.9
Agree	61.1	54.2	67.7	61.6	64.6
I wish I had more friends:					
Disagree	20.8%	20.4%	21.5%	20.7%	21.4%
Mostly disagree	15.2	16.0	14.0	17.0	9.3
Neither	18.9	21.1	16.6	19.1	17.8
Mostly agree	24.1	24.2	24.1	24.8	19.4
Agree	21.0	18.4	23.7	18.4	32.1

Note: N indicates sample size. Percents may not add to 100 due to rounding.

Source: Bachman, Jerald G., Lloyd D. Johnston, and Patrick M. O'Malley. 1993.*b Monitoring the Future: Questionnaire Responses from the Nation's High School Seniors, 1992.* Ann Arbor, MI: Survey Research Center, Institute for Social Research, The University of Michigan, p. 206.

F4-2. Parents' Report of Adolescents' Interaction with Others, by Mother's Marital Status, Race, and Education, 1987

Survey question: Now I am going to read some statements that describe the behavior of many children. Please tell me whether each statement has been often true, sometimes true, or not true of (child) during the past three months: a) feels others are out to get (child)? b) hangs around with kids who get into trouble?

		Percent of Parents Who Feel:					
		Others Are Out to Get (Child)			Child Hangs Around with Troublemakers		
	N	Often	Sometimes	Never	Often	Sometimes	Never
Child							
Age							
12-17	5,224	1%	6%	93%	2%	10%	88%
Sex:							
Male	2,723	1	7	92	3	11	86
Female	2,501	1	6	93	2	9	89
	5,224						
Race:							
White	3,772	1	6	93	2	10	88
Black	747	1	7	92	3	11	86
Hispanic*	539	2	7	91	3	11	86
Other	165	0	5	95	1	8	91
	5,224						
Mother							
Marital Status:							
Married	4,016	1	6	93	2	9	89
Divorced	775	1	7	92	3	14	83
Widowed	119	3	9	88	4	10	86
Never married	189	1	8	91	4	18	78
	5,099						
Education:							
Less than high school	1,106	2	7	91	4	14	82
High school graduate	2,211	1	7	92	2	11	87
Some college	1,064	1	6	93	2	8	90
College graduate	426	0	5	95	0	6	94
Post graduate	290	0	4	96	1	4	95
	5,097						

*May be of any race. N indicates sample size.

Source: National Survey of Families and Households, 1988 [machine-readable data file] James Sweet and Larry Bumpass, principal investigators. Distributed by the Center for Demography and Ecology, University of Wisconsin-Madison, Madison, WI. For a description of this study see James Sweet, Larry Bumpass, and Vaughn Call. *The Design and Content of the National Survey of Families and Households.* Working Paper NSFH-1, Center for Demography and Ecology, University of Wisconsin-Madison, 1988.

F4-3. Parents' Report of Children's Interactions with Others, by Mother's Marital Status, Race, and Education, 1987

Survey question: Now I am going to read some statements that describe the behavior of many children. Please tell me whether each statement has been often true, sometimes true, or not true of (child) during the past three months: a) bullies or is cruel or mean to others? b) has trouble getting along with other children? c) is not liked by other children?

	N	Bullies/Cruel/Mean to Others			Trouble Getting Along			Not Liked by Others		
		Sometimes	Never	Often	Sometimes	Never	Often	Sometimes	Never	Often
Child										
Age:										
1-5 years	951	3%	16%	82%	1%	10%	90%	0%	5%	95%
6-11 years	5,494	1	13	86	1	10	90	1	6	93
12-17 years	5,264	2	11	87	1	9	90	1	6	93
	11,709									
Sex:										
Male	5,957	2	14	84	1	10	89	1	7	92
Female	5,752	1	11	88	1	8	91	1	6	93
	11,709									
Race:										
White	8,410	1	12	86	1	9	90	1	6	93
Black	1,652	3	12	85	1	11	88	1	7	92
Hispanic*	1,280	3	13	84	1	9	90	1	5	94
Other	368	0	10	90	0	6	94	0	4	96
	11,709									
Mother										
Marital status:										
Married	9,130	1	12	87	1	9	91	1	6	93
Divorced	1,666	3	13	84	2	11	88	1	7	92
Widowed	197	4	11	85	3	10	87	2	7	91
Never married	493	3	15	82	3	15	83	1	10	89
	11,485									
Education:										
Less than high school	2,329	3	14	83	1	10	88	1	7	92
High school graduate	5,038	2	13	86	1	9	90	1	6	93
Some college	2,331	1	12	87	1	10	90	0	6	94
College graduate	1,060	1	11	88	0	8	92	0	5	95
Post graduate	716	1	7	92	0	9	91	1	7	92
	11,473									

*May be of any race.
Note: Percents may not add to 100 due to rounding.

Source: K. Maguire, A. L. Pastore, and T. J. Flanagan (eds.). 1993. *Sourcebook of Criminal Justice Statistics 1992.* U.S. Department of Justice, Bureau of Justice Statistics. Washington, DC: U.S. Government Printing Office.

F4-4. Mothers' Report of Their Adolescent Getting Along Well with Other Kids, by Mother's Marital Status, Race, and Education, 1987

Mother's Characteristic	N	Never	Sometimes	Often
Marital Status:				
Married	1444	1%	12%	87%
Divorced/separated	202	1	17	82
Cohabiting	47	3	12	85
Never married	26	2	18	80
	1,719			0
Race:				
White	1298	1	12	87
Black	187	1	13	86
Hispanic*	111	0	23	77
Other	158	3	12	87
	1,754			0
Education:				
Less than high school	90	1	17	82
High school graduate	261	2	10	88
Some college	141	1	10	89
College graduate	61	0	15	85
Post graduate	125	1	11	88
	678			0

*May be of any race.
Note: N indicates sample size.

Source: National Survey of Families and Households, 1988 [machine-readable data file] James Sweet and Larry Bumpass, principal investigators. Distributed by the Center for Demography and Ecology, University of Wisconsin-Madison, Madison, WI. For a description of this study see James Sweet, Larry Bumpass, and Vaughn Call. *The Design and Content of the National Survey of Families and Households.* Working Paper NSFH-1, Center for Demography and Ecology, University of Wisconsin-Madison, 1988.

F4-5. Adolescents' Rating of Neighborhood as a Place to Grow Up, 1990

Survey question: I'd like to start by asking you about the neighborhood you live in now. How is your neighborhood as a place for children to grow up?

Rating	Percent (N=929)
Excellent	21%
Very good	25
Good	33
Fair	17
Poor	4

Note: N indicates sample size

Source: Moore, K. A. 1992. *National Commission on Children: 1990 Survey of Parents and Children.* (Data Set 19, H. M. Daley, E. C. Peterson, E. L. Lang, & J. J. Card, Archivists) [machine-readable data file and documentation]. Washington, DC: Child Trends, Inc. (Producer). Los Altos, CA: Sociometrics Corporation, American Family Data Archive (Producer & Distributor).

F4-6. Adolescents' Report of Influences in Their Lives, 1990

Survey question: Do you feel today's teenagers are influenced a great deal, some, a little, or very little by...?

Influenced by . . .	Great deal	Some	Little	Very little
Friends	87%	11%	1%	1%
Home	51	31	14	4
School	45	36	14	5
Music	41	35	17	7
Television	32	43	18	7
Movies	19	48	22	11
Religion	13	30	28	28
Magazines	9	41	32	17
Books	3	23	41	32

Note: Percentages may not add to 100 due to rounding.

Source: Bezilla, Robert (ed.). 1993. *American's Youth in the 1990s.* Princeton, NJ: The George H. Gallup International Institute, page 30.

F4-7. Adolescents' Report of Person Who Was the Greatest Influence in Their Lives, 1990

Survey question: What person has been the greatest influence in your life?

Person of Greatest Influence	N	Percent
Mother	299	26
Father	190	16
Parents	152	13
Friend	136	12
Brother/sister	88	8
Boyfriend/girlfriend	36	3
Grandparent	30	3
Other (each 2% or less)	145	13
Don't know or no answer	76	6

Note: 1152 respondents.

Source: The George H. Gallup International Institute. 1991. *The Gallup Survey on Teenage Suicide.* Princeton, NY: The George H. Gallup International Institute, page 22.

F5. CHALLENGES AND PROBLEMS

F5-1 Adolescents' Perceptions of the Biggest Problem Facing Them, 1977–1992

Survey question: What do you feel is the biggest problem facing people your age?				
Problem	1977	1983	1987	1992
Drug abuse	27%	35%	54%	40%
Alcohol abuse	7	10	12	7
Peer pressures	5	8	10	15
AIDS	—	—	5	11
Teen pregnancy	—	—	11	9
Sex	—	—	—	6
Crime, gangs	—	—	—	6
School problems	3	5	1	5
Getting along with parents	20	5	2	2
Problem in growing up	6	1	2	2
Financing college	—	1	1	2
Unemployment	6	16	2	1
Fear of war	—	4	1	—
Economic problems	3	2	1	1
Career uncertainties	3	3	—	1
Teen suicide	—	—	2	—
Miscellaneous	12	5	5	4
Don't know	14	18	8	6
Columns add to more than 100% because some teens marked more than one problem. —This question was not asked that particular year.				

Source: Bezilla, Robert (ed.). 1993. *American's Youth in the 1990s.* Princeton, NJ: The George H. Gallup International Institute, page 33.

F5-2. Adolescents' Report of Greatest Problems They and Their Friends Face, 1991

Survey question: Which of the following is the single greatest problem you face today? In addition to the above, what are the next two most important problems you face? What are the three biggest problems your best friend faces?		
	Percent (N=1152)	
Problem	Teen's own top three problems	Best friend's top three problems
School grades	33%	27%
Career uncertainties	25	11
Growing pains	18	14
Fears	18	7
Getting along with parents	16	31
Being liked	15	15
Financing college	15	9
School problems	14	20
Drug abuse	12	10
Fear of war	12	5
Peer pressures	11	11
Weight problems	11	8
Concern about AIDS	10	5
Economic problems	10	8
Alcohol abuse	9	15
Depression	8	8
Teen pregnancy	7	8
Other	7	7
No response	2	7
Note: N Indicates sample size		

Source: Bezilla, Robert (ed.). 1993. *American's Youth in the 1990s.* Princeton, NJ: The George H. Gallup International Institute, page 31.

G.   Leisure and Recreation

Adolescence is seen by most Americans as a period of life that should include time for play and recreation. Government agencies and health organizations, however, continue to criticize American youth's leisure habits, accusing them of watching too much television among other things. In this chapter, we review the television habits of children and teenagers, as well as their participation in other leisure activities such as sports. Information about the music-related behavior of young people is also presented. Their reading habits are discussed, and data about exposure to books, magazines, and newspapers are shown. Finally, we report on the religious beliefs and behavior of adolescents.

G1. TELEVISION AND MOVIES

Public attention has focused on the extensive time that young Americans spend before a television set. Adolescents are frequently depicted as "couch potatoes" who spend hours with the television. And the national data seems to support this claim. Young children spend nearly 26 hours per week watching television, while older children and teens devote around 22 hours to this activity. Young women watch the most TV—29 hours per week. Of the shows broadcast on television, children under 12 favor situational comedies, while teens divide their attention between comedies, dramas, and feature films.

Adolescents reported that when they watch movies, they most often watch them in their homes with a VCR. When not watching movies on a VCR, they most often watch movies at theaters, on television, or on cable television.

G2. SPORTS AND CLUBS

The data in this chapter show that adolescents and young adults participate in a wide array of sports. Younger children favor bicycle riding and swimming, followed by camping, baseball, basketball, and fishing. Teenagers participate in the same activities, but also enjoy volleyball, football, softball, bowling, and running. Young adults, age 18 to 24 years, still like to swim but cut back on bike riding and football. Aerobics and exercising with equipment are also taken up by substantial numbers of young adults.

The data also indicates that adolescents' favorite spectator sports are football, basketball, and baseball. These three sports are the favorite of 76 percent of the surveyed teens.

G3. MUSIC

Rap music emerged in 1992 as adolescents' favorite music. Rock, top 40, and country and western were also popular types of music. Most adolescents listen to their music via FM radio and tape and CD recordings, but music videos are also a significant source of music for adolescents.

G4. BOOKS, MAGAZINES, AND NEWS-PAPERS

A majority of teenagers reported they had read a newspaper (68 percent) and a magazine (58 percent) the previous day, and half of the teens in a Gallup survey claimed they read a newspaper daily. The headlines are the most popular part of the paper for adolescents, followed by the movie reviews, comics, sports page, and TV listings.

Also, reading books has not totally been abandoned by teenagers. Thirty-five percent of a national sample reported they had read for pleasure the previous day. Twenty-two percent had read for at least one hour.

G5. RELIGION

When a national sample of teens were asked their religious preference, the largest number (29 percent) identified themselves as Roman Catholic. Twenty-one percent replied Baptist, while only 7 percent preferred the Methodist church. Also, only 7 percent failed to report a preference. A very large majority (95 percent) believe in God. Also, roughly 40 percent of the national sample indicated they regularly attend Sunday school. Finally, a sizable proportion of adolescents, approximately one-third, reported they had exposure to religious broadcasting during the previous month.

G6. OTHER RECREATION AND LEISURE

In addition to the specific activities detailed in this chapter, there are other, less easily categorized adolescent activities. High school sophomores reported they spend considerable time talking with friends on the telephone, visiting with friends at a local hangout, and just driving around. Also, a sizable percent of teenagers have attended a professional sporting event, visited an art museum, or attended a rock concert during the previous year. Fewer reveal they have attended a symphony concert, ballet, or opera.

As the American business community is well aware, adolescents are a very large market segment. It is estimated that younger adolescents, those aged 12 to 14, spend an average of $22 per week, while older teens, 15- to 17-year-olds, spend $43 each week. Manufacturers such as shoe companies, fast-food franchises, audio-tape and CD producers, video-game manufacturers, and other industries continue to target the teen market. Adolescents accommodate by spending most of their money on food, snacks, and clothing, followed by entertainment expenses, tapes and CDs, and cosmetics and grooming.

G1.   TELEVISION AND MOVIES

G1-1. Children's and Adolescents' Weekly Television Viewing, by Age, November 1992

Age	Hours per week
2 to 5 years	25 hours 32 minutes
6 to 11 years	21 hours 30 minutes
12 to 17 years	
Men	22 hours 39 minutes
Women	21 hours 00 minutes
18 to 24 years:	
Men	23 hours 31 minutes
Women	28 hours 54 minutes

Source: Johnson, O. (ed.). 1993. *Information Please Almanac, 1994.* Boston, MA: Houghton, Mifflin Co.

G1-2. Adolescents' Time Spent Watching TV Each Day, by Sex, Age, Race, and Social Class, 1992

Survey question: About how much time, if any, did you spend yesterday watching TV?

Characteristic	None	Less than 1 hour	1–2 hours	3 or more hours
National	**12%**	**22%**	**47%**	**17%**
Sex:				
Male	9	21	50	16
Female	15	23	44	15
Age:				
13-15 years	11	19	50	18
16-17 years	14	26	44	17
Race:				
White	12	24	47	17
Non-white	12	15	50	21
Social Class:*				
White-collar background	13	24	51	12
Blue-collar background	13	20	42	23

* Primary wage earner in the family occupied a white- or blue-collar job.
Note: Percents may not add to 100 due to rounding.

Source: Bezilla, Robert (ed.). 1993. *American's Youth in the 1990s.* Princeton, NJ: The George H. Gallup International Institute, page 234.

G1-3. High School Seniors' TV Watching and Movie Attendance, by Sex and Race, 1992

Question: How often do you . . . watch TV? Go to movies?					
		Sex		Race	
	Total (N=2,727)	Males (N=1,270)	Females (N=1,360)	White (N=1,847)	Black (N=378)
Watch TV:					
Almost every day	73.2%	77.4%	69.3%	70.3%	86.8%
At least once a week	22.2	18.6	25.4	24.6	10.6
Once or twice a month	3.1	2.2	4.0	3.7	0.9
A few times a year	0.9	0.9	1.0	0.9	1.1
Never	0.6	0.8	0.3	0.5	0.7
Go to movies:					
Almost every day	0.1%	0.0%	0.1%	0.1%	0.0%
At least once a week	8.2	9.1	7.3	7.5	9.2
Once or twice a month	56.3	53.0	60.1	48.8	51.0
A few times a year	33.0	34.7	30.9	31.8	37.6
Never	2.4	3.2	1.6	1.8	2.3

Note: N represents sample size. Percents may not add to 100 due to rounding.

Source: Bachman, Jerald G., Lloyd D. Johnston, and Patrick M. O'Malley. 1993. *Monitoring the Future: Questionnaire Responses from the Nation's High School Seniors, 1992.* Ann Arbor, MI: Survey Research Center, Institute for Social Research, The University of Michigan, page 221.

G1-4. Hours Spent Watching Television on Weekdays by High School Seniors, by Sex and Race, 1992

Question: How much TV do you estimate you watch on an average weekday?					
		Sex		Race	
	Total (N=2,727)	Males (N=1,270)	Females (N=1,360)	White (N=1,847)	Black (N=378)
Average TV watching on weekday:					
None	3.6%	4.0%	3.3%	4.0%	1.0%
Half-hour or less	14.1	13.8	14.6	16.5	8.5
About one hour	20.9	19.9	22.0	23.9	8.2
About two hours	21.5	21.5	21.6	22.6	13.6
About three hours	16.7	16.8	16.6	16.1	17.2
About four hours	10.3	10.8	9.8	8.5	16.1
Five hours or more	12.9	13.3	12.2	8.4	35.4

Note: N represents sample size. Percents may not add to 100 due to rounding.

Source: Bachman, Jerald G., Lloyd D. Johnston, and Patrick M. O'Malley. 1993. *Monitoring the Future: Questionnaire Responses from the Nation's High School Seniors, 1992.* Ann Arbor, MI: Survey Research Center, Institute for Social Research, The University of Michigan, page 169.

G1-5. Where Teenagers Watch Movies, 1985–1991

Survey question: About how many times, if any, did you, yourself, go out to the movies within the last 12 months? About how many times, if any, in the past 12 months have you seen movies in each of the following ways—On cable television? On regular television? On a videocassette recorder (VCR)?

| Year | Percent of teens using each medium to view movies | | | |
	VCR	Theater	Broadcast television	Cable TV
1985	75%	92%	88%	69%
1988	93	74	94	76
1991	97	95	93	82
	Average annual number seen			
1985	20	15	28	38
1988	34	12	31	32
1991	26	9	26	28

Source: Bezilla, Robert (ed.). 1993. *American's Youth in the 1990s.* Princeton, NJ: The George H. Gallup International Institute, page 246.

G1-6. How Adolescents Watch Movies, by Sex, Age, Race, and Social Class, 1991

Survey question: About how many times, if any, did you, yourself, go out to the movies within the last 12 months? About how many times, if any, in the past 12 months have you seen movies in each of the following ways—On cable television? On regular television? On a videocassette recorder (VCR)?

Characteristics	VCR	Theater	Broadcast television	Cable TV
National	**97%**	**95%**	**93%**	**82%**
Sex:				
Male	98	93	91	81
Female	97	96	94	83
Age:				
13-15 years	97	95	92	83
16-17 years	98	94	94	83
Race:				
White	98	95	92	81
Non-white	96	95	94	93
Social Class:*				
White-collar background	97	97	93	85
Blue-collar background	99	93	96	78

* Primary wage earner in the family occupied a white- or blue-collar job.

Source: Bezilla, Robert (ed.). 1993. *American's Youth in the 1990s.* Princeton, NJ: The George H. Gallup International Institute, page 247.

G1-7. Family Time Spent Watching Movies on VCR or on TV Programs, 1985

	Percent
Survey question: How often does your whole household family get together to watch movies on a VCR or TV program?	
Very often	41
Sometimes	30
Not very often	20
Never	8

Note: 1,612 respondents.

Source: Ethan Allen, Inc. 1986. *The Ethan Allen Report: The Status and Future of the American Family.* Danbury, CT: Ethan Allen, Inc., page 72.

G2. SPORTS AND CLUBS

G2-1. Children and Adolescents' Participation in Sports Activities, by Age, 1991

Activity (in 1,000s)	7-11 years	12-17 years	18-24 years
Total	**18,613**	**20,716**	**25,273**
Number participated in:			
Aerobic exercising	1,005	1,541	5,241
Backpacking	883	1,603	1,737
Baseball	5,205	4,835	2,177
Basketball	4,970	7,990	4,440
Bicycle riding	11,084	9,327	4,942
Bowling	4,004	4,735	7,321
Calisthenics	1,247	1,782	1,831
Camping	5,740	5,244	4,967
Exercise walking	2,022	2,850	5,579
Exercising with equipment	510	2,827	6,985
Fishing—fresh water	4,356	4,054	4,799
Fishing—salt water	665	866	1,362
Football	2,806	4,463	2,767
Golf	758	1,696	3,100
Hiking	2,097	2,567	2,516
Hunting with firearms	356	1,329	2,455
Racquetball	121	451	1,862
Running/jogging	2,262	4,063	4,153
Skiing—alpine/downhill	689	1,615	2,333
Skiing—cross country	253	444	718
Soccer	3,741	3,581	1,167
Softball	2,358	4,286	3,671
Swimming	10,244	9,959	9,152
Target shooting	689	1,451	1,813
Tennis	1,060	2,993	3,549
Volleyball	1,774	5,089	4,625

Source: U.S. Bureau of the Census, *Statistical Abstract of the United States: 1993* (113th edition). Washington, DC, 1993, page 254.

G2-2. Adolescents' Participation in Sports, 1978–1991

Survey question: Which of these sports or activities have you, yourself participated in or played within the past 12 months?

Sport	Year			
	1978	1983	1987	1991
Aerobic dancing	NA	NA	28%	26%
Basketball	68	75	76	56
Bicycling	NA	78	78	47
Bowling	59	50	48	41
Fishing	51	48	44	36
Football (touch)	NA	64	60	45
Golf	16	19	18	16
Horseback riding	16	32	20	19
Hunting	27	22	21	19
Ice skating	34	26	21	NA
Jogging	NA	55	55	46
Racquetball	14	NA	14	NA
Regular fitness program	NA	NA	NA	42
Rollerskating	52	68	55	31
Sailing	NA	NA	8	NA
Skateboarding	NA	NA	NA	12
Snow skiing	22	24	23	16
Softball	64	77	71	28
Soccer	NA	NA	NA	30
Tennis	47	52	46	34
Weight training	NA	NA	49	43

Note: NA indicates not available. All numbers are percents. Sample was 1,000.

Source: Bezilla, Robert (ed.). 1993. *American's Youth in the 1990s.* Princeton, NJ: The George H. Gallup International Institute, page 228.

G2-3. High School Seniors' Participation in Sports and Athletics, by Sex and Race, 1992

Actively participate in sports, athletics, or exercising	Total (N=2,727)	Sex		Race	
		Males (N=1,270)	Females (N=1,360)	White (N=1,847)	Black (N=378)
Almost every day	44.5	52.9	36.4	46.6	38.0
At least once a week	22.2	22.4	21.9	22.5	15.1
Once or twice a month	12.3	9.7	15.4	12.7	15.3
A few times a year	11.7	8.1	15.2	10.7	18.0
Never	9.2	6.9	11.1	7.6	13.6

Note: N indicates sample size. Percents may not add to 100 due to rounding.

Source: Bachman, Jerald G., Lloyd D. Johnston, and Patrick M. O'Malley. 1993. *Monitoring the Future: Questionnaire Responses from the Nation's High School Seniors, 1992.* Ann Arbor, MI: Survey Research Center, Institute for Social Research, The University of Michigan, p. 222.

G2-4. Consumer Purchases of Sporting Goods, by Age of Consumer, 1991

		FOOTWEAR				EQUIPMENT					
Age	Total house-holds	Aerobic shoes	Gym shoes/ sneakers	Jogging/ running shoes	Walking shoes	Fishing tackle	Camping equip-ment	Exercise equip-ment	Rifles	Shotguns	Golf equip-ment
Under 14 yrs	20.6%	6.6%	39.3%	8.8%	3.3%	6.0%	12.0%	1.0%	3.1%	2.9%	2.0%
14–17	5.3	3.5	10.7	11.7	1.9	3.0	6.0	2.0	4.2	6.0	3.0
18–24 years	10.1	11.7	8.5	8.4	2.7	6.0	7.0	5.0	9.2	10.8	5.0
25 and over	64.0	78.2	41.5	71.1	92.1	85.0	75.0	92.0	83.5	80.3	89.0

Source: U.S. Bureau of the Census, *Statistical Abstract of the United States: 1993* (113th edition). Washington, DC, 1993, page 255.

G2-5. Boy Scouts and Girl Scouts—Membership and Units, 1970–1991

Item (in 1,000s)	1970	1975	1980	1985	1990	1991
Boy Scouts of America						
Membership	6,287	5,318	4,318	4,845	5,448	5,319
Boys	4,683	3,933	3,207	3,755	4,293	4,150
Adults	1,604	1,385	1,110	1,090	1,155	1,170
Total units (packs, troops, posts)	157	150	129	134	130	129
Girl Scouts of the U.S.A.						
Membership	3,922	3,234	2,784	2,802	3,269	3,383
Girls	3,248	2,723	2,250	2,172	2,480	2,561
Adults	674	511	534	630	788	822
Total units (troops, groups)	164	159	154	166	202	210

Source: U.S. Bureau of the Census, *Statistical Abstract of the United States: 1993* (113th edition). Washington, DC, 1993, p. 256.

G2-6. Adolescents' Favorite Spectator Sports, by Sex, 1991

		Sex	
Sport	Total	Male	Female
Football	41%	49%	33%
Basketball	22	18	25
Baseball	13	12	13
Hockey	4	5	3
Tennis	3	1	5
Soccer	2	0	4
Volleyball	2	0	4
Wrestling	2	2	1
Swimming, diving	2	1	2
Miscellaneous	7	10	5
None	1	1	2

Note: Total adds to more than 100 percent because some teens named more than one favorite sport.

Source: Bezilla, Robert (ed.). 1993. *American's Youth in the 1990s.* Princeton, NJ: The George H. Gallup International Institute, page 229.

G3. MUSIC

G3-1. Adolescents' Musical Taste, 1981–1992

Survey question: What is your favorite form of music?

Type of Music	Years 1981	1986	1992
Rap	NA	NA	26%
Top 40	25%	34%	16
Rock	30	22	25
New wave	16	18	4
Easy listening	NA	8	4
Country and western	13	7	12
Rhythm 'n' blues	6	4	4
Classical	3	3	3
Jazz	6	3	1

Note: NA indicates not available. Percents may not add to 100 due to rounding.

Source: Bezilla, Robert (ed.). 1993. *American's Youth in the 1990s.* Princeton, NJ: The George H. Gallup International Institute, page 254.

G3-2. Adolescents' Sources of Music, by Sex, Age, Race, and Social Class, 1992

Survey question: Did you, yourself, listen to music yesterday in any of the following ways—Listening to a recording such as a CD, record, tape, or cassette? FM radio? AM radio? Music video on cable TV? Music video on regular TV? Attended a live concert?

Characteristic	Source FM radio	AM radio	Record-ing	Cable video	TV video	Live concert
National	**92%**	**17%**	**88%**	**55%**	**43%**	**4%**
Sex:						
Male	90	19	87	57	43	4
Female	95	16	89	54	43	3
Age:						
13-15 years	91	19	85	53	43	4
16-17 years	95	16	92	58	44	4
Race:						
White	92	15	85	53	43	4
Non-white	95	25	92	69	51	6
Social Class:*						
White-collar background	94	17	91	55	45	3
Blue-collar background	91	17	84	56	44	3

* Primary wage earner in the family occupied a white- or blue-collar job.
Note: 1 percent of teens said they did not hear music from any of these sources on the previous day.

Source: Bezilla, Robert (ed.). 1993. *American's Youth in the 1990s.* Princeton, NJ: The George H. Gallup International Institute, page 257.

G3-3. Adolescents' Favorite Form of Music, by Sex, Age, Race, and Social Class, 1992

Survey question: What is your favorite form of music?

Characteristic	Rap	Hard rock	Top 40	Country & western	Rhythm 'n' blues
National	**26%**	**25%**	**16%**	**12%**	**4%**
Sex:					
Male	29	27	10	14	2
Female	23	23	22	11	6
Age:					
13-15 years	33	25	17	10	2
16-17 years	18	24	13	15	7
Race:					
White	17	30	19	15	2
Non-white	55	9	6	5	12
Black	67	4	4	2	17
Social Class:*					
White-collar background	22	25	19	9	6
Blue-collar background	31	21	13	16	4

* Primary wage earner in the family occupied a white- or blue-collar job.

Source: Bezilla, Robert (ed.). 1993. *American's Youth in the 1990s.* Princeton, NJ: The George H. Gallup International Institute, page 255.

G3-4. High School Seniors' Attendance at Rock Concerts, by Sex, and Race, 1992

Question: How often do you . . .

Go to rock concerts	Total (N=2,727)	Sex		Race	
		Males (N=1,270)	Females (N=1,360)	White (N=1,847)	Black (N=378)
Almost every day	0.1	0.2	0.0	0.1	0.3
At least once a week	0.5	0.5	0.5	0.3	0.3
Once or twice a month	2.9	4.1	1.9	3.4	1.2
A few times a year	46.2	47.2	45.8	51.4	29.3
Never	50.3	48.0	51.9	44.8	68.8

Note: N indicates size of sample. Percent totals may not add to 100 due to rounding.

Source: Bachman, Jerald G., Lloyd D. Johnston, and Patrick M. O'Malley. 1993. *Monitoring the Future: Questionnaire Responses from the Nation's High School Seniors, 1992.* Ann Arbor, MI: Survey Research Center, Institute for Social Research, The University of Michigan, p. 221.

G4. BOOKS, MAGAZINES, AND NEWSPAPERS

G4-1. Adolescents' Readership of Newspapers, Magazines, and Comic Books, by Sex, Age, and Social Class, 1991

Survey question: Did you, yourself, do any of the following yesterday—read or look at a newspaper, read or look at a magazine, read or look at a comic book?

Characteristic	Newspapers	Magazines	Comic books
National	**68%**	**58%**	**11**
Sex:			
Male	68	58	12
Female	69	57	9
Age:			
13-15 years	64	62	14
16-17 years	75	52	6
Social Class:*			
White-collar background	71	60	11
Blue-collar background	70	58	10

* Primary wage earner in the family occupied a white- or blue-collar job.

Source: Bezilla, Robert (ed.). 1993. *American's Youth in the 1990s.* Princeton, NJ: The George H. Gallup International Institute, page 238.

G4-2. Adolescent Newspaper Readership, by Sex, Age, Race, and Social Class, 1991

Survey question: About how often would you say you read or look at anything in a daily newspaper?

Characteristic	Frequency			
	About daily	1–2 times weekly	1–2 times monthly	Seldom or never
National	52%	36%	6%	5%
Sex:				
Male	55	34	6	5
Female	48	39	6	6
Age:				
13-15 years	48	38	6	6
16-17 years	56	33	5	5
Race:				
White	54	35	6	4
Non-white	45	38	4	10
Social Class:*				
White-collar background	56	33	3	6
Blue-collar background	49	40	9	2

* Primary wage earner in the family occupied a white- or blue-collar job.

Source: Bezilla, Robert (ed.). 1993. *American's Youth in the 1990s.* Princeton, NJ: The George H. Gallup International Institute, page 239.

G4-3. Adolescent Readership of Daily Newspaper Sections, by Sex, Age, Race, and Social Class, 1991

Survey question: Which of these, if any, have you read or looked at in a daily newspaper in the past seven days—front page headlines, movie reviews, comics, sports, TV listings, help wanted ads?

| | Section Read Last Week | | | | | |
Characteristics	Head-lines	Movie review	Comics	Sports	TV listings	Want ads
National	**71%**	**60%**	**55%**	**54%**	**53%**	**43%**
Sex:						
Male	68	60	55	71	53	41
Female	73	61	56	37	53	44
Age:						
13-15 years	58	61	61	53	56	39
16-17 years	75	59	47	56	50	48
Race:						
White	73	60	58	56	53	43
Non-white	63	59	47	50	56	42
Social Class:*						
White-collar background	74	64	59	58	57	38
Blue-collar background	72	58	54	54	52	49

* Primary wage earner in the family occupied a white- or blue-collar job.

Source: Bezilla, Robert (ed.). 1993. *American's Youth in the 1990s.* Princeton, NJ: The George H. Gallup International Institute, page 240.

G4-4. Frequency of Magazine and Newspaper Reading among High School Seniors, by Sex and Race, 1992

Question: How often do you do each of the following?

| | | Sex | | Race | |
	Total (N=2,727)	Males (N=1,270)	Females (N=1,360)	White (N=1,847)	Black (N=378)
Read magazines:					
Almost every day	11.6%	14.6%	8.9%	11.1%	14.2%
At least once a week	43.5	43.9	43.2	44.0	46.6
Once or twice a month	32.1	26.7	37.5	33.0	29.7
A few times a year	8.2	8.9	7.5	8.0	5.4
Never	4.6	6.0	2.9	3.9	4.0
Read newspapers:					
Almost every day	36.0%	42.6%	30.2%	38.1%	34.7%
At least once a week	35.2	31.7	38.6	34.1	37.3
Once or twice a month	16.4	13.8	18.9	15.2	17.8
A few times a year	7.8	7.6	7.6	8.0	6.6
Never	4.5	4.3	4.8	4.5	3.6

Note: N indicates sample size. Percents may not add to 100 due to rounding.

Source: Bachman, Jerald G., Lloyd D. Johnston, and Patrick M. O'Malley. 1993. *Monitoring the Future: Questionnaire Responses from the Nation's High School Seniors, 1992.* Ann Arbor, MI: Survey Research Center, Institute for Social Research, The University of Michigan, page 222.

G4-5. Time Adolescents Spent Reading Books, by Sex, Age, Race, and Social Class, 1992

Survey question: About how much time, if any, did you spend yesterday at each of these activities—reading for fun or pleasure?

Characteristic	None	Less than 1 hour	1-2 hours	3 or more hours
National	**43%**	**35%**	**20%**	**2%**
Sex:				
Male	42	37	19	2
Female	43	34	22	2
Age:				
13-15 years	40	39	19	2
16-17 years	45	31	22	2
Race:				
White	45	35	18	2
Non-white	31	38	28	3
Social Class:*				
White-collar background	39	40	18	2
Blue-collar background	49	31	19	1

* Primary wage earner in the family occupied a white- or blue-collar job.

Source: Bezilla, Robert (ed.). 1993. *American's Youth in the 1990s.* Princeton, NJ: The George H. Gallup International Institute, page 237.

G4-6. Books Read by High School Seniors, by Sex and Race, 1992

Question: In the past year, how many books have you read just because you wanted to; that is, without their being assigned?

Books read for pleasure in last year:	Total (N=2,727)	Sex		Race	
		Males (N=1,270)	Females (N=1,360)	White (N=1,847)	Black (N=378)
None	23.1%	28.5%	18.2%	23.1%	22.0%
One	14.1	14.6	13.7	15.1	11.7
Two to five	36.1	34.8	37.0	33.8	42.0
Six to ten	12.3	12.4	12.5	11.9	13.7
Ten or more	14.4	9.7	18.7	16.1	10.7

Note: N indicates sample size. Percents may not add to 100 due to rounding.

Source: Bachman, Jerald G., Lloyd D. Johnston, and Patrick M. O'Malley. 1993. *Monitoring the Future: Questionnaire Responses from the Nation's High School Seniors, 1992.* Ann Arbor, MI: Survey Research Center, Institute for Social Research, The University of Michigan, p. 169.

G5. RELIGION

G5-1. Adolescents' Religious Preference, by Region, 1988

Survey question: What is your religious preference? What specific denomination or faith is that?

	National (N=500)	East (N=114)	Midwest (N=171)	South (N=123)	West (N=92)
Protestant	59%	54%	59%	75%	59%
Baptist	21	10	16	42	7
Methodist	7	8	8	7	3
Presbyterian	2	2	4	1	3
Lutheran	4	3	14	*	*
Episcopalian	*	1	1	*	*
Other Protestant	25	20	16	25	46
Roman Catholic	29	48	31	17	23
Orthodox Catholic	1	1	*	1	1
Other Christian	1	1	*	1	2
Jewish	2	3	1	2	2
Other	1	1	1	*	1
No response	7	2	8	4	12

*Less than one-half of 1 percent.
Note: N indicates sample size. This question was posed to 13- to 17-year-olds.

Source: The George H. Gallup International Institute. 1992. *The Religious Life of Young Americans.* Princeton, NJ: The George H. Gallup International Institute, page 53.

G5-2. Adolescents' Belief in God and Resurrection, by Sex, Age, Region, Race, and Religion, 1988

Survey question: Do you believe in God or a universal spirit? Do you believe that this God or universal spirit observes your actions and rewards or punishes you for them? Do you believe that God loves you? Do you believe in life after death, or not?

	Believe in God (N=500)	Believe in a personal God (N=500)	Believe God loves you (N=513)	Belief in life after death (N=500)
National	**95%**	**76%**	**93%**	**67%**
Gender:				
Male	96	76	92	69
Female	95	77	94	65
Age:				
13-15 years	94	77	96	64
16-17 years	96	76	88	71
Region:				
East	96	79	87	66
Midwest	94	67	93	69
South	96	84	96	61
West	95	74	93	76
Race:				
White	94	74	92	69
Non-white	99	90	96	60
Religion:				
Protestant	98	79	96	64
Catholic	94	77	94	74

Note: N indicates sample size. This question was posed to a national sample of teenagers, 13–17 years old.

Source: The George H. Gallup International Institute. 1992. *The Religious Life of Young Americans.* Princeton, NJ: The George H. Gallup International Institute, page 23.

G5-3. Adolescents' Personal Experience with the Presence of God, by Sex, Age, Region, Race, and Religion, 1991

Survey question: Have you ever personally experienced the presence of God?					
	Yes	No	Not sure	Non-Believer	Number of believer interviews
National	**29%**	**65%**	**4%**	**2%**	**513**
Gender:					
Male	28	67	3	2	245
Female	30	63	6	1	268
Age:					
13-15 years	27	67	5	1	305
16-17 years	32	62	3	3	204
Region:					
East	21	69	6	4	103
Midwest	30	67	2	1	141
South	33	61	5	1	157
West	31	63	5	1	111
Race:					
White	29	65	5	1	364
Non-white	32	65		*	144
Religion:					
Protestant	33	61	5	1	249
Catholic	27	70	3	*	162

*Less than one-half of 1 percent.
Note: This question was posed to a national sample of teenagers, 13–17 years old.

Source: The George H. Gallup International Institute. 1992. *The Religious Life of Young Americans.* Princeton, NJ: The George H. Gallup International Institute, page 28.

G5-4. Adolescents' Current Church Activities, by Sex, Age, Region, Race, and Religion, 1991

Survey question: For each of the following activities please tell me if you are now involved in this kind of activity, would like to be involved, or have no interest in it...Sunday school or Bible study group? Church youth group, other than Sunday school? Choir or music group at church? Church-sponsored activities to help less fortunate people?					
	Sunday school	Church youth group	Church charity activity	Church choir	Number of interviewees
National	**41%**	**36%**	**23%**	**18%**	**500**
Gender:					
Male	40	34	20	15	230
Female	42	38	27	22	270
Age:					
13-15 years	42	35	22	19	303
16-17 years	39	36	25	17	197
Region:					
East	32	31	21	12	114
Midwest	29	26	13	11	171
South	54	43	32	29	123
West	45	43	14	30	92
Race:					
White	40	37	25	17	432
Non-white	45	31	18	27	67
Religion:					
Protestant	54	47	29	23	295
Catholic	20	18	11	8	153

Note: This question was posed to a national sample of teenagers, 13–17 years old.

Source: The George H. Gallup International Institute. 1992. *The Religious Life of Young Americans.* Princeton, NJ: The George H. Gallup International Institute, page 33.

G5-5. Adolescents' Experience with Religious Broadcasting, by Sex, Age, Region, Race, and Religion, 1988

Survey question: In the past 30 days have you watched any religious programs on television? ... listened to any on radio?

	Radio or TV	TV	Radio	Number of interviews
National	**35%**	**24%**	**20%**	**500**
Gender:				
Male	38	27	20	230
Female	32	20	21	270
Age:				
13-15 years	34	22	18	303
16-17 years	37	25	23	197
Region:				
East	27	17	13	114
Midwest	34	20	21	171
South	47	34	28	123
West	28	21	15	92
Race:				
White	32	22	16	432
Non-white	51	33	40	144
Religion:				
Protestant	42	26	28	295
Catholic	28	22	9	153

Note: This question was posed to a national sample of teenagers, 13–17 years old.

Source: The George H. Gallup International Institute. 1992. *The Religious Life of Young Americans.* Princeton, NJ: The George H. Gallup International Institute, page 48.

G6.   OTHER RECREATION AND LIESURE

G6-1. Percent of High School Sophomores Who Say They Engage in Various Activities at Least Once or Twice a Week, and Amount of TV Watched, by Student Characteristics, 1990

Student Characteristics	Percent				
	Just driving/ riding around	Visiting friends at local hangout	Talking to friends on the telephone	Reading for pleasure	Hours of TV watched on school nights
All Sophomores	56.1%	66.3%	80.1%	41.0%	9.1
Male	57.9	69.5	72.5	33.8	10.2
Female	54.3	63.1	87.7	48.2	8.0
Race/ethnicity					
White	58.9	68.7	81.7	41.5	6.7
Black	50.1	59.1	79.6	41.2	23.0
Hispanic	47.6	59.3	72.4	38.2	10.2
Asian	44.0	57.1	78.3	40.2	6.9
American Indian	53.3	70.4	65.1	39.5	15.8
Test performance					
Lowest test quartile[1]	59.6	66.1	74.8	27.7	17.9
Second test quartile	62.0	69.0	80.9	36.3	11.8
Third test quartile	57.8	68.5	83.9	42.4	5.9
Highest test quartile	45.8	61.1	80.4	55.8	3.2
Socioeconomic status					
Low quartile[1]	55.1	62.6	72.2	37.4	13.5
Middle 2 quartiles	58.3	68.0	81.9	40.4	9.5
High quartile	52.0	66.2	83.5	46.1	3.4

[1] A quartile is one-fourth of the respondents. Thus the "lowest test quartile" is the fourth of the respondents with the lowest scores on the achievement test.

Source: Snyder, T. D., and C. M. Hoffman. 1993. *Digest of Educatin Statistics.* Washington, DC: National Center for Education Statistics, page 13.

G6-2. Adolescents' Participation in Various Activities, 1990

Activity	Percent (N=929)	Percent (N=782)
Played team sport at school	84%	79%
Attended activity at church or temple	74	82
Taken special lessons in music, dance, karate, etc.	72	73
Participated in extra school activity: play, choir	70	79
Attended Scouts, 4H, YM(W)CA, Boys (Girls) Clubs	54	55

Note: N indicates sample size. This question was posed to 13–17 years olds.

Source: Moore, K. A. 1992. *Natinal Commission on Children: 1990 Survey of Parents and Children.* (Data Set 19, H. M. Daley, E. C. Peterson, E. L. Lang, & J. J. Card, Archivists) [machine-readable data file and documentation]. Washington, DC: Child Trends, Inc. (Producer). Los Altos, CA: Sociometrics Corporation, American Family Data Archive (Producer & Distributor).

G6-3. Adolescents' Attendance at Entertainment Events during Previous Year, by Sex, Age, Race, and Social Class, 1992

Survey question: Which of the following have you, yourself gone to or attended in the past 12 months?

Characteristic	Pro sports	Art museum	Other museum	Rock concert	Symph. concert	Ballet	Opera
National	**44%**	**31%**	**26%**	**28%**	**11%**	**7%**	**4%**
Sex:							
Male	51	34	28	20	11	6	5
Female	36	28	23	26	11	8	4
Age:							
13-15 years	42	32	24	27	16	9	5
16-17 years	46	30	23	35	7	6	3
Race:							
White	46	31	27	29	12	6	4
Non-white	37	32	22	22	6	9	6
Social Class:*							
White-collar background	50	32	30	31	13	8	4
Blue-collar background	36	30	20	26	9	6	3

* Primary wage earner in the family occupied a white- or blue-collar job.

Source: Bezilla, Robert (ed.). 1993. *American's Youth in the 1990s.* Princeton, NJ: The George H. Gallup International Institute, page 226.

G6-4. Party Attendance of High School Seniors during Previous Year, by Sex and Race, 1992

		Sex		Race	
Question: Over the last 12 months, about how often have you gone to parties?	Total (N=2,736)	Males (N=1,248)	Females (N=1,352)	White (N=1,886)	Black (N=387)
Not at all	15.6%	14.4%	16.8%	15.0%	22.5%
Once a month or less	34.2	30.3	38.3	34.6	33.2
2 or 3 times a month	26.9	25.8	27.3	25.9	25.7
About once a week	13.1	16.8	9.9	14.2	9.9
2 or 3 times a week	8.1	9.4	6.6	8.3	7.4
Over 3 times a week	2.2	3.4	1.1	2.0	1.3

Note: N indicates sample size. Percents may not add to 100 due to rounding.

Source: Bachman, Jerald G., Lloyd D. Johnston, and Patrick M. O'Malley. 1993. *Monitoring the Future: Questionnaire Responses from the Nation's High School Seniors, 1992.* Ann Arbor, MI: Survey Research Center, Institute for Social Research, The Univeristy of Michigan, page 216.

G6-5. Leisure Activities of High School Seniors, by Sex and Race, 1992

		Sex		Race	
Question: How often do you do each of the following?	Total (N=2,727)	Males (N=1,270)	Females (N=1,360)	White (N=1,847)	Black (N=378)
Participate in community affairs or volunteer work:					
Almost every day	3.1%	2.0%	4.2%	2.5%	6.2%
At least once a week	7.8	6.0	9.2	7.2	9.2
Once or twice a month	16.8	15.1	18.6	17.5	16.8
A few times a year	41.7	41.2	42.7	43.7	36.7
Never	30.6	35.7	25.3	29.1	31.1
Go to taverns, bars, or nightclubs:					
Almost every day	1.3%	2.1%	0.2%	1.3%	0.8%
At least once a week	9.5	10.2	8.7	9.2	9.6
Once or twice a month	16.6	18.5	14.8	15.5	21.8
A few times a year	20.1	20.0	20.3	21.8	16.2
Never	52.5	49.2	56.0	52.2	51.6
Go to parties/social affairs:					
Almost every day	2.9%	3.2%	2.2%	2.9%	2.0%
At least once a week	33.2	37.7	29.2	35.7	23.3
Once or twice a month	35.4	33.7	37.5	35.2	40.5
A few times a year	23.6	20.8	26.5	21.9	27.6
Never	4.9	4.6	4.7	4.3	6.7
Get together informally with friends:					
Almost every day	45.9%	53.7%	38.3%	47.6%	40.1%
At least once a week	40.8	36.6	45.1	41.4	39.2
Once or twice a month	9.5	6.4	12.6	8.6	12.9
A few times a year	2.7	2.3	2.9	1.9	5.1
Never	1.1	0.9	1.2	0.5	2.8

G6-5. Leisure Activities of High School Seniors, by Sex and Race, 1992 (continued)

	Total (N=2,727)	Sex		Race	
		Males (N=1,270)	Females (N=1,360)	White (N=1,847)	Black (N=378)
Go shopping or window shopping:					
Almost every day	3.3%	1.8%	4.6%	2.6%	5.8%
At least once a week	31.5	23.7	39.0	29.8	43.1
Once or twice a month	48.6	48.7	48.4	50.3	41.4
A few times a year	12.5	18.7	6.8	12.9	7.2
Never	4.1	7.1	1.2	4.4	2.5
Spend at least an hour of leisure time alone:					
Almost every day	41.8%	42.2%	41.7%	39.7%	57.6%
At least once a week	34.4	34.7	34.1	36.1	26.1
Once or twice a month	11.8	10.7	12.8	12.9	7.9
A few times a year	5.7	6.7	4.9	5.5	4.1
Never	6.2	5.6	6.6	5.7	4.2
Ride around in a car (or motorcycle) just for fun:					
Almost every day	30.2%	35.5%	24.5%	28.6%	35.4%
At least once a week	33.2	34.1	32.8	33.4	35.3
Once or twice a month	17.7	15.7	19.7	19.6	12.5
A few times a year	10.7	8.4	13.2	11.2	8.0
Never	8.2	6.3	9.8	7.1	8.8

Note: N indicates sample size. Percents may not add to 100 due to rounding.

Source: Bachman, Jerald G., Lloyd D. Johnston, and Patrick M. O'Malley. 1993. *Monitoring the Future: Questionnaire Responses from the Nation's High School Seniors, 1992.* Ann Arbor, MI: Survey Research Center, Institute for Social Research, The Univeristy of Michigan, page 221–223.

G6-6. Adolescent's Enjoyment of Family Activities, 1992

Survey question: Of all the activities you do with a family member or members, which three do you enjoy the most?

Activities	Percent
Outdoor activities	26%
Travel/vacations	19
Just being together	19
Watching television	16
Talking	14
Playing non-team sports	14
Family meals	12
Going out to eat	11
Visiting family members	11
Religious activities	10
Family gatherinsg/events/holidays	9
Going to movies	9
Shopping	9
Partying/socializing/entertaining	8
Family outings/day trips	7
Playing team sports	7
Watching sports	7
Indoor games	7
Taking walks	6
Picnics	6
Playing/activities with children	5
Reading/doing homework	4
Water sports/ sailing, boating	4
Driving around/taking rides	4

Note: 1,706 respondents.

Source: Bachman, Jerald G., Lloyd D. Johnston, and Patrick M. O'Malley. 1993. *Monitoring the Future: Questionnaire Responses from the Nation's High School Seniors, 1992.* Ann Arbor, MI: Survey Research Center, Institute for Social Research, The University of Michigan, p. 194.

G6-7. High School Seniors' Concerns with Clothes and Possessions, by Sex and Race, 1992

Question: How do you feel about each of the following?

	Total (N=2,727)	Sex		Race	
		Males (N=1,270)	Females (N=1,360)	White (N=1,847)	Black (N=378)
Shopping for clothes, records, sporting goods, books:					
Not at all	1.6%	2.8%	0.5%	1.7%	0.5%
Not very much	11.2	15.6	6.8	12.4	4.8
Pretty much	34.1	42.7	25.4	36.8	20.6
Very much	53.2	39.0	67.4	49.1	74.2
How much you care about having latest fashion:					
Not at all	7.2%	9.4%	4.7%	7.7%	3.1%
Not very much	28.8	28.9	28.4	30.6	20.4
Pretty much	40.0	39.8	40.3	40.8	39.1
Very much	24.0	21.8	26.5	20.9	37.3
How much you care whether your family has things your friends/neighbors have:					
Not at all	28.1%	27.1%	29.0%	26.8%	32.5%
Not very much	49.4	47.8	50.9	50.8	47.8
Pretty much	17.2	18.8	15.6	18.4	13.8
Very much	5.3	6.3	4.5	4.0	6.0

Note: N indicates sample size. Percents may not add to 100 due to rounding.

Source: Bachman, Jerald G., Lloyd D. Johnston, and Patrick M. O'Malley. 1993. *Monitoring the Future: Questionnaire Respnses from the Nation's High School Seniors, 1992.* Ann Arbor, MI: Survey Research Center, Institute for Social Research, The University of Michigan, p. 193.

G6-8. High School Seniors' Access to an Automobile, by Sex and Race, 1992

	Total (N=2,727)	Sex		Race	
		Males (N=1,270)	Females (N=1,360)	White (N=1,847)	Black (N=378)
Do you have a driver's license:					
Yes	86.9%	90.7%	83.5%	92.0%	70.3%
No, but I soon will	11.2	8.0	13.9	6.8	24.0
No	1.9	1.3	2.6	1.2	5.7
Do you own a car:					
Yes	61.4%	67.8%	54.1%	64.7%	31.9%
No, but I expect to own one in another year or two	25.1	20.9	29.7	20.3	58.2
No	13.5	11.3	16.2	15.0	10.0
Able to use someone else's car when wanted:					
Yes, whenever I wish	32.7%	31.9%	33.4%	34.5%	29.2%
Yes, most of the time	42.1	39.5	44.9	43.6	35.7
Sometimes	17.5	19.7	15.2	15.4	23.0
Rarely	5.3	6.4	4.3	4.3	9.3
Never	2.5	2.6	2.2	2.1	2.8

Note: N indicates sample size. Percents may not add to 100 due to rounding.

Source: Bachman, Jerald G., Lloyd D. Johnston, and Patrick M. O'Malley. 1993. *Monitoring the Future: Questionnaire Respnses from the Nation's High School Seniors, 1992.* Ann Arbor, MI: Survey Research Center, Institute for Social Research, The University of Michigan, p. 206.

G6-9. Trend in Media Used by Adolescents, 1983–1991

Type of Media	Percent Who Used			
	1983	1986	1990	1991
Radio	93%	91%	90%	88%
TV	91	89	76	88
Cable TV	NA	NA	63	na
VCR	NA	NA	39	na
Newspaper	73	68	63	88
Magazine	54	54	71	58
Comic book	15	17	10	11

Note: NA indicates not available.

Source: Bezilla, Robert (ed.). 1993. *American's Youth in the 1990s.* Princeton, NJ: The George H. Gallup International Institute, page 232.

G6-10. Adolescents' Entertainment Spending, by Sex, 1994

Goods or Services	Amount Spent per Week	
	Boys	Girls
Food, snacks	$10.10	$6.50
Clothing	6.19	10.65
Entertainment	4.35	3.45
Records, tapes, CDs	1.55	1.80
Grooming/cosmetics	1.10	3.35

Source: *Newsweek* (Summer/Fall, 1994). Special issue, "The New Teens," page 35.

H. Deviance

Several national surveys have asked the general public what it thinks are the major problems currently facing American society. Crime, violence in the schools, and drug abuse top the list. Newspapers tell of children as young as six years of age committing heinous crimes, including brutal murders. There are also accounts of rampant drug use and irresponsible sexual behavior among American adolescents. All of which stimulates concern in the American public.

In this chapter, we present arrest rates for juvenile offenders as well as the self-reported frequency of different delinquent activities. Detailed information is also presented about both drug and alcohol abuse among adolescents, as is conflict in the home among family members, especially between parents and their children.

Violence in the schools has become such a major problem that many urban schools now have police officers assigned to them during school hours. In this chapter, we present data about the actual frequency and prevalence of school violence. We also include information about how often teens feel their friends pressure them to engage in delinquent behavior. In addition, data presented here from the juvenile courts reveals the disposition of juvenile offenders who have been arrested. Finally, we include data on children as victims of violence, either from the actions of those their own age or from adults.

H1. DELINQUENCY

Over 11 million people under the age of 25 were arrested in 1992. It is frightening to note that 304 youngsters under 15 and nearly 7,000 under 21 years of age were arrested for murder. Young men accounted for most of the arrests, although over 2 million young women were also charged with various crimes in 1992.

Of all the states in the U.S., California has the highest rate of arrest for individuals under 18 years, followed by Texas, Florida, and New York. Vermont, Delaware, and Wyoming reported the lowest rates of juvenile arrest.

In a national sample of high school seniors, a large majority reported fighting with their parents, and a third admitted stealing something worth under 50 dollars during the previous 12 months. In addition, 30 percent acknowledged that they had shoplifted, and 26 percent claimed to have taken a car without the owner's permission.

Finally, over three-fourths of young men and two-thirds of young women in the twelfth grade have experienced sexual intercourse at least once. Over half of both have done so four or more times. Only about half of these sexually active teens practice contraception. We include data on premarital sex in this chapter on deviance because of its close association with teen pregnancy, venereal disease, abortion, and single-parent families. (For more detail, see Chapter I on sexual behavior.)

H2. SUBSTANCE ABUSE

Alcohol consumption has long been a practice of high school students. In 1959, nearly a fourth of a sample of teenagers admitted they had drunk alcohol during the previous month. That figure rose to 38 percent in 1979, 41 percent in 1982, and then dropped to a little over 20 percent in the late 1980s. A recent survey in 1992, reported that over 50 percent of young people interviewed had drunk in the past month. The same survey of high school seniors also noted that 77 percent had consumed alcohol beverages during the preceding year. Adolescents' favorite alcoholic beverage is beer, followed by wine, with few favoring liquor. More boys than girls drink alcohol, but the gap is narrowing.

Drug abuse and the popularity of specific drugs has varied over the past 25 years. Marijuana was smoked by half of all high school seniors in 1980, but that number steadily declined to 22 percent in 1992. A similar decrease was noted for cocaine use. It appears that overall drug use among high school seniors has dropped during the past two decades.

The most frequent site for drug or alcohol use is a friend's home, followed by the young person's own home. Around 15 percent consume their drugs or alcohol in a car, and only a few do so at school.

Drunk driving has declined among teenagers but continues to be a problem. In 1980, nearly 20 percent of the seniors surveyed reported being ticketed by police for driving under the influence of drugs or alcohol. Ticketing for drunk driving dropped to nine percent among seniors by 1992.

H3. FAMILY PROBLEM BEHAVIOR

Adolescence is a time of emerging independence from the family; nevertheless, teenagers are still greatly influenced by family life. One important aspect of family life that has an impact on children is alcohol abuse by their parents. In 1992, 29 percent of a sample of teenagers reported that liquor had been a source of trouble in the family. Drugs had been a family problem for 11 percent and gambling for 6 percent of the sample.

Family problems, however, do not necessarily begin or end with the parents' behavior. Parents must also deal with their teenage children's inappropriate behavior within the home and outside the home to a degree. Approximately 5 to 10 percent of parents report that their children disobey them, lie to them, don't have remorse for deviant behavior, and don't get along with others very well. But when asked what they worry about the most, parents said they worried about their children becoming victims of others' deviant behavior. Over a fourth of the parents were concerned that their child would be kidnapped, hit by a car, get beaten up, ride in a car with a drunk driver, or be shot. Less than 30 percent of the parents worried their children would catch AIDS, drink heavily, do drugs, get pregnant, or catch a venereal disease.

H4. SCHOOL PROBLEM BEHAVIOR

Only a small percent of parents reported their children have problems in school. Less than three percent indicated their children were disobedient at school or had trouble with their teachers. Approximately one-fourth of the parents in a national survey admitted that one of their children had repeated a grade and that they, the parents, had met with a teacher about a specific problem. Fifteen percent of the parents revealed one of their children had been expelled from school for a period of time.

Parents are also concerned about the safety of their children while they are in junior high and high school. Forty-five percent of a sample of eighth graders reported

they had been in a fight, 38 percent had been threatened, 18 percent had been robbed, and 16 percent had been attacked. Similar frequencies were reported by tenth grade students.

H5. PEER PRESSURE

Teenagers in a national survey reported that a substantial number of their friends participate in delinquent behavior, including skipping school, using drugs, and stealing. When asked about the direct influence from friends to behave a certain way, between 10 and 15 percent said they felt pressured to engage in delinquent behavior, while, conversely, 59 percent said they were pressured by their friends to work hard in school.

H6. TREATMENT OF JUVENILE OFFENDERS

Most arrested juveniles are referred to the juvenile court and are released on some type of probation. A few are referred to criminal or adult court, to another police agency, or to a welfare agency. At this time in American society, however, juveniles are committing more serious crimes such as murder and rape and, consequently, more are being certified to stand trial as adults.

H7. JUVENILE VICTIMS

Children are often the victims of an adult's violent behavior as well as that of those their own age. Children in female-headed families are especially vulnerable to violence. In 1992, over 8,000 people under the age of 25 were murdered. Over two-thirds of the robberies and assaults against teenagers were committed in either the street or school.

Juvenile victimization has led to an increase in the amount adolescents worry about their personal and social situations. When adolescents were asked what worried them most, they answered that what worried them was the state of the earth's environment and the possibility of international war. School grades, the possibility of catching AIDS, being in a car accident, or being hurt by someone on drugs were also issues of concern.

H1. DELINQUENCY

H1-1. Total Arrests of Persons under 15, 18, 21, and 25 Years of Age, 1992

Offense Charged	Number of persons arrested					Percent of total, all ages			
	Total all ages	Under 15	Under 18	Under 21	Under 25	Under 15	Under 18	Under 21	Under 25
TOTAL	11,893,153	689,877	1,943,138	3,474,226	5,300,253	5.8	16.3	29.2	44.6
Murder and nonnegligent manslaughter	19,491	304	2,829	6,857	10,729	1.6	14.5	35.2	55.0
Forcible rape	33,385	2,049	5,369	9,519	14,616	6.1	16.1	28.5	43.8
Robbery	153,456	11,514	40,434	68,541	94,666	7.5	26.3	44.7	61.7
Aggravated assault	434,918	20,366	63,777	115,926	184,354	4.7	14.7	26.7	42.4
Burglary	359,699	50,131	122,567	181,932	229,919	13.9	34.1	50.6	63.9
Larceny-theft	1,291,984	182,623	402,066	564,883	714,795	14.1	31.1	43.7	55.3
Motor vehicle theft	171,269	22,010	75,800	105,361	126,915	12.9	44.3	61.5	74.1
Arson	16,322	5,210	7,968	9,527	10,923	31.9	48.8	58.4	66.9
Violent crime	641,250	34,233	112,409	200,843	304,365	5.3	17.5	31.3	47.5
Property crime	1,839,274	259,974	608,401	861,703	1,802,552	14.1	33.1	46.9	58.9
Crime Index total*	2,480,524	294,207	720,810	1,062,546	1,386,917	11.9	29.1	42.8	55.9

Note: 10,962 agencies; 1992 estimated population 213,392,000.
* Total for murder, rape, robbery, aggravated assault, burglary, larceny-theft, motor vehicle theft, and arson.

Source: Whitaker, C. J., and L. D. Bastian. 1991. *Teenage Victims: A National Crime Survey Report.* Washington, DC: U.S. Department of Justice, page 233.

H1-2. Male and Female Arrests, Distribution by Age, 1992

Offense Charged	Total all ages		Ages under 15		Ages under 18	
	Male	Female	Male	Female	Male	Female
TOTAL	9,633,809	2,259,344	511,870	178,007	1,496,866	446,272
Percent distribution	100.0	100.0	5.3	7.9	15.5	19.8
Murder and nonnegligent manslaughter	17,592	1,899	269	35	2,670	159
Forcible rape	32,965	420	1,988	61	5,258	111
Robbery	140,374	13,082	10,197	1,317	36,987	3,447
Aggravated assault	370,379	64,539	16,433	3,933	53,280	10,497
Burglary	326,570	33,129	44,718	5,413	111,663	10,904
Larceny-theft	876,736	415,248	129,761	52,862	283,662	118,404
Motor vehicle theft	152,753	18,516	18,381	3,629	66,418	9,382
Arson	14,139	2,183	4,658	552	7,121	847
Violent crime	561,310	79,940	28,887	5,346	98,195	14,214
Percent distribution	100.0	100.0	5.1	6.7	17.5	17.8
Property crime	1,370,198	469,076	197,518	62,456	468,864	139,537
Percent distribution	100.0	100.0	14.4	13.3	34.2	29.7
Crime Index total	1,931,508	549,016	226,405	67,802	567,059	153,751
Percent distribution	100.0	100.0	11.7	12.3	29.4	28.0

Note: 10,962 agencies; 1992 estimated population 213,392,000.

Source: Whitaker, C. J., and L. D. Bastian. 1991. *Teenage Victims: A National Crime Survey Report.* Washington, DC: U.S. Department of Justice, pages 229, 231.

H1-3. Adolescent Arrests, by State, 1992

State	Total	Index[1]	Violent crime[2]	Property crime[3]
Alabama	13,263	5,858	1,001	4,857
Alaska	4,904	2,609	142	2,467
Arizona	51,000	18,750	2,128	16,622
Arkansas	16,576	6,179	758	5,421
California	246,332	110,683	20,930	89,753
Colorado	52,073	17,398	1,794	15,604
Connecticut	25,348	9,407	1,292	8,115
Delaware	2,014	815	131	684
District of Columbia	3,741	1,412	586	826
Florida	82,150	48,294	8,812	39,482
Georgia	29,531	10,446	1,408	9,038
Hawaii	18,841	5,058	334	4,724
Idaho	17,323	6,171	417	5,754
Illinois	54,481	19,818	2,527	17,291
Indiana	30,085	10,372	1,629	8,743
Iowa	9,796	3,038	340	2,698
Kansas	21,587	8,199	865	7,334
Kentucky	20,977	8,957	1,419	7,538
Louisiana	24,823	9,720	1,873	7,847

Notes at end of table

H1-3. Adolescent Arrests, by States, 1992 *(continued)*

State	Total	Index[1]	Violent crime[2]	Property crime[3]
Maine	8,920	4,042	144	3,898
Maryland	41,260	18,437	3,202	15,235
Massachusetts	16,204	6,451	2,029	4,422
Michigan	53,290	22,862	3,794	19,068
Minnesota	39,923	15,673	932	14,741
Mississippi	7,052	2,941	267	2,674
Missouri	22,573	7,727	1,458	6,269
Montana	8,460	3,158	88	3,070
Nebraska	11,482	3,705	148	3,557
Nevada	12,530	4,116	426	3,690
New Hampshire	5,626	1,796	96	1,700
New Jersey	86,785	25,135	5,243	19,892
New Mexico	11,061	4,754	433	4,321
New York	151,694	42,680	15,608	27,072
North Carolina	41,484	15,828	2,772	13,056
North Dakota	5,854	2,112	35	2,077
Ohio	71,656	21,245	3,077	18,168
Oklahoma	25,672	11,294	1,326	9,968
Oregon	39,132	14,935	1,093	13,842
Pennsylvania	84,133	24,233	4,791	19,442
Rhode Island	9,139	3,156	595	2,561
South Carolina	9,669	3,272	798	2,474
South Dakota	7,773	2,375	78	2,297
Tennessee	23,955	7,125	807	6,318
Texas	175,075	61,506	8,216	53,290
Utah	31,023	13,216	861	12,355
Vermont	466	240	12	228
Virginia	46,298	15,420	1,502	13,918
Washington	46,746	22,898	1,790	21,108
West Virginia	6,547	2,543	167	2,376
Wisconsin	111,311	31,136	2,184	28,952
Wyoming	6,023	1,613	50	1,503

Note: Arrests of individuals under 18 years of age.

[1] Includes arson.

[2] Violent crime includes offenses of murder, forcible rape, robbery, and aggravated assault.

[3] Property crime includes offenses of burglary, larceny-theft, motor vehicle theft, and arson.

Source: Whitaker, C. J., and L. D. Bastian. 1991. *Teenage Victims: A National Crime Survey Report.* Washington, DC: U.S. Department of Justice, page 274–280.

H1-4. Child Murder Offenders, by Sex and Race, 1992

| | Age | | | | |
Offender	5 to 9 years	10 to 14 years	15 to 19 years	20 to 24 years	Total
SEX					
Males	3	228	4,029	3,611	7,871
Females	0	33	208	316	557
Unknown	1	2	12	2	17
Total	4	263	4,249	3,929	8,445
RACE					
White	1	117	1,493	1,494	3,105
Black	1	133	2,622	2,339	5,095
Other	1	9	100	83	193
Unknown	1	4	34	13	52
Total	4	263	4,249	3,929	8,445

Source: Whitaker, C. J., and L. D. Bastian. 1991. *Teenage Victims: A National Crime Survey Report.* Washington, DC: U.S. Department of Justice, page 16.

H1-5. High School Seniors Reported Delinquent Behavior during Previous 12 Months, 1991

Delinquent Activity	Class of 1980 (N=3,327)	Class of 1985 (N=3,327)	Class of 1990 (N=2,627)	Class of 1992 (N=2,690)
Argued or had a fight with a parent	86%	89%	91%	91%
Hit an instructor or supervisor	3	3	3	3
Got into a serious fight in school/work	16	19	19	19
Taken part in a fight where a group of your friends were against another group	18	21	21	21
Hurt someone badly enough to need bandages or a doctor	12	11	13	13
Used a knife or gun or some other thing to get something from a person	3	3	3	4
Taken somthing not belonging to you worth under $50	33	30	32	33
Taken something not belonging to you worth over $50	7	7	10	10
Taken something from a store without paying for it	31	24	32	30
Taken a car that didn't belong to someone in your family without permission from owner	5	6	7	6
Taken part of a car without permission of the owner	7	7	7	6
Gone into some house or building when you weren't supposed to be there	25	26	26	26
Damaged school property on purpose	13	14	13	15
Damaged property at work on purpose	7	5	6	6
Have gotten into trouble with police because of something you did	22	22	24	22

Note: N indicates sample size.

Source: K. Maguire, A. L. Pastore, and T. J. Flanagan (eds.). 1993. *Sourcebook of Criminal Justice Statistics 1992.* U.S. Department of Justice, Bureau of Justice Statistics. Washington, DC: U.S. Government Printing Office, page 308.

H1-6. High School Seniors Reported Delinquent Behavior during Previous 12 Months, by Sex, 1992

Delinquent Activity	Females (N=1,308)			Males (N=1,276)		
	Not at all	Once or twice	Three or more	Not at all	Once or twice	Three or more
Argued or had a fight with either parent	7%	18%	75%	12%	23%	66%
Hit an instructor or supervisor	99	1	0	95	4	1
Gotten into a serious fight at school or work	86	13	2	77	18	5
Taken part in a fight where a group of your friends were against another group	85	12	3	73	19	8
Hurt someone badly enough to need bandages or a doctor	96	3	1	79	17	4
Used a knife or gun or some other thing to get something from a person	99	1	0	93	5	2
Taken something not belonging to you worth under $50	75	17	8	60	26	14
Taken something not belonging to you worth over $50	95	4	1	85	11	5
Taken something from a store without paying for it	77	16	7	63	23	15
Taken a car that didn't belong to someone in your family without owner's permission	97	3	1	92	6	3
Taken part of a car without permission from owner	98	2	0	90	7	3
Gone into some house or building when you weren't supposed to	80	16	4	69	22	10
Damaged school property on purpose	92	7	1	80	15	5
Damaged property at work on purpose	98	2	0	91	6	4
Have gotten into trouble with police because of something you did	87	12	1	69	22	9

Note: N indicates sample size. Percents may not add to 100 due to rounding.

Source: K. Maguire, A. L. Pastore, and T. J. Flanagan (eds.). 1993. *Sourcebook of Criminal Justice Statistics 1992.* U.S. Department of Justice, Bureau of Justice Statistics. Washington, DC: U.S. Government Printing Office, page 311

H1-7. High School Seniors Reported Delinquent Behavior during Previous 12 Months, by Race, 1992

Delinquent Activity	Whites (N=1,806)			Blacks (N=368)		
	Not at all	Once or twice	Three or more	Not at all	Once or twice	Three or more
Argued or had a fight with either parent	6%	19%	76%	24%	23%	53%
Hit an instructor or supervisor	97	2	1	96	3	1
Gotten into a serious fight at school or work	82	15	3	81	16	4
Taken part in a fight where a group of your friends were against another group	79	16	5	76	17	7
Hurt someone badly enough to need bandages or a doctor	88	10	2	85	11	4
Used a knife or gun or some other thing to get something from a person	97	2	1	93	4	3
Taken something not belonging to you worth under $50	65	24	11	79	12	9
Taken something not belonging to you worth over $50	90	7	3	92	5	3
Taken something from a store without paying for it	70	19	11	74	16	10
Taken a car that didn't belong to someone in your family without owner's permission	95	4	1	92	6	3
Taken part of a car without permission from owner	95	4	2	95	4	1
Gone into some house or building when you weren't supposed to	72	21	7	81	12	7
Damaged school property on purpose	86	11	3	88	10	2
Damaged property at work on purpose	94	4	2	96	2	2
Have gotten into trouble with police because of something you did	76	19	5	84	12	3

Note: N indicates sample size. Percents may not add to 100 due to rounding.

Source: K. Maguire, A. L. Pastore, and T. J. Flanagan (eds.). 1993. *Sourcebook of Criminal Justice Statistics 1992.* U.S. Department of Justice, Bureau of Justice Statistics. Washington, DC: U.S. Government Printing Office, page 314–317.

H1-8. Sexual and Contraceptive Behavior, by Sex and Grade In School, 1989

Grade	Percent Sexually Active				If Sexually Active, Percent Using Contraceptives	
	1 or more times		4 or more times		At 1st intercourse (partner or self)	All of the time now (partner or self)
	Boys	Girls	Boys	Girls		
7	22%	10%	7%	3%	36%	41%
8	32	17	12	4	40	45
9	41	27	17	14	46	46
10	50	43	26	27	49	47
11	58	54	37	41	53	51
12	77	66	51	54	54	53

Source: Benson, P. L. 1990. *The Troubled Journey: A Portrait of 6th-12th Grade Youth.* Minneapolis, MN: Search Institute, page 54.

H1-9. High School Seniors Reported Receiving a Traffic Ticket or Warning for a Moving Violation in the Last 12 Months, by Sex, 1980–1992

Survey Question: Within the last 12 months, how many times, if any, have you received a ticket (or been stopped and warned) for moving violations, such as speeding, running a stop light, or improper passing?

Number of tickets/warnings	Class of 1980		Class of 1985		Class of 1990		Class of 1992	
	Male (N=7,744)	Female (N=8,078)	Male (N=7,776)	Female (N=8,164)	Male (N=7,862)	Female (N=7,241)	Male (N=7,582)	Female (N=8,053)
None	60.3%	82.8%	62.6%	81.5%	59.3%	76.7%	61.1%	76.5%
One	22.1	12.7	21.3	13.5	21.8	16.8	21.6	15.9
Two	9.4	3.1	9.1	3.2	10.9	4.4	9.5	4.8
Three	4.3	1.0	4.2	1.2	4.3	1.4	4.2	1.7
Four or more	3.9	0.5	2.8	0.6	3.7	0.8	3.7	1.0

Note: N indicates sample size. Percents may not add to 100 due to rounding.

Source: K. Maguire, A. L. Pastore, and T. J. Flanagan (eds.). 1993. *Sourcebook of Criminal Justice Statistics 1992.* U.S. Department of Justice, Bureau of Justice Statistics. Washington, DC: U.S. Government Printing Office, p. 319.

H1-10. High School Seniors Reported Receiving a Traffic Ticket or Warning for a Moving Violation in the Last 12 Months, by Race, 1980–1992

Survey Question: Within the last 12 months, how many times, if any, have you received a ticket (or been stopped and warned) for moving violations, such as speeding, running a stop light, or improper passing?

Number of tickets/warnings	Class of 1980		Class of 1985		Class of 1990		Class of 1992	
	White (N=12,846)	Black (N=2,098)	White (N=12,291)	Black (N=1,995)	White (N=11,410)	Black (N=1,614)	White (N=11,029)	Black (N=2,244)
None	70.1%	84.1%	69.8%	86.7%	64.3%	82.9%	65.4%	82.9%
One	18.2	11.1	19.0	9.1	21.5	11.2	21.2	10.3
Two	6.6	3.2	6.5	2.9	8.5	3.8	7.5	4.8
Three	2.8	1.0	2.9	1.0	3.3	0.9	3.3	1.4
Four or more	2.3	0.5	1.8	0.3	2.5	1.2	2.6	0.6

Note: N indicates sample size. Percents may not add to 100 due to rounding.

Source: K. Maguire, A. L. Pastore, and T. J. Flanagan (eds.). 1993. *Sourcebook of Criminal Justice Statistics 1992.* U.S. Department of Justice, Bureau of Justice Statistics. Washington, DC: U.S. Government Printing Office, pages 320–321.

H1-11. High School Seniors' Reported Involvement in Driving Accidents in Last 12 Months, 1980–1992

Survey question: During the last 12 months, how many accidents have you had while you were driving (whether or not you were responsible)?				
Number of Accidents	Class of 1980 (N=16,524)	Class of 1985 (N=16,502)	Class of 1990 (N=15,676)	Class of 1992 (N=16,251)
None	74.8%	75.6%	73.9%	76.9%
One	19.4	18.5	19.4	17.5
Two or more	5.8	5.9	6.7	5.5
Note: N indicates sample size. Percents may not add to 100 due to rounding.				

Source: K. Maguire, A. L. Pastore, and T. J. Flanagan (eds.). 1993. *Sourcebook of Criminal Justice Statistics 1992.* U.S. Department of Justice, Bureau of Justice Statistics. Washington, DC: U.S. Government Printing Office, pp. 320–321.

H1-12. Parents Report of Frequency that Children Engaged in Violent Behavior, 1985

Survey question: Within the past year, did (child) have any special difficulties, such as	
Violent Behavior	Percent Yes (N=3,235)
Had temper tantrums	11%
Had disciplinary problem in school	5
Misbehaved at home	9
Had physical fight with other children at home	5
Had physical fight with children outside home	2
Had physical fight with adults at home	1
Had physical fight with adults outside home	0
Deliberately vandalized or destroyed property	2
Stole money or objects	1
Been arrested	1
Had other problems	1
Note: N indicates sample size.	

Source: K. Maguire, A. L. Pastore, and T. J. Flanagan (eds.). 1993. *Sourcebook of Criminal Justice Statistics 1992.* U.S. Department of Justice, Bureau of Justice Statistics. Washington, DC: U.S. Government Printing Office, p. 324.

H2. SUBSTANCE ABUSE

H2-1. Adolescents' Reported Alcohol Consumption, 1959–1989, Selected Years

Survey question: We are trying to find out what teens like yourself are currently doing in several areas. Please tell me if you personally have or have not done each of the following activities in the past 30 days. Have you drank alcohol such as beer, wine, or liquor?

Year	Drink	Beer	Wine	Liquor
1959	22%	14%	6%	2%
1979	38	26	16	10
1982	41	32	15	14
1987	22	16	9	7
1989	21	14	8	3

Source: Bezilla, Robert (ed.). 1993. *American's Youth in the 1990s.* Princeton, NJ: The George H. Gallup International Institute, 179.

H2-2. Reported Alcohol Use and Most Recent Use among High School Seniors, by Sex, Region, and College Plans, 1992

Survey question: "On how many occasions have you had alcoholic beverages to drink in your lifetime? On how many occasions have you had alcoholic beverages to drink during the last 12 months? On how many occasions have you had alcoholic beverages to drink during the last 30 days?"

Characteristics	Ever used	Most Recent Use		
		Within last 30 days	Within last 12 months, but not last 30 days	Not within last 12 months
All Seniors	87.5%	51.3%	25.5%	10.7%
Sex:				
Male	87.6	55.8	21.4	10.4
Female	87.6	46.8	29.4	11.4
Region:				
Northeast	89.3	51.5	27.8	10.0
North Central	90.1	58.0	22.8	9.3
South	86.4	48.1	26.2	12.1
West	84.3	46.7	26.2	11.4
College Plans:				
None or < 4 years	90.2	54.9	24.8	10.5
Complete 4 years	86.9	50.0	25.9	11.0

Source: K. Maguire, A. L. Pastore, and T. J. Flanagan (eds.). 1993. *Sourcebook of Criminal Justice Statistics 1992.* U.S. Department of Justice, Bureau of Justice Statistics. Washington, DC: U.S. Government printing Office, page 326.

H2-3. Reported Drug Use and Alcohol Use within Last 12 Months among High School Seniors, by Type of Drug, 1980–1992

Survey question: "On how many occasions, if any, have you used . . . during the last 12 months?"

Type of Drug	Class of 1980 (N=15,900)	Class of 1985 (N=16,000)	Class of 1990 (N=15,200)	Class of 1992 (N=15,800)
Marijuana/hashish	48.8%	40.6%	27.0%	21.9%
Inhalants	4.6	5.7	6.9	6.2
Hallucinogens	9.3	6.3	5.9	5.9
Cocaine	12.3	13.1	5.3	3.1
Heroin	0.5	0.6	0.5	0.6
Stimulants	20.8	NA	NA	NA
Sedatives	10.3	5.8	3.6	2.9
Tranquilizers	8.7	6.1	3.5	2.8
Alcohol	87.9	85.6	80.6	76.8
Steroids	NA	NA	1.7	1.1

Note: N indicates sample size. NA indicates not available.

Source: K. Maguire, A. L. Pastore, and T. J. Flanagan (eds.). 1993. *Sourcebook of Criminal Justice Statistics 1992.* U.S. Department of Justice, Bureau of Justice Statistics. Washington, DC: U.S. Government Printing Office, page 328.

H2-4. Reported Marijuana and Cocaine Use and Most Recent Use among High School Seniors, by Sex, Region, and College Plans, 1992

Survey question: On how many occasions, if any, have you had (marijuana, cocaine) in your lifetime? On how many occasions, if any, have you had (marijuana, cocaine) during the last 12 months? On how many occasions, if any, have you had (marijuana, cocaine) during the last 30 days?

	Marijuana				Cocaine			
		Most recent use				Most recent use		
	Ever used	Within last 30 days	Within last 12 months, but not last 30 days	Not within last 12 months	Ever used	Within last 30 days	Within last 12 months but not last 30 days	Not within last 12 months
All seniors								
(N=15,000)	32.6%	11.9%	10.0%	10.7%	6.1%	1.3%	1.8%	3.0%
Sex:								
Male	36.3	13.4	11.0	11.9	7.0	1.5	2.2	3.3
Female	28.6	10.2	8.7	9.7	5.1	0.9	1.5	2.7
Region:								
Northeast	34.5	14.4	9.5	10.6	5.6	1.1	1.7	2.8
North Central	32.1	12.2	10.5	9.4	4.8	1.2	1.3	2.3
South	29.9	9.4	8.7	11.8	6.0	1.1	2.1	2.8
West	36.8	14.0	12.1	10.7	8.7	1.8	2.5	4.4
College Plans:								
None or < 4 years	41.8	15.0	12.5	14.3	10.0	2.3	2.8	4.9
Complete 4 years	28.8	10.4	9.0	9.4	4.7	0.8	1.6	2.3

Note: N indicates sample size.

Source: K. Maguire, A. L. Pastore, and T. J. Flanagan (eds.). 1993. *Sourcebook of Criminal Justice Statistics 1992.* U.S. Department of Justice, Bureau of Justice Statistics. Washington, DC: U.S. Government Printing Office, page 327.

H2-5. Students' (Grades 6 to 12) Reported Location of Alcohol and Drug Use, 1991–1992

Where do you . . .?	Percent of Users				
	At home	At school	In car	Friend's home	Other
Drink beer	23.4%	2.5%	13.9%	31.5%	27.9%
Drink liquor	21.5	3.3	13.2	33.1	28.8
Smoke marijuana	14.2	8.3	20.6	28.9	28.0
Use cocaine	19.3	7.5	15.8	24.6	22.8
Use hallucinogens	19.5	14.9	16.1	25.3	24.1

Note: Percents may not add to 100 due to rounding.

Source: K. Maguire, A. L. Pastore, and T. J. Flanagan (eds.). 1993. *Sourcebook of Criminal Justice Statistics 1992.* U.S. Department of Justice, Bureau of Justice Statistics. Washington, DC: U.S. Government Printing Office, page 334.

H2-6. Adolescents' Reported Cigarette Smoking, by Sex, Age, Race, and Social Class, 1992

In the past 30 days have you smoked a cigarette?	Percent Yes (N=1,008)
National	**14%**
Sex:	
Male	14
Female	13
Age:	
12-13 years	3
14-15 years	14
16-17 years	25
Race:	
White	15
Non-white	6
Black	4
Hispanic	11
Social Class:*	
White-collar background	14
Blue-collar background	13

* Primary wage earner in the family occupies a white- or blue-collar job.
Note: N indicates sample size.

Source: Bezilla, Robert (ed.). 1993. *American's Youth in the 1990s.* Princeton, NJ: The George H. Gallup International Institute, page 187.

H2-7. Adolescents' Reported Reasons for Smoking, 1992

Survey question: What are your reasons for smoking?			
		Percent (N=1,000)	
Reasons	Very true	Somewhat true	Not at all true
It helps to calm you when you feel a lot of stress	54%	32%	14%
You enjoy smoking when you go out to have a good time	46	32	22
You enjoy the taste	28	43	28
You can't help it, you just have to keep smoking	25	28	47
It helps you to concentrate	14	28	57
It helps you to wake up in the morning	12	15	72
It helps you to control your weight	7	16	76
It is part of growing up and makes you feel older	5	20	75
You like the way you look when you smoke	2	15	82

Note: N indicates sample size. Percents may not add to 100 due to rounding.

Source: Bezilla, Robert (ed.). 1993. *American's Youth in the 1990s.* Princeton, NJ: The George H. Gallup International Institute, page 189.

H2-8. High School Seniors' Report of Receiving a Traffic Ticket or Warning for a Moving Violation in Last 12 Months While under the Influence of Drugs, by Type of Drug, 1980–1992

Survey question: "How many of these tickets or warnings occurred after you were ...?"				
	Class of 1980 (N=16,524)	Class of 1985 (N=16,502)	Class of 1990 (N=15,676)	Class of 1992 (N=16,251)
Drinking alcoholic beverages?				
None	81.1%	84.2%	89.8%	91.2%
One	13.9	12.1	8.1	6.3
Two or more	4.9	3.6	2.1	2.5
Smoking marijuana or hashish?				
None	90.3	94.4	96.9	97.9
One	6.7	3.9	2.2	1.1
Two or more	3.1	1.8	0.9	1.1
Using other illegal drugs?				
None	97.6	97.8	98.9	99.0
One	1.6	1.3	0.7	0.3
Two or more	0.9	1.0	0.4	0.7

Note: N indicates sample size. Percents may not add to 100 due to rounding.

Source: K. Maguire, A. L. Pastore, and T. J. Flanagan (eds.). 1993. *Sourcebook of Criminal Justice Statistics 1992.* U.S. Department of Justice, Bureau of Justice Statistics. Washington, DC: U.S. Government Printing Office, page 322.

H2-9. High School Seniors' Report of Receiving a Traffic Ticket or Warning for a Moving Violation in Last 12 Months While under the Influence of Drugs, by Type Of Drug and Sex, 1980–1992

Survey question: "How many of these tickets or warnings occurred after you were ... ?"

	Class of 1980		Class of 1985		Class of 1990		Class of 1992	
	Male	Female	Male	Female	Male	Female	Male	Female
	(N=7,744)	(N=8,078)	(N=7,776)	(N=8,164)	(N=7,862)	(N=7,241)	(N=7,582)	(N=8,053)
Drinking alcoholic beverages?								
None	78.2%	84.6%	82.2%	87.7%	88.4%	92.9%	89.1%	94.8%
One	15.7	10.2	13.3	10.1	9.3	5.8	7.6	4.2
Two or more	6.1	5.2	4.5	2.2	2.4	1.3	3.3	1.1
Smoking marijuana or hashish?								
None	89.3	92.9	93.2	96.8	96.3	98.3	97.3	98.8
One	6.9	6.1	4.3	2.9	2.7	1.2	1.2	0.7
Two or more	3.8	1.1	2.6	0.3	1.1	0.5	1.5	0.5
Using other illegal drugs?								
None	97.3	98.3	97.4	98.7	99.0	98.7	99.0	99.4
One	1.7	1.3	1.4	1.1	0.6	1.0	0.3	0.3
Two or more	1.0	0.4	1.3	0.2	0.4	0.3	0.7	0.3

Note: N indicates sample size. Percents may not add to 100 due to rounding.

Source: K. Maguire, A. L. Pastore, and T. J. Flanagan (eds.). 1993. *Sourcebook of Criminal Justice Statistics 1992.* U.S. Department of Justice, Bureau of Justice Statistics. Washington, DC: U.S. Government Printing Office, pp. 322–323.

H2-10. High School Seniors' Report of Receiving a Traffic Ticket or Warning for a Moving Violation in Last 12 Months While under the Influence of Drugs, by Type of Drug and Race, 1980–1992

	Class of 1980		Class of 1985		Class of 1990		Class of 1992	
	White	Black	White	Black	White	Black	White	Black
	(N=12,846)	(N=2,098)	(N=12,291)	(N=1,995)	(N=11,410)	(N=1,614)	(N=11,029)	(N=2,244)
Drinking alcoholic beverages?								
None	80.0%	93.6%	83.2%	94.3%	89.4%	91.6%	91.3%	95.2%
One	14.8	3.9	12.8	3.6	8.4	7.0	6.3	2.7
Two or more	5.1	2.2	3.9	2.0	2.2	1.4	2.4	2.1
Smoking marijuana or hashish?								
None	90.1	95.2	94.3	97.0	96.9	97.8	98.0	98.2
One	6.9	2.6	4.0	1.3	2.2	1.0	1.2	0.4
Two or more	2.9	2.3	1.7	1.7	1.0	1.2	0.9	1.4
Using other illegal drugs?								
None	97.6	98.9	98.1	98.0	98.9	99.0	99.2	98.7
One	1.7	0.0	1.2	0.7	0.7	0.6	0.2	1.2
Two or more	0.7	1.1	0.8	1.3	0.4	0.5	0.5	0.1

Note: N indicates sample size. Percents may not add to 100 due to rounding.

Source: K. Maguire, A. L. Pastore, and T. J. Flanagan (eds.). 1993. *Sourcebook of Criminal Justice Statistics 1992.* U.S. Department of Justice, Bureau of Justice Statistics. Washington, DC: U.S. Government Printing Office, pp. 324–325.

H2-11. High School Seniors' Report of Involvement in Driving Accidents While under the Influence of Drugs in Last 12 Months, by Type of Drug, 1980–1992

	Class of 1980 (N=16,524)	Class of 1985 (N=16,502)	Class of 1990 (N=15,676)	Class of 1992 (N=16,257)
Drinking alcoholic beverages?				
None	84.6%	89.0%	92.2%	93.4%
One	13.1	9.4	6.7	5.4
Two or more	2.3	1.6	1.2	1.3
Smoking marijuana or hashash?				
None	91.8	95.4	97.9	98.2
One	6.7	3.8	1.7	1.2
Two or more	1.4	0.7	0.3	0.6
Using other illegal drugs?				
None	98.1	98.5	99.4	98.9
One	1.5	1.0	0.4	0.6
Two or more	0.4	0.4	0.2	0.6

Note: N indicates sample size. Percents may not add to 100 due to rounding.

Source: K. Maguire, A. L. Pastore, and T. J. Flanagan (eds.). 1993. *Sourcebook of Criminal Justice Statistics 1992*. U.S. Department of Justice, Bureau of Justice Statistics. Washington, DC: U.S. Government Printing Office, page 325.

H2-12. Adolescents' Reported Driving and Drinking Behavior, 1978–1992

Survey question: Have you, yourself, ever driven a car shortly after drinking alcoholic beverages? Have you ever been a passenger in a car when a driver about your own age was under the influence of alcohol?

Year	Driven under the influence	Passenger with driver under the influence
1978	10%	NA
1985	8	28%
1988	7	22
1992	7	21

Note: NA indicates data not available.

Source: Bezilla, Robert (ed.). 1993. *American's Youth in the 1990s*. Princeton, NJ: The George H. Gallup International Institute, page 181.

H3. FAMILY PROBLEM BEHAVIOR

H3-1. Adolescents' Report of Family Addictions, 1977–1992

Survey question: Have any of the following ever been a cause of trouble in your family—Liquor? Drugs? Gambling?			
Year	Liquor problems	Drug problems	Gambling problems
1977	18%	NA	NA
1985	16	NA	NA
1992	29	11%	6%
Note: NA indicates data not available			

Source: Bezilla, Robert (ed.). 1993. *American's Youth in the 1990s.* Princeton, NJ: The George H. Gallup International Institute, page 174.

H3-2. Adolescents' Report of Family Addiction, by Sex, Age, Race, and Social Class, 1992

Survey question: Have any of the following ever been a cause of trouble in your family—Drugs? Gambling? Liquor?			
Adolescent's Characteristics	Liquor	Family Addiction Drugs	Gambling
National	**29%**	**11%**	**6%**
Sex:			
Male	28	8	7
Female	30	14	6
Age:			
13–15 years	27	9	7
16–17 years	32	13	7
Race:			
White	31	11	5
Nonwhite	22	12	11
Black	24	13	14
Hispanic	33	10	12
Social Class:*			
White-collar background	26	9	4
Blue-collar background	37	16	8
* Primary wage earner in family occupies a white- or blue-collar job.			

Source: Bezilla, Robert (ed.). 1993. *American's Youth in the 1990s.* Princeton, NJ: The George H. Gallup International Institute, page 175.

H3-3. Frequency that Parents Worry about Adolescent Children's Delinquent Behavior, 1990

Survey question: There are many things that parents worry about when they have (children/teenagers). As I read a list of things that sometimes happen to (children/teenagers), please tell me whether you worry a lot, a little, or not at all that this will happen to (child). First, how much do you worry that (he/she) will...

Worry that child/teen will:	Percent of Time Worry (N=1,366)		
	A lot	A little	Not at all
Get involved with trouble makers	29%	45%	26%
Use drugs	27	35	38
Get AIDS	28	32	39
Drink a lot of alcohol	21	32	47
Get beat up, attacked, or molested	34	43	23
Not get a good job after finishing school	28	37	35
Drop out of high school	19	16	65
Ride in car with drunk driver	28	37	35
Get shot	25	25	50
Sell drugs	17	10	73
(Girl) get pregnant	26	40	34
(Boy) get a girl pregnant	20	46	34
Get venereal disease	20	40	40
Get kidnapped	42	38	20
Get hit by a car	37	45	18

Note: N indicates sample size. Percents may not add to 100 due to rounding.

Source: Moore, K. A. 1992. *National Commission on Children: 1990 Survey of Parents and Children.* (Data Set 19, H. M. Daley, E. C. Peterson, E. L. Lang, & J. J. Card, Archivists) [machine-readable data file and documentation]. Washington, DC: Child Trends, Inc. (Producer). Los Altos, CA: Sociometrics Corporation, American Family Data Archive (Producer & Distributor).

H3-4. Parents' Report of Children's Violent Behavior, by Child's Age, Sex, and Race, and Mother's Marital Status and Education, 1987

Survey question: Now I am going to read some statements that describe the behavior or many children. Please tell me whether each statement has been often true, sometimes true, or not true of (child) during the past 3 months: a) Argues too much? b) Has a very strong temper and loses it easily? c) Breaks things on purpose, deliberately destroys (child's) own or others' things?

	N	Argues too Much			Loses Strong Temper			Purposely Destroys Things		
		Often	Some-times	Never	Often	Some-times	Never	Often	Some-times	Never
Child										
Age:										
1–5	952	14%	35%	51%	7%	24%	69%	1%	9%	91%
6–11	5,493	14	38	48	6	23	72	1	5	94
12–17	5,255	15	33	52	7	22	71	0	0	0
	11,700									
Sex:										
Male	5,957	15	36	50	7	25	68	1	8	91
Female	5,743	14	35	51	5	20	75	0	3	97
	11,700									
Race:										
White	8,396	13	37	50	6	23	72	0	6	94
Black	1,652	16	32	53	7	22	71	1	7	92
Hispanic	1,283	18	36	46	9	25	66	2	7	92
Other	369	11	31	58	7	19	74	1	1	98
	11,700									
Mother										
Marital Status:										
Married	9,122	13	36	51	6	22	73	0	5	94
Divorced	1,661	18	34	48	9	27	64	1	8	91
Widowed	197	20	28	52	12	25	63	1	4	95
Never married	496	20	36	45	12	27	62	2	7	91
	11,476									
Education:										
Less than high school	2,329	19	35	46	10	27	64	2	8	90
High school graduate	5,033	15	36	49	7	22	71	0	6	94
Some college	2,327	13	37	50	5	22	73	0	5	95
College graduate	1,061	9	35	56	3	20	77	0	3	97
Post grad	714	7	34	59	2	19	79	0	5	95
	11,464									

Note: N indicates sample size.

Source: Holmes, B. C., A. S. Kaplan, E. L. Lang, and J. J. Card. 1991. *National Health Interview Survey on Children, 1988: A User's Guide to the Machine-readable Files and Documentation* (Data Set 33-34). Los Altos, CA: Sociometrics Corporation, American Family Data Archive.

H3-5. Parents' Perception of Children's Dishonest Behavior, by Child's Age, Sex, and Race, and Mother's Marital Status and Education, 1987

Survey question: Now I am going to read some statements that describe the behavior or many children. Please tell me whether each statement has been often true, sometimes true, or not true of (child) during the past 3 months: a) Cheats or tells lies? b) Is disobedient at home? c) Doesn't seem to feel worry after (child) misbehaves?

| | | Cheats, Tells Lies | | | Disobeys Parents | | | No Remorse for Behavior | | |
	N	Often	Some-times	Never	Often	Some-times	Never	Often	Some-times	Never
Child										
Age:										
1–5	952	3%	28%	69%	4%	37%	58%	3%	15%	82%
6–11	5,501	3	25	72	2	31	67	2	13	85
12–17	5,264	4	19	77	3	23	74	4	14	83
	11,717									
Sex:										
Male	5,963	4	26	70	3	30	67	3	15	82
Female	5,754	2	20	78	2	25	73	3	12	85
	11,717									
Race:										
White	8,410	2	21	77	2	28	70	3	13	85
Black	1,653	5	30	65	3	25	72	4	17	79
Hispanic	1,286	5	28	67	5	28	67	4	13	82
Other	368	2	20	78	2	23	75	1	11	89
	11,717									
Mother										
Marital Status:										
Married	9,136	3	21	76	2	27	71	2	13	85
Divorced	1,665	4	27	69	4	31	65	4	15	81
Widowed	196	5	24	71	6	26	68	6	14	80
Never married	496	8	33	59	6	31	63	8	20	72
	11,493									
Education:										
Less than High School	2,334	5	29	66	5	27	69	5	16	79
High school graduate	5,039	3	22	75	2	29	69	3	13	82
Some college	2,330	3	21	76	2	28	70	2	13	85
College graduate	1,061	1	17	82	1	27	72	1	10	89
Post graduate	718	1	16	83	1	26	73	1	13	86
	11,482									

Note: N indicates sample size.

Source: Holmes, B. C., A. S. Kaplan, E. L. Lang, and J. J. Card. 1991. *National Health Interview Survey on Children, 1988: A User's Guide to the Machine-readable Files and Documentation* (Data Set 33-34). Los Altos, CA: Sociometrics Corporation, American Family Data Archive.

H3-6. Mothers' Report of Adolescent Bullies, Is Cruel, and Is Mean to Others, by Mother's Marital Status, Race, and Education, 1987–1988

Survey question: I am going to read some statements that might describe a child's behavior. Please tell me whether each statement has been often true, sometimes true, or has not been true of (child) during the past three months: a) Bullies, or is cruel or mean to others?

| | | 12–18 Years | | |
Mother	N	Never	Sometimes	Often
Marital Status:				
Married	1444	83%	13%	4%
Divorced/separated	202	75	20	5
Cohabiting	47	79	14	7
Never married	26	66	27	7
	1,719			
Race:				
White	1298	81	15	4
Black	187	84	13	3
Hispanic	111	87	9	4
Other	158	82	15	3
	1,754			
Education:				
Less than high school	90	84	10	6
High school graduate	261	83	14	3
Some college	141	82	14	4
College graduate	61	84	14	2
Post graduate	125	86	11	3
	665			

Note: N indicates sample size.

Source: National Survey of Families and Households, 1988 [machine-readable data file] James Sweet and Larry Bumpass, principal investigators. Distributed by the Center for Demography and Ecology, University of Wisconsin-Madison, Madison, WI. For a description of this study see James Sweet, Larry Bumpass, and Vaughn Call. *The Design and Content of the National Survey of Families and Households.* Working Paper NSFH-1, Center for Demography and Ecology, University of Wisconsin-Madison, 1988.

H4. SCHOOL PROBLEM BEHAVIOR

H4-1. Problem with School-Aged Children, by Mother's Marital Status, Race, and Education, 1988

Mother's Characteristics	N	Children in School	Problem with School-Aged Child							
			Repeated Grade	Met with Teacher for a Problem	Child Expelled	Ran away from Home	Trouble with Police	Seen Dr. for emotional Problem	Difficult to Raise	Easy to Raise
Mother's Marital Status:										
Married	3140	92%	18%	16%	9%	2%	5%	11%	14%	62%
Divorced/separated	363	94	31	26	15	6	11	26	22	58
Cohabiting	146	94	23	23	14	3	7	16	14	53
Never married	102	89	33	32	15	2	6	11	16	69
Race of Mother:										
White	2701	92	18	16	9	3	7	15	16	60
Black	440	91	27	25	15	1	5	6	10	67
Hispanic	306	94	27	22	8	2	3	7	13	72
Other	356	91	19	19	12	3	7	9	8	60
Mother's Education:										
Less than high school	225	92	32	16	11	3	3	7	12	66
High school graduate	546	92	15	16	9	2	4	11	13	60
Some college	324	91	14	15	4	1	4	10	13	67
College graduate	156	94	6	11	4	0	5	9	16	51
Post graduate	278	97	10	14	7	2	5	17	14	59

Note: N indicates sample size.

Source: National Survey of Families and Households, 1988 [machine-readable data file] James Sweet and Larry Bumpass, principal investigators. Distributed by the Center for Demography and Ecology, University of Wisconsin-Madison, Madison, WI. For a description of this study see James Sweet, Larry Bumpass, and Vaughn Call. *The Design and Content of the National Survey of Families and Households.* Working Paper NSFH-1, Center for Demography and Ecology, University of Wisconsin-Madison, 1988.

H4-2. Parents' Perceptions of Children's Interactions with School Teacher, by Mother's Marital Status and Education, 1988

Survey question: Now I am going to read some statements that describe the behavior of many children. Please tell me whether each statement has been often true, sometimes true, or not true of (child) during the past 3 months: a) Is disobedient at school? b) Has trouble getting along with teachers?

	N	Disobedient at School			Trouble with Teacher		
		Often	Sometimes	Never	Often	Sometimes	Never
Child							
Age:							
1–5 years	930	1%	11%	88%	1%	3%	97%
6–11 years	5,487	1	13	86	1	6	94
12–17 years	5,253	2	14	84	1	11	87
	11,670						
Sex:							
Male	5,939	2	18	80	1	10	89
Female	5,731	1	9	91	1	6	93
	11,670						
Race:							
White	8,379	1	11	88	1	7	92
Black	1,650	2	21	77	2	12	86
Hispanic	1,271	2	17	81	1	8	91
Other	369	0	14	86	0	7	93
	11,670						
Mother							
Marital Status:							
Married	9,100	1	12	87	1	7	92
Divorced	1,662	2	19	79	1	12	87
Widowed	191	3	18	79	3	12	85
Never married	494	4	21	75	3	12	85
	11,448						
Education:							
Less than high School	2,304	2	17	81	2	9	89
High school graduate	5,028	1	13	86	1	8	91
Some college	2,326	1	14	85	1	8	91
College graduate	1,060	1	8	91	0	5	95
Post graduate	718	0	10	90	1	6	93
	11,435						

Note: N indicates sample size. Percents may not add to 100 due to rounding.

Source: Holmes, B. C., A. S. Kaplan, E. L. Lang, and J. J. Card. 1991. *National Health Interview Survey on Children, 1988: A User's Guide to the Machine-readable Files and Documentation* (Data Set 33-34). Los Altos, CA: Sociometrics Corporation, American Family Data Archive.

H4-3. Percent of Adolescents' Violent Behavior in School, by Grade and Sex, 1987

Survey question: While at school were you or have you... a) Been involved in physical fights? b) Been robbed? c) Been threatened? d) Been attacked? e) Carried a knife? f) Carried a handgun?

Type of Violence	8th Graders Total	Females	Males	10th Graders Total	Females	Males
Been involved in physical fights:						
0 times	55.8%	68.6%	43.5%	66.2%	74.7%	58.0%
1 time	16.5	13.2	19.6	14.9	12.7	16.9
2 times	10.0	6.4	13.4	8.1	4.8	11.3
3 or more times	17.8	11.8	23.4	10.9	7.7	13.8
Been robbed:						
0 times	82.4	86.5	78.5	89.2	89.1	89.2
1 time	8.8	6.8	10.8	6.2	6.8	5.6
2 times	3.6	3.1	4.0	2.6	2.5	2.7
3 or more times	5.2	3.6	6.7	2.1	1.7	2.5
Been threatened:						
0 times	62.3	69.4	55.4	68.8	70.8	66.9
1 time	19.0	16.3	21.5	16.8	16.7	16.9
2 times	5.5	4.7	6.4	5.6	5.4	5.8
3 or more times	13.2	9.6	16.7	8.8	7.1	10.4
Been attacked:						
0 times	83.6	90.0	77.5	91.9	91.9	88.6
1 time	9.5	6.6	12.3	5.9	5.9	7.2
2 times	3.9	2.0	5.7	0.4	0.4	1.9
3 or more times	3.0	1.4	4.5	1.8	1.8	2.3
Carried a knife:						
Never	86.4	95.5	77.7	85.2	94.5	76.2
Less than monthly	5.6	2.0	9.0	4.9	1.6	8.1
More than monthly	8.0	2.6	13.3	9.9	3.9	15.7
Carried a handgun:						
Never	98.3	98.9	97.7	98.4	99.6	97.1
Less than monthly	0.5	0.2	0.8	0.6	0.1	1.0
More than monthly	1.3	1.0	1.6	1.0	0.2	1.8

Note: Percents may not add to 100 due to rounding.

Source: Snyder, T. D., and C. M. Hoffman. 1993. *Digest of Education Statistics.* Washington, DC: National Center for Education Statistics, page 139.

H4-4. High School Students' Report of Carrying a Weapon during Previous 30 Days, by Sex, 1991

Survey question: Students were asked whether they carried a weapon, such as a gun, knife, or club at least one day during the 30 days preceding the survey, and, among those who carried a weapon, whether that weapon was a handgun, rather than any other weapon such as a rifle, shotgun, inife, razor, or club.

Percent Carried Weapon	(N=12,272)
Total	26%
Sex:	
Male	41
Female	11

Note: N indicates sample size.

Source: K. Maguire, A. L. Pastore, and T. J. Flanagan (eds.). 1993. *Sourcebook of Criminal Justice Statistics 1992.* U.S. Department of Justice, Bureau of Justice Statistics. Washington, DC: U.S. Government Printing Office, page 319.

H5. PEER PRESSURE

H5-1. Friends' Delinquent Behavior, 1990

Survey question: Now I'll read a list of things that kids sometimes do. For each one I read, please tell me, as far as you know, how many of your friends have done something like this. Tell me whether you think most of them, some of them, or none of them have done each thing. First...

Number of Friends Who Have:	Percent (N=928)			
	All/Most	Some	None	Don't Know
Cheated on a test	19%	44%	35%	2%
Skipped school	31	51	18	0
Been sent to principal for doing wrong	12	43	46	0
Worked hard in school	65	32	3	0
Tried cigarettes	20	37	43	0
Drank beer or wine	17	30	53	1
Smoked marijuana	3	16	81	1
Used crack or cocaine	0	3	96	1
Had sex	33	42	23	2
(Girls) got pregnant	4	33	63	0
(Boys) got someone pregnant	1	14	83	2
Stolen something from a store	5	27	66	2
Got in trouble with police	3	25	71	1

Note: N indicates sample size. Percents may not add to 100 due to rounding.

Source: Moore, K. A. 1992. *National Commission on Children: 1990 Survey of Parents and Children.* (Data Set 19, H. M. Daley, E. C. Peterson, E. L. Lang, & J. J. Card, Archivists) [machine-readable data file and documentation]. Washington, DC: Child Trends, Inc. (Producer). Los Altos, CA: Sociometrics Corporation, American Family Data Archive (Producer & Distributor).

H5-2. Perceived Peer Pressure to Engage in Delinquent Behavior, 1990

Survey question: Do you ever feel pressure from your friends to do any of the following things?

(N=810)	Percent Yes
Skip school	16%
Work hard in school	59
Try cigarettes	11
Drink beer, wine, or liquor	13
Smoke marijuana	5
Have sex	15
Commit a crime or violent acts	10

Note: N indicates sample size.

Source: Moore, K. A. 1992. *National Commission on Children: 1990 Survey of Parents and Children.* (Data Set 19, H. M. Daley, E. C. Peterson, E. L. Lang, & J. J. Card, Archivists) [machine-readable data file and documentation]. Washington, DC: Child Trends, Inc. (Producer). Los Altos, CA: Sociometrics Corporation, American Family Data Archive (Producer & Distributor).

H6. TREATMENT OF JUVENILE OFFENDERS

H6-1. Percent Distribution of Juveniles Taken into Police Custody, by Method of Disposition, 1972–1991

Year	Referred to juvenile court juris- diction	Handled within depart- ment and released	Referred to criminal or adult court	Referred to other police agency	Referred to welfare agency
1972	50.8%	45.0%	1.3%	1.6%	1.3%
1975	52.7	41.6	2.3	1.9	1.4
1980	58.1	33.8	4.8	1.7	1.6
1985	61.8	30.7	4.4	1.2	1.9
1990	64.5	28.3	4.5	1.1	1.6
1991	64.2	28.1	5.0	1.0	1.7

Note: Percents may not add to 100 due to rounding.

Source: K. Maguire, A. L. Pastore, and T. J. Flanagan (eds.). 1993. *Sourcebook of Criminal Justice Statistics 1992.* U.S. Department of Justice, Bureau of Justice Statistics. Washington, DC: U.S. Government Printing Office, page 456.

H6-2. Police Disposition of Juvenile Offenders Taken into Custody, 1992

	Total	Handled within department and released	Referred to juvenile court jurisdiction	Referred to welfare agency	Referred to other police agency	Referred to criminal or adult court
Total, all agencies:						
Number	1,330,455	399,856	831,696	22,400	14,323	62,180
Percent	100.0	30.1	62.5	1.7	1.1	4.7

Note: 9,158 agencies; population 185,129,000.

Source: Federal Bureau of Investigation. 1992. *Uniform Crime Reports for the United States, 1992.* Washington, DC: U.S. Department of Justice, page 282.

H6-3. Characteristics of Juvenile Offenders in Cases Disposed by Juvenile Courts, by Type of Offense, 1990

Characteristics	Type of Offense				
	All offenses (N=1,264,800)	Personal (N=239,700)	Property (N=731,700)	Drug (N=68,200)	Public-order (N=225,200)
Total	100%	100%	100%	100%	100%
Sex:					
Male	81.2	80.2	81.3	86.6	80.5
Female	18.8	19.8	18.7	13.4	19.5
Race:					
White	66.1	55.5	70.1	53.9	67.9
Black	30.8	42.1	36.4	44.7	28.9
Other	3.2	2.4	3.5	1.4	3.2

Note: N indicates sample size.

Source: K. Maguire, A. L. Pastore, and T. J. Flanagan (eds.). 1993. *Sourcebook of Criminal Justice Statistics 1992.* U.S. Department of Justice, Bureau of Justice Statistics. Washington, DC: U.S. Government Printing Office, page 540.

H7. JUVENILE VICTIMS

H7-1. Trends in Annual Victimization Rates, by Age of Victim, 1979–1988

Year	Crimes per 1000 Individuals					
	Crimes of Violence			Crimes of Theft		
	12–15 years	16–19 years	20 or older	12–15 years	16–19 years	20 or older
1979	59.2	77.4	32.2	147.4	148.3	82.5
1980	53.5	73.9	31.1	122.8	126.9	76.7
1981	64.8	74.6	33.1	133.5	135.3	77.7
1982	56.2	76.2	32.8	132.9	130.2	75.1
1983	55.9	70.9	29.3	130.8	121.1	69.9
1984	57.4	71.4	28.6	124.3	122.4	64.2
1985	59.3	71.3	26.6	112.7	123.9	62.5
1986	59.7	65.7	25.6	112.4	119.4	60.8
1987	64.4	73.8	25.6	112.1	123.9	61.9
1988	63.3	78.9	26.1	117.5	123.0	64.2

Source: Whitaker, C. J., and L. D. Bastian. 1991. *Teenage Victims: A National Crime Survey Report.* Washington, DC: U.S. Department of Justice, page 3.

H7-2. Victimization Rates and Number of Victimizations, by Age of Victim and Type of Crime, 1982–1984

	Age of Victim		
TYPE OF CRIME	12–15	16–19	20 or older
Crimes of violence	56.6	72.9	30.2
Rape	1.6	2.1	0.7
Robbery	9.7	11.6	5.6
Aggravated assault	11.0	21.3	8.5
Simple assault	34.3	37.8	15.4
Crimes of theft	129.3	124.6	69.7
Personal larceny:			
With contact	3.0	3.0	3.0
Without contact	126.3	121.6	66.8
NUMBER OF VICTIMIZATIONS*			
Crimes of violence	819,199	1,105,296	4,850,851
Rape	22,527	32,466	113,004
Robbery	140,444	176,592	903,372
Aggravated assault	159,410	323,142	1,359,524
Simple assault	496,819	573,097	2,474,950
Crimes of theft	1,875,700	1,889,956	11,198,304
Personal larceny:			
With contact	43,510	45,909	475,302
Without contact	1,832,190	1,844,047	10,723,002
Total number of persons	14,501,994	15,163,374	160,630,831

Note: Detail may not add to total because of rounding.
* Annual average for 1982–1984.
Rates are per 1,000 persons.

Source: Whitaker, C. J., and L. D. Bastian. 1991. *Teenage Victims: A National Crime Survey Report.* Washington, DC: U.S. Department of Justice, page 12.

H7-3. Homicide Rate Committed against Various Age Groups, 1988

Age of Victim	Adjusted rate of homicide per 100,000
Total	8.5
1–11	2.1
12–15	2.4
16–19	10.1
20–24	17.0
25–34	15.4
35–49	10.3
50–64	5.8
65 or older	4.3

Source: Whitaker, C. J., and L. D. Bastian. 1991. *Teenage Victims: A National Crime Survey Report.* Washington, DC: U.S. Department of Justice, page 10.

H7-4. Age of Adolescent and Young Adult Victims of Murder, by Sex and Race, 1992

Characteristics	Age of Victim			
	10 to 14 years	15 to 19 years	20 to 24 years	Total
Sex:				
Males	230	2,444	3,551	6,663
Female	121	407	630	1,507
Total	351	2,851	4,181	8,170
Race:				
White	163	1,114	1,614	3,302
Black	171	1,664	2,451	4,633
Other	14	60	97	196
Unknown	3	13	19	40
Total	351	2,851	4,181	8,171

Source: Whitaker, C. J., and L. D. Bastian. 1991. *Teenage Victims: A National Crime Survey Report.* Washington, Dc: U.S. Department of Justice, page 3.

H7-5. Violent Crime Rates, by Household Composition and Age of Victim, 1985–1987

| | Annual Rate of Crime per 1,000 Persons | | | | | | | |
| | Crimes of violence | | Robbery | | Aggravated assault | | Simple assault | |
Household Composition	12–15 years	16–19 years	12–15 years	16–19 years	12–15 years	16–19 years	12–15 years	16–19 years
Household headed by:								
Married couple/children	48.3	51.5	7.2	5.8	8.6	14.8	31.7	30.0
Children only	48.0	53.8	7.2	5.1	8.4	16.0	31.7	32.0
Children and others	49.7	48.0	7.0	6.9	9.5	12.9	31.8	26.8
Single father/children	84.4	95.0	19.5	21.3	9.2	30.8	52.0	37.1
Children only	76.3	109.9	6.7	31.1	11.3	30.6	54.6	45.0
Children and others	95.2	82.4	36.3	13.1	6.5	31.0	48.6	30.4
Single mother/children	91.3	90.3	15.2	13.8	21.9	33.0	53.3	40.7
Children only	102.8	94.7	15.2	13.2	24.2	34.3	62.7	42.3
Children and others	61.2	85.0	15.1	13.4	15.7	31.5	28.5	38.9

Source: Whitaker, C. J., and L. D. Bastian. 1991. *Teenage Victims: A National Crime Survey Report.* Washington, DC: U.S. Department of Justice, page 8.

H7-6. Place of Occurrence of Robberies and Assaults against Adolescents, 1985–1988

| | Type of Crime and Age of Victim | | | | | |
| | Robbery | | Aggravated assault | | Simple assault | |
Place of Occurrence	12–15 years	16–19 years	12–15 years	16–19 years	12–15 years	16–19 years
At school	32	9	23	9	43	24
in building	19	4	9	4	24	13
on property	13	5	14	5	19	11
Street	35	38	28	27	21	22
Near victim's home	9	6	13	9	11	7
At victim's home	4	10	5	7	4	7
Home of friend, relative, or neighbor	4	9	12	11	7	11
Park, field, or playground	5	5	6	8	5	4
Public transporation, parking lot	5	15	7	15	4	12
Resurant, commercial bldg	4	5	1	9	3	9
Other place	2	4	5	5	2	5

Source: Whitaker, C. J., and L. D. Bastian. 1991. *Teenage Victims: A National Crime Survey Report.* Washington, DC: U.S. Department of Justice, page 8.

H7-7. Place of Occurrence of Personal Crimes, by Age of Victim, 1985–1988

	Type of Crime and Age of Victim					
	Crimes of Violence			Crimes of Theft		
Place of Occurrence	12–15 years	16–19 years	20 years or older	12–15 years	16–19 years	20 years or older
At school	37	17	2	81	39	6
in building	20	9	1	74	30	3
on property	17	8	1	7	9	3
Street	25	26	22	2	6	12
Near victim's home	11	7	13	0	0	0
At victim's home	4	8	18	0	0	0
Home of friend, relative, or neighbor	8	11	9	3	11	9
Park, field, or playground	5	5	2	2	2	2
Public transportation, parking lot	5	13	11	3	21	39
Restaurant, commercial bldg	2	8	15	4	12	19
Other place	3	5	8	5	8	13

Note: Numbers are percents.

Source: Whitaker, C. J., and L. D. Bastian. 1991. *Teenage Victims: A National Crime Survey Report.* Washington, DC: U.S. Department of Justice, page 7.

H7-8. Victim-Offender Relationship, by Age of Victim, 1987–1988

	Age of Victim		
Type of crime and victim-offender relationship	12–15	16–19	20 or older
Crimes of violence[†]			
Spouse, ex-spouse	—*	1%*	7%
Parent	1%	2	—*
Other relative	2	2	3
Well known	23	19	18
Causal acquaintance	26	19	13
Stranger	44	52	53
Unknown or not ascertained	4	5	5
Robbery			
Spouse, ex-spouse	—*	2	4
Parent	1*	1*	—*
Other relative	—*	1*	2
Well known	16	15	10
Casual acquaintance	12	13	5
Stranger	68	62	73
Unknown or not ascertained	3	7	7
Aggravated assault			
Spouse, ex-spouse	—*	—*	6
Parent	2*	2*	1*
Other relative	1*	2*	3
Well known	18	18	15
Casual acquaintance	25	14	13
Stranger	48	56	55
Unknown or not ascertained	7	8	7
Simple assault			
Spouse, ex-spouse	—*	1	9
Parent	1*	2	—*
Other relative	3	2	4
Well known	26	21	22
Casual acquaintance	29	24	15
Stranger	37	49	46
Unknown or not ascertained	4	2	4

Note: Percentages may not total 100% because of rounding. Multiple-offender victimizations are classified by the most intimate relationship between the victim and one of the offenders.
—less than 0.5%
*Estimate is based on 10 or fewer sample cases
[†]Includes data on rape, not displayed as a separate category

Source: Whitaker, C. J., and L. D. Bastian. 1991. *Teenage Victims: A National Crime Survey Report.* Washington, DC: U.S. Department of Justice, page 9.

H7-9. Frequency that Adolescents Worry that They Will Be the Victim of Delinquent or Unpleasant Events, 1990

How much do you worry that:	Percent of Frequency (N=929)		
	A lot	A little	Not at all
You will get beaten up by someone	11%	34%	55%
You will be in a car accident	25	45	30
Someone on drugs will hurt you	25	27	48
Family member will lose his/her job	19	34	47
You will not be safe in home	11	23	66
You will be sexually abused or raped	14	20	66
You won't get good grades in school	36	39	25
You won't know what to do with life	23	40	36
You will get AIDS some day	26	30	44
Your parents will separate or divorce	19	23	58
The world's environment bad when you grow up	46	42	11
This country will be in a war	45	42	14

Note: N indicates sample size. Percents may not add to 100 due to rounding.

Source: Whitaker, C. J., and L. D. Bastian. 1991. *Teenage Victims: A National Crime Survey Report.* Washington, DC: U.S. Department of Justice, page 9.

I. Sex, Childbearing, and Marriage

The patterns through which one starts a family have changed dramatically in recent years, affecting both the living arrangements of children and the social experiences of adolescents. The sexual revolution combined with altered patterns of marriage and childbearing in the teenage years have created a new context for the beginning stages of the forming of one's own family. For example, the average age at first sexual intercourse has decreased while the age at marriage has increased. This chapter examines several aspects related to adolescent sexual behavior including sexual activity, contraceptive use, pregnancy and childbearing, educational and economic outcomes of early childbearing, and attitudes regarding sexual behavior.

I1. SEXUAL BEHAVIOR

While the age at which most children begin puberty has decreased over the last 100 years, the average age at marriage has increased, creating a longer period of time in which adolescents are be sexually active but not married. A majority of teens now report having sex for the first time before age 17, and over 80 percent are sexually experienced by age 19. Blacks tend to have sexual intercourse at younger ages than whites, and Hispanics also begin somewhat earlier than non-Hispanic whites. The likelihood of sexual experience also varies by income and religion.

Some researchers contend that the first act of intercourse does not necessarily represent a transition to sexual activity. Attention must also be given to frequency of intercourse and number of partners. Accordingly, the percentage of teens who have had sex two or more times increases steadily with age, reaching 60 percent of twelfth graders. Over 50 percent of twelfth graders also say they have had sex four or more times. Of those who are sexually experienced, many have sex on a fairly regular basis. About one-fifth report having sex at least once a week, a fourth say several times a week, a third say two to three times a month, and about one-fourth say once a month or less. Only about 10 percent of the sexu-

ally active women report having more than one partner in the last three months. Whites are a little more likely than blacks to either be monogamous or to have had at least six partners. The most recent national survey of sexual behavior indicates that a majority of those in late adolescence have had only one sexual partner in the last 12 months, have had sex at least a few times per month, and have experienced oral sex. Orgasms are more common for men than women, and two-fifths of men and two-thirds of women say they never masturbate. About one-fifth of women report they have been forced to do something sexual.

I2. CONTRACEPTIVE USE

According to a study by the Search Institute, about one half of sexually active adolescents are not using contraceptives. This percentage declines with age, but remains above 45 percent for twelfth graders. Other studies suggest higher percentages of contraceptive use among teens who are at risk of an unintended pregnancy. Methods of contraception used vary by age, ethnicity, and income level. Contraceptive use at first intercourse improved substantially between 1982 and 1988. The improvement between 1988 and 1991 was less marked, however. Most of this improvement involved use of condoms. Roughly 50 percent of sexually active young men report consistent use of condoms.

About 4 percent of women aged 15 to19 have had an abortion. Most young women who have an abortion do so because they feel they are too young or cannot afford to have a baby. Many adolescents also want to keep the pregnancy a secret. Most parents know about the abortion only if their daughter is under 15; older teens are more likely too keep it a secret. Also, mothers are more likely to know about their daughter's abortion than are fathers.

Teenage girls' risk of pregnancy is linked to numerous factors, but those who are engaged in other risky behaviors such as drug use, anti-social tendencies, misbehavior at school, or unsafe driving are significantly more likely to be at risk of pregnancy. Drug use, in particular, is associated with greater risks of pregnancy.

I3. PREGNANCY, CHILDBEARING, AND MARRIAGE

Teenage pregnancy has increased moderately since 1972. This increase is due to higher rates of sexual activity among adolescents. In other words, if only sexually active women are included in the denominator and not the entire female population, then the pregnancy rate has declined noticeably. Because of the increasing numbers of abortions, the proportion of pregnancies ending in birth declined between 1979 and 1986, but has increased somewhat since 1986. Whether a pregnancy ends in birth or abortion generally depends on the mother's marital status. An unintended birth is the most common outcome for married teens, but abortion is the most common outcome for the unmarried. Pregnancy, abortion, and birth rates vary substantially by region and state of residence. Also, teenage birth and abortion rates in the United States are substantially higher than in most other industrialized countries.

Even so, the teenage birth rate has remained relatively stable over the last 20 years. The rate is substantially higher for blacks and Hispanics that for non-Hispanic whites. And teens from poor and low income families are more likely to give birth than are teens from high income families. It is also interesting to note that a significant proportion of teens who give birth have partners who are at least six years older. A large majority of teen births are to unmarried women, something that has become much more common since the early 1960s. Another related trend is the declining percentage of never-married women who place their children up for adoption.

Teenage marriage is very uncommon. Only about six percent of the population has married by their twentieth birthday. And of the women who marry before age 20, nearly one-third of them are pregnant or have children when they marry. Teen marriage is comparatively low among blacks, but high among Hispanics. In addition, age at marriage decreased over the first half of the century, but has risen sharply since 1970. It also appears that the age difference between spouses is declining.

I4. NEGATIVE OUTCOMES OF EARLY CHILDBEARING

While not always the case, teenage childbearing can have long term negative consequences for the mother and child. Babies of younger mothers are more likely to have health problems and to require hospitalization. Women who have their first birth before age 20 have much lower incomes in their 30s than do women who delay childbearing. Adolescents are also less likely to complete high school if they have a child. Likewise, adolescent parents are much less likely to ever attend college or receive a college diploma.

Of the over 8 million teens aged 15 to 19, 5.4 million are sexually experienced, and for 1.7 million, their first act of sexual intercourse was not contraceptively protected. Over 1 million became pregnant, and over 300,000 became unwed mothers. In addition, teens who come from poor or low income families are more likely to be represented at each subsequent stage in this process.

I5. SEXUAL VALUES AND FUTURE EXPECTATIONS

A majority of children in grades six through twelve do not place a high value on sexual restraint. Over half of sixth and seventh graders do value restraint, but only a fifth of twelfth graders do. Correspondingly, a majority of teens think it is better to promote safe sex than abstinence. In addition, nearly two-thirds of teens favor laws requiring women under 18 to get parental consent before they are allowed to have an abortion.

Most teenagers say they intend to marry and have children, and the percentages have remained relatively stable since 1977. Contrary to current fertility rates, black adolescents intend to have fewer children than do whites. Adolescents who are below average students or from blue-collar backgrounds are less likely to say they will marry. Also, the percent who intend to have children is somewhat lower than the percent who intend to marry. Most of the major subgroups in the population contain a high percentage of people who intend to have children. The number of children desired is declining, however.

I1. SEXUAL BEHAVIOR

I1-1. Age at Menarche/Spermarche, First Intercourse, Marriage, and Childbearing, 1890 and 1988

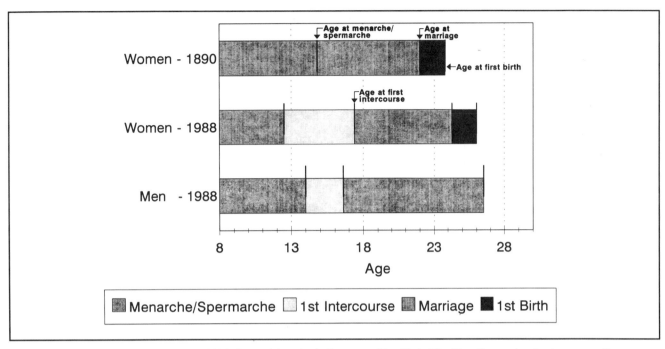

Source: The Alan Guttmacher Institute. 1994. *Sex and America's Teenagers.* New York: The Alan Guttmacher Institute, page 7.

I1-2. Percent Reporting They Ever Had Sexual Intercourse, by Age 12–19, 1988–1990

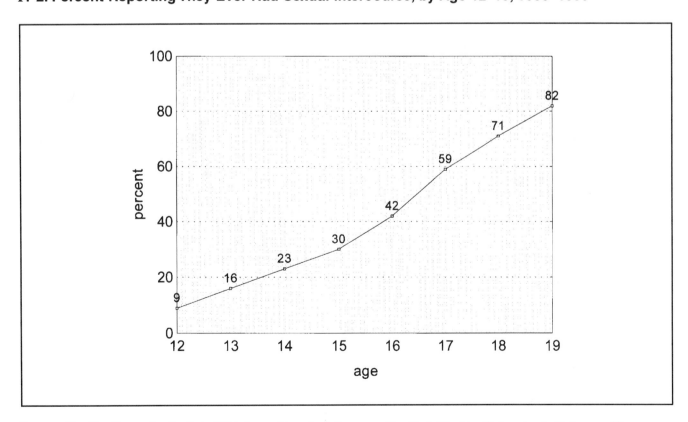

Source: The Alan Guttmacher Institute. 1994. *Sex and America's Teenagers.* New York: The Alan Guttmacher Institute, page 19.

I1-3. Intercourse Status of Women, by Age 20, by Race, 1956–1960 and 1985–1987

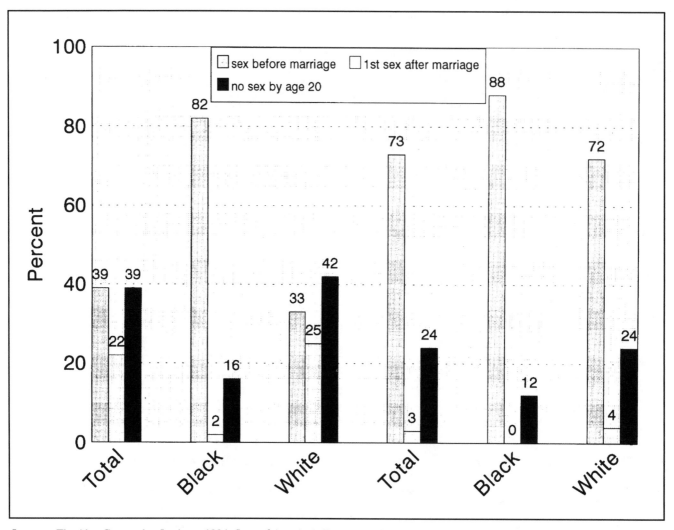

Source: The Alan Guttmacher Institute. 1994. *Sex and America's Teenagers.* New York: The Alan Guttmacher Institute, page 25.

I1-4. Cumulative Percentage of Never Married U.S. Males Aged 15–19, Who Have Had Sexual Intercourse, by Age, According to Racial or Ethnic Group, 1988

Age	All Races	Black	White	Hispanic*
13	5.4	19.8	2.9	3.9
14	11.0	34.6	7.1	6.3
15	21.1	47.8	16.2	19.4
16	37.8	63.5	33.0	37.7
17	57.5	78.4	53.0	63.2
18	67.4	84.7	69.8	60.9
19	79.0	95.8	75.9	80.5

*Persons of Hispanic origin may be of any race.

Source: *Family Planning Perspectives* 23 (4) 1991, page 163.

I1-5. Percent of Men and Women Who Have Had Intercourse By Age 18, 1956–1988

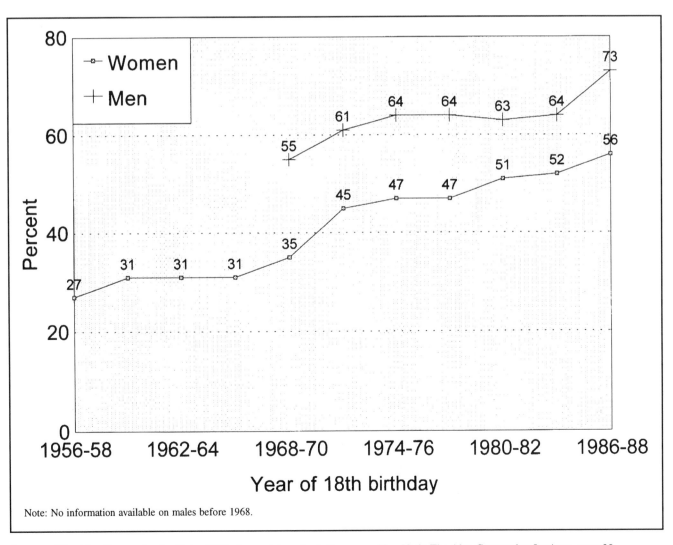

Note: No information available on males before 1968.

Source: The Alan Guttmacher Institute. 1994. *Sex and America's Teenagers.* New York: The Alan Guttmacher Institute, page 20.

I1-6. Percent of Women Aged 15–19 Who Have Had Intercourse, by Race, Income, Religion, and Urban Status, 1988

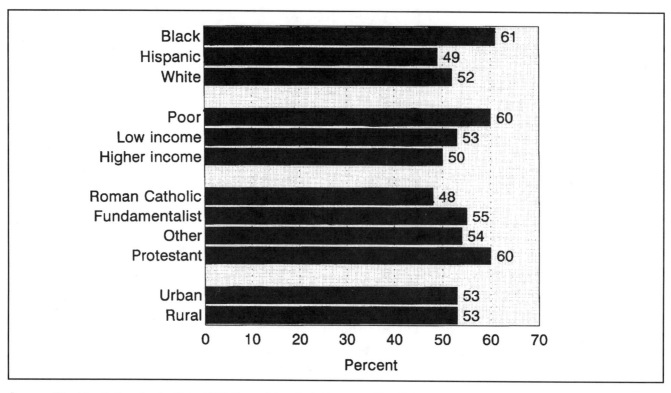

Source: The Alan Guttmacher Institute. 1994. *Sex and America's Teenagers.* New York: The Alan Guttmacher Institute, page 26.

I1-7. Percent of Youth Who Are Sexually Active (2+ times), by Grade in School, 1990

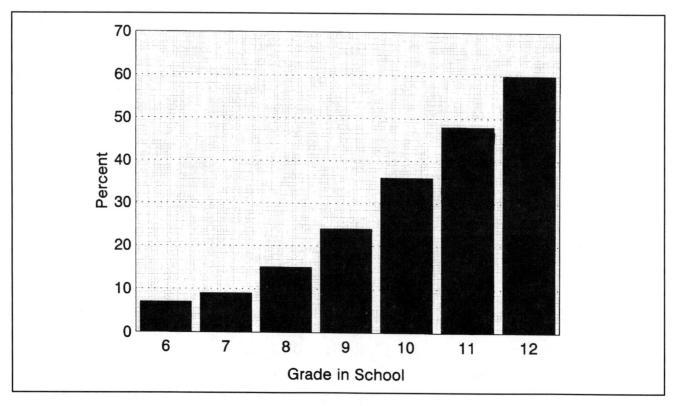

Source: Benson, Peter L. 1993. *The Troubled Journey: A Portrait of 6th-12th Grade Youth.* Minneapolis, MN: Search Institute, page 43.

I1-8. Percent of Youth Who Have Had Sex Four or More Times, by Gender and Grade in School, 1990

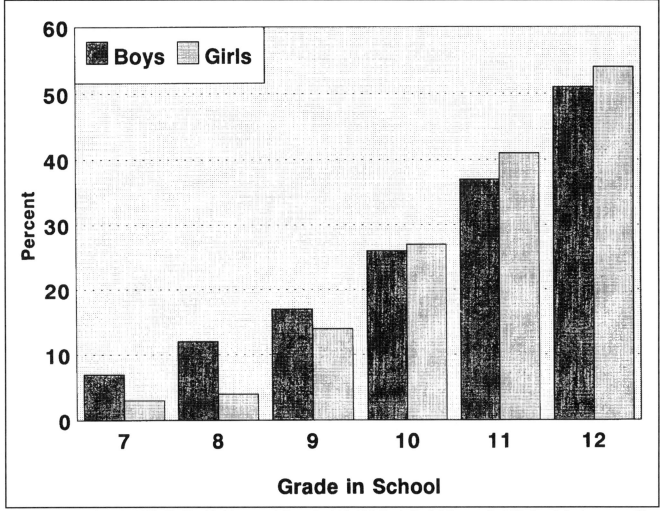

Source: Benson, Peter L. 1993. *The Troubled Journey: A Portrait of 6th-12th Grade Youth.* Minneapolis, MN: Search Institute, page 54.

I1-9. Frequency of Intercourse among Sexually Experienced Teens Aged 15–19, 1988

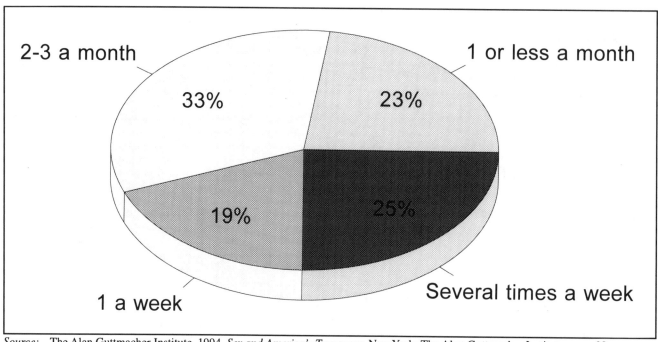

Source: The Alan Guttmacher Institute. 1994. *Sex and America's Teenagers.* New York: The Alan Guttmacher Institute, page 29.

I1-10. Percent of Women Sexually Active in the Last Three Months Who Had More than One Partner in that Time Period, by Age and Marital Status, 1988

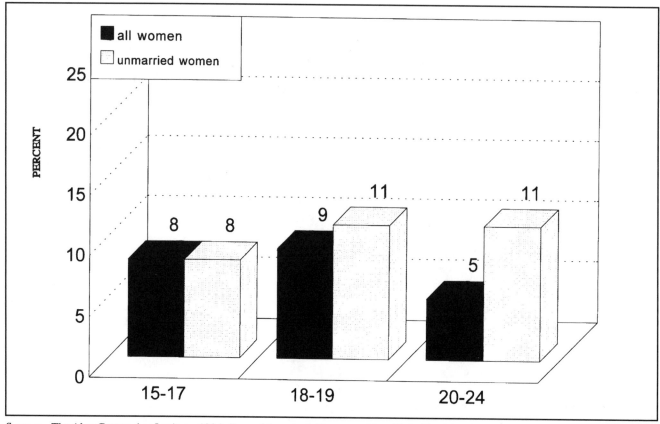

Source: The Alan Guttmacher Institute. 1994. *Sex and America's Teenagers.* New York: The Alan Guttmacher Institute, page 32.

I1-11. Percentage Distribution of Number of Sexual Partners among Sexually Active Women Aged 15–19 Living in Metropolitan Areas, by Race, 1971–1979

Race and no. of partners	1971	1976	1979	1988
All				
1	62	53	49	39
2-3	25	28	35	31
4-5	7	9	8	17
6 or more	7	11	8	14
Whites*				
1	62	56	51	40
2-3	23	23	33	30
4-5	7	8	7	17
6 or more	8	13	9	14
Blacks				
1	61	43	41	35
2-3	30	40	43	35
4-5	5	12	11	18
6 or more	4	6	5	12

*Includes a small number of women of races other than black.
Note: The National Surveys of Young Women asked respondents about their number of premarital partners; the 1988 National Survey of Family Growth asked respondents for their lifetime number of partners.

Source: Family Planning Perspectives 24 (6) 1992, page 248.

I1-12. Mean Number of Sexual Partners since First Intercourse and in the Last 12 Months among Sexually Experienced, Never-Married U.S. Males Aged 15–19, by Age and Race, 1988

Time Period and Age	All Races	Black	White	Hispanic
Since First Intercourse	(N=1,251)	(N=533)	(N=440)	(N=228)
15-19	5.11	8.30	4.29	5.15
15	4.10	6.40	3.55	1.98
16	4.25	6.68	3.55	3.66
17	4.76	8.99	3.60	4.23
18	5.51	8.00	4.73	8.43
19	6.12	11.34	5.22	5.80
In Last 12 Months	(N=1,262)	(N=559)	(N=444)	(N=228)
15-19	1.92	2.37	1.85	1.57
15	1.92	2.11	2.04	1.13
16	1.93	2.82	1.67	1.87
17	1.77	2.49	1.58	1.52
18	1.90	2.01	1.91	1.82
19	2.08	2.47	2.11	1.39

Note: N indicates sample size.

Source: Family Planning Perspectives 23 (4) 1991, page 163.

I1-13. Sex Behavior of 18- to 24-Year-Olds, 1992

		Men	Women	Total
			Percent	
Number of partners:	0	—	—	11
(past 12 months)	1	—	—	57
	2-4	—	—	24
	5+	—	—	9
Frequency of sex:	None	15	11	—
(past 12 months)	A few times per year	21	16	—
	A few times per month	24	32	—
	2-3 times per week	28	29	—
	4+ times per week	12	12	—
Frequency of orgasm	Always	70	22	—
during sex:	Usually	22	39	—
	Sometimes	6	26	—
	Rarely	0	5	—
	Never	2	8	—
Duration of last	15 min. or less	5	7	—
sexual event:	15 min. to 1 hour	65	70	—
	1 hour or more	31	23	—
Percent engaging in	Active: lifetime	72	69	—
oral sex:	last sex event	28	19	—
	Passive: lifetime	74	75	—
	last sex event	29	24	—
Percent ever forced to				
do something sexual by a man:		—	—	22
Frequency of masturbation:	Never	42	66	—
	Sometimes	29	26	—
	Once a week or more	29	8	—

— Not reported for this group.

Source: Michael, Robert O., John H. Gagnon, Edward O. Laumann, and Gina Kolata. 1994. *Sex in America: A Definitive Survey.* Boston, MA: Little, Brown, & Company.

I2. CONTRACEPTIVE USE

I2-1. Percent of Sexually Active Youth Not Using Contraceptives, by Grade in School, 1990

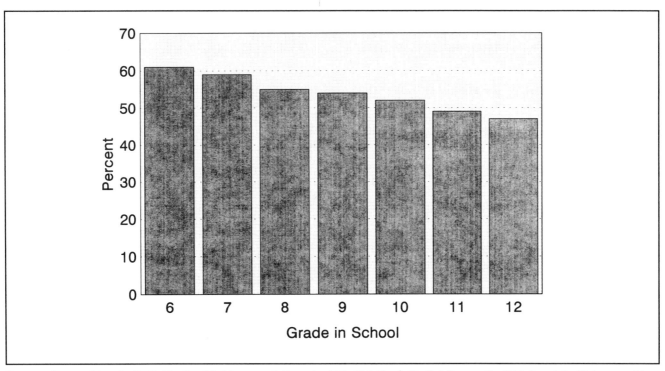

Source: Benson, Peter L. 1993. *The Troubled Journey: A Portrait of 6th-12th Grade Youth.* Minneapolis, MN: Search Institute, page 54.

I2-2. Percent of Women Aged 15–19 at Risk of Unintended Pregnancy Who Are Using a Contraceptive, by Age, Race, and Income, 1988

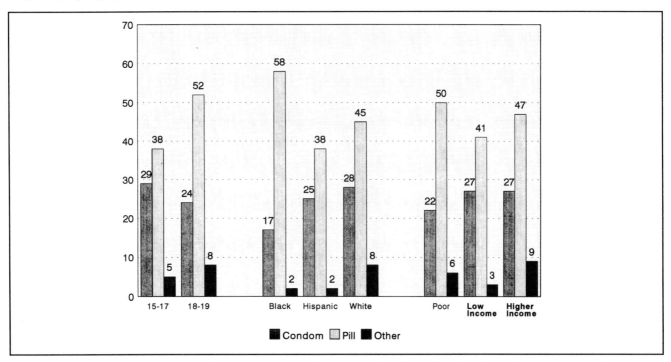

Source: The Alan Guttmacher Institute. 1994. *Sex and America's Teenagers.* New York: The Alan Guttmacher Institute, page 34.

I2-3. Contraceptive Use at First Intercourse, Women Aged 15–19, 1982 and 1988

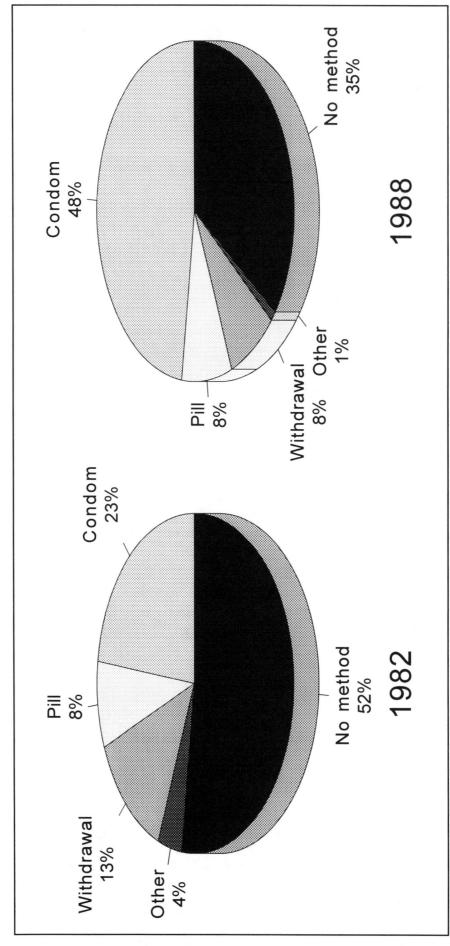

Source: The Alan Guttmacher Institute. 1994. *Sex and America's Teenagers.* New York: The Alan Guttmacher Institute, page 33.

I2-4. Measures of Condom Use, by Race or Ethnicity, Young Men Aged 17.5–19, 1988 and 1991

Condom Use	1988	1991
Percent who used at last intercourse		
All	53.0	56.1
Black	63.4	60.5
White	50.8	55.9
Hispanic	43.2	57.3
Consistency of use with last partner		
All	50.4	55.5
Black	58.5	60.9
White	48.6	56.1
Hispanic	43.9	45.7

Source: Family Planning Perspectives 25 (3) 1993, page 108.

I2-5. Reasons for Abortion, by Age of Women Having Abortions, 1987

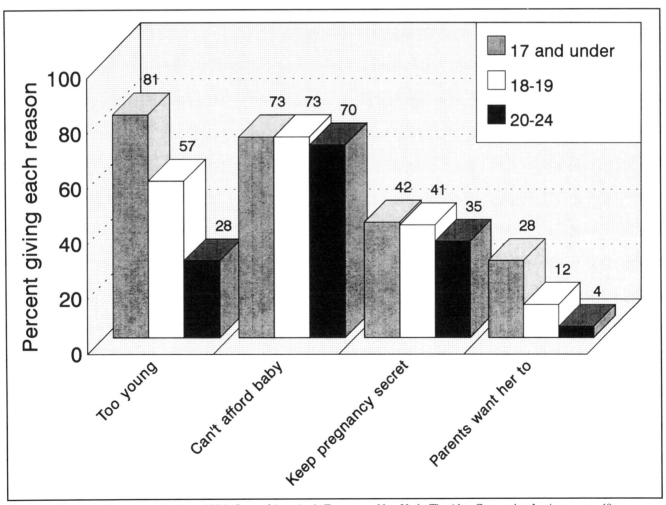

Source: The Alan Guttmacher Institute. 1994. *Sex and America's Teenagers.* New York: The Alan Guttmacher Institute, page 48.

I2-6. Parents' Knowledge of Minor's Abortions, 1991–1992

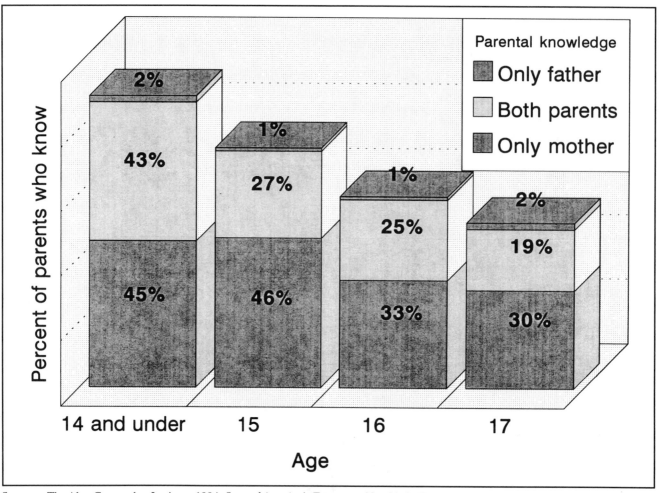

Source: The Alan Guttmacher Institute. 1994. *Sex and America's Teenagers.* New York: The Alan Guttmacher Institute, page 49.

I2-7. Amount of Information about Sex and Reproduction Given to Those Aged 15–19, 1988

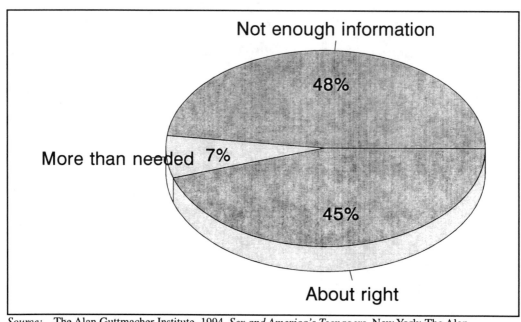

Source: The Alan Guttmacher Institute. 1994. *Sex and America's Teenagers.* New York: The Alan Guttmacher Institute, page 18.

I2-8. Percent of Youth at Risk Sexually, (Sex 2+ Times and/or Nonuse of Contraceptives), by Other At-Risk Behaviors, 1990

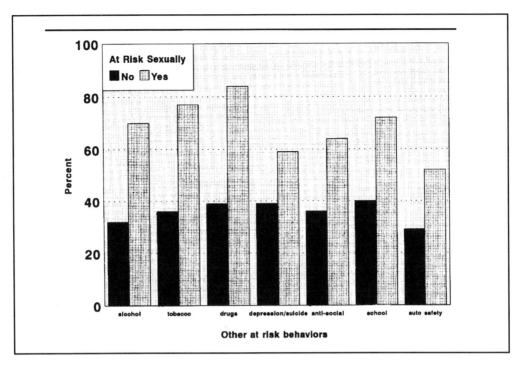

Source: Benson, Peter L. 1993. *The Troubled Journey: A Portrait of 6th-12th Grade Youth.* Minneapolis, MN: Search Institute, page 51.

I3. PREGNANCY, CHILDBEARING, AND MARRIAGE

I3-1. Pregnancies per 1,000 Women Aged 15–19, 1972–1990

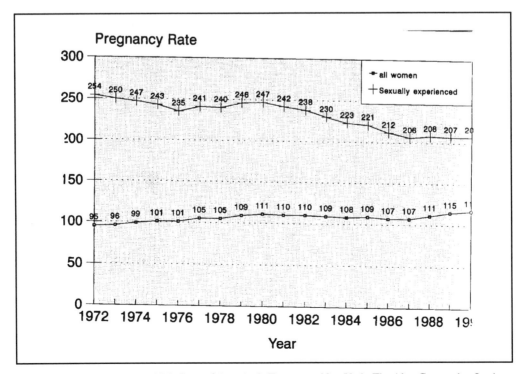

Source: The Alan Guttmacher Institute. 1994. *Sex and America's Teenagers.* New York: The Alan Guttmacher Institute, page 41.

I3-2. Percent of Teenage Pregnancies Ending in Birth, 1972–1990

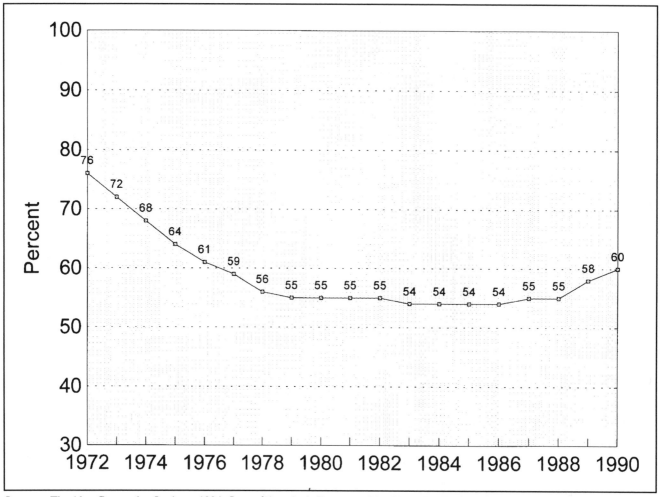

Source: The Alan Guttmacher Institute. 1994. *Sex and America's Teenagers.* New York: The Alan Guttmacher Institute, page 44.

I3-3. Pregnancy Outcomes among Women under 19, by Marriage Status, 1988

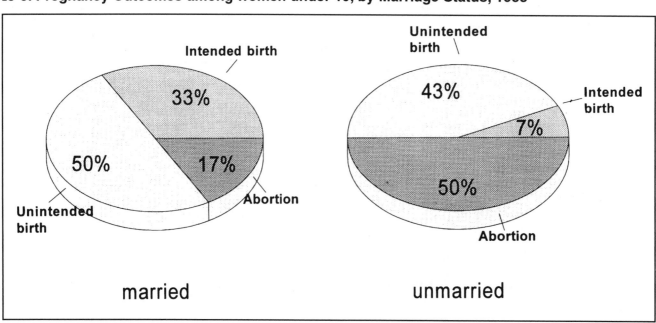

Source: The Alan Guttmacher Institute. 1994. *Sex and America's Teenagers.* New York: The Alan Guttmacher Institute, page 43.

I3-4. Pregnancy, Birth, and Abortion Rates, by Age Group and State, 1988

Rate per 1,000 Women	Pregnancy Rate			Birthrate			Abortion Rate		
	15-19	15-17	18-19	15-19	15-17	18-19	15-19	15-17	18-19
U.S.	**111**	**74**	**164**	**53**	**34**	**80**	**43**	**30**	**62**
Alabama	110	77	158	63	42	92	32	24	43
Alaska	111	65	179	57	31	97	38	26	57
Arizona	127	79	195	69	44	105	40	24	62
Arkansas	115	75	176	70	45	110	27	19	40
California	154	99	232	58	35	91	76	51	112
Colorado	102	68	147	49	29	75	39	29	52
Connecticut	107	74	158	36	23	57	58	43	82
Delaware	117	82	164	53	34	77	49	37	65
District of Columbia	209	191	228	74	68	80	110	100	120
Florida	133	92	194	63	42	94	52	38	73
Georgia	122	84	180	69	45	104	37	27	50
Hawaii	134	97	168	49	30	68	68	56	79
Idaho	73	43	111	45	26	69	17	11	26
Illinois	112	72	169	54	36	80	43	26	67
Indiana	89	54	137	52	31	80	25	15	38
Iowa	69	44	101	33	20	51	27	19	37
Kansas	88	58	128	49	28	77	27	22	32
Kentucky	96	65	142	60	38	92	22	17	29
Louisiana	107	69	160	68	45	101	23	14	35
Maine	82	54	123	41	22	69	30	25	37
Maryland	129	86	195	51	32	81	61	43	89
Massachusetts	97	62	142	32	21	48	53	34	77
Michigan	111	75	163	47	30	73	49	36	69
Minnesota	69	41	106	31	17	50	29	19	42
Mississippi	106	77	148	73	52	104	16	13	21
Missouri	99	60	152	55	34	84	30	18	47
Montana	74	48	112	39	23	64	24	19	31
Nebraska	75	48	110	37	22	57	27	20	38
Nevada	142	87	228	65	38	106	59	37	92
New Hampshire	87	55	130	33	17	53	43	31	60
New Jersey	112	72	177	39	24	63	60	39	93
New Mexico	124	81	189	72	44	114	35	26	48
New York	116	75	175	40	24	64	61	42	90
North Carolina	122	85	174	61	39	91	45	34	59
North Dakota	57	29	92	31	16	49	18	9	30
Ohio	96	59	149	52	31	81	31	20	47
Oklahoma	105	68	155	62	39	94	27	19	38
Oregon	105	68	148	48	28	76	43	31	61
Pennsylvania	87	57	128	41	26	62	34	23	48
Rhode Island	86	50	129	38	25	54	36	18	58
South Carolina	114	80	161	65	44	94	33	25	44
South Dakota	69	44	101	44	26	67	15	11	19
Tennessee	110	73	164	64	41	97	31	21	43
Texas	117	76	174	69	45	102	31	19	47
Utah	69	45	98	44	28	62	15	10	21
Vermont	81	53	113	33	19	50	37	28	48
Virginia	106	69	159	46	27	73	46	33	65
Washington	109	68	166	47	27	77	47	32	68
West Virginia	78	50	118	50	31	76	17	12	24
Wisconsin	74	47	111	38	22	59	26	19	37
Wyoming	82	51	125	48	26	78	23	18	29

Source: Family Planning Perspectives 25 (3) 1993, page 123.

I3-5. Pregnancy Rate and Outcome in Various Countries, 1988

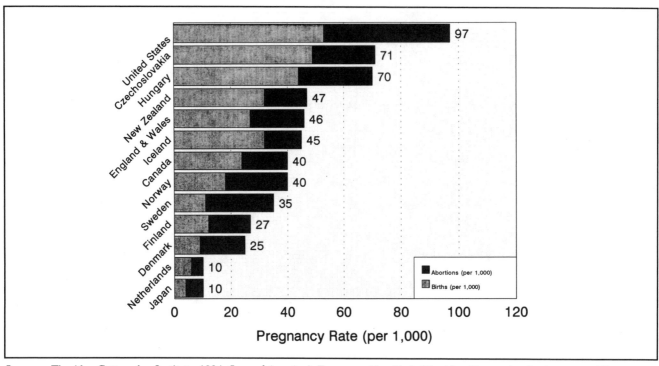

Source: The Alan Guttmacher Institute. 1994. *Sex and America's Teenagers.* New York: The Alan Guttmacher Institute, page 76.

I3-6. Birth Rates per 1,000 Women Aged 15–19, 1972 to 1990

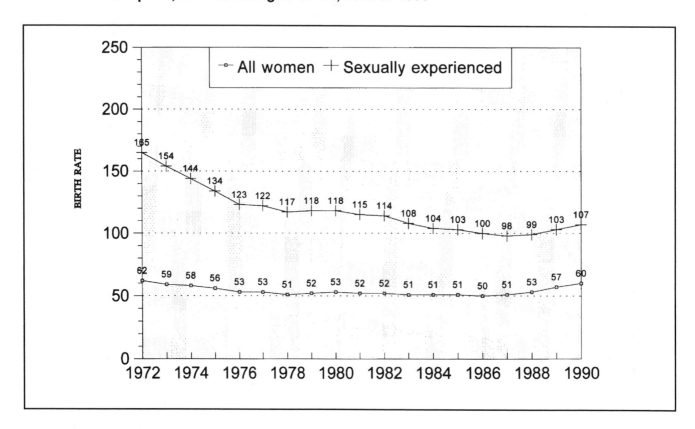

Source: The Alan Guttmacher Institute. 1994. *Sex and America's Teenagers.* New York: The Alan Guttmacher Institute, page 51.

I3-7. Births per 1,000 Women, by Age, 1990

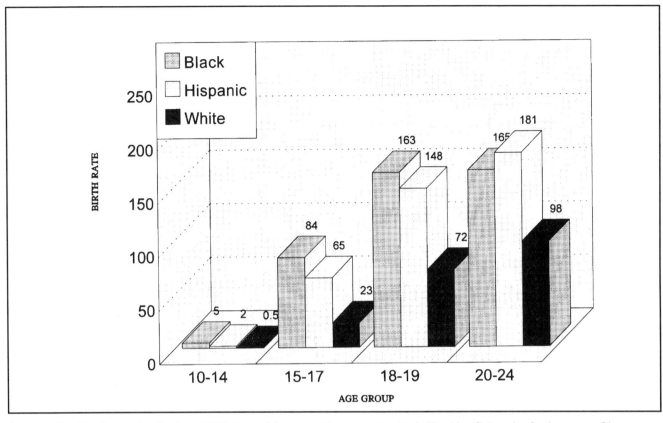

Source: The Alan Guttmacher Institute. 1994. *Sex and America's Teenagers.* New York: The Alan Guttmacher Institute, page 54.

I3-8. Percent of Women Giving Birth Who Have Partners at Least Six Years Older, by Age, 1988

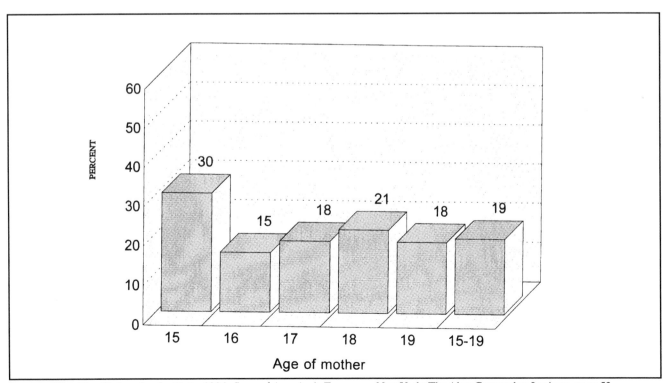

Source: The Alan Guttmacher Institute. 1994. *Sex and America's Teenagers.* New York: The Alan Guttmacher Institute, page 53.

I3-9. Status of First Births to Women Aged 15–17, 1960–64 and 1985–89

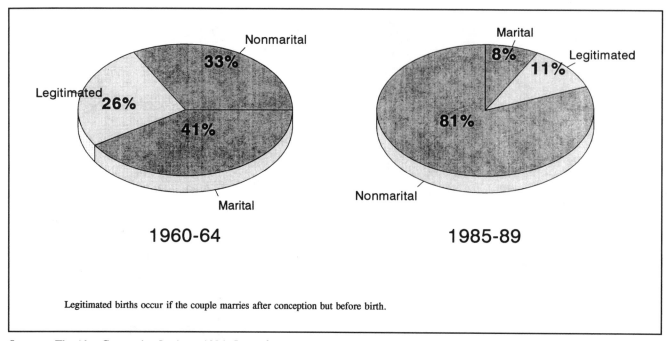

Legitimated births occur if the couple marries after conception but before birth.

Source: The Alan Guttmacher Institute. 1994. *Sex and America's Teenagers.* New York: The Alan Guttmacher Institute, page 55.

I3-10. Percent of Babies Born to Never-Married Women Placed for Adoption, by Race and Year

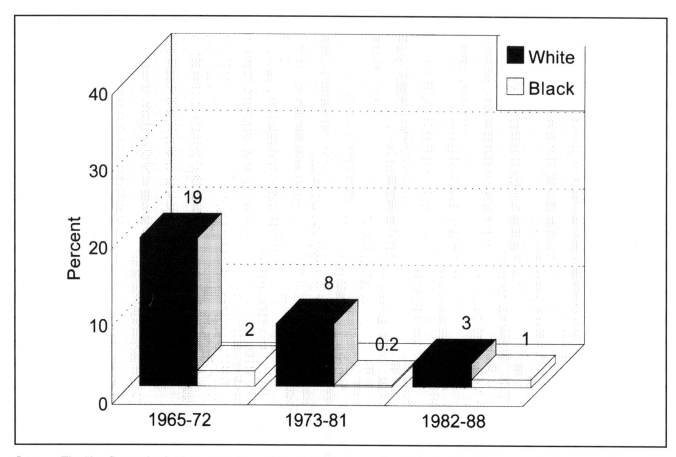

Source: The Alan Guttmacher Institute. 1994. *Sex and America's Teenagers.* New York: The Alan Guttmacher Institute, page 50.

I3-11. Income Status of Teens Who Gave Birth or Had an Abortion Compared to All Teens, 1988

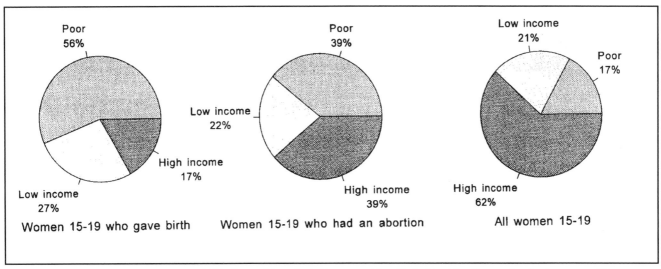

Source: The Alan Guttmacher Institute. 1994. *Sex and America's Teenagers.* New York: The Alan Guttmacher Institute, page 58

I3-12. Percent of Adolescents Ever Married, by Age, Gender, and Ethnicity, 1992

| Ethnicity | Gender | Percent Ever-Married | | |
		15-17	18-19	20-24
White	Female	1.8	11.2	37.3
	Male	0.4	2.4	21.5
	Total	1.1	6.8	29.5
Black	Female	0.2	4.4	19.7
	Male	0.0	1.1	11.7
	Total	0.1	2.8	16.0
Hispanic*	Female	5.1	20.4	42.8
	Male	1.2	6.4	28.2
	Total	3.1	13.4	35.2
Total	Female	1.5	10.0	34.3
	Male	0.3	2.3	19.7
	Total	0.9	6.1	27.1

*May be of any race.

Source: U.S. Bureau of the Census. Current Population Reports, Series P20, No. 468. *Marital Status and Living Arrangements: March 1992.* U. S. Government Printing Office, Washington, DC, 1992, page 1.

I3-13. Age by which 50 Percent of the Ever-Married Population Have Married, 1890–1990

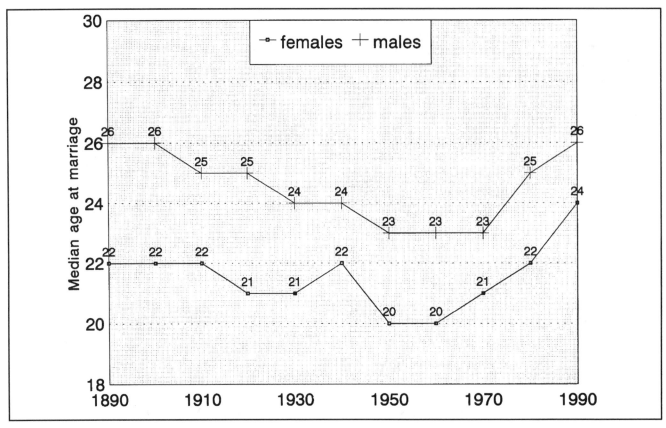

Source: The Alan Guttmacher Institute. 1994. *Sex and America's Teenagers.* New York: The Alan Guttmacher Institute, page 24.

I3-14. Parental Status of Women Who Marry before Age 20, Based on Women Age 25 or Younger, 1988

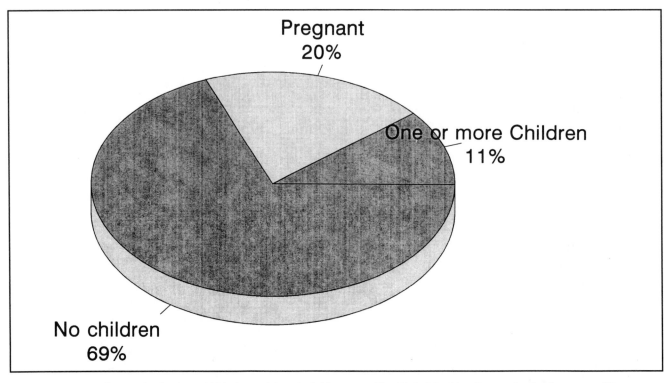

Source: The Alan Guttmacher Institute. 1994. *Sex and America's Teenagers.* New York: The Alan Guttmacher Institute, page 57.

I3-15. Marital Status of Persons 15–24, by Sex, Race, and Hispanic Origin, 1990

		Percent Never Married	Percent Married Spouse Present	Percent Separated	Percent Divorced	Percent Widowed
All races:						
Age 15-17	Males	99.7	0.2	—	—	—
	Females	98.5	1.1	0.1	0.1	—
Age 18-19	Males	97.7	2.1	0.1	—	—
	Females	90.0	8.2	0.8	0.6	—
Age 20-24	Males	80.3	16.9	0.9	1.3	—
	Females	65.7	28.7	2.7	2.2	0.1
White:						
Age 15-17	Males	99.6	0.3	—	—	—
	Females	98.2	1.4	0.1	0.1	—
Age 18-19	Males	97.6	2.1	0.1	—	—
	Females	88.8	9.5	0.8	0.6	—
Age 20-24	Males	78.5	18.7	0.9	1.4	—
	Females	62.7	31.5	2.7	2.4	0.1
Black:						
Age 15-17	Males	100.0	—	—	—	—
	Females	99.8	—	0.1	0.1	—
Age 18-19	Males	98.9	1.1	—	—	—
	Females	95.6	2.5	1.0	0.9	—
Age 20-24	Males	88.3	8.9	1.3	1.5	—
	Females	80.3	14.1	3.6	1.3	0.1
Hispanic:*						
Age 15-17	Males	98.8	1.0	—	—	—
	Females	94.9	4.7	—	—	—
Age 18-19	Males	93.6	5.2	—	—	—
	Females	79.6	17.9	1.5	0.6	—
Age 20-24	Males	71.8	24.5	1.1	0.5	—
	Females	57.2	37.2	3.0	0.9	0.2

*May be of any race.
— Too few cases for reliable information.

Source: U.S. Bureau of the Census. Current Population Reports, Series P20, No. 468. *Marital Status and Living Arrangements: March 1992.* U.S. Government Printing Office, Washington, DC, 1992, pages 1–3.

I4. NEGATIVE OUTCOMES OF EARLY CHILDBEARING

I4-1. Babies' Health Problems, by Age of Mother at First Birth (Children under 5), 1988

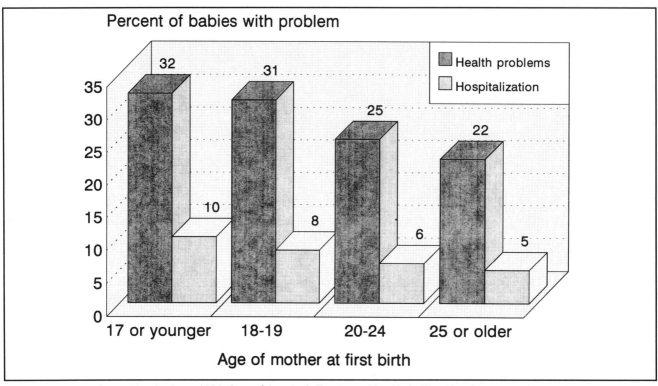

Source: The Alan Guttmacher Institute. 1994. *Sex and America's Teenagers.* New York: The Alan Guttmacher Institute, page 63.

I4-2. Median Family Income of Teenage Mothers' Income in Later Life, Women Aged 30–39, 1986

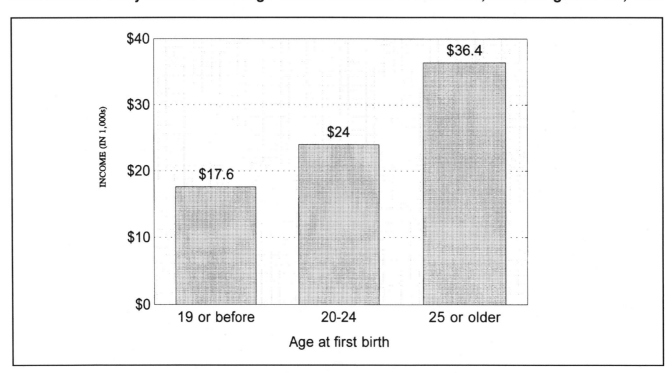

Source: The Alan Guttmacher Institute. 1994. *Sex and America's Teenagers.* New York: The Alan Guttmacher Institute, page 61.

I4-3. Estimated Ratios of High School Completion between Women with a Teenage Birth and Those without, by Race, 1993

Age	White	Black	Hispanic*
15.5	.48	.68	.55
16.0	.47	.66	.54
16.5	.45	.62	.52
17.0	.42	.57	.49
17.5	.39	.54	.46
18.0	.40	.53	.43
18.5	.35	.50	.39
19.0	.34	.48	.37
19.5	.32	.47	.35
20.0	.32	.47	.35

*May be of any race.

Source: *Family Planning Perspectives* 26 (1) 1994, page 20.

I4-4. Educational Attainment of Women Aged 35–39, by Age at First Birth, 1987

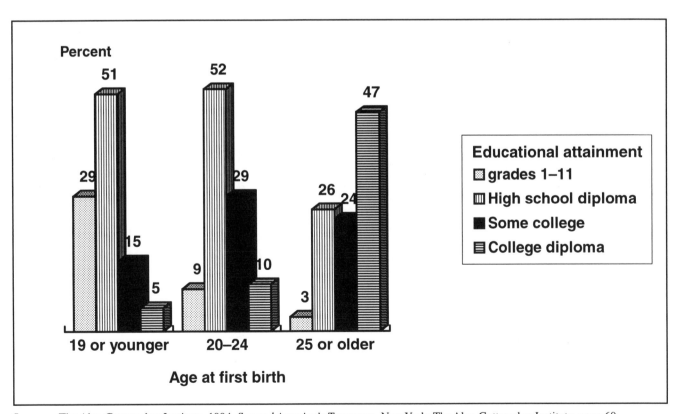

Source: The Alan Guttmacher Institute. 1994. *Sex and America's Teenagers.* New York: The Alan Guttmacher Institute, page 60.

I4-5. Number of Women Aged 15–19 Reaching Each Reproductive Stage and Percent Who Are Poor or of Low Income, 1994

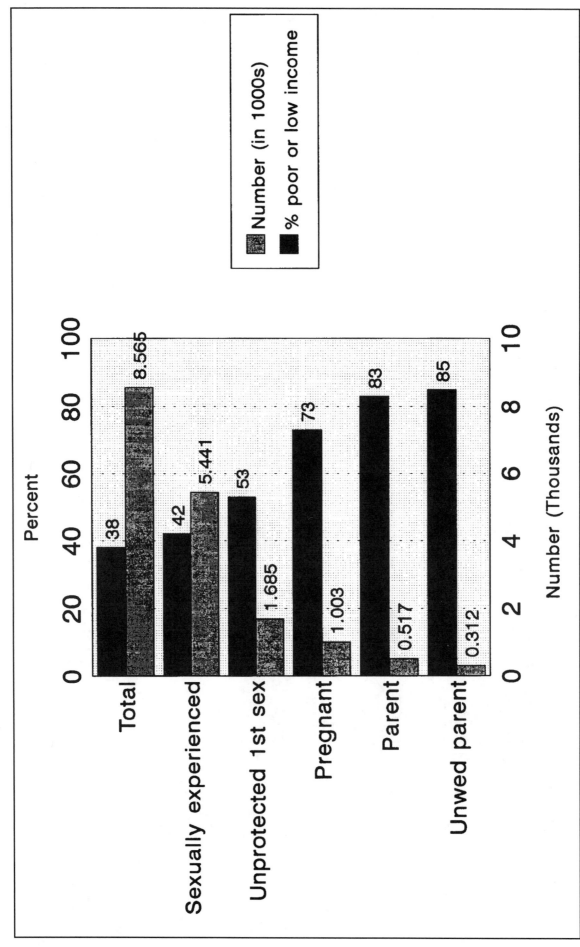

Source: The Alan Guttmacher Institute. 1994. *Sex and America's Teenagers.* New York: The Alan Guttmacher Institute, page 70.

I5. SEXUAL VALUES AND FUTURE EXPECTATIONS

I5-1. Percent of Youth Who Value Sexual Restraint, by Grade in School, 1990

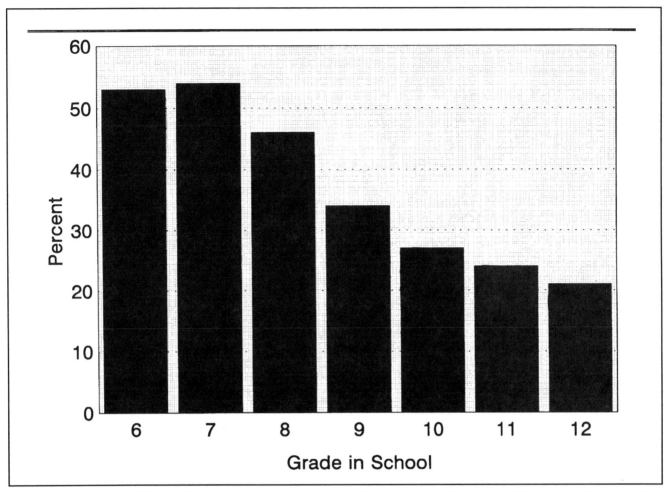

Source: Benson, Peter L. 1993. *The Troubled Journey: A Portrait of 6th-12th Grade Youth.* Minneapolis, MN: Search Institute, page 86.

I5-2. Those Who Believe in Practicing Safe Sex or Abstinence, by Sex, Age, and Race, 1991

Characteristic	Safe Sex	Abstinence
National	**64%**	**31%**
Sex:		
Male	67	29
Female	61	33
Age:		
13 to 15 years	63	32
16 to 17 years	65	29
Race:		
White	64	31
Non-white	66	31

Source: Bezilla, Robert (Ed.). *America's Youth in the 1990s.* Princeton, NJ: The George H. Gallup International Institute, 1993, page 54.

I5-3. Young Men's Reactions to an Unplanned Pregnancy, by Neighborhood Conditions and Race or Ethnicity, 1992

Neighborhood conditions and race	N	Reactions to an Unplanned Pregnancy					
		Feel like a real man			Emotional response		
		Not at all	A lot	N	Very upset	Very pleased	
Total	**1,805**	**60.4%**	**4.6**	**1,791**	**68.9%**	**4.1**	
Poor	**276**	**45.0**	**7.6**	**274**	**46.2**	**11.5**	
Black	143	40.0	10.7	141	38.2	15.0	
White	61	49.3	4.1	62	45.3	8.2	
Hispanic*	66	36.4	11.4	65	59.7	11.1	
Average	**690**	**54.1**	**7.5**	**681**	**57.5**	**8.3**	
Black	275	47.5	11.9	269	39.4	8.0	
White	218	55.9	6.4	216	62.6	8.3	
Hispanic*	172	58.2	5.6	171	63.8	3.1	
Very Good	**839**	**65.1**	**3.2**	**836**	**77.0**	**1.5**	
Black	230	52.7	10.2	229	64.7	5.1	
White	443	67.5	2.4	442	79.9	1.2	
Hispanic*	136	58.3	4.3	135	61.1	0.9	

Note: N indicates the sample size.
*May be of any race.
Neighborhood quality was measured by interviewers' assessments of the condition of buildings in the neighborhood.

Source: Family Planning Perspectives 25 (1) 1993, page 25.

I5-4. Lifetime Expected Births of Women, by Age and Race, 1992

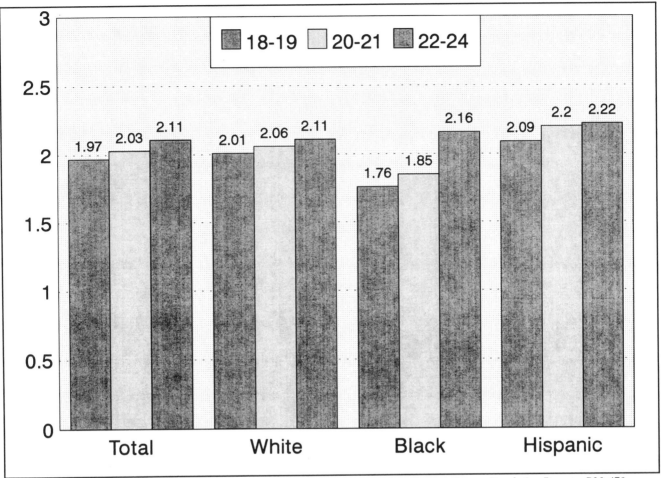

Source: Bachu, Amara. *Fertility of American Women: June 1992, U.S. Bureau of the Census, Current Population Reports, P20-470.* U.S. Government Printing Office, Washington, DC, 1993, page 17.

I5-5. Opinion of Parental Approval Laws for Abortion, by Sex, Age, and Race, 1990

Survey question: Would you favor or oppose a restriction in your state that would require women under 18 years of age to get parental consent before they are allowed to have an abortion?

Characteristic	Favor	Oppose
National	**64%**	**32%**
Sex:		
Male	64	32
Female	64	32
Age:		
13-15 years	68	27
16-17 years	58	38
Race:		
White	65	32
Non-white	61	33

Source: Bezilla, Robert (Ed.). *America's Youth in the 1900s.* Princeton, NJ: The George H. Gallup International Institute, 1993, page 50.

I5-6. Marriage and Children Trend, 1977–1992

Year	Like to Marry	Want to have Children
1992	88%	84%
1988	86	76
1987	85	80
1986	88	83
1984	88	83
1983	82	79
1977	84	79

Source: Bezilla, Robert (Ed.). *America's Youth in the 1990s.* Princeton, NJ: The George H. Gallup International Institute, 1993, page 42.

I5-7. Marriage Intentions, by Sex, Age, Race, and Social Class, 1992

Survey question: Do you think you will get married some day, or do you think you will remain single?

Characteristic	Get married	Stay single	Not sure
National	**88%**	**9%**	**3%**
Sex:			
Male	86	11	3
Female	88	8	4
Age:			
13-15 years	88	8	4
16-17 years	88	10	2
Race:			
White	89	8	3
Non-white	85	11	4
Social Class:			
White-collar background	94	4	2
Blue-collar background	83	13	4

Source: Bezilla, Robert (Ed.). *America's Youth in the 1990s.* Princeton, NJ: The George H. Gallup International Institute, 1993, page 43.

I5-8. Marriage Aspirations of American High School Seniors, 1976 and 1986

| Variable | Sex | Percent | | Change |
		1976	1986	1976-86
Likely to get married	Total	74.2	77.7	3.5
	Males	69.4	74.7	5.3
	Females	80.0	80.8	0.8
Timing of marriage	Total	25.8	37.4	11.6
(percent answering	Males	32.4	45.2	12.8
over 5 years from	Females	19.5	30.5	11.0
now)				
Questions marriage	Total	14.1	12.8	-1.3
as way of life	Males	14.8	11.0	-3.8
(agree)	Females	13.5	13.8	0.3
One partner too	Total	27.6	21.4	-6.2
restrictive (agree or	Males	33.7	25.3	
mostly agree)	Females	20.9	18.0	-2.9

Source: Crimmins, Eileen M., Richard A. Easterlin, and Yasuhiko Saito. 1991. "Preference changes among American youth: Family, work, and good aspirations, 1976-86." *Population and Development Review* 17 (1) page 119.

I5-9. Child Planning, by Sex, Age, Race, and Social Class, 1992

Survey question: When you do get married, would you like to have children, or not? [Question was asked of only those who said they planned to marry some day.]

Characteristic	Yes, want to have children	Average number wanted
National	**84%**	**2.3**
Sex:		
Male	81	2.1
Female	88	2.4
Age:		
13-15 years	85	2.2
16-17 years	83	2.4
Race:		
White	85	2.2
Non-white	84	2.4
Social Class:		
White-collar background	88	2.3
Blue-collar background	82	2.2

Source: Bezilla, Robert (Ed.). *America's Youth in the 1990s.* Princeton, NJ: The George H. Gallup International Institute, 1993, page 44.

I5-10. Childbearing Aspirations of American High School Seniors, 1976 and 1986

| Variable | Sex | Percent | | Change |
		1976	1986	1976-86
Likely to have	Total	77.8	81.5	3.7
children (very or	Males	80.5	82.6	2.1
fairly)	Females	76.0	80.2	4.2
Being a father is fulfilling (agree or mostly agree)	Males	69.7	71.2	1.5
Being a mother is fulfilling (agree or mostly agree)	Females	65.9	68.2	2.3
Timing of first	Total	28.8	31.5	2.7
child (1 year or	Males	34.7	37.9	3.2
less after marriage)	Females	22.8	25.5	2.7

Source: Crimmins, Eileen M., Richard A. Easterlin, and Yasuhiko Saito. 1991. "Preference changes among American youth: Family, work, and good aspirations, 1976-86." *Population and Development Review* 17 (1) page 120.

I5-11. Average Number of Children Wanted by American High School Seniors, by Sex and Percent Distribution of Both Sexes, 1976 and 1986

Survey question: All things considered, if you could have exactly the number of children you want, what number would you choose to have?

| Variable | Percent | | Change |
	1976	1986	1976-86
Average number of children wanted:			
Total	2.63	2.37	-0.26
Males	2.57	2.32	-0.25
Females	2.68	2.42	-0.26
Percent distribution by number of children wanted:			
Total	100.0	100.0	0.0
None	3.3	4.5	1.2
One	3.2	7.2	4.0
Two	44.9	47.8	2.9
Three	20.4	20.8	0.4
Four	12.5	9.6	-2.9
Five	2.6	1.7	-0.9
Six or more	3.4	1.4	-2.0
Don't know	9.7	7.0	-2.7
Fewer than two	6.5	11.7	5.2
Four or more	18.5	12.7	-5.8

Source: Crimmins, Eileen M., Richard A. Easterlin, and Yasuhiko Saito. 1991. "Preference changes among American youth: Family, work, and good aspirations, 1976-86." *Population and Development Review* 17 (1) page 121.

I5-12. Opinion on Abortion by Adolescents, June–July, 1991

Characteristic	Allow abortions for any reason	Outlaw all abortions
National	**47%**	**44%**
Sex:		
Male	50	45
Female	43	43
Age:		
13-15 years	47	48
16-17 years	46	40
Race:		
White	45	44
Non-white	53	45
Student Type:		
Above-average students	43	46
Average and below	51	42
Region:		
East	47	43
Midwest	48	49
South	40	47
West	52	34
Religion:		
Protestant	46	44
Catholic	48	45
Church Attendance:		
Attender	37	51
Non-attender	56	38

Source: Bezilla, Robert (Ed.). *America's Youth in the 1990s.* Princeton, NJ: The George H. Gallup International Institute, 1993, page 48.

I5-13. Opinion on Divorce Trends by Adolescents, 1977–1992

Year	Believe divorce laws are too lax	Believe divorced couples try hard to save marriages
1992	76%	23%
1988	72	30
1987	73	25
1986	79	25
1984	75	22
1983	66	23
1981	73	24
1977	55	29

Source: Bezilla, Robert (Ed.). *America's Youth in the 1990s.* Princeton, NJ: The George H. Gallup International Institute, 1993, page 45.

I5-14. High School Seniors' Attitude about Sex Education in High School, by Sex and Race, 1992

Survey question: High schools should offer instruction in birth control methods.

Response	Total (N=2,342)	Sex		Race	
		Males (N=1,099)	Females (N=1,197)	White (N=1,679)	Black (N=298)
Disagree	6%	6%	5%	6%	4%
Mostly disagree	3	4	3	3	5
Neither	16	19	12	15	18
Mostly agree	24	24	24	24	19
Agree	52	47	56	53	55

Note: N indicates sample size. Percentages may not add to 100 due to rounding.

Source: Bachman, Jerald G., Lloyd D. Johnston, and Patrick M. O'Malley. 1993. *Monitoring the Future: Questionnaire Responses from the Nation's High School Seniors, 1992*. Ann Arbor, MI: Survey Research Center, Institute for Social Research, The University of Michigan, page 150.

Index

by Linda Webster